Canaletto & Bellotto

Mateusz Mayer

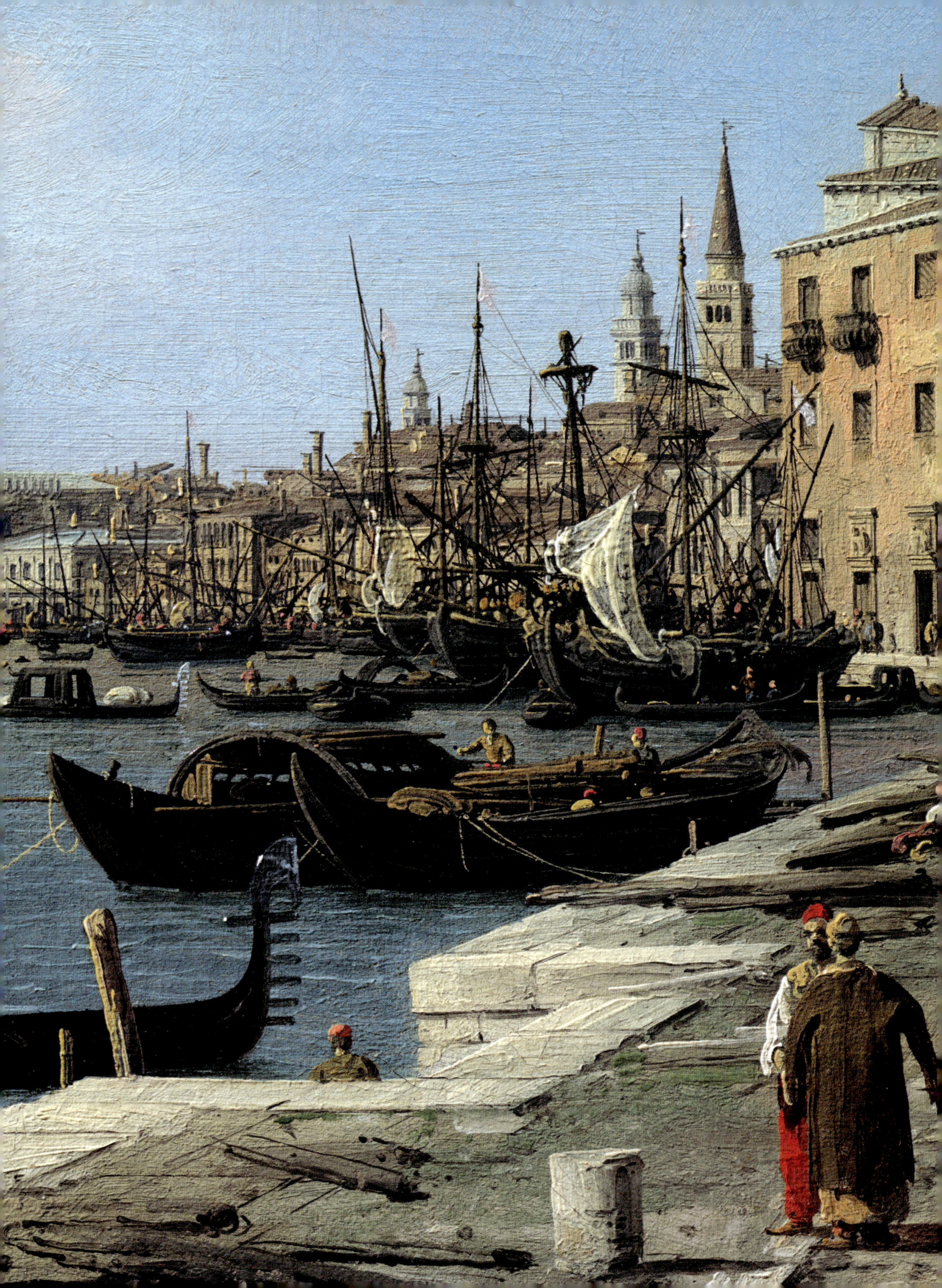

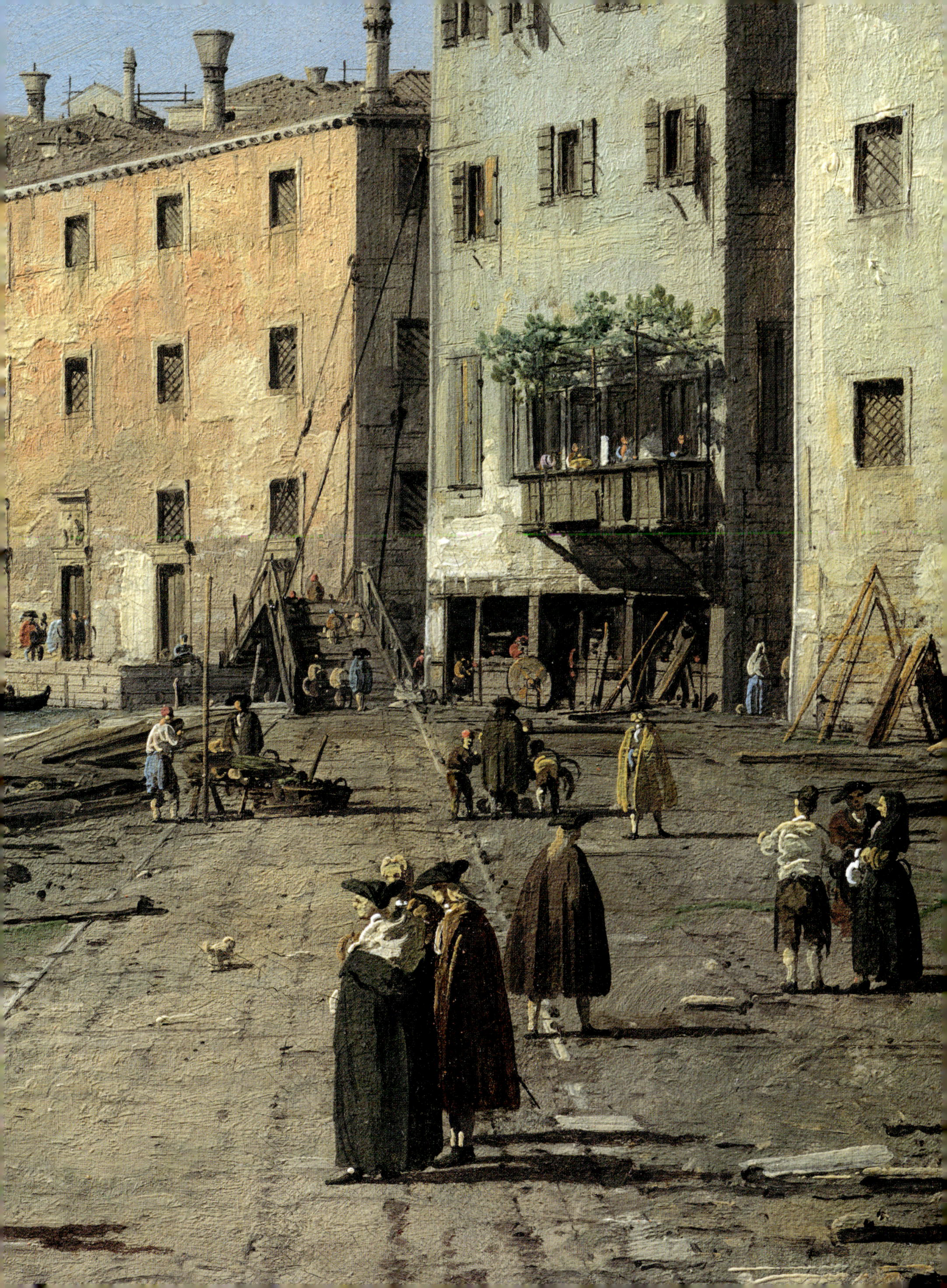

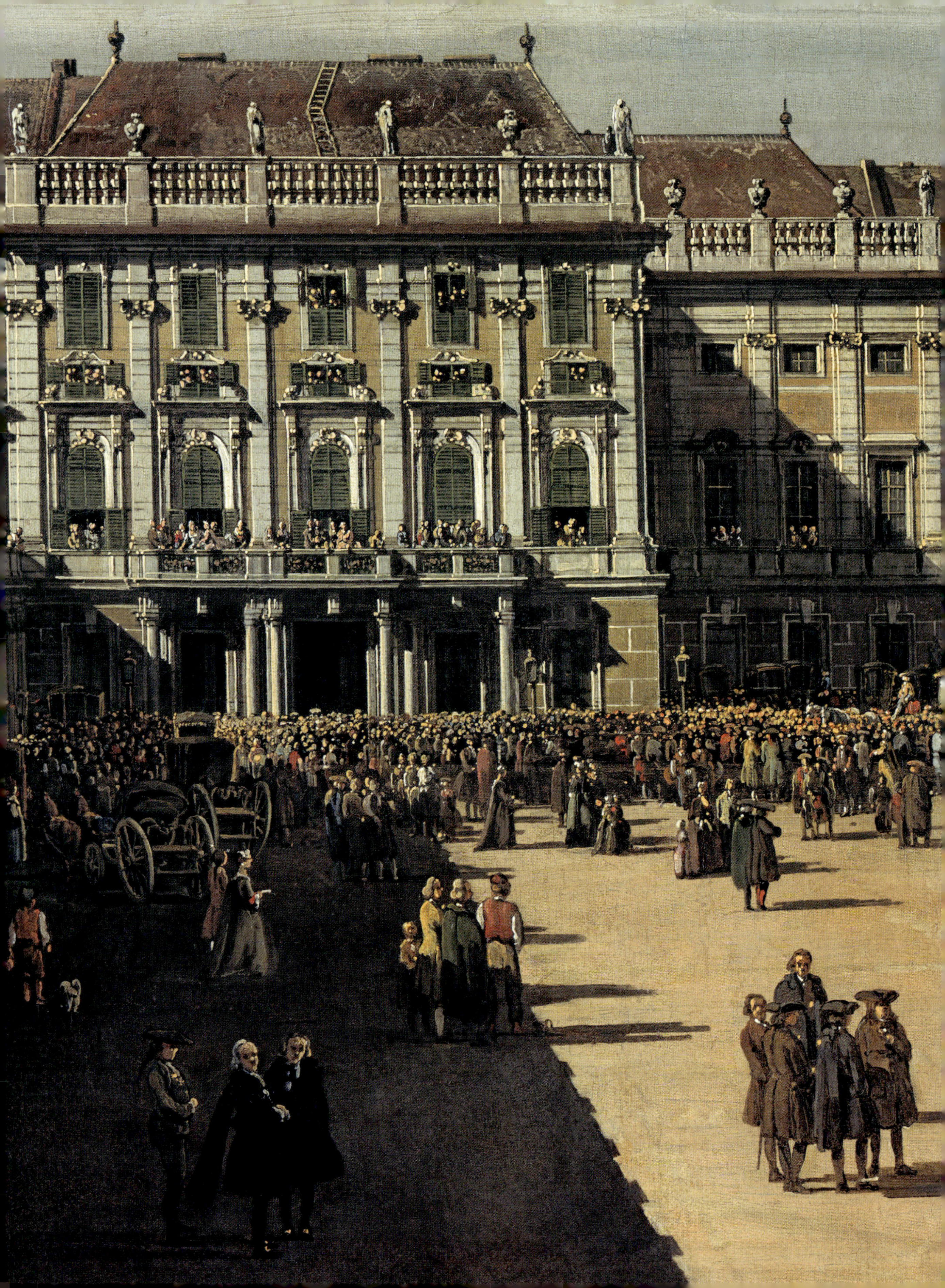

Canaletto & Bellotto

OBSERVATION AND INVENTION IN VENICE, LONDON, AND VIENNA

Mateusz Mayer

KUNST
HISTORISCHES
MUSEUM

HIRMER

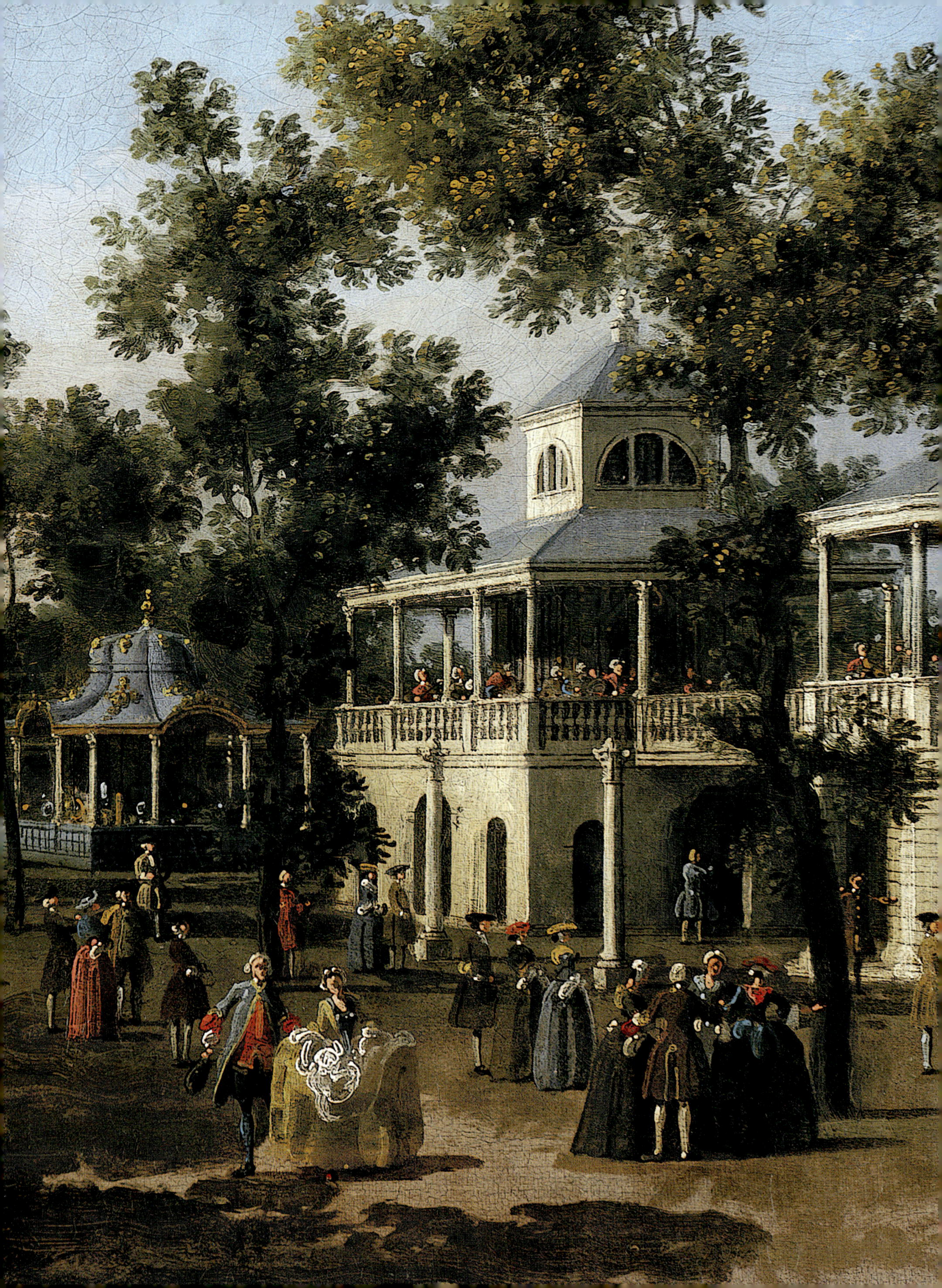

Contents

Director's Foreword

Our collective perceptions of eighteenth-century Venice, London, and Vienna have been shaped by the iconic views of these metropolises painted by two of the period's leading artists: Giovanni Antonio Canal, called Canaletto, and his nephew and pupil, Bernardo Bellotto (who often called himself Canaletto, too, to emphasize his connection to his celebrated uncle). Even today, I believe, we are not fully aware of how deeply their paintings influence our idea of the eighteenth-century city. Both artists focus not only on atmosphere, light, and transience, but also architectural verisimilitude and the texture of urban life. Indeed, their works perfectly capture the essence of the period, the social, cultural, and intellectual changes of the time, depicting, as Virginia Woolf put it so beautifully in *Orlando*, the "positive landscapes of the eighteenth century"[1] where "in the extreme clearness of the atmosphere the line of every roof, the cowl of every chimney was perceptible. Even the cobbles in the streets showed distinct one from another."[2]

This exhibition, the first in Austria to juxtapose the works of these two *vedutisti*, explores both their shared outlooks along with the differences in their techniques, approaches, and compositions. Both artists were fascinated by optical phenomena, scientific instruments, and everyday scenes, as well as capturing the essence of urban society—some of the reasons why these great artworks remain relevant for today.

The exhibition was curated by Mateusz Mayer, the newest member of the Picture Gallery's curatorial staff. Despite the short time available to him, he has conceived a splendid show that explores different aspects of the work of these two artists, as well as the time in which they lived and depicted in their compositions. To him, I wish to express my heartfelt thanks.

I also want to thank Elke Oberthaler, head of the Restoration Studio, who served as the interim director of the Picture Gallery, and Jennifer Sliwka, its new director, for their tireless and enthusiastic support of this project. Exhibition management was in the capable hands of Elisabeth Kainberger, and the elegant exhibition design is by Serenella Zoppolat and Tilo Perkmann.

Although the Kunsthistorisches Museum has a splendid collection of views of Vienna and its environs by Bellotto, we have but two small Venetian *vedute* by Canaletto. Many of the paintings on show come from other marvelous European public and private collections, and I am most grateful for their willingness to loan them.

I also want to express my sincere gratitude to our partner Uniqa and our sponsor Dorotheum, without whose generous support we could not have realized this exhibition.

Thank you all for making this spectacular show possible. All that remains for me now is to wish you a memorable "grand tour" of these fabulous eighteenth-century metropolises.

Jonathan Fine
Director General
Kunsthistorisches Museum

Author's Acknowledgments

When I was invited to curate an exhibition devoted to the Kunsthistorisches Museum's paintings by Bernardo Bellotto (also known as Canaletto), two guiding concerns quickly emerged: first, to clarify that there were in fact two artists working under the name "Canaletto" (that is, uncle and nephew, both of whom travelled widely across Europe); and second, to show that eighteenth-century city views — often perceived as straight-forward, almost photographic records of reality — were in fact carefully staged constructions, offering pointed insights into the social and political worlds they depict.

This project could not have been realized without the generosity, expertise, and encouragement of many colleagues and collaborators, far more than can be named individually here. I extend my sincere thanks to everyone who contributed — often behind the scenes — to the realization of this exhibition and publication. I am especially grateful to Jonathan Fine for his trust and guidance throughout the project, and to Agnes Stillfried, Elke Oberthaler, Jennifer Sliwka, and Gudrun Swoboda for their steadfast support. I also wish to thank my curatorial colleagues throughout the museum. Special thanks are due to Elisabeth Kainberger for expertly overseeing the organizational aspects of the exhibition.

I am equally grateful to the museum's conservators and collection specialists—especially Anneliese Földes, Eva Götz, and Flaminia Rukavina Vidovgrad for their sensitive conservation work; Markus Geyer for his care of the frames; and Andreas Uldrich for the new photography. My thanks extend as well to the departments Exhibitions, Research Services, Education, Information Technology, Library and Archives, Branding, Press, Sales, Guest Services, and Security, whose professionalism and collaboration were essential to the project's success.

My sincere gratitude further goes to Christopher Apostle, Charles Beddington, Deborah Howard, Angel Jiang, David Pullins, Daniel Ralston, and Letizia Treves for sharing their knowledge, insights, and enthusiasm. Finally, I warmly thank all lending institutions and collectors who so generously agreed to part, for a time, with their paintings, drawings, prints, and scientific instruments, thereby enabling this exhibition and the conversations and questions that, I hope, emerge when these works are seen together.

Mateusz Mayer
Exhibition Curator

LENDERS TO THE EXHIBITION

Academy of Fine Arts Vienna
ALBERTINA, Vienna
Andrew Lloyd Webber Foundation supported by Tate, UK
Austrian National Library, Vienna
Compton Verney, UK
Fondazione Musei Civici di Venezia, Museo Correr, Venice
Gallerie dell'Accademia, Venice
Kunsthistorisches Museum, Vienna
Leica Microsystems GmbH
LIECHTENSTEIN. The Princely Collections, Vaduz–Vienna
Musée des Beaux-Arts et d'Archéologie, Troyes
Museo Nacional Thyssen-Bornemisza, Madrid
Museu Nacional d'Art de Catalunya, Barcelona
National Gallery of Ireland, Dublin
Nationalmuseum, Stockholm
Sächsisches Staatsarchiv, Hauptstaatsarchiv Dresden
Schottenstift, Vienna
Technisches Museum Wien, Vienna
The British Museum, London
The Dean and Chapter of Westminster, London
The Lobkowicz Collections, Lobkowicz Palace, Prague Castle, Czech Republic
The Royal Castle in Warsaw – Museum
The Wallace Collection, London
Wien Museum, Vienna

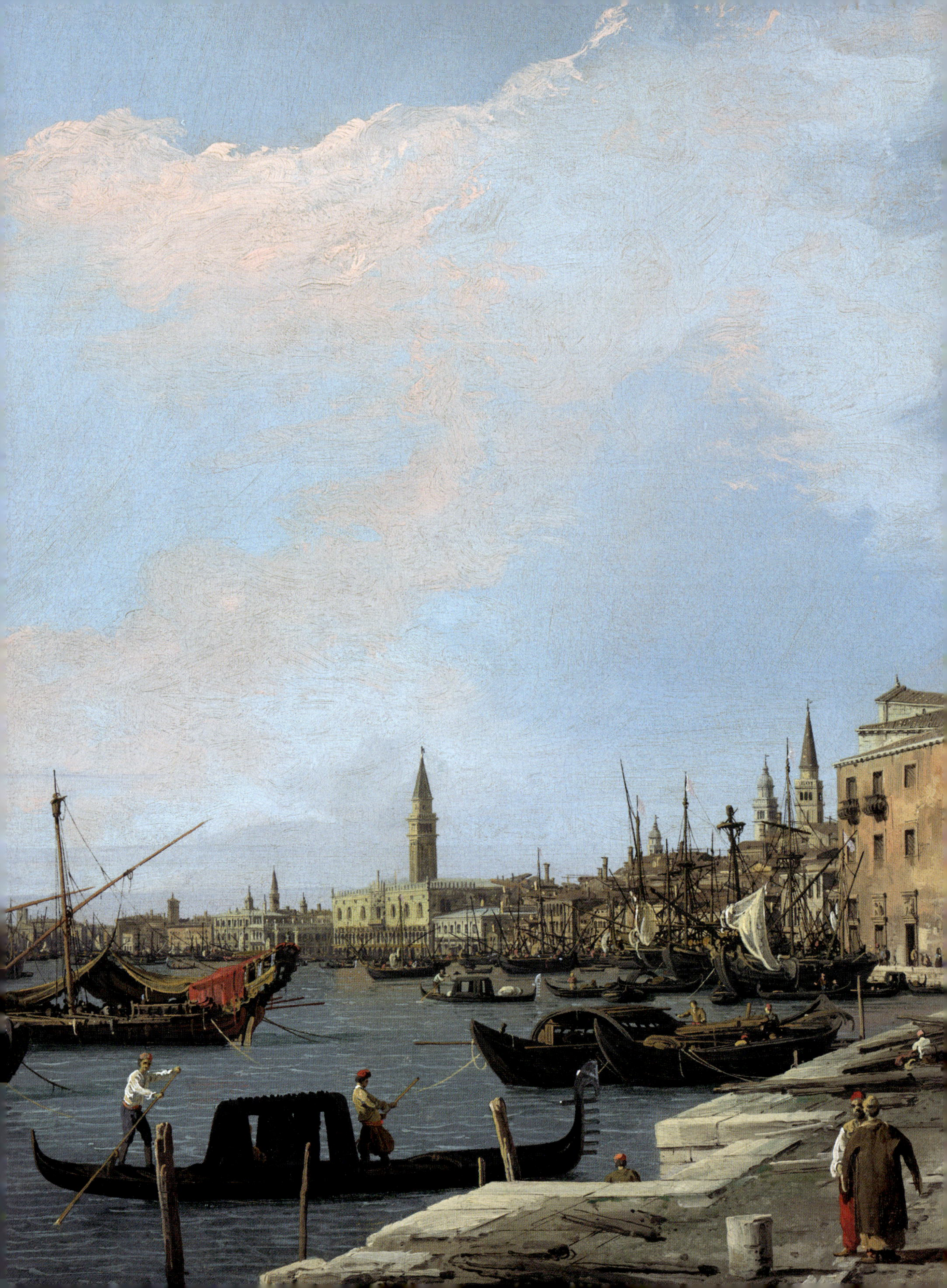

Venetian Beginnings

One of Canaletto's paintings at the Kunsthistorisches Museum presents a panoramic view of Venice's bustling waterfront (fig. 1).[1] Seen from a vantage point near the church of San Biagio, the composition extends west along the gently curving *Riva degli Schiavoni*, the city's southern quay. Painted around 1730, it captures a sweep of urban architecture, from the modest dwellings at right to civic landmarks like the Doge's Palace and the Campanile of San Marco at center. Toward the left, between the Grand Canal and the Giudecca Canal, rises the splendid dome of Santa Maria della Salute; furthest left lies San Giorgio Maggiore, with its elegant dome and multi-arched façade of its dormitory (the *Manica Lunga*). On the right, the third building from the edge are the *Forni*, Venice's military bakeries, their plain orange façade contrasting with the ornate architecture beyond. Behind them rise the *campanili* (church towers) of San Giovanni in Bragora (since demolished) and San Giorgio dei Greci, their vertical form echoing the masts animating Venice's famed water basin, the *Bacino*. The waters teem with gondolas, barges, and a schooner flying a crimson flag, all vivid with watermen at work. Along the waterfront, groups of Venetians pass and interact, their gestures and clothing rendered in swift, economical brushwork. At once urban record, marine view, and genre scene, the painting combines topographical precision and social observation in a harmonious whole.

In eighteenth-century Europe, this type of city view, or *veduta*, was immensely popular, and the name "Canaletto" became synonymous with the genre. Yet it is perhaps confusing that not one, but two artists used this name. The first is Giovanni Antonio Canal (1697–1768), known as Canaletto proper. The second is his nephew and pupil, Bernardo Bellotto (1722–1780), who is best known for his views of Dresden, Vienna, and Warsaw, and who adopted his uncle's name, signing some works "Bernardo Bellotto called Canaletto."[2] Bellotto surely did so not only to emphasize his artistic ties to his famous kinsman, from whom he had learned, but also to enhance his own market value.[3] To distinguish them in what follows, we shall refer to Canal as "Canaletto" and his nephew as "Bellotto."

Both artists emerged from the vibrant urban fabric of Venice. Built on islands separated by canals and only partly linked by bridges, the aquatic composition of Venice's built environment is unique. For centuries, this venerated maritime republic maintained strong mercantile ties across the Mediterranean, fostering a cultural milieu bridging East and West. Her tripartite government comprising a Doge, a Great Council, and a Senate, made Venice a model of stable republican governance, earning her the name *La Serenissima*—the most serene. This blend of natural environment, mercantile outlook, and political structure shaped a distinctive artistic legacy, merging classical traditions with a Venetian flair for light and color. In earlier centuries, artists like Giovanni Bellini, Titian, and Paolo Veronese carried the city's artistic fame. By the eighteenth century, however, the republic had passed her political zenith, with her population now reduced to around 145,000 and the 1797 collapse looming. Nevertheless, a new generation of artists, among them Giovanni Battista Tiepolo, Sebastiano Ricci, Giovanni Battista Pittoni, and Giovanni Antonio Canal, boldly reinvigorated Venetian painting.

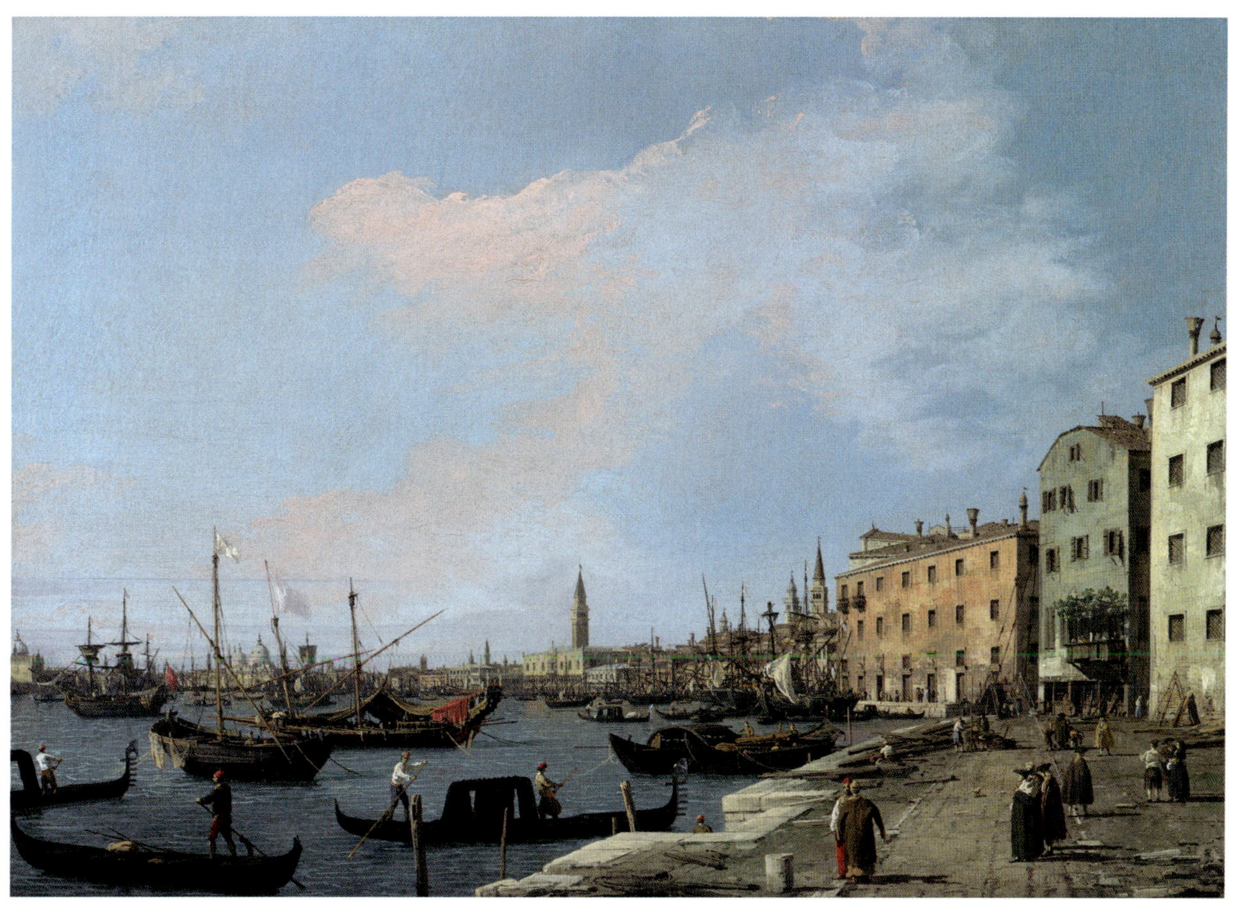

Fig. 1: Canaletto, *The Riva degli Schiavoni in Venice*, c.1730, oil on canvas, 46 × 63 cm. Kunsthistorisches Museum, Vienna, Picture Gallery, inv. 6332

Canal, or Canaletto, was born on 28 October 1697. His family belonged to the *cittadini originari*, a respected social class just below the Venetian patriciate. The only confirmed portrait of him notes this status: a print showing the artist in his 30s (fig. 2), bearing his coat of arms and inscribed *Origine Civis Venetus*—a citizen of Venice by birth. He did not, however, invent the genre of urban views (consider, for instance, Jan Vermeer's famous *View of Delft* of c. 1660 or Gaspar van Wittel's Roman vistas from 1681 onward). Nor was he alone among Venetian painters portraying their city. Luca Carlevarijs, Michele Marieschi, and Francesco Guardi produced many such views. But Canaletto's

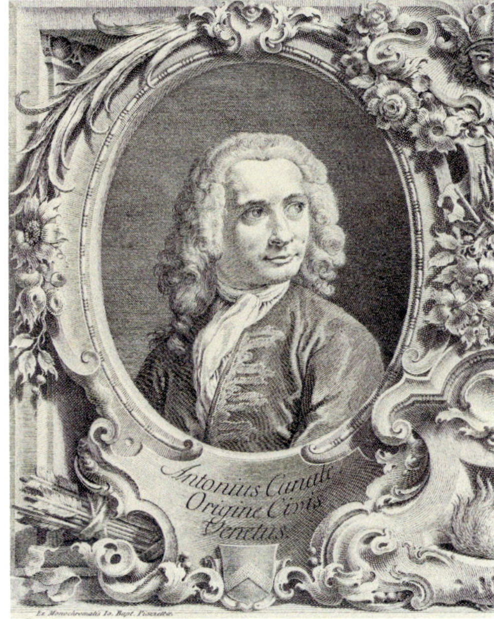

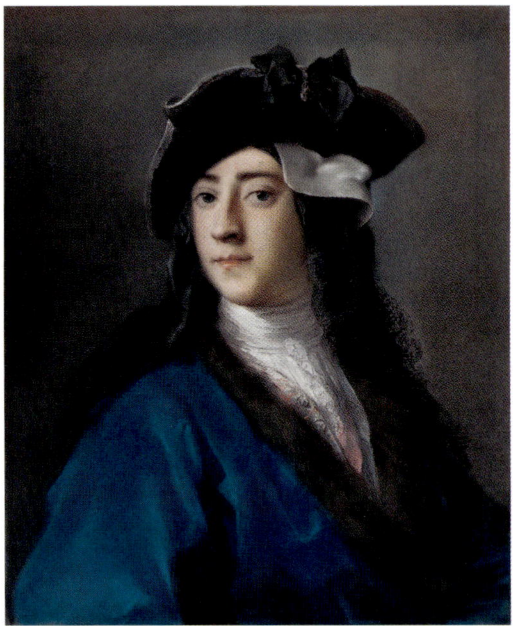

Fig. 2: Antonio Visentini,
Portrait of Canaletto from the frontispiece of *Prospectus Magni Canalis Venetiarum* (detail), 1735, etching, 384 × 543 mm. The Metropolitan Museum of Art, New York, Gift of David and Elizabeth Tunick 1991, inv. 1991.1206.6

Fig. 3: Rosalba Carriera, *Gustavus Hamilton, Second Viscount Boyne, in Masquerade Costume*, 1730/31, pastel on paper, 565 × 429 mm. The Metropolitan Museum of Art, New York, Purchase, George Delacorte Fund Gift, in memory of George T. Delacorte Jr., and Gwynne Andrews, Victor Wilbour Memorial, and Marquand Funds, 2002, inv. 2002.22

luminous, crisp, and architecturally precise renderings stood apart and became the most coveted *vedute* of the eighteenth century.[4]

Canaletto's rise to fame was fueled above all by interest from outside Venice. Although members of the local elite — such as Giambattista Recanati, Jacopo Pedozzi, and Zaccaria Sagredo — are known to have collected his paintings, it was external demand that transformed his career.[5] In 1725, the painter turned art agent, Alessandro Marchesini, reported that Canaletto had publicly exhibited a view of the church Santi Giovanni e Paolo at the Scuola di San Rocco, where it "amazed everyone" and was immediately purchased by the Imperial ambassador, Count Colloredo.[6] That same year, when Stefano Conti, a wealthy textile merchant from

Lucca, sought additional paintings to complement those he owned by Carlevarijs, Marchesini recommended Canaletto instead, noting that his pictures possessed such luminous clarity that it was as if sunlight itself shone from within them.[7] Such praise helped accelerate Canaletto's growing reputation and soon affected the pace and pricing of his work. In 1727, Owen McSwiney—an Irish impresario turned art agent—noted in a letter to Lord March (later 2nd Duke of Richmond) that Canaletto "has more work than he can do in any reasonable time," while criticizing his "whimsical" pricing.[8] Despite such frustrations, his appeal was clear, especially among British aristocrats who flocked to Venice as part of their educational journey across Italy: the so-called Grand Tour.

Indeed, Venice's uniqueness attracted travelers eager to experience not only her art and architecture but also her vibrant social life, musical and theatrical offerings, masked balls, and notorious courtesans.[9] The city's allure, especially during carnival season, is epitomized best by a pastel portrait of Gustavus Hamilton, Second Viscount Boyne, produced in 1730/31 by Rosalba Carriera, Venice's most prominent female portraitist (fig. 3). It shows Hamilton in masquerade costume, having donned the traditional Venetian *bauta*, comprising a mask, veil, and tricorn. Alongside such portraits, painted views of Venice became increasingly popular souvenirs, status symbols, and tokens of refined taste among visiting noblemen. The 1730s, in particular, saw the Grand Tour fuel a robust market for *vedute*, and Canaletto was deeply involved in meeting this demand.

He did so notably under the patronage of Joseph Smith, a merchant, collector, and art dealer who served as the British consul in Venice from 1744 to 1760. Smith, who acquired around fifty-four of Canaletto's paintings, played a crucial role in facilitating sales to British collectors. In 1762, he sold his copious collection of Canaletto's works to the young King George III.[10] Other aristocrats likewise sought to purchase Canaletto's paintings in bulk, often commissioning works through Smith. In 1731, the 21-year-old Duke of Bedford ordered twenty-four paintings, which still hang together today at Woburn Abbey.[11] Similarly, the Earl of Carlisle acquired seventeen for his "Canaletto Room"

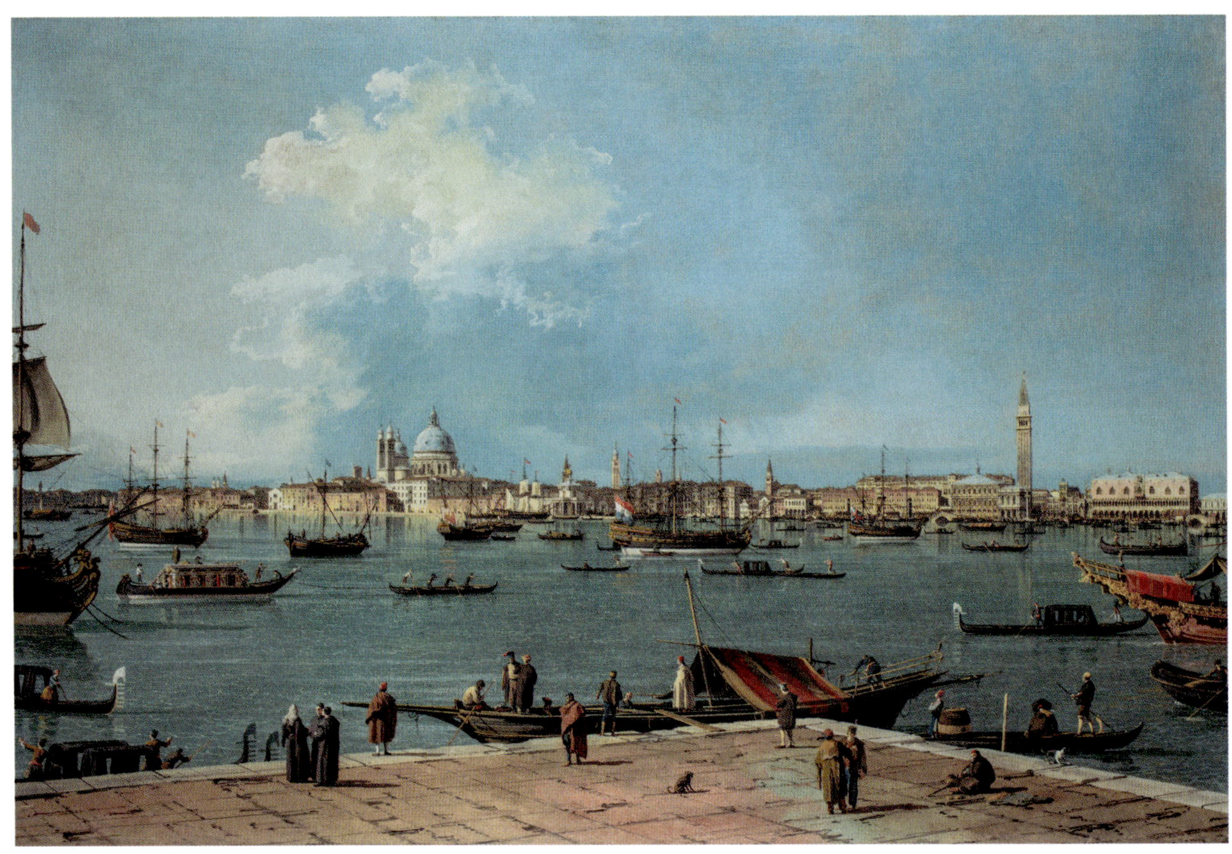

Fig. 4: Canaletto, *Venice: The Bacino di San Marco from San Giorgio Maggiore*, 1735/44, oil on canvas, 129.2 × 188.9 cm, detail on pp. 20–21. The Wallace Collection, London, inv. P497

at Castle Howard. To meet the expectations of such illustrious patrons, Canaletto gradually refined his style: whereas his early paintings displayed thick, frayed, almost sketch-like brushwork that lent them a raw, exploratory character, his later canvases became brighter, more meticulously detailed, and more compact and portable, as exemplified by the *Riva degli Schiavoni* mentioned earlier.[12]

Among Canaletto's mature works, his *Bacino di San Marco from San Giorgio Maggiore*, now in the Wallace Collection, stands out as one of his most ambitious Venetian vistas (fig. 4). Likely commissioned by Francis Seymour-Conway—later 1st Marquess of Hertford—during his Grand Tour from 1737 to 1740, the painting demonstrates that while many of Canaletto's works became smaller, he continued to use large formats for the most elite patrons. It depicts the *Bacino* from the island of San Giorgio Maggiore, with the opening of the Grand Canal at center and the Giudecca Canal to the left. The architectural landmarks are meticulously rendered, including the Palazzo Ducale, the Campanile di San Marco, Santa Maria della Salute, and the Dogana da Mar—Venice's customs building erected between 1678 and 1682.[13] The dynamic interplay of foreground, middle ground, and background enhances the composition's visual rhythm. The triangular terrace in the foreground, for instance, is animated by figures representing a range of Venetian society: a seated beggar on the right, Ottoman merchants in the center, and two priests engaged in conversation with a lawyer on the left. In the middle ground, the lagoon is alive with gondolas, a *burchiello* passenger barge being towed by a *barca*, and ships bearing Dutch, British, and Venetian flags. These maritime elements, alongside the monumental architecture behind them, underscore Venice's identity as a thriving mercantile hub. Compositional harmony is evident: the verticals of boat masts echo the church towers and domes on the horizon; several vessels are cropped by the canvas edge, suggesting the bustling waters extend well beyond the frame. The curved sails counterbalance the scene's horizontal expanse filled with Canaletto's famous bright blue sky and dramatic white clouds.

As with many of Canaletto's successful compositions, the Wallace picture owes much to its theatrical flair. Canaletto would have been well-acquainted with stagecraft: his father, Bernardo Canal (1664–1744), was a respected theatrical set designer with whom he trained from 1716 to 1718, before joining the Venetian painters' guild, the *Fraglia dei Pittori*, as an independent artist in 1720.[14] Through this apprenticeship, he most probably learned principles of perspective and geometry as applied to stage design—a tradition grounded in treatises by Sebastiano Serlio, Nicola Sabbattini, and Andrea Pozzo. Each of them addressed the challenge of creating illusionistic depth—which later culminated in more advanced approaches to *prospettiva per angolo* (oblique perspective), elaborated by Ferdinando Galli Bibiena in his *L'Architettura civile* (1711), that breaks with the single-point

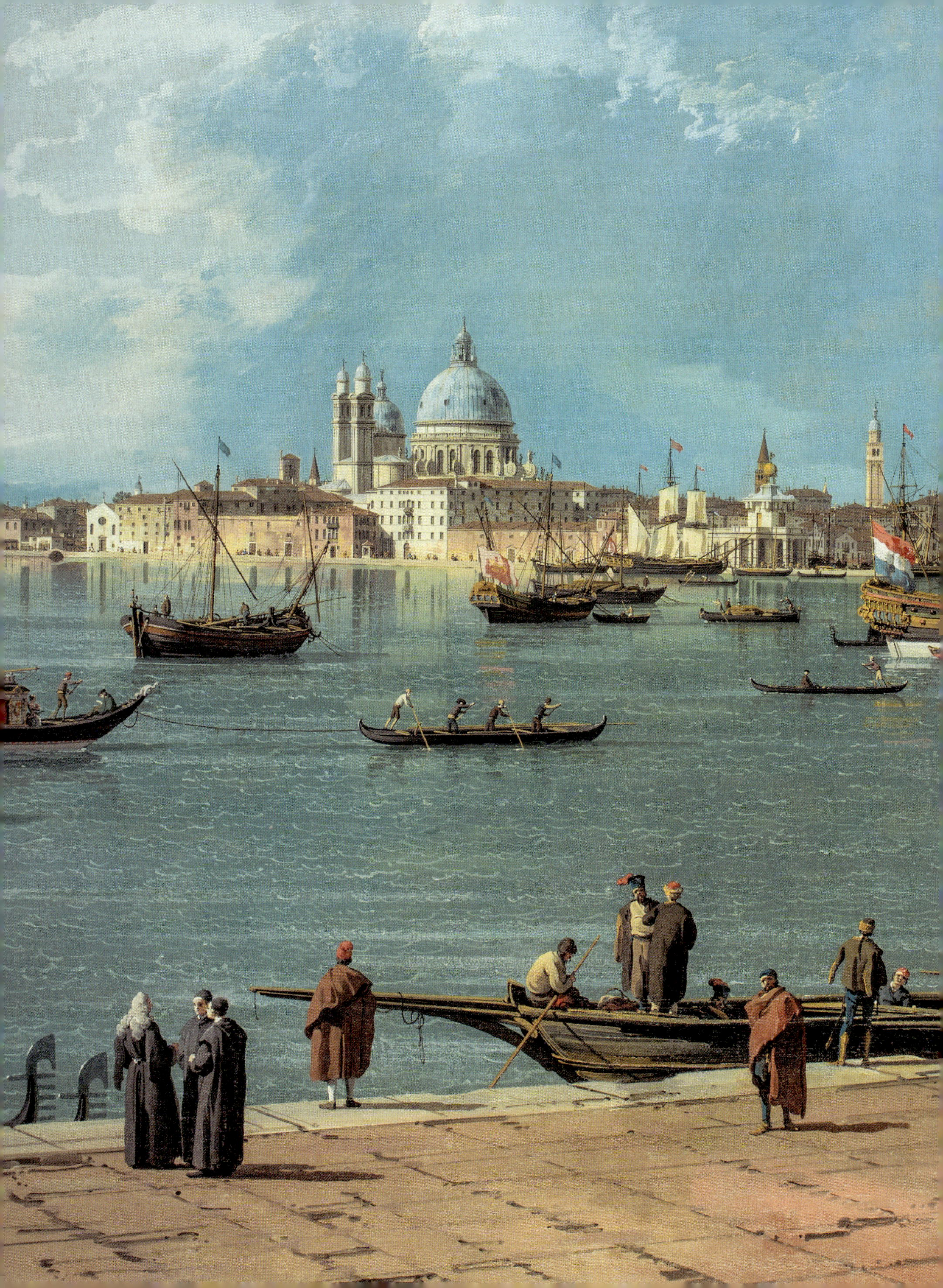

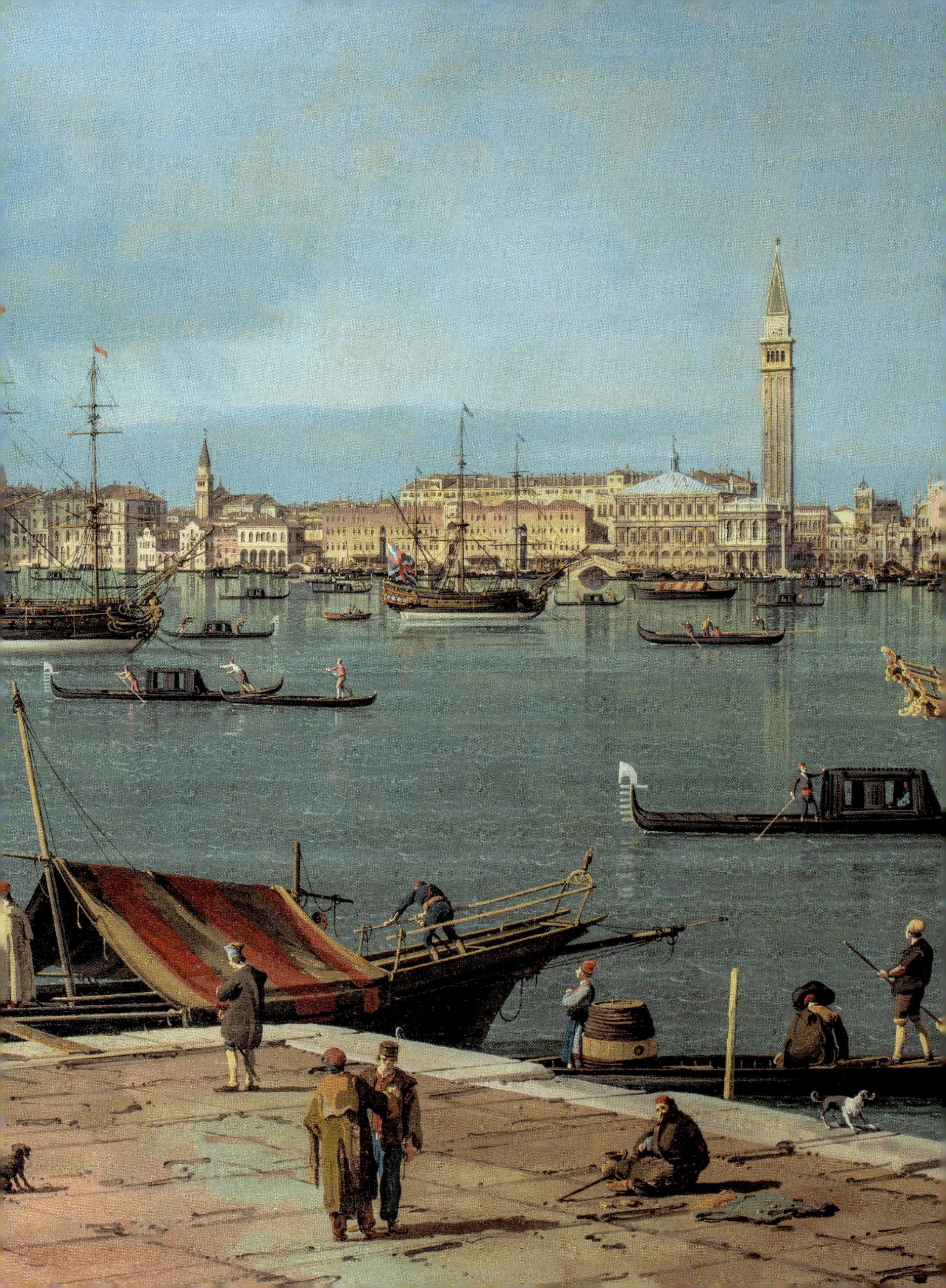

perspective of the Renaissance in favor of multiple vanishing points projecting into corners, generating a more immersive space.[15] While Canaletto did not—as technical studies suggest—compose his paintings geometrically, his scenographic sensibility is plainly evident in his spatial understanding.[16] In the Wallace picture, the triangular terrace acts like a stage, its receding lines diverging toward opposite vanishing points and pulling the viewer into the scene.

Another theatrically conceived work is Canaletto's depiction of the *Bucintoro* returning to the Molo on Ascension Day, one version of which, from the Thyssen-Bornemisza collection, was probably painted around 1745 (fig. 5). The *Bucintoro*—Venice's lavish state galley—was used for the annual *Sposalizio del Mare*, or "Marriage of the Sea," a symbolic ceremony wherein the Doge would sail out to the Adriatic and cast a gold ring into the water, reaffirming Venice's union with the sea. This ritual, accompanied by religious rites and civic fanfare, was one of Venice's grandest spectacles. In Canaletto's canvas, the *Bucintoro* returns to the Molo, the pier near the Palazzo Ducale. Its red-and-gold ornamentation, crowned by a figure of Justice and the Venetian flag with the golden lion of Saint Mark, stands out among a flotilla of escorting gondolas. Seen again from across the *Bacino*, the scene unfolds along a strong diagonal linking the Doge's Palace, the Biblioteca Marciana, the mint (*la Zecca*), and the distant dome of Santa Maria della Salute. Like a set designer crafting a theatrical tableau, Canaletto marshals spatial depth, rhythmic movement, and architectural clarity to produce a carefully orchestrated image of Venetian pageantry. Indeed, the warm afternoon light, drifting clouds, and the vivid brushwork heighten the sense of ceremonial grandeur. The enduring popularity of this subject—reflected in nearly a dozen surviving versions from Canaletto's hand and studio—attests to its appeal among Grand Tour patrons.[17]

Returning to the Wallace painting (fig. 4), we find that its theatrical sensibility expresses itself not through public ritual, as in the *Bucintoro* canvas, but through a more subtle manipulation of spatial illusion. The composition's oblique viewpoint—marked by the bank jutting into the foreground—and the abrupt cropping of ships at the canvas's edge already signal a play with

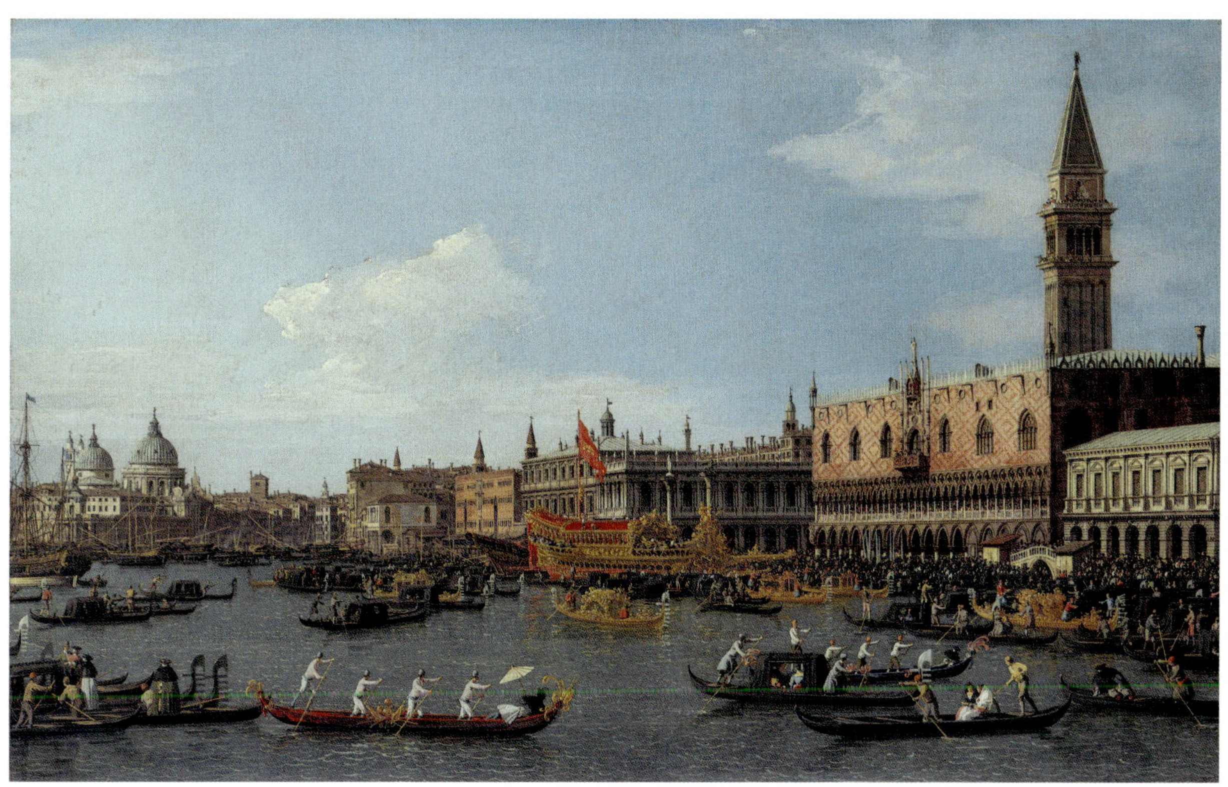

Fig. 5: Canaletto, *The Bucintoro*, 1745/50, oil on canvas, 57 × 93 cm. Museu Nacional d'Art de Catalunya, Barcelona (Thyssen-Bornemisza Collection on deposit at the MNAC, 2004), inv. 212851

spatial logic, one that recalls the angled perspectives championed by Bibiena. Moreover, the painting cleverly weaves together a composite of viewpoints: Though it seems to depict the Venetian skyline as seen from San Giorgio Maggiore, it subtly departs from topographical accuracy by including architectural elements—such as several church towers—not visible from that vantage point. In the aforementioned *Riva degli Schiavoni* (fig. 1), on the other hand, Canaletto omits entire buildings along the eastern waterfront, moves the city's landmarks closer together (essentially compressing the view), and elevates the middle arch of San Giorgio's dormitory façade. These calculated reconfigurations are not lapses in accuracy but, rather, aesthetic strategies: deliberate orchestrations of visual elements that heighten a composition's

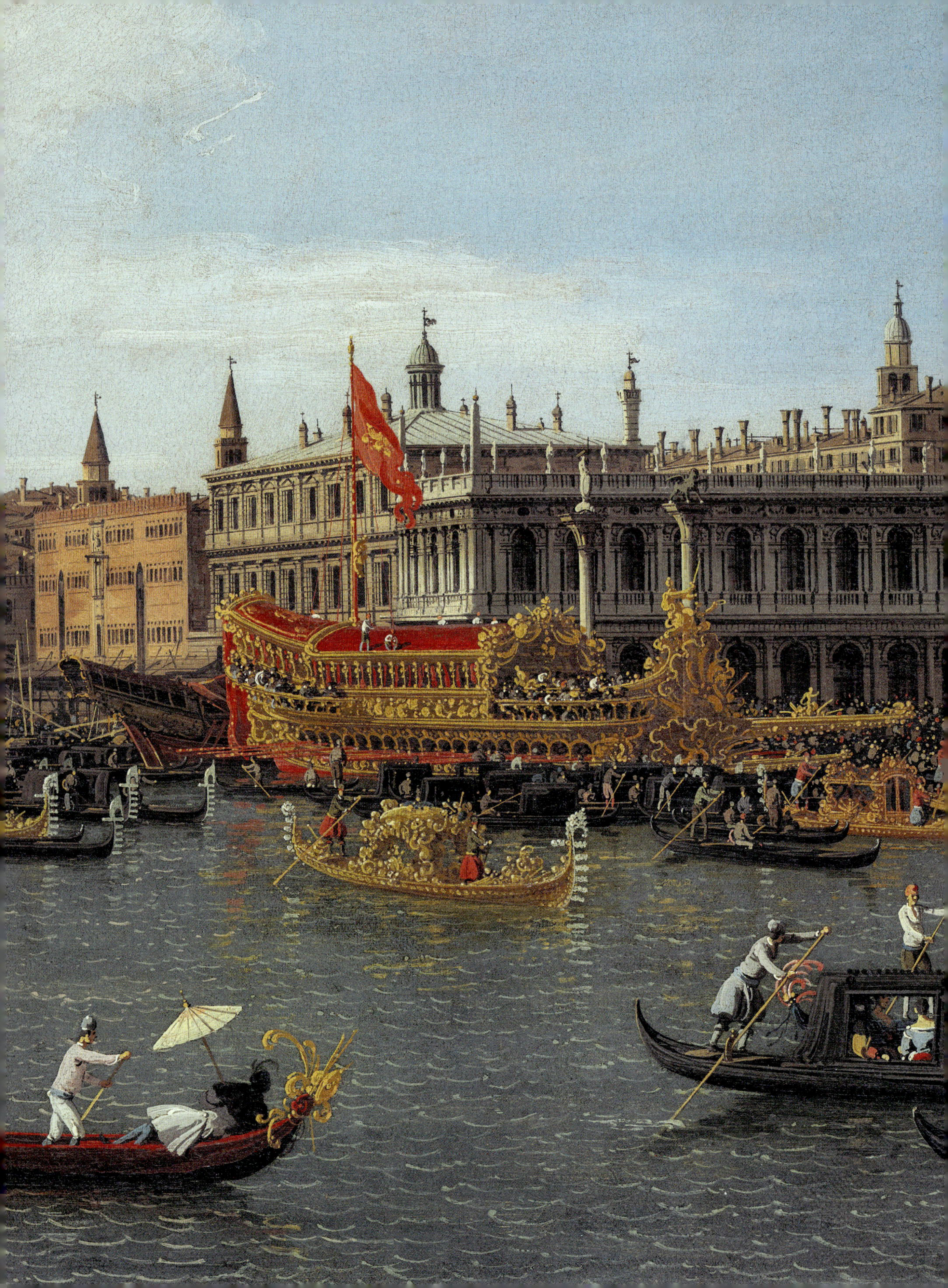

clarity and harmony. In synthesizing observation and invention, he adjusts the city's iconic contours and distills her social vibrancy into a painterly spectacle—transforming Venice into a luminous cultural ideal.

THE CAMERA OBSCURA

The balance between topographical accuracy and artistic license was not achieved through intuition alone. Behind the precision of Canaletto's vistas lay a methodical process rooted in the use of optical instruments—above all, the *camera obscura*.[18] Far from diminishing his artistic creativity, this device helped him translate Venice's urban complexity into pictorial form. It anchored his compositions in topographical verisimilitude while allowing him to rearrange architectural elements according to aesthetic priorities. In doing so, his use of optical tools was never merely mechanical but reflected a broader intellectual engagement with the scientific culture of his time that sought to reconcile empirical observation with the ideals of artistic expression.

The camera obscura was, in essence, a darkened enclosure where an external scene was projected through a lens onto a flat surface. Although artists had long used such devices—Vermeer is frequently cited as an early practitioner—the eighteenth century witnessed a significant surge in scientific interest in optics.[19] Publications on the subject proliferated, from practical manuals to philosophical treatises, the most influential being Isaac Newton's *Opticks* (1704).[20] Most of these works compared the eye to a camera obscura, including Jean Antoine Nollet's 1764 *Leçons de physique expérimentale* (fig. 6).[21] In doing so, Nollet shows a box-type model resembling one now housed in Venice's Museo Correr that, bearing on its hood the stamped name "A[NTONIO]. CANAL" (see cat. 4), may have belonged to Canaletto.[22] Dating from the eighteenth century, it features an adjustable lens tube and an interior 45-degree mirror that reflected the image upward onto a glass screen. With the hood lifted to block ambient light, an artist could place transparent paper over the screen and trace the projection coming from below. However, no tracings on

Detail of fig. 5

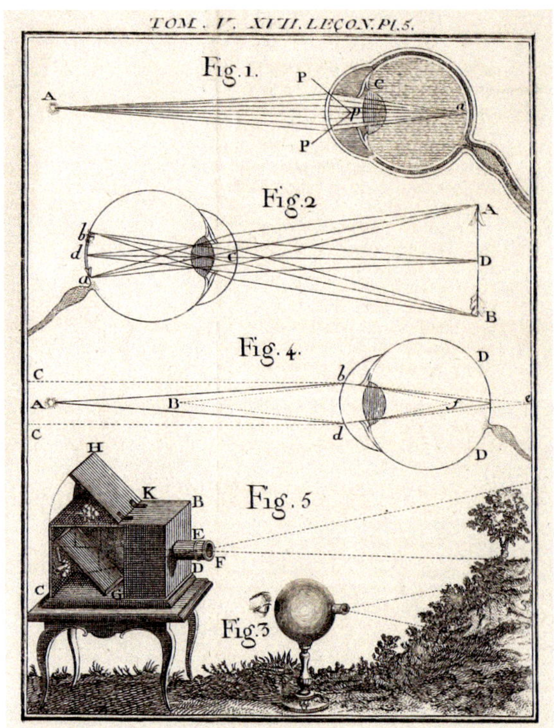

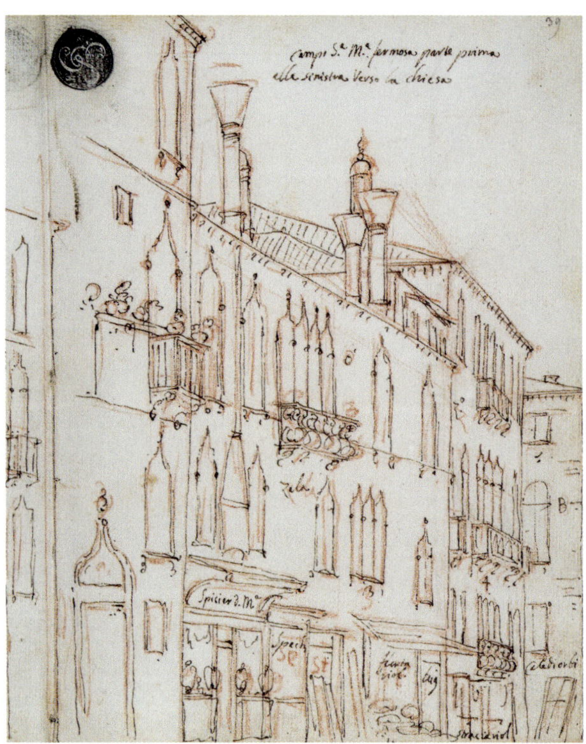

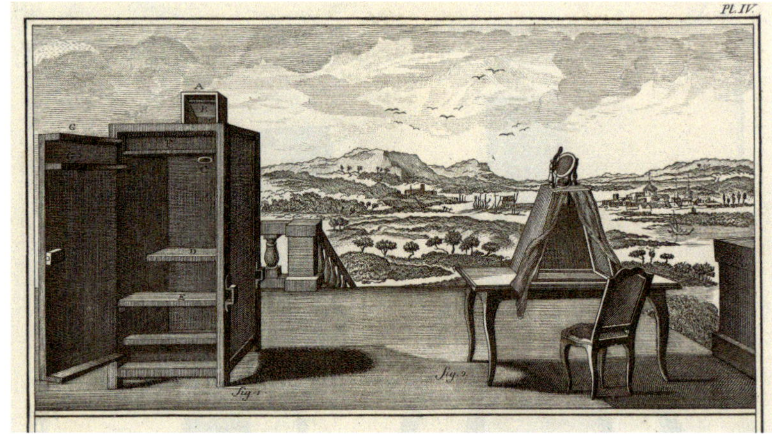

Fig. 6: Jean Antoine Nollet, *Leçons de physique expérimentale*, vol. 5 (Paris, 1764). Getty Research Institute, Los Angeles, inv. 1385-117

Fig. 7: Canaletto, *Quaderno Veneziano*: buildings on one side of the Campo Santa Maria Formosa, 1720/40, red crayon and ink, 175 × 235 mm. Gallerie dell'Accademia, Venice, cat. dis. 1839; foglio 39 recto

Fig. 8: Detail from: Denis Diderot, *Encyclopédie* (Paris, 1770/79). Austrian National Library, Vienna, 56.Q.1.(Vol.Planches,3), Pl. 4, Dessein, Chambre Obscure

translucent paper survive by Canaletto's hand. All extant camera drawings, including those in the so-called *quaderno*—that is, Canaletto's sketchbook now held at the Gallerie dell'Accademia in Venice (fig. 7)—are on opaque paper.[23] Recently, Philip Steadman has reaffirmed that Canaletto more likely used booth- or tent-type cameras that projected images downward.[24] Such devices frequently appear in contemporary treatises, from Willem Jacob 's Gravesande's *Essai de perspective* (1711) and Alexandre Julien Savérien's *Dictionnaire universel de mathematique et de physique* (1753) to Denis Diderot's *Encyclopédie* (1770/79, fig. 8).[25] Some models were lightweight and portable, with a pyramidal frame covered with cloth, large enough for the artist to insert his head and sketch through hand slots. Others were booth-like structures in which one could sit to work. Eighteenth-century examples rarely survive, but their frequent appearance in contemporary treatises attests to how widespread and accessible such devices must have been to artists like Canaletto.[26]

Yet, although Canaletto made use of a camera obscura, he was never beholden to its mechanical projection. He was, after all, a painter. Rather, his sketches provided a visual archive that he

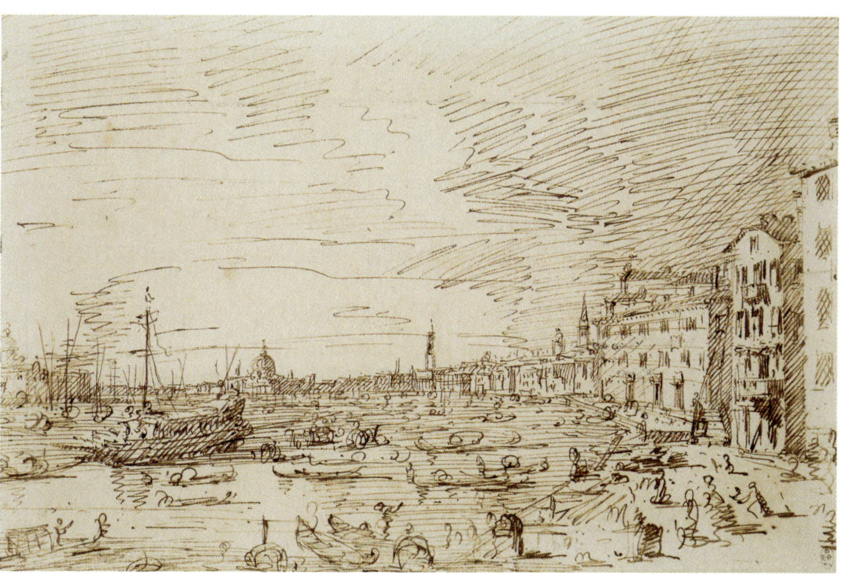

Fig. 9: Canaletto, *The Bacino Looking West from San Biagio*, 1729, pen and ink over pencil, 213 × 318 mm. Royal Collection Trust, inv. RCIN 907457

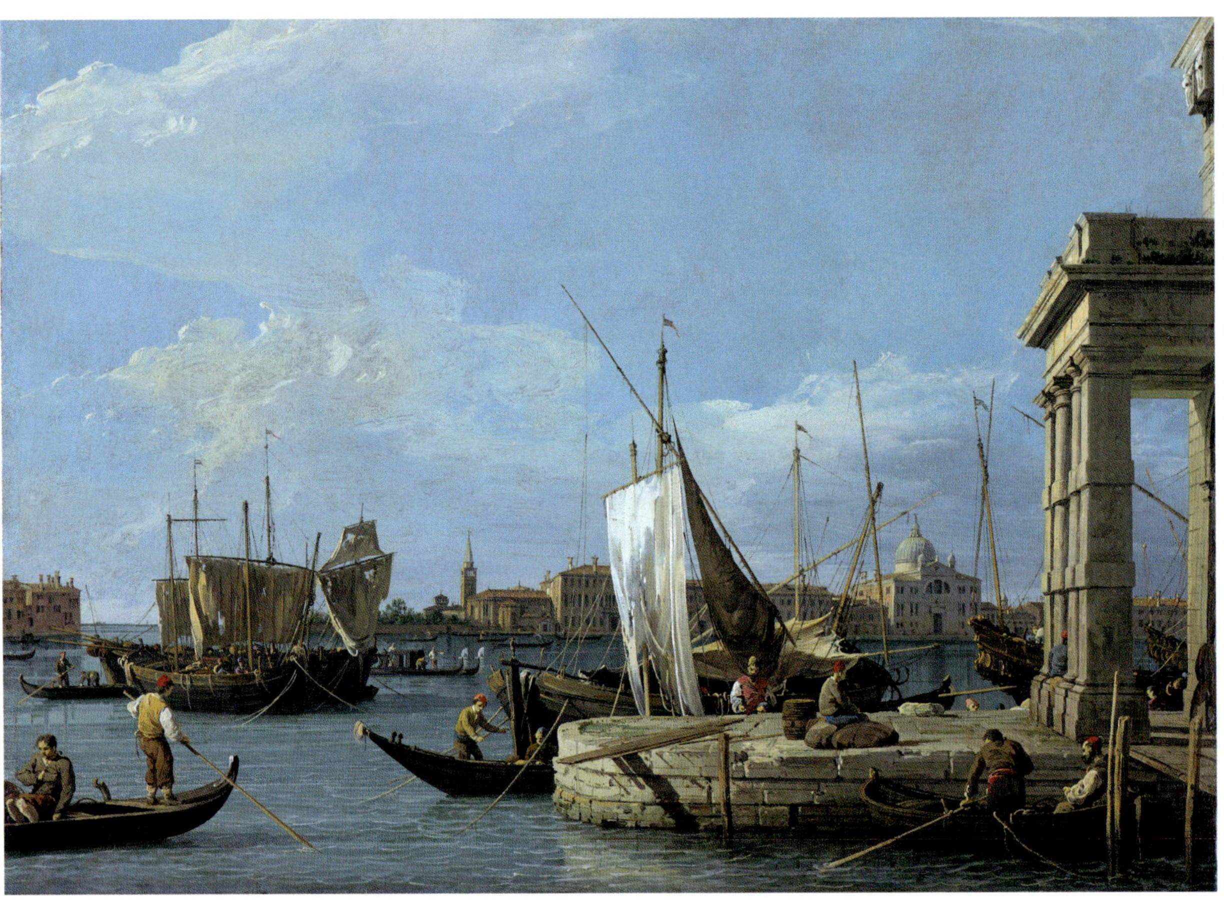

Fig. 10: Canaletto, *The Dogana in Venice*, c.1730, oil on canvas, 45.8 × 63.4 cm, detail on pp. 36–37. Kunsthistorisches Museum, Vienna, Picture Gallery, inv. 6331

combined and expanded into elaborate compositions on canvas in his studio, subtly adjusting proportions to suit pictorial logic—shifting buildings, emphasizing domes or towers, or omitting structures altogether. The Campanile di San Marco, in particular, is rarely depicted in its true proportions; Canaletto often elongates it to make it appear taller and more elegant. Even the number of windows on a given façade might vary from one painting to another. Beyond his camera-aided drawings, he also produced free hand studies that demonstrate compositional autonomy. One such sheet in the Royal Collection (fig. 9), related to his views of the *Riva degli Schiavoni*, exemplifies this intuitive approach rendered in vivid hatching.[27]

In his paintings, Canaletto often combined elements from multiple viewpoints, modifying the real to suit the ideal. His

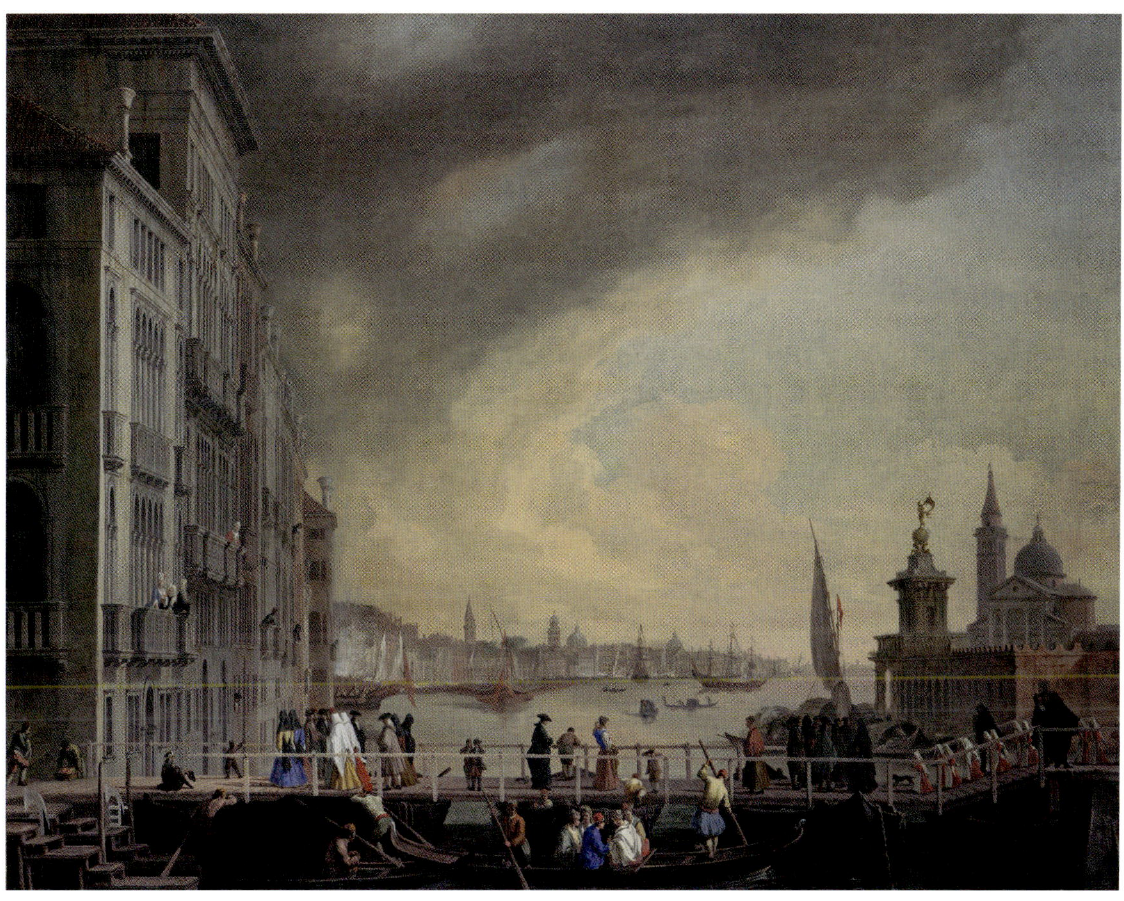

Fig. 11: Johan Richter (attr.), *Feast of Santa Maria della Salute*, c.1720, oil on canvas, 121 × 151 cm. Wadsworth Atheneum Museum of Art, Hartford, The Ella Gallup Sumner and Mary Catlin Sumner Collection Fund, inv. 1939.268

c. 1730 view of the Dogana (fig. 10) now at the Kunsthistorisches Museum is a case in point.[28] It fuses two vantage points: one from the center of the Grand Canal, offering a frontal view of the Dogana's loggia, and another from the Dogana's quay, looking across the Giudecca Canal toward the churches of San Giovanni Battista and the Zitelle. While the shallow lagoon could support pole-anchored rafts, the deeper Grand Canal posed greater challenges — making this seamless dual perspective all the more remarkable. To reach this vantage point, Canaletto must have used a temporary platform, perhaps similar to Venice's pontoon bridges built for votive festivals like the *Festa della Salute*, as documented in a painting attributed to Johan Richter from 1720 (fig. 11). Yet this particular bridge over the Grand Canal lay too far west for a frontal Dogana view, and so Canaletto must have stood on an extended or floating pier opposite it. How exactly remains unknown. In any case, in the final canvas he concealed his composite method through careful architectural alignment, calibrated placement of boats and figures, and a luminous palette of soft greys, cool blues, and warm accents that unite the scene. The result is as technically sophisticated as it is visually elegant.

CANALETTO'S PAINTERLY LANGUAGE

While Canaletto's use of the camera obscura enabled him to achieve a striking degree of realism, his success as a *vedutista* hinged on ensuring his paintings did not appear as mechanical copies of optical projections. Indeed, Diderot, in his 1753 discussion of the camera obscura, noted how "with this instrument ... someone who does not know how to draw will nevertheless be able to draw things with the utmost precision."[29] Thus, for artists this circumstance posed a serious question about their skill. A telling reflection of this concern is a satirical drawing by Antonio Maria Zanetti the Elder, mocking Canaletto's contemporary, Michele Marieschi (fig. 12): It shows Marieschi with a camera behind him projecting a clumsy, block-like cityscape on the wall, an image by which the artist hopes—as suggested in the depiction of low hanging fruits above—to harvest the rewards of art.[30] Yet, his concealed drawing hand, along with a puzzled gaze at a figure sketch, imply complete reliance on the device and an inability to draw unaided. The caricature reflects a prevailing bias: within the traditional hierarchy of genres, *veduta* painting ranked far below history painting full of carefully studied human figures. Mere optical accuracy thus risked being read as artistic incompetence. For a painter like Canaletto, the challenge was therefore to elevate view painting above mechanical reproduction—to prove, through painterly refinement and compositional wit, that the camera was a means, not an end.[31]

Canaletto's contemporaries indeed noted how he manipulated the visual data the camera provided. In his book, *Abecedario*, the great connoisseur Pierre-Jean Mariette observed that Canaletto "made use of the camera obscura, whose faults he was able to mitigate."[32] Likewise, Antonio Maria Zanetti the Younger—a cousin of Zanetti the Elder who satirized Marieschi—praised Canaletto for showing its limitations: "Canal taught the proper use of the *camera ottica* and showed what defects can be introduced into a painting when its whole view is taken from what can be seen in the camera, particularly the colors of the atmosphere, and when one does not eliminate things offensive to the senses."[33] A decade later, when Johann Dallinger von Dalling catalogued two of Canaletto's paintings in the Liechtenstein collection in 1780, he similarly remarked that the artist "must have made shrewd use of the camera obscura, which can make objects too bright and harsh if not correctly used."[34] For Canaletto, then, the camera was only a starting point. It was an optical instrument whose images were to be refined through artistic discernment.

This intersection of optics and aesthetics reflects Canaletto's association with Venice's enlightened milieu. Through his patron Joseph Smith, he would have moved in circles that comprised not

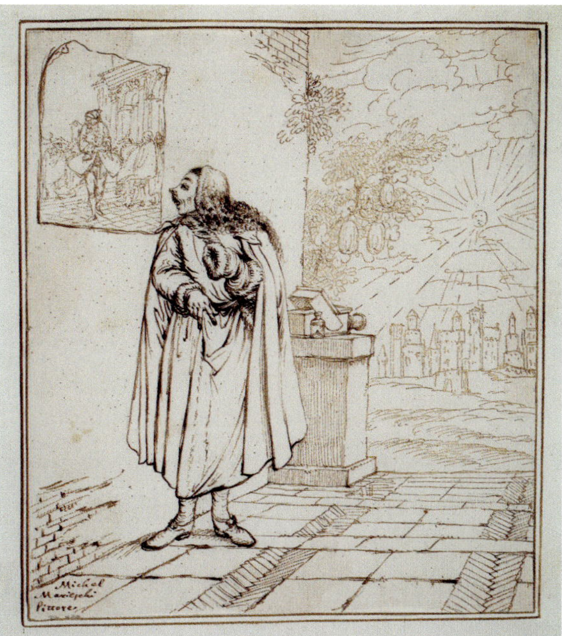

Fig. 12: Antonio Maria Zanetti the Elder, *Caricature of Michele Marieschi*, c.1740, pen and brown ink with brown wash over pencil, 231 × 200 mm. Fondazione Giorgio Cini, Venice, inv. 36726

only international collectors but also scientists and academicians.[35] Among them was Francesco Algarotti—polymath, Royal Society member, and Newtonian advocate—who knew Canaletto personally and owned four of his paintings. In his *Il newtonianismo per le dame*, a playful dialogue on Newton's optical experiments first published in Italian in 1737 and reissued in English in 1739, Algarotti repeatedly invoked the camera obscura. At one point, he described its image as so vivid and soft that "a landskip drawn by Claude Lorrain, or a visto by Canaletto, appear faint and languid."[36] A related view is offered by Antonio Conti, a Paduan priest, physicist, and acquaintance of Smith. In his posthumous *Prose e Poesie* (1756), he reflects on the limits of painted realism:

> *The camera obscura might be used to make the perspective of a canal in Venice with its buildings: Canaletto, thanks to his sagacity, may transfer more points to his painting than any other; but it is not possible that he will ever transfer them all. Nevertheless, those he doth transfer strike the eye with so lively an impression, that, at the first glance upon his canvas, I am persuaded I behold the very scene.*[37]

While Algarotti and Conti invoke Canaletto in the context of optical fidelity, their assessments are framed by a scientific mindset that imagined nature—and its technological capture—as more precise than even the most gifted painter's hand. Their views contrast with Zanetti's, who had warned against the camera's "defects," and show how contemporaries read Canaletto's pictures through empirical language, even when scientists believed technology to surpass the brush.

Given this context, Canaletto's clarity and exacting detail has prompted André Corboz to characterize his mature style as "Newtonian."[38] Indeed, Algarotti, in his *Essay on Painting* (1764), urged painters (albeit without naming Canaletto) to ground their practice in empirical observation and the science of optics—whether through the study of color or the use of instruments like the camera obscura: "In short, painters should make the same use of the camera obscura, which naturalists and astronomers make of the microscope and telescope, for all these instruments equally contribute to make known, and represent nature."[39] Whether consciously or not, Canaletto's paintings seem to embody this imperative. They render the city with a level of exactitude that often surpasses the capacity of the unaided eye. Distant windows, church towers, gondoliers at the water's edge, even clouds, are depicted with uncanny precision. Some art historians likened this heightened realism to a telescopic gaze and a compression of physical distance into legible detail.[40] His contemporaries, too, remarked on this intensity of vision: McSwiney, in his aforementioned letter to the Duke of Richmond, noted that Canaletto's "excellence lies in painting things which fall immediately under his eye."[41] While this comment is often read as evidence that he worked without optical devices, it can equally be interpreted as reflecting Enlightenment ideals of close empirical observation, both aided and unaided by cameras, telescopes, and magnifying glasses.

Eighteenth-century engagement with optics in Venice was far from theoretical: it was embedded in the city's material and cultural fabric. Algarotti maintained ties with leading opticians such as Domenico Selva and his son Lorenzo, whose workshop near San Marco was, by 1725, producing telescopes, microscopes, and camera obscuras.[42] Other craftsmen, such as Biagio Burlini on the Fondamenta Osmarin, ran similar well-appointed shops.[43] Their catalogues listed a wide range of optical devices sought by scientists and artists alike, often stressing—as with the scientific treatises of the time—the analogies between the physiology of the human eye and the workings of the camera obscura.[44] Selva's portable tent-cameras even featured internal tables at which one could comfortably sit, and it was suggested that these might well have been the kind of gadgets Canaletto employed in the field.[45]

Yet, although ample circumstantial evidence confirms that Canaletto used optical devices, no contemporary eyewitness accounts record him employing them outdoors. In June 1749, the English antiquarian George Vertue even noted his surprise that Canaletto "is remarkable for reservedness & shyness in being seen at work, at any time, or anywhere."[46] But rather than indicating the absence of his use of optical instruments, such discretion may instead reveal a wish to protect trade secrets and the need to preserve the delicate balance between mechanical reproduction and artistic invention. When sketching in public, moreover, he may have worked inside booth-type cameras resembling the temporary wooden *casotti* common in Venetian squares, used for small-scale commerce or storage.[47] These would have allowed him to operate unnoticed, even in crowded spaces. This idea gains plausibility from later intelligence about his nephew Bellotto, who in 1754, while preparing views of Pirna and the fortress of Sonnenstein, formally requested permission to erect a small wooden hut for his work, guarded by sentries.[48] The Dresden record offers rare documentary confirmation of such temporary structures, suggesting that Bellotto — and perhaps Canaletto before him — relied on booth-type cameras. Further context is provided by the fact that during carnival the Selva family constructed large-scale versions of *casotti* as theatrical camera

Fig. 13: Biagio Burlini, *Raccolta di macchine, ed istrumenti d'ottica* (Venice, 1758). Wellcome Collection, London, inv. EPB/B/16206

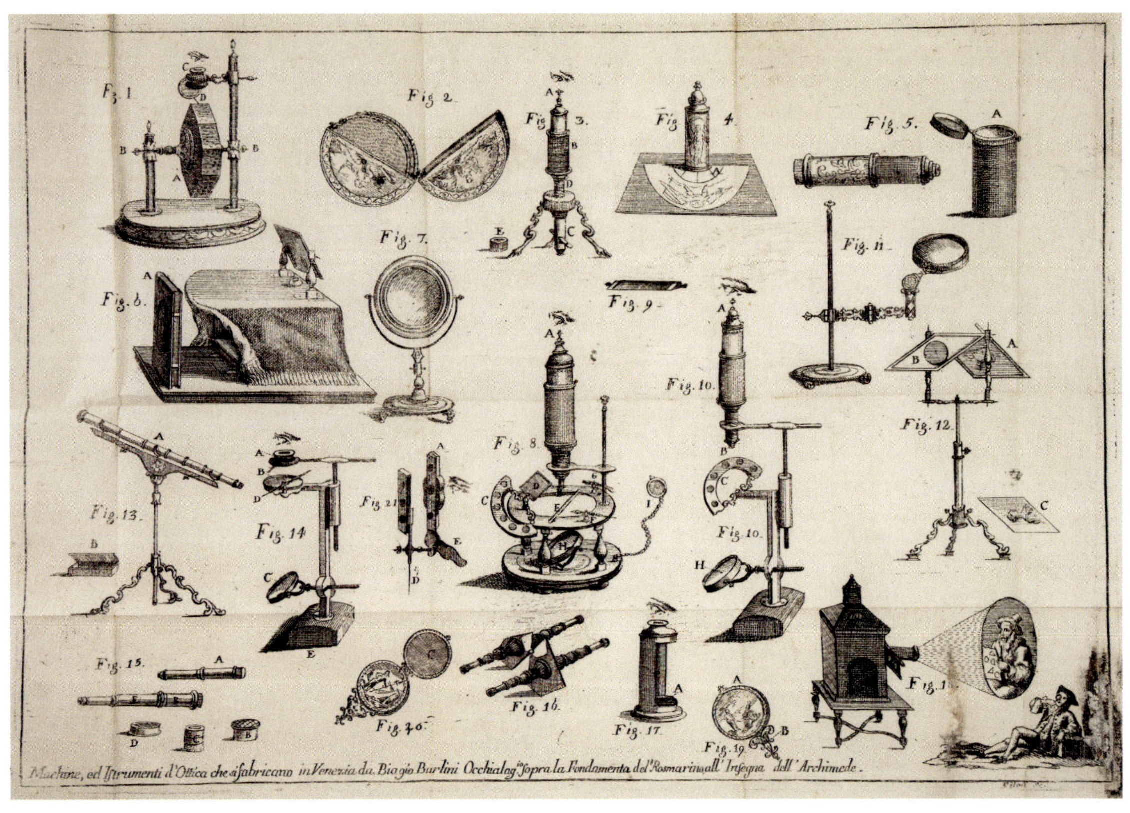

obscuras, equipping them with lenses and mirrors to project exterior scenes onto interior walls.[49] These immersive spaces, large enough to hold entire audiences, exemplified the era's fascination with illusion and optical wonder. Canaletto's practice unfolded within just such an atmosphere of empirical spectacle, where art, science, and entertainment converged.

Building upon this environment of experimentation, Philip Steadman has recently suggested that Canaletto may also have used the camera to transfer compositional elements onto canvas. In a series of trials, he demonstrated how preparatory drawings or architectural prints could be placed before the camera's mirror and, by adjusting lenses and distances, scaled and projected onto the painting surface without recourse to underdrawings—which, as technical studies suggest, are absent from Canaletto's paintings.[50] Indeed, no carbon-based underdrawings have ever been detected on his canvases: neither graphite, black chalk, nor ink lines appear beneath the paint surface. While it remains possible that he used media difficult to detect via infrared reflectography (such as red chalk), the evidence suggests he generally sketched compositions directly in paint. He may also have employed magic lanterns as illustrated in Burlini's 1758 *Raccolta di macchine, ed istrumenti d'ottica* (fig. 13). In their essence, magic lanterns projected images onto a wall through translucent drawings much like a modern slide projector. While there is no evidence Canaletto employed such an apparatus, Burlini's publication demonstrates the range and sophistication of optical tools available at mid-century. The precision of Canaletto's architectural renderings suggests that, in principle, he may have drawn on such technologies, perhaps in conjunction with more traditional aids like the pantograph, a mechanical device used to copy images.[51]

However, as mentioned, reducing Canaletto's practice to a mere replication of projections would be a profound misreading: once in the studio, he synthesized empirical observation, theoretical study, and painterly technique, extending his mastery beyond optical devices into the very materiality of painting. He typically combined multiple viewpoints, subtly altered the appearance of single buildings, and worked in deliberate stages,

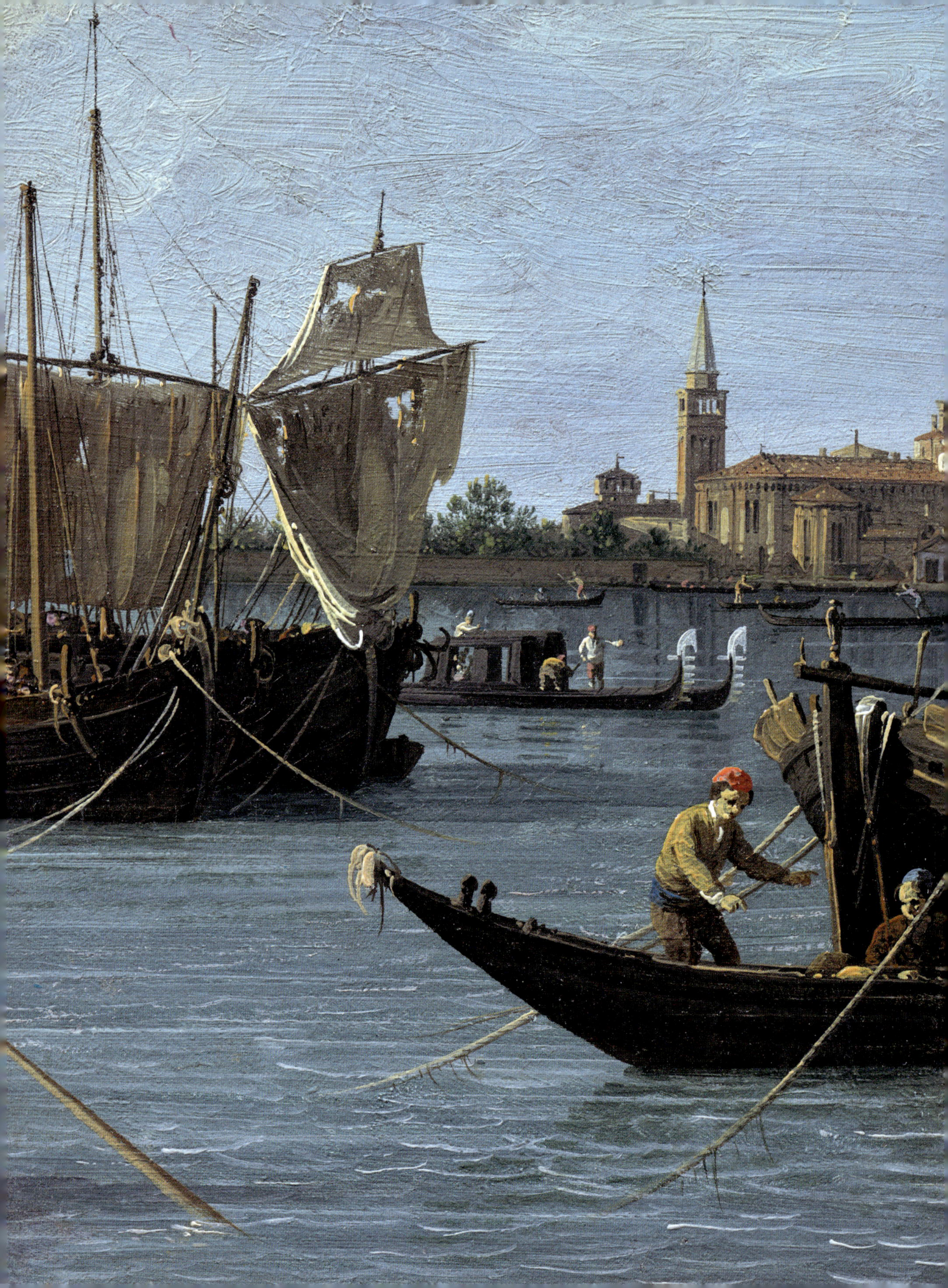

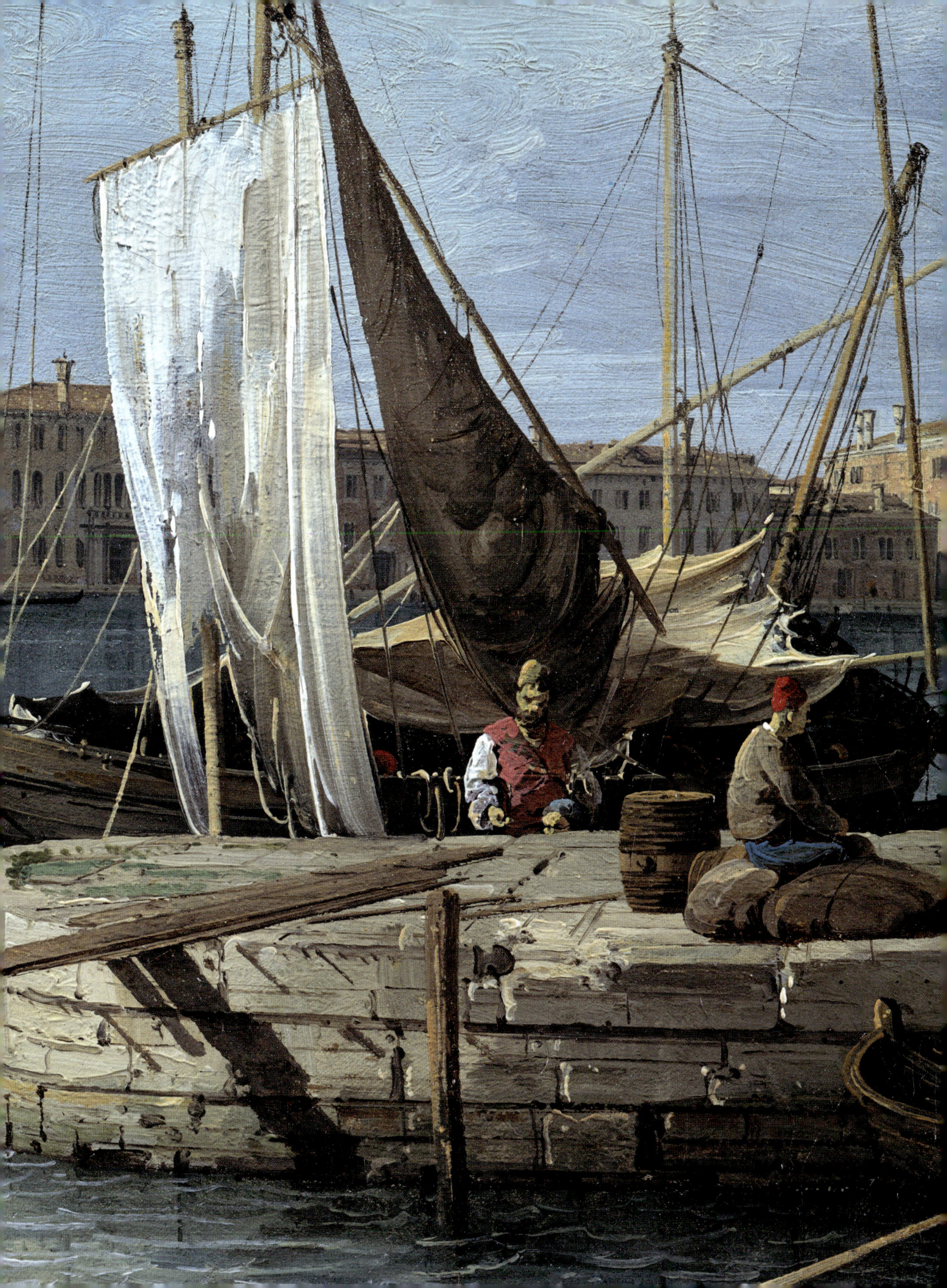

layering paint progressively from broadly blocked-in areas to a finely detailed surface. To save time, he seems to have often purchased pre-primed canvases that featured a dual ground: a warm brown base layer overlaid with a paler beige-gray which provided chromatic depth and a stable painting surface.[52] On this base, he blocked in major elements — sky, water, architecture — before refining details and finally adding animated staffage figures. In passages such as the sails' ropes in the *Dogana* canvas (fig. 10), he painted wet-in-wet, pulling new color across underlying, wet paint to create vivid effects — other ropes were added only after the underlying layer had completely dried. When composing his architectural elements, he often incised lines into wet paint using a stylus or the end of his brush. These grooves appear in various paint layers — sometimes already etched into the preparatory layer, other times added only as a final step for texture. Some, left without added color to catch the light, naturally cast subtle shadows; others were retraced with dark paint for emphasis. In the *Dogana* view, this search for precision is especially evident: he used a compass to inscribe the thermal window of the Zitelle and marked out the loggia's contours with a ruler before adding details. In the *Riva degli Schiavoni* canvas (fig. 1), shallow grooves on the right-hand façade evoke ashlars while others guide the (later painted over) perspectival foreshortening. As for the buildings in the far distance, he dispensed with incisions altogether, painting free hand.[53] Consequently, his practice emerges as a hybrid one: combining firsthand observation, mechanical recording, optical projection, invention, and modulating paint two- and three-dimensionally — all filtered through a visual language fully his own.

BELLOTTO LEARNS FROM CANALETTO

Given the high demand for his paintings, Canaletto likely employed at least one or two assistants. Among the most gifted artists to emerge from this circle was his nephew, Bernardo Bellotto. Born on 20 May 1722 to Fiorenza Domenica Canal — Canaletto's younger sister — and her husband Lorenzo Bellotto,

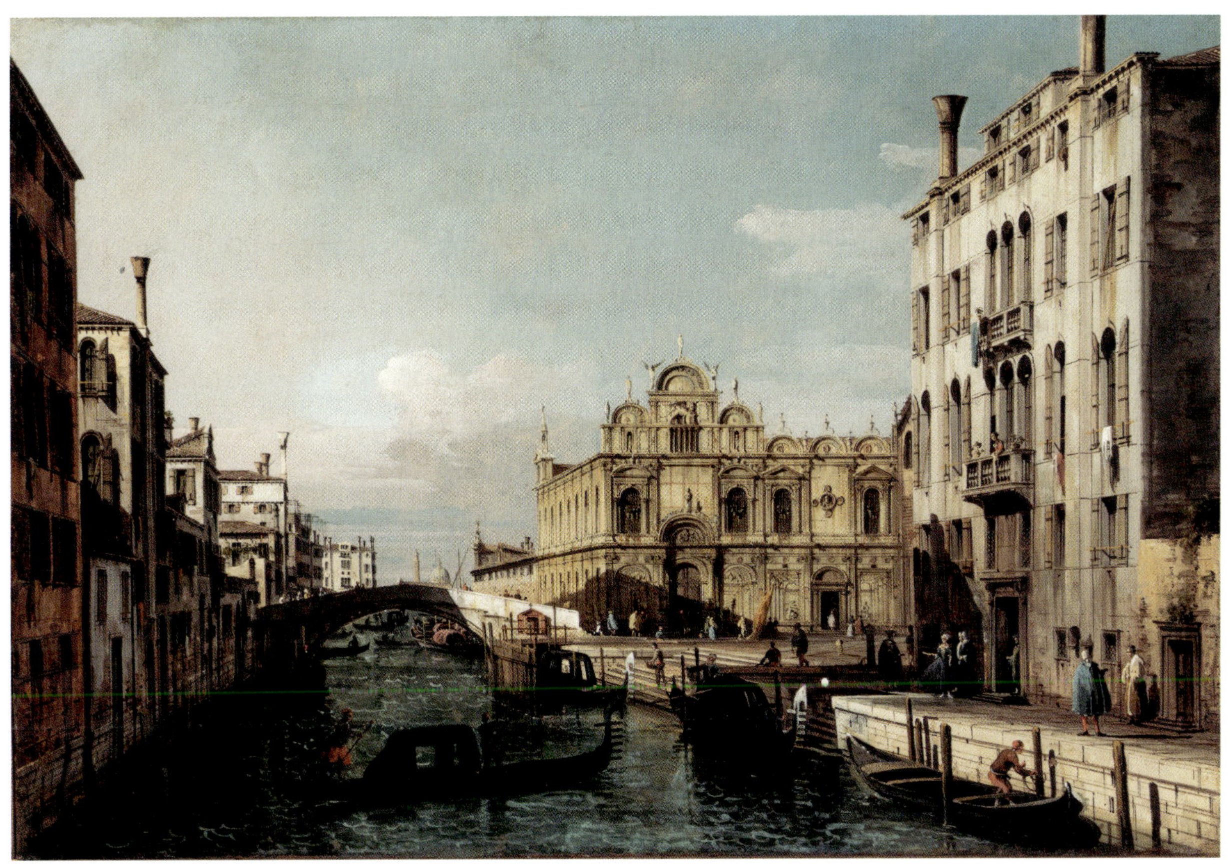

Fig. 14: Bernardo Bellotto, *The Rio dei Mendicanti and the Scuola di San Marco*, c.1740, oil on canvas, 41 × 59 cm. Gallerie dell'Accademia, Venice, inv. 494

the young Bernardo entered his uncle's workshop around 1735, at the age of thirteen.[54] His arrival coincided with the height of Canaletto's popularity, at a moment when demand for Venetian *vedute* was reaching its peak. It is safe to assume Bellotto's early role involved grinding pigments, priming canvases, and assisting with preparatory sketches, perhaps even filling in elements on the canvases Canaletto did not wish (or have the time) to complete himself. In the process, he adopted his uncle's rigorous working methods, including the use of the camera obscura. In 1738 he joined the Venetian painters' guild, the *Fraglia*, where he remained listed until 1743.

While training in his uncle's style, Bellotto gradually developed a distinct artistic language.[55] A key work from this early period is his c. 1740 view of the Rio dei Mendicanti (fig. 14),

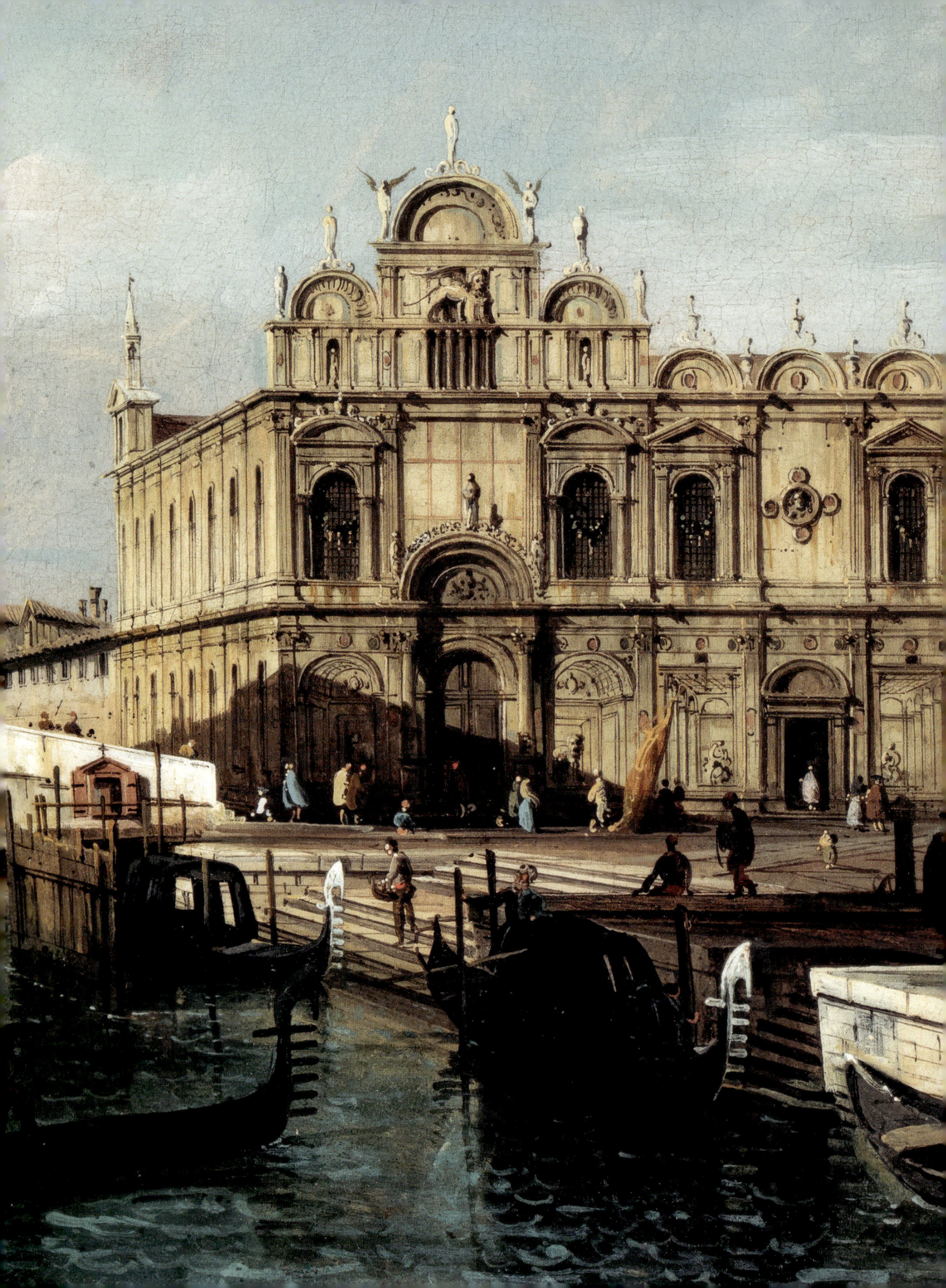

a painting that marks a decisive step in his emerging pictorial voice, especially when contrasted with Canaletto's *Riva degli Schiavoni* (fig. 1). While Canaletto preferred evenly lit scenes and pastel tones, Bellotto embraced dramatic tonal contrasts and earthier, deeper hues. In the *Rio dei Mendicanti*, chiaroscuro defines the mood: façades on the left cast deep shadows across the canal, while sunlit buildings on the opposite side glow warmly. This contrast heightens dramatic tension and visually links both canal banks through shifting shade. The composition centers on the Scuola Grande di San Marco, home to a prominent lay confraternity. Its renowned Renaissance façade—rebuilt after a fire in 1485—is crisply lit at the top, while an angled shadow from across the canal cuts into its base, animating its architectural form. In the far distance, the dome and campanile of San Michele—Venice's cemetery island—appear on the horizon, guiding the eye along the canal's recession. This diagonal is suddenly halted by the Ponte Cavallo, which acts as a visual barricade, compressing the space into a stage-like setting, keeping the viewer's attention on the foreground. There, at right, the Palazzo Dandolo anchors a subtle narrative: a finely dressed couple emerges from its doorway to greet a cloaked figure. Some speculate these figures reference the now-unknown patron (perhaps tied to the Dandolo family).[56] While this remains hypothetical, the painting's dramatic contrasts, warm hues, and compact spatial structure confirm it as an early yet remarkably self-assured work by eighteen-year-old Bellotto.

Another important milestone from this formative period is the *View of the Grand Canal with the Palazzi Foscari and Moro Lin* (fig. 15), also painted around 1740. It depicts gondolas and barges navigating the Grand Canal, flanked by Palazzo Moro Lin on the left and Palazzo Foscari on the right, with a view toward Santa Maria della Carità (today's Gallerie dell'Accademia) at center. Though the composition follows Canaletto's models, Bellotto subtly departs from them, imbuing the scene with his own sensibility: buildings and water are rendered in deeper hues and with more dramatic shadowing, demonstrating Bellotto's technical precocity and emerging stylistic independence, even if the perspective is geometrically rigid. Intriguingly, it has been

Detail of fig. 14

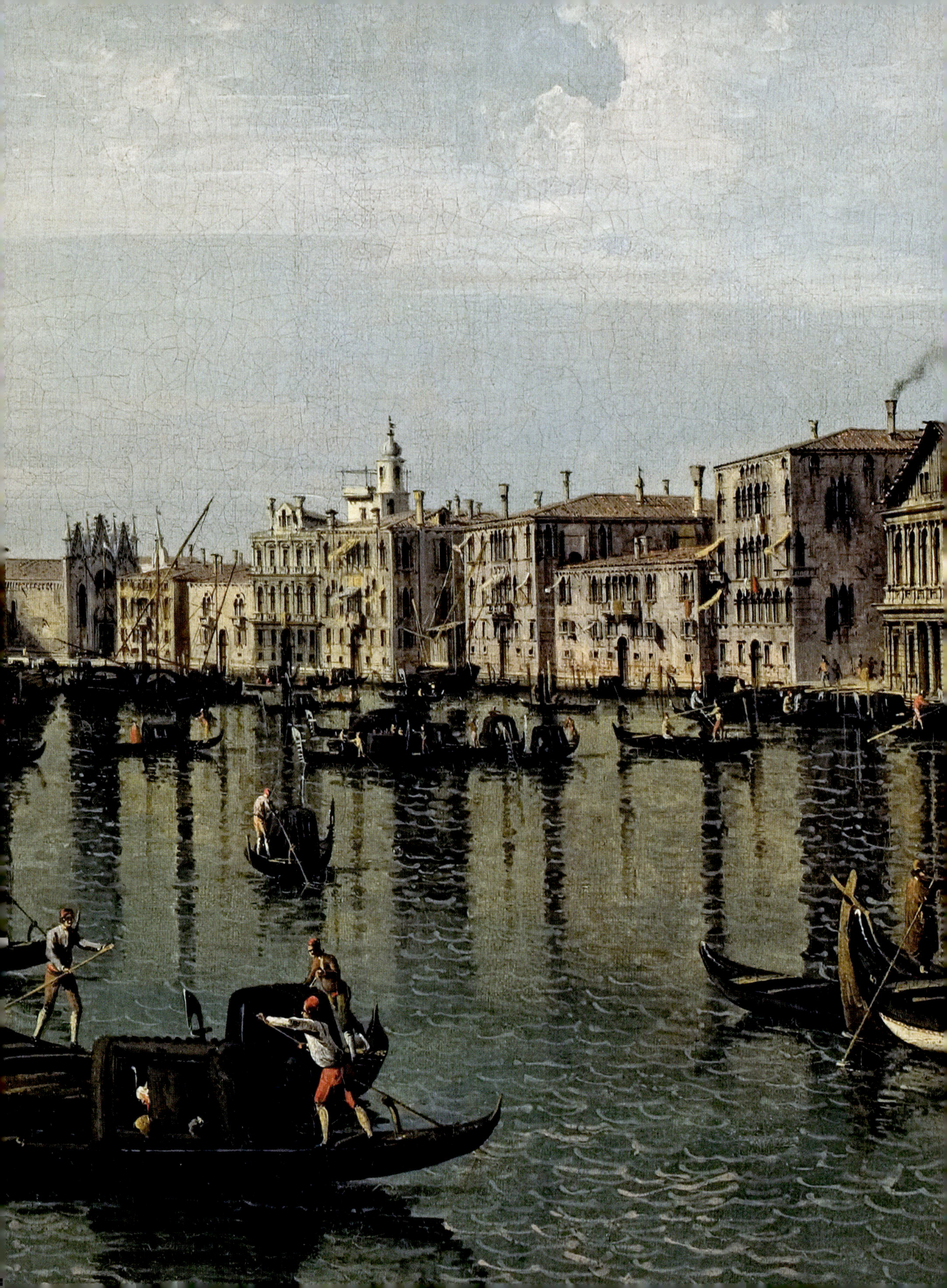

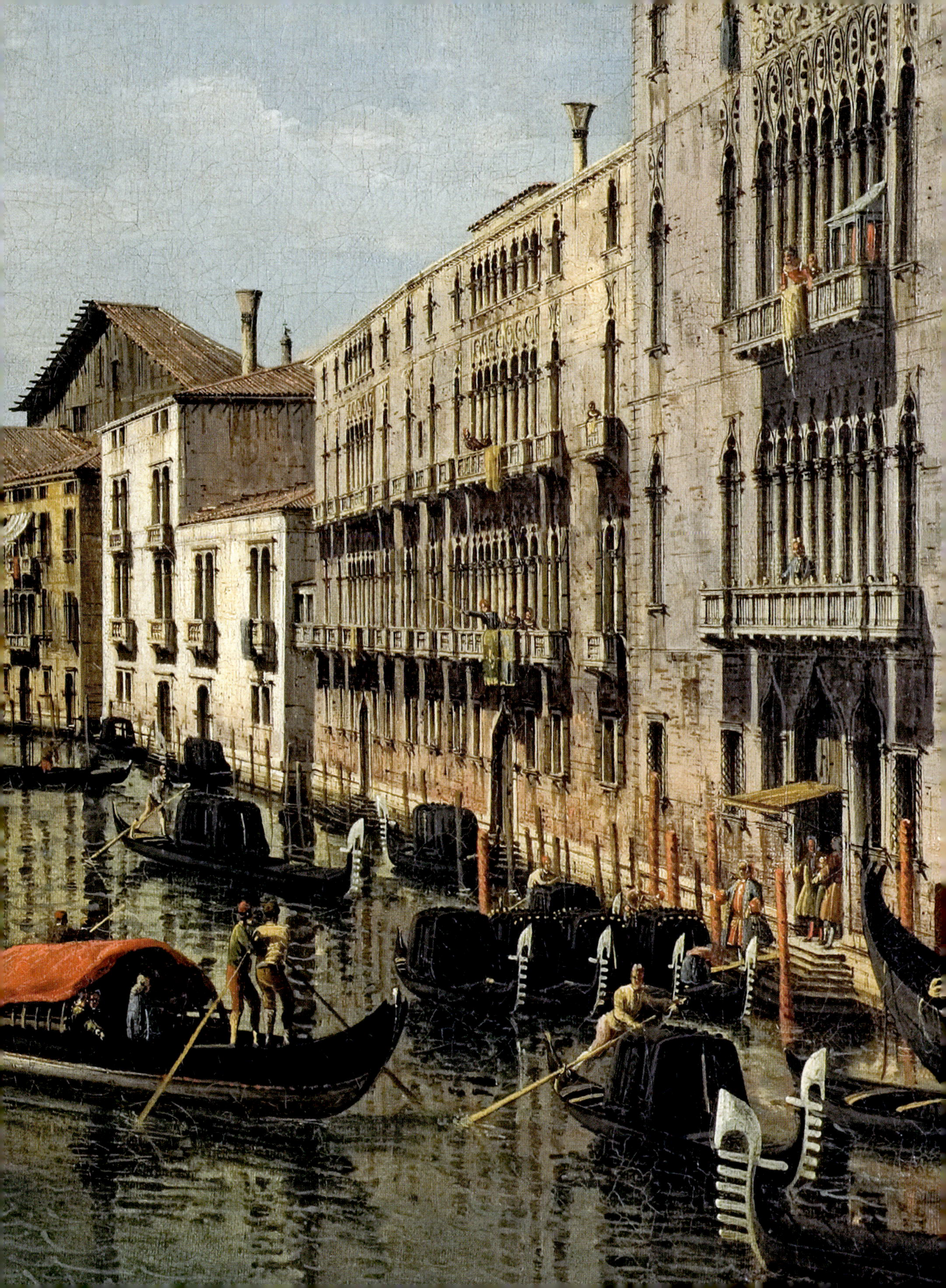

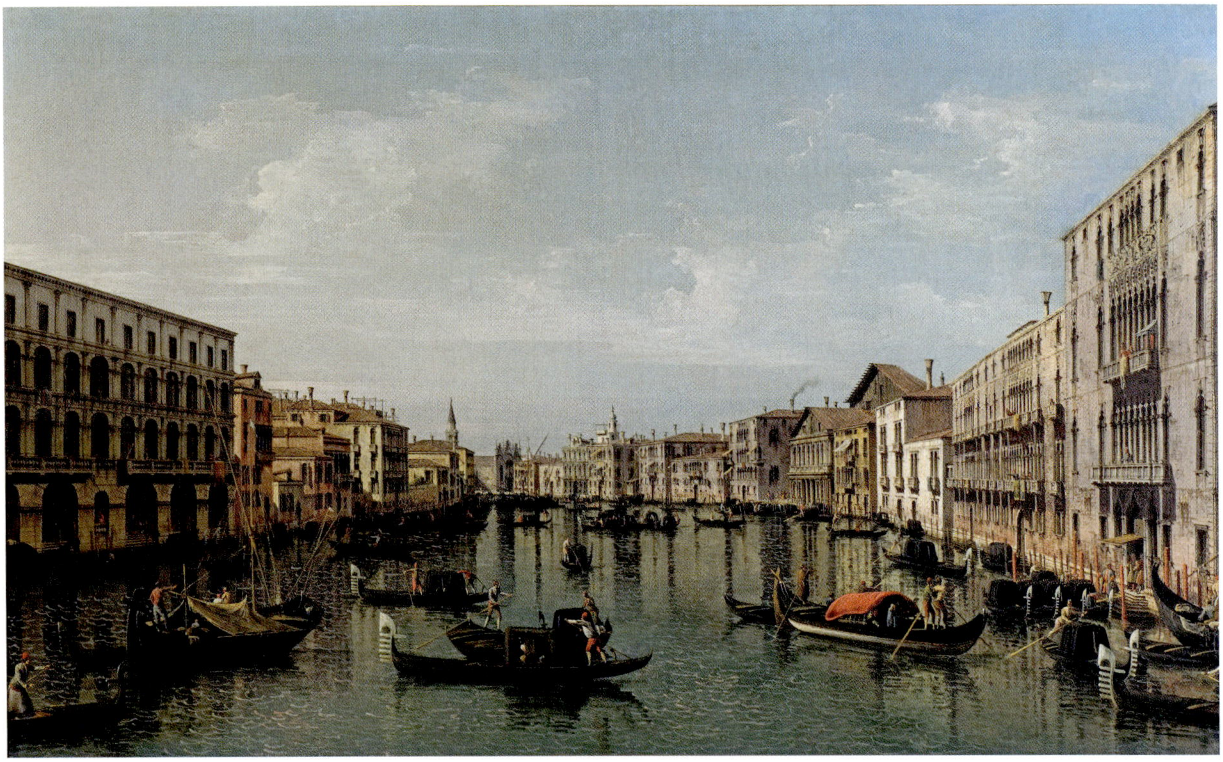

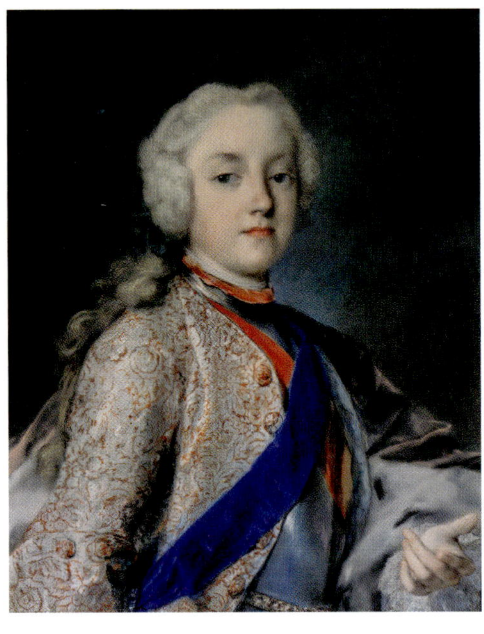

Fig. 15: Bernardo Bellotto, *View of the Grand Canal with the Palazzi Foscari and Moro Lin*, c. 1740, oil on canvas, 101 × 162 cm, detail on pp. 42–43. Nationalmuseum, Stockholm, inv. NM 49

Fig. 16 : Rosalba Carriera, *Crown Prince Friedrich Christian of Saxony*, 1740, pastel on paper, 635 × 515 mm. Gemäldegalerie Alte Meister, Dresden, inv. P 2

suggested that the figure flanked by attendants at the portal of Palazzo Foscari at lower right may depict the young Friedrich Christian of Saxony, whose family would later become Bellotto's most important patrons.[57] If so, the painting may commemorate the prince's extended visit to Venice from December 1739 to June 1740.[58] As the son of Augustus III, King of Poland and Elector of Saxony, Friedrich Christian was a prominent diplomatic figure and future ruler and accordingly took residence in the prestigious Palazzo Foscari, overlooking the Grand Canal. Lady Montagu, who lived across the canal, described him as "a beautiful person from the waist upwards" but chair-bound—a detail Bellotto tactfully omits.[59] During his stay, the prince also sat for a portrait by Rosalba Carriera in April 1740 (fig. 16), where his appearance differs markedly from the corpulent figure in Bellotto's scene. While the identification thus remains hypothetical, if correct, it would suggest that Bellotto already had an eye toward Central European patronage, setting him apart from his uncle's focus on English clients. These early works thus mark the emergence of a painter who, though indebted to Canaletto, would soon carry the Venetian *veduta* tradition far beyond the lagoon.

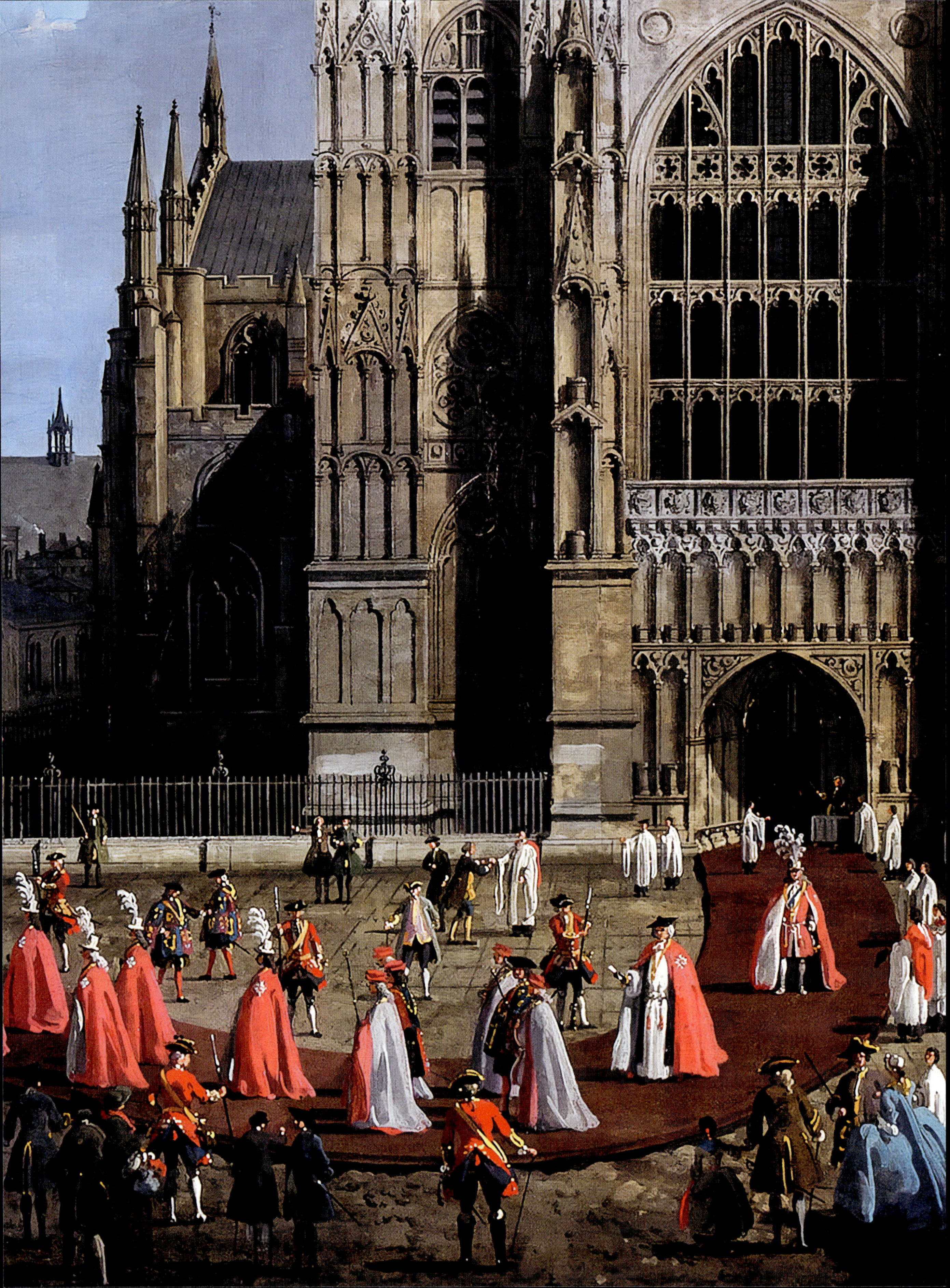

Leaving Venice for England and Saxony

Although Canaletto's paintings commanded extraordinary prices in Venice—especially among English Grand Tourists throughout the 1730s—the outbreak of the War of the Austrian Succession (1740–48) disrupted continental travel and dealt a significant blow to the Venetian art market. As George Vertue observed in 1746, "of late few persons travel to Italy from hence during the wars."[60] With the flow of wealthy visitors dwindling, Canaletto and Bellotto appear to have altered focus—supplementing their iconic Venetian views with depictions of towns on the Italian mainland and with fantastical architectural *capricci* that combined real and imagined elements to foreground artistic invention.[61] However, by the mid-1740s uncle and nephew must have realized that sustaining their careers would require a more radical step—and that better prospects lay not only beyond Venice, but beyond Italy herself. In 1746, Canaletto relocated to London, leveraging his network of British patrons. The following year, Bellotto departed for Dresden, where he became court painter to Frederick

Augustus II, Elector of Saxony and simultaneously King of Poland (ruling as August III). While Canaletto returned to Venice in 1755, Bellotto never went back to the lagoon. Instead, his career extended to Vienna, Munich, and Warsaw. Despite working in different cultural and political settings, both artists skillfully adapted their Venetian sensibilities to new audiences. Through their hands the *veduta* became a pan-European genre that articulated civic identity, Imperial ambition, and social order.

CANALETTO IN ENGLAND

With the Grand Tour disrupted, Canaletto seems to have reasoned that if his English patrons could no longer come to him, he must go to them. According to George Vertue, he arrived in London in May 1746 and took lodgings on Silver Street (now Beak Street), just off Golden Square.[62] Likely operating from a studio behind a cabinetmaker's shop, he painted both on commission and for the market. With the exception of a brief return to Venice in 1750/51, when he purchased a house on the Zattere, he remained in England for nine years, producing around fifty English views on canvas and paper, alongside Italian subjects and *capricci*.[63]

By the mid-eighteenth century, London was one of Europe's largest cities—a sprawling metropolis of around 675,000 inhabitants, shaped by commerce, empire, and Enlightenment ideals. Unlike Venice, London was on the rise, energized by political stability under the Hanoverian monarchy, expanding global trade, and a booming financial sector. Her prosperity was bound up with the reach of the British Empire, which brought in exotic goods and wealth, together with the exploitation and atrocities of colonialism. The Thames, carrying both goods and people, was central to this Imperial network, while the skyline—reimagined by architects like Christopher Wren with domes and spires in the classical idiom—bore the legacy of the Great Fire of 1666. London grew and aspired to modern grandeur while remaining a city of contrasts: neoclassical projects coexisted with earlier remnants, and orderly Georgian squares abutted chaotic, unplanned neighborhoods. Critics lamented the city's lack of

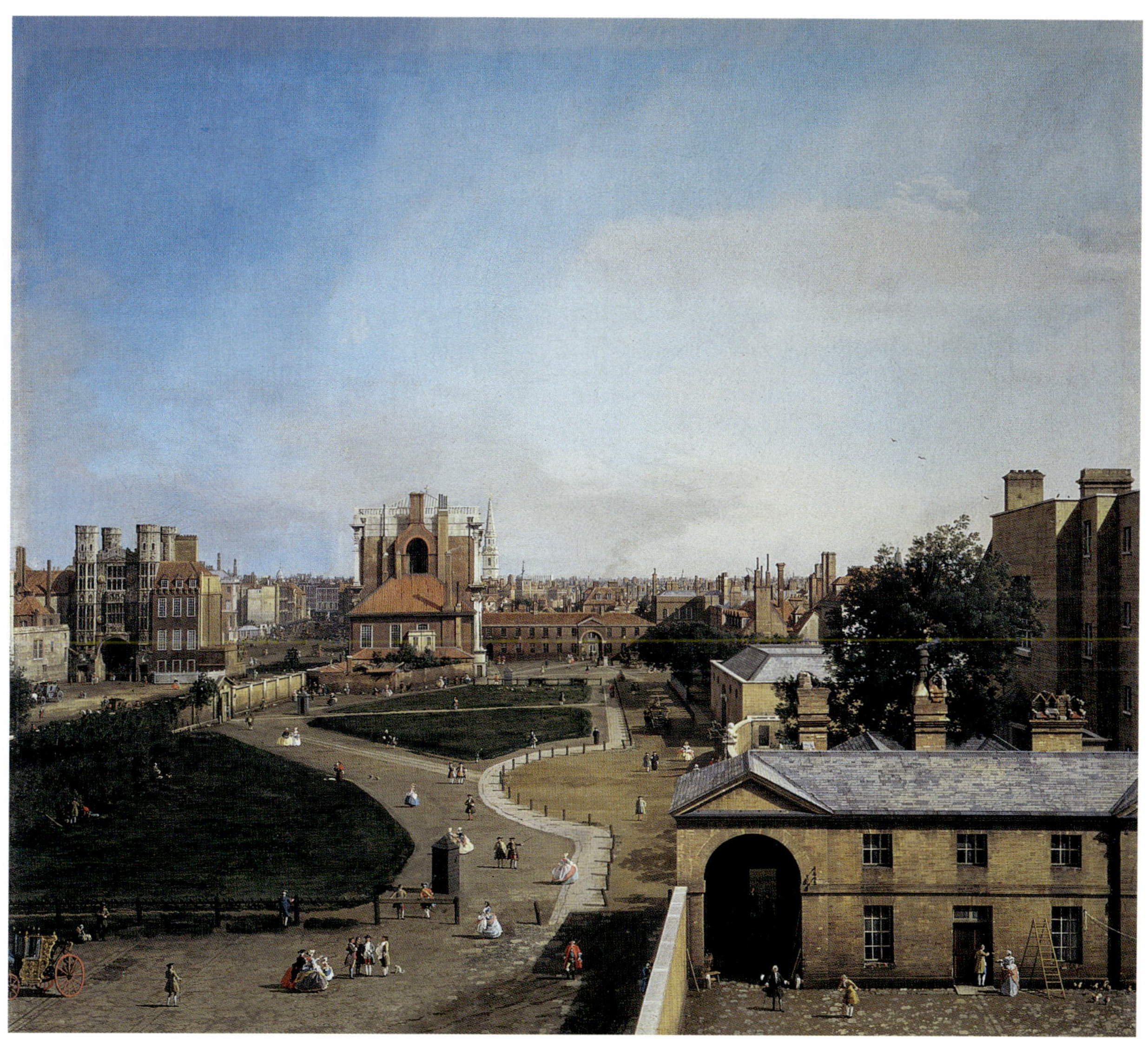

Fig. 17: Canaletto, *Whitehall and the Privy Garden from Richmond House*, probably 1747, oil on canvas, 106.7 × 116.8 cm. The Trustees of the Goodwood Collection

magnificence: in 1734, an anonymous writer complained that while no nation could reproach England for her lavish expenditure on public buildings, all might fault her for the "want of elegance and discernment in the execution," urging instead that the nation should strive "to vie with our neighbours in politeness, as well as power and empire."[64] Three decades later, in *London and Westminster Improved* (1766), the architect John Gwynn echoed this ambition, insisting that beautiful buildings embodied "a refinement of taste, which in a nobleman produces true magnificence and elegance" and "in a mechanic produce at least cleanliness and decorum."[65] If designed well, therefore, London's architecture had the potential to beautify the city as well as elevate the condition of her inhabitants. It was in this contradictory world that Canaletto applied his pictorial language to craft an idealized vision of this metropolis.

Smith brokered one of Canaletto's early engagements with the city, arranging an introduction—via McSwiney—to the Duke of Richmond, who already owned Venetian views by the artist.[66] In 1747, the Duke granted Canaletto access to an upper room at Richmond House, his Thames-side residence near Whitehall. The two paintings produced from this privileged vantage point are widely considered masterpieces of Canaletto's English period.[67] One of them, *Whitehall and the Privy Garden* (Fig. 17), reads as a meditation on London's urban fabric in a moment of flux. Its composition juxtaposes layers of architectural periods and styles: the skyline centers on Inigo Jones's Banqueting House of 1622—the sole survivor of Whitehall Palace, largely destroyed by fire in 1698—flanked by the spire of James Gibbs's St. Martin-in-the-Fields (completed 1726). To the left stands the Holbein Gate, a Tudor relic from the 1530s about to be demolished in 1759 to ease traffic congestion. The foreground contrasts the modest courtyard of Richmond House at right—complete with washing line, chickens, and perhaps the Duke himself, greeted by a servant—with the ordered Privy Garden, enlivened by polite pedestrians, carriages, and gardeners. Its lawns are divided by neat paths, bollards, and wooden barriers regulating movement, while several figures echo the Duke's open-armed gesture, turning the garden into a stage for Georgian cordiality.[68] Workers and poorer families are visible yet rendered harmless, pushed to the margins and absorbed into a picturesque backdrop.[69] This near absence of London's less palatable realities—its crowds, dirt, and sizable underclass—leaves an impression of order and harmony. Yet Canaletto's irregular compositional arrangement also subtly disrupts this curated vision, suggesting a keen awareness of the city's transitional state.

If the Richmond view contemplates architectural tensions of a city in flux, Canaletto's c. 1748 *London: The River Thames on Lord Mayor's Day* (fig. 18) revels in civic spectacle. Likely commissioned by Ferdinand Philip, 6th Prince Lobkowicz, during his English sojourn from 1745 to 1748, the monumental canvas ranks among the grandest records of eighteenth-century London.[70] The Thames flows through the scene with emblematic force, animated by livery company vessels escorting the newly elected Lord Mayor, proceeding upriver to Westminster by state barge to swear allegiance to the Crown. Spectators throng the water in smaller boats, smoke from cannon fire drifts across the scene, and bright pennants enliven the festive air. The skyline—defined by a forest of church spires born of Wren's post-Fire reconstruction—forms a commanding backdrop. Also among the prominent features is the Monument, London's soaring column of 1677 commemorating the Great Fire that had necessitated such extensive rebuilding. In the distance at right, the Tower of London comes into view. Most prominently, to the left, St. Paul's Cathedral rises above the scene, a symbol of Protestant identity and civic renewal. Designed by

Fig. 18: Canaletto, *London: The River Thames on Lord Mayor's Day*, c.1748, oil on canvas, 118.5 × 237.5 cm, detail on pp. 52–53. The Lobkowicz Collections, Prague

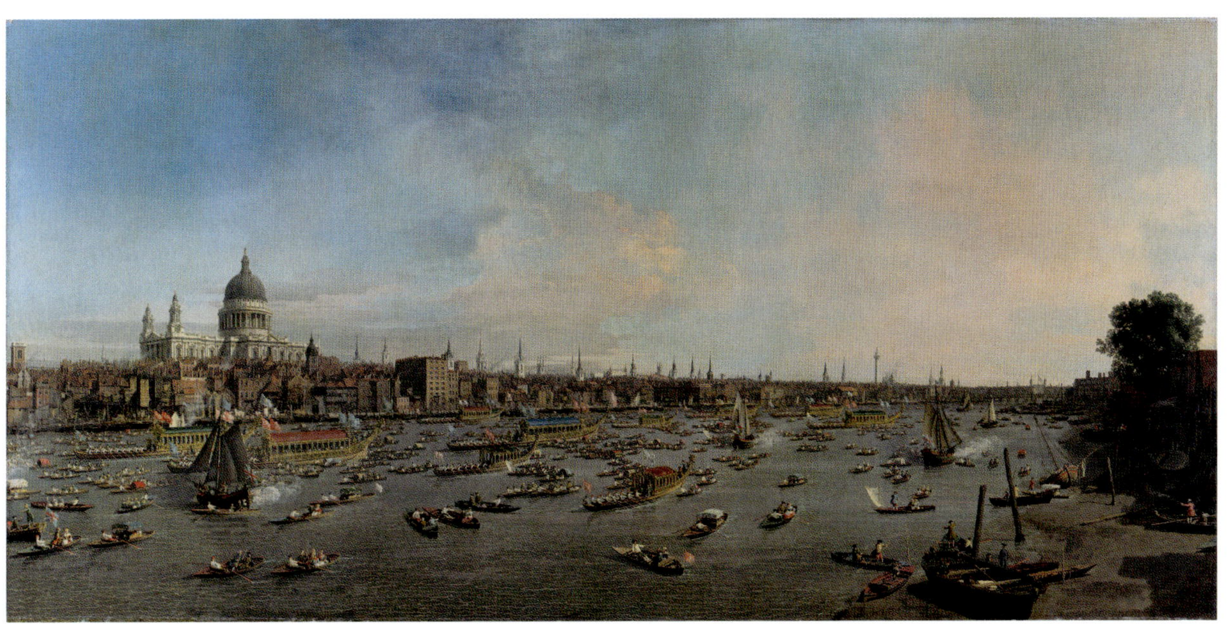

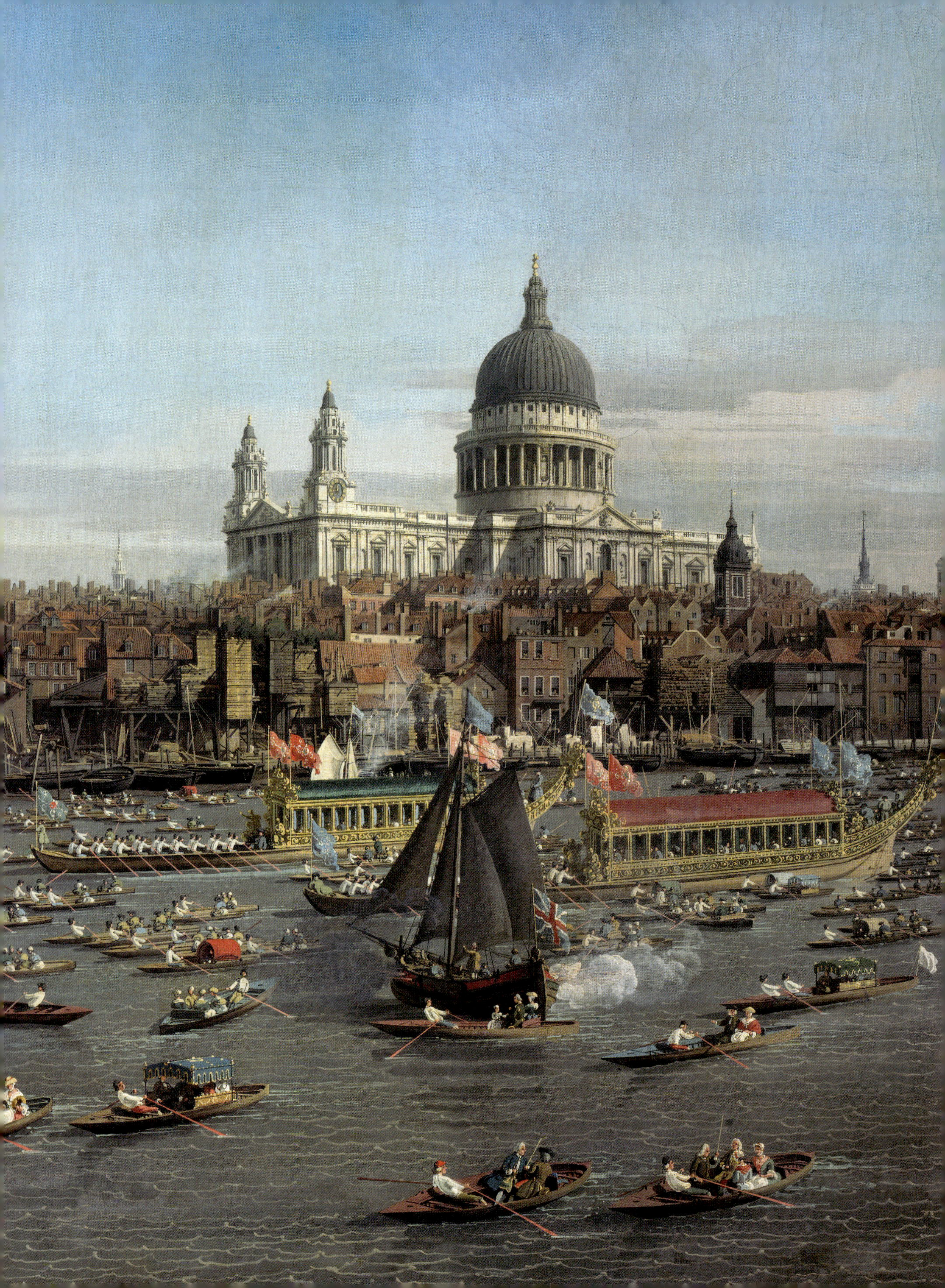

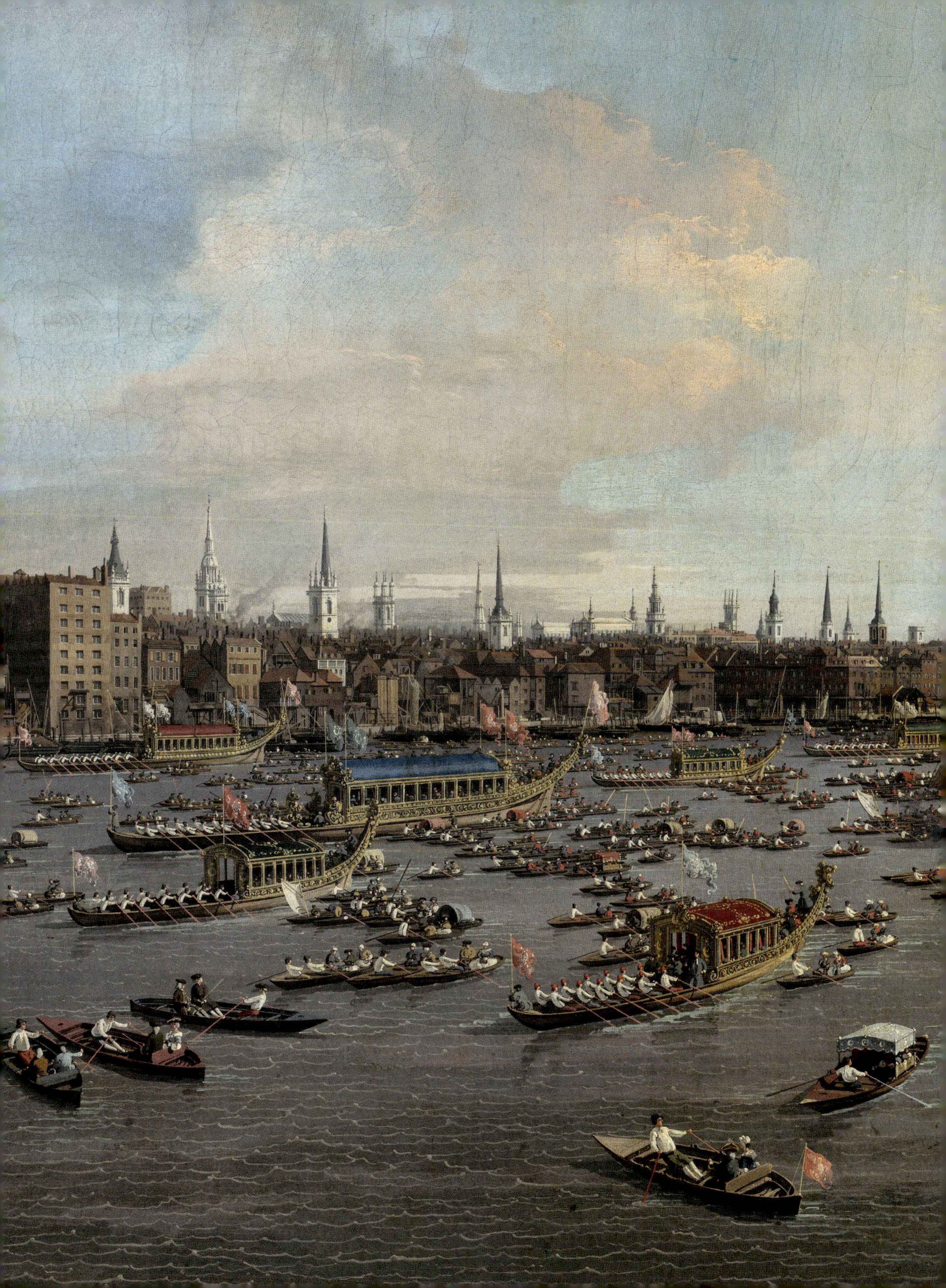

Wren and completed around 1711, its great dome—deliberately conceived to rival St. Peter's in Rome—reflects London's growing confidence as an Imperial capital, modeling herself as a new Rome for the modern age.[71] As John Gwynn observed in 1766: "The English are now what the Romans were of old."[72]

Canaletto would have been attuned to this analogy. During his apprenticeship with his father, he traveled to Rome around 1719/20, producing drawings after the city's monuments that would later inform his grand Roman vistas of the early 1740s.[73] He would have been aware of London's ancient roots as Roman Londinium, and how her history reinforced St. Paul's analogy to St. Peter's. At the same time, the crowded procession of rivercraft and spectators echoes the ceremonial vitality of Venetian pageantry. Whig patrons in particular might have encouraged London's comparison to Venice, for it has been argued that they displayed in their homes Canaletto's Venetian views to proclaim their admiration for Venice's political order.[74] Aligning the Lord Mayor's barge with the Doge's *Bucintoro*, Canaletto merges Venetian spectacle with British civic ritual, casting London as the capital of both a rising empire and a modern republic.

If St. Paul's epitomized London's modern aspirations in the City, further west, Westminster Abbey embodied her historic and ceremonial core, one that had recently undergone considerable change. As the coronation site and burial church of English monarchs, it symbolized the enduring bond between Crown and State. Its distinctive silhouette anchors many of Canaletto's London views. Only once, however, did he devote an entire canvas to its exterior: *Westminster Abbey with a Procession of the Knights of the Bath* (Fig. 19). Painted in 1749, the work captures the newly completed west towers, which are among the earliest milestones of the Gothic Revival. First proposed by Wren in 1713, who advised they be built "in the Gothick form" to avoid a "disagreeable mixture, which no person of good taste could relish," the towers were designed by Nicholas Hawksmoor in the 1730s and completed by John James around 1745.[75] Canaletto, painting only a few years later, thus captures a moment when London's medieval heritage was consciously woven into her modern reshaping.

Fig. 19: Canaletto, *Westminster Abbey with a Procession of the Knights of the Bath*, 1749, oil on canvas, 99 × 101.5 cm. The Dean and Chapter of Westminster, London

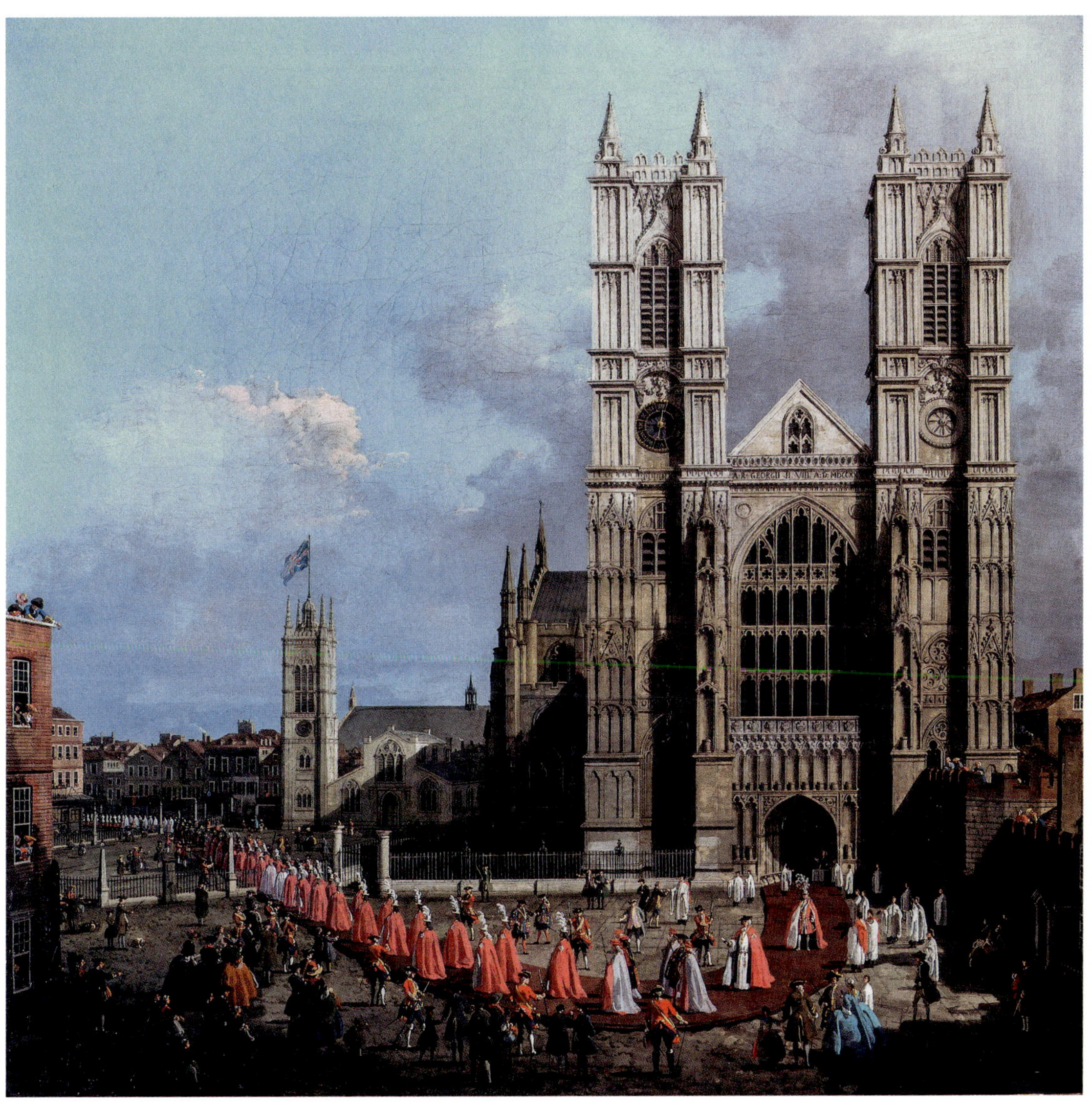

Against the newly completed façade with its clock set just after midday, Canaletto renders the installation procession of the Knights of the Order of the Bath on 20 June 1749, as they moved from their chapel in the Abbey to the House of Lords. Revived in 1725 by King George I, the Order represented ideals of chivalry and was limited to the sovereign, the Great Master, and thirty-six Knights Companions. The painting's unusual square format—rather rare for Canaletto—may reflect its intended placement, possibly above a fireplace, similar to the Duke of Richmond's

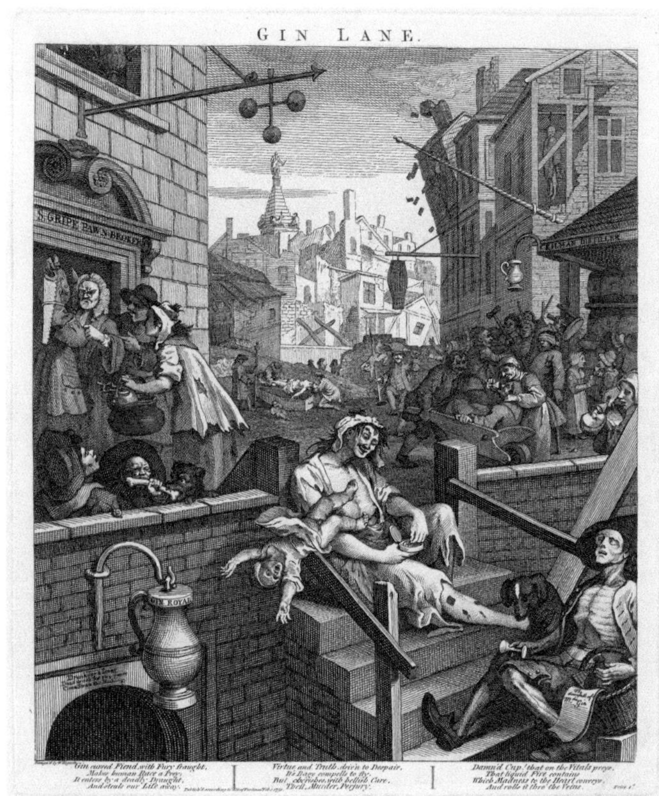

Fig. 20: William Hogarth, *Gin Lane*, 1751, etching and engraving, 406 × 337 mm. The Metropolitan Museum of Art, New York, Gift of Sarah Lazarus 1891, inv. 91.1.140

paintings. He skillfully tailored the composition to this difficult format, shifting the Abbey to the right and arranging the crimson- and white-cloaked knights, their hats topped with white ostrich plumes, into a sweeping U-shape. This formation anchors the scene visually and metaphorically links the Abbey's medieval past to modern London, as the knights, preceded by their esquires and the Abbey's canons, process over a red carpet past St. Margaret's Church and along the former houses of King Street in the left background. At the procession's end, in front of the Abbey, stand two notable figures: Joseph Wilcocks, Dean of Westminster and of the Order, who is thought to have commissioned the painting, followed by John West, 7th Baron De La Warr, who stood in for the ailing Great Master, the Duke of Montagu.[76] Additionally, Canaletto emphasizes this area through his orchestration of light: the sun illuminates both the Abbey's west front and the knights, while much of the surrounding crowd (though seemingly content and cheerful) remains in shadow.

Yet, like his Venetian *vedute*, Canaletto's ceremonial visions were carefully curated. Contemporaries described Lord Mayor's Day, for instance, as raucous and even dangerous: In 1726, César-François de Saussure observed insolent crowds and foreigners pelted with filth.[77] Others remarked that London generally presented a "dismal prospect of an universal poverty, and crowds of miserable people, either rack'd with the agonies of their own guilt or folly, or groaning under the intolerable want of bread."[78] Canaletto chose to depict none of such social turmoil or hardship, translating instead the city's recognizable topography and festivities into a cultural ideal. This approach contrasts to that of his British contemporary William Hogarth, whose works often expose the unruly, sordid realities of London life. Hogarth's famous 1751 *Gin Lane* (fig. 20), for instance, brims with the noise, disorder, and ambiguities of the capital's streets, offering a satirical and moralizing counterpoint.[79] Where Hogarth exposed the frictions of urban life, Canaletto distilled London's public space and ritual into a vision of grandeur and Imperial promise—bathed, tellingly, in clear and luminous light, rather than the grey, rain-streaked skies too familiar to Londoners. Canaletto thus follows a mode of the pastoral as described in *The Guardian* in 1713, which urged:

> *It is indeed commonly affirmed, that truth well painted will certainly please the imagination; but it is sometimes convenient not to discover the whole truth, but that part which only is delightful. We must sometimes show only half an image to the fancy; which if we display in a lively manner, the mind is so dexterously deluded, that it doth not readily perceive that the other half is concealed. This in writing Pastorals, let the tranquility of that life appear full and plain, but hide the meanness of it; represent its simplicity as clear as you please, but cover its misery.*[80]

Still, in the *Lord Mayor's Day* canvas, the distant silhouette of Old London Bridge at right hints at some of the city's problems. Since the Middle Ages, the bridge had been the only fixed Thames

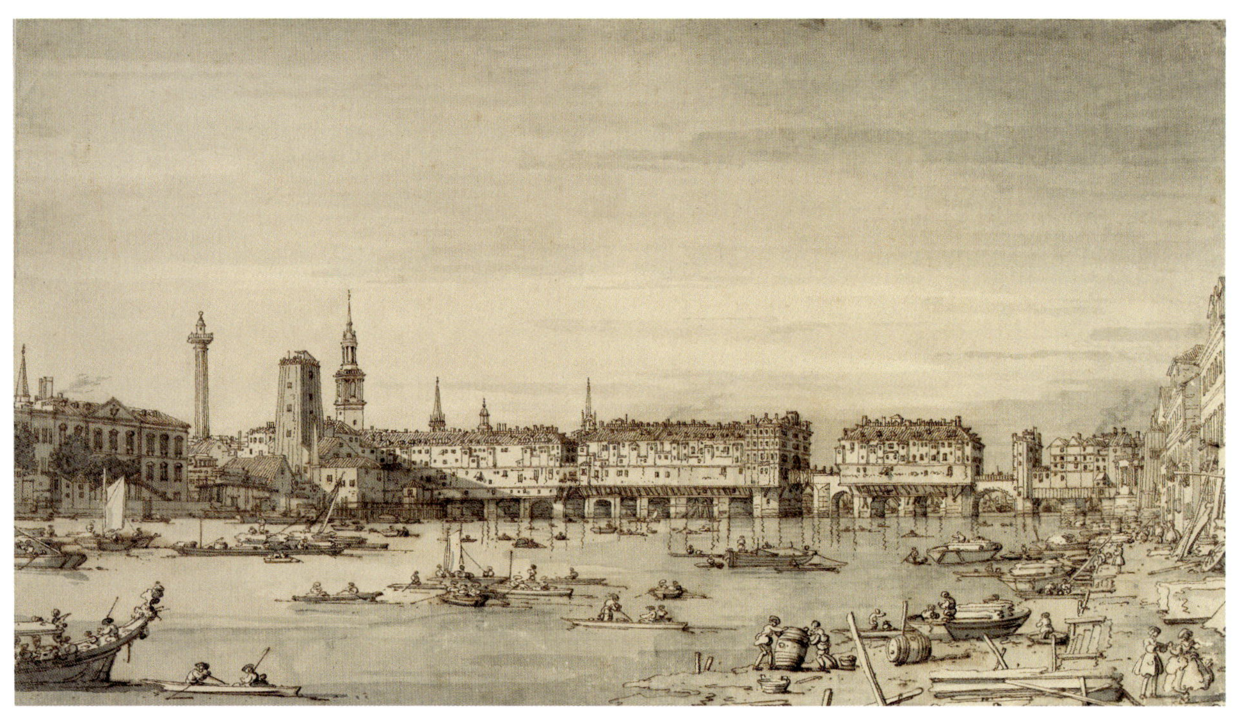

crossing between the sea and Kingston. By Canaletto's time, it was a notorious bottleneck—an emblem of outdated infrastructure in a capital striving for efficiency. He likewise captured the bridge's extraordinary density in a detailed drawing (fig. 21): houses crammed shoulder to shoulder, narrow passageways threading through them, and a timber tower supplying piped water to the city. Depicted from the west, the sheet further shows Fishmongers' Hall (opened 1671), the Monument (1677), and Wren's tower of St. Magnus Martyr (1671–87), scattered somewhat incoherently across the skyline. In the foreground, groupings of barges and boats drift across the Thames while workmen bustle along the untidy foreshore—minor signs of disorder that nonetheless unfold within a generally calm atmosphere. Yet this surface tranquillity belies the bridge's notoriety: clustered piers created treacherous, even deadly currents, and its central gateway caused

Fig. 21: Canaletto, *Old London Bridge*, 1746/52, pen and brown ink, with grey wash, over ruled black chalk lines, 307 × 539 mm. The British Museum, London, inv. 1909,0406.4

Detail of fig. 18

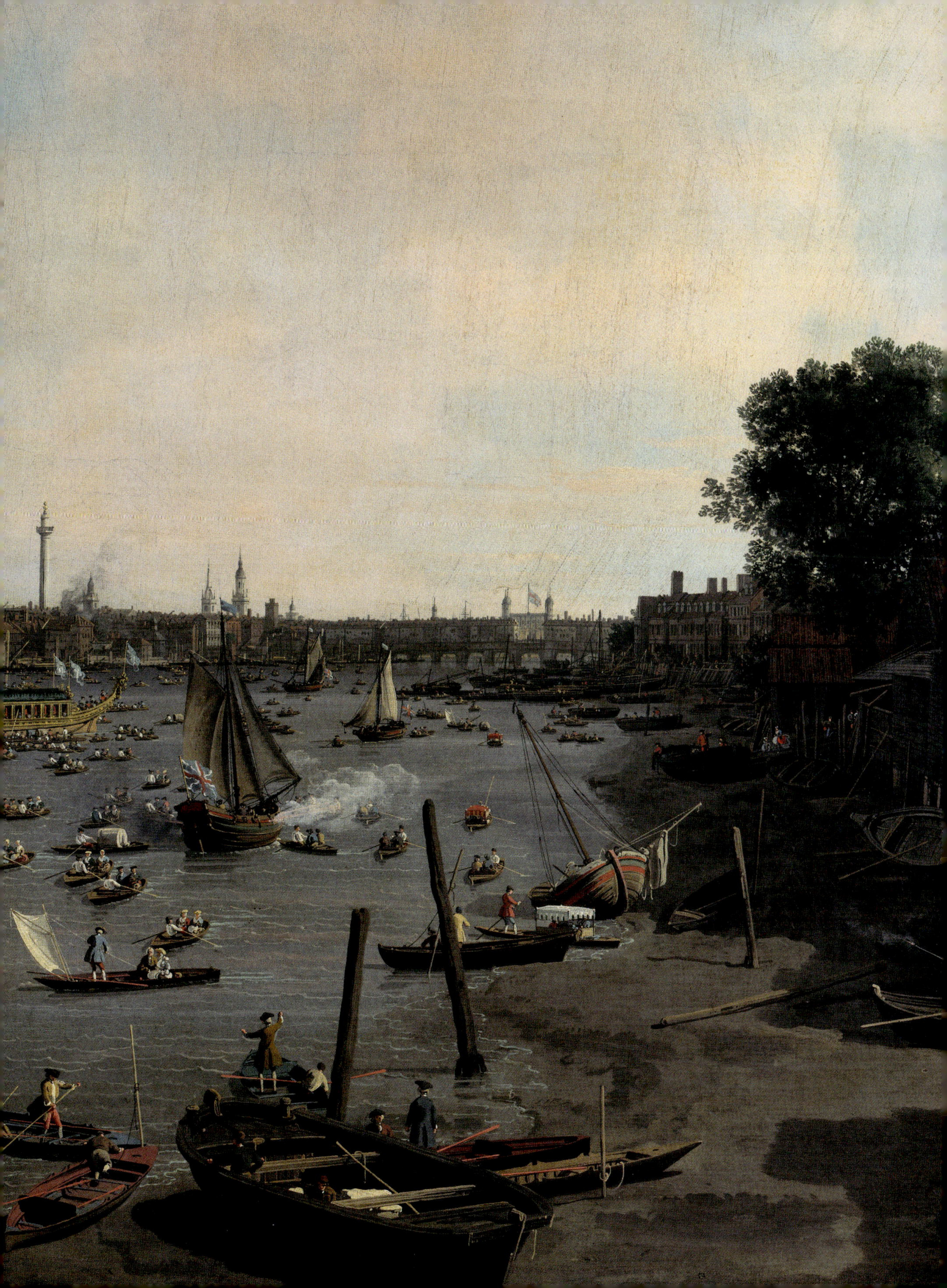

chronic traffic jams. By the 1730s, its future was under review, and in 1746 a committee convened to decide its fate. The houses were removed between 1758 and 1762, and two central arches were replaced with a single span to ease navigation. Ultimately, the entire structure was demolished in 1830.[81] Canaletto was in all likelihood aware of these debates; thus his painting and drawing can be read both as topographical studies and as visual elegies for a cityscape on the cusp of transformation.

As the limitations of Old London Bridge had become untenable, proposals for a second crossing further up the Thames were under debate to link Westminster and Lambeth. Few projects of eighteenth-century London more forcefully captured elite imagination and sparked arguments about how construction might enhance the city's magnificence. Parliament's Westminster Bridge Act of 1736 authorized construction as a work of urgent public benefit. Funding came through a lottery and a parliamentary grant, and while first planned in wood, the bridge was ultimately built of costly Portland stone to the plans of Swiss engineer Charles Labelye, who drew on newly invented machinery in its construction. Oversight fell to a body of 175 commissioners—aristocrats, merchants, and politicians—including several of Canaletto's past and future patrons such as the Duke of Richmond, the Duke of Bedford, and Sir Hugh Smithson (later 1st Duke of Northumberland). Built between 1739 and 1750, Westminster Bridge—at the time the longest stone bridge in Britain—ultimately spanned the river with fifteen arches on fourteen piers. Its form, evoking the arches and viaducts of ancient Rome, aligned the structure with classical grandeur, allowing London—already crowned by Wren's dome of St. Paul's—to present herself as heir to the Roman tradition and a capital of modern empire.[82]

One of Canaletto's most commanding early renderings, *The Thames and the City of Westminster from Lambeth*, executed just months after his arrival in 1746 and also acquired by the 6th Prince Lobkowicz, offers a measured, almost meditative depiction of this new structure (fig. 22).[83] The large canvas looks downstream from Lambeth Palace: to the left rise the four towers of St. John's Smith Square (1728), Westminster Abbey, and (marked by a flag) St. Margaret's Church. To their right lies the site

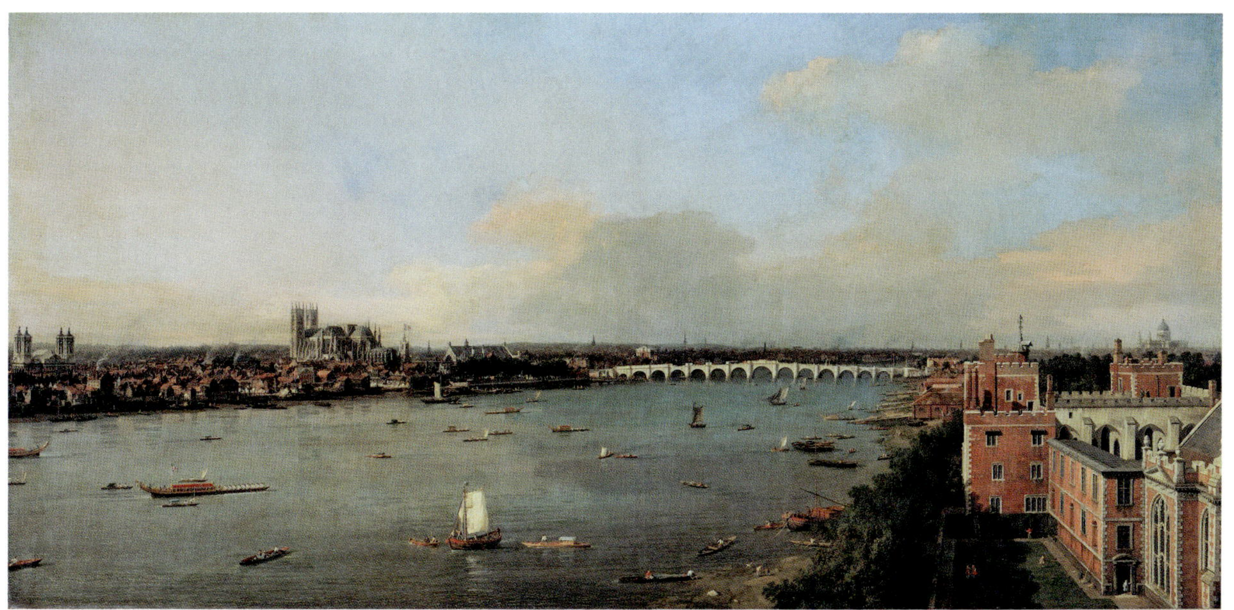

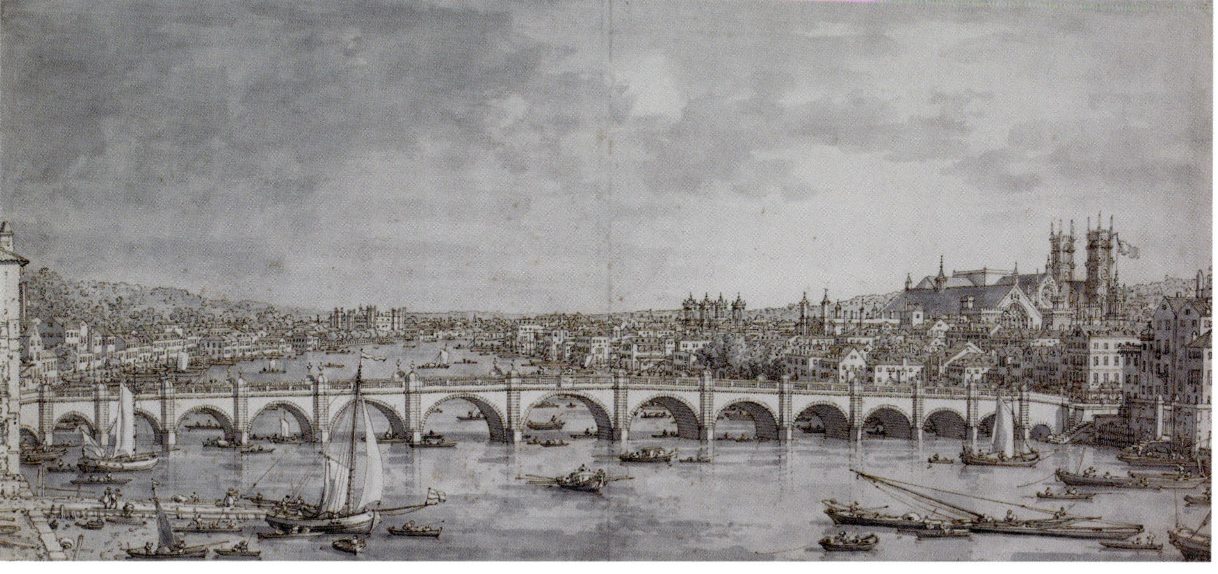

Fig. 22: Canaletto, *The Thames and the City of Westminster from Lambeth*, probably 1746, oil on canvas, 118 × 238 cm. The Lobkowicz Collections, Prague

Fig. 23: Canaletto, *View of the River Thames and Westminster Bridge from the North*, c.1750, pen and brown ink, with grey wash, over ruled black chalk lines, 345 × 738 mm. The British Museum, London, inv. 1868,0328.306

now occupied by the nineteenth-century Palace of Westminster, but in Canaletto's time dominated by the medieval St. Stephen's Chapel and Westminster Hall. In the far distance to the right, the dome of St. Paul's punctuates the skyline. This time, river traffic is sparse—just a few ceremonial barges and a handful of smaller sailing and rowing boats animate the Thames—setting a subdued mood compared to *Lord Mayor's Day*. Canaletto's careful attention to construction details, including the timber centering still supporting several arches, matches the bridge's documented state in the summer of 1746. Yet despite its near completion, structural problems arose a year later: by September 1747, one of the piers had begun to subside, forcing the dismantling and rebuilding of two arches. The bridge remained closed for several more years and was not opened to traffic until 1750.

Canaletto's sustained fascination with Westminster Bridge is also evident in a drawing in the British Museum (fig. 23). Likely executed before the bridge's opening to the public, it shows the structure as if completed, spanning the full width of the composition. Canaletto depicts a semi-octagonal, half-domed shelter over every pier—an inaccuracy, since only twelve, positioned at the corners of the central arch and the outermost arches at each end, were ultimately built.[84] The river below teems with activity as watermen ferry passengers, while sailing vessels navigate the current. A larger one in the foreground has just lowered its mast to pass beneath the arches. In the background, familiar landmarks reappear: Lambeth Palace on the left, the four towers of St. John's across the river, the medieval core of the Palace of Westminster, and Westminster Abbey, linking London's civic and religious institutions to the modern architectural ambitions symbolized by Westminster Bridge.

While Canaletto repeatedly returned to Westminster Bridge in both paintings and drawings, he arguably offers his most radical response in his 1747 *London Seen through an Arch of Westminster Bridge* (fig. 24). Likely commissioned by Sir Hugh Smithson—one of the bridge's leading commissioners—the canvas records the completion of one of the arches in April 1747, just before the removal of the timber centering that July.[85] The composition is bold and unconventional: instead of adopting the

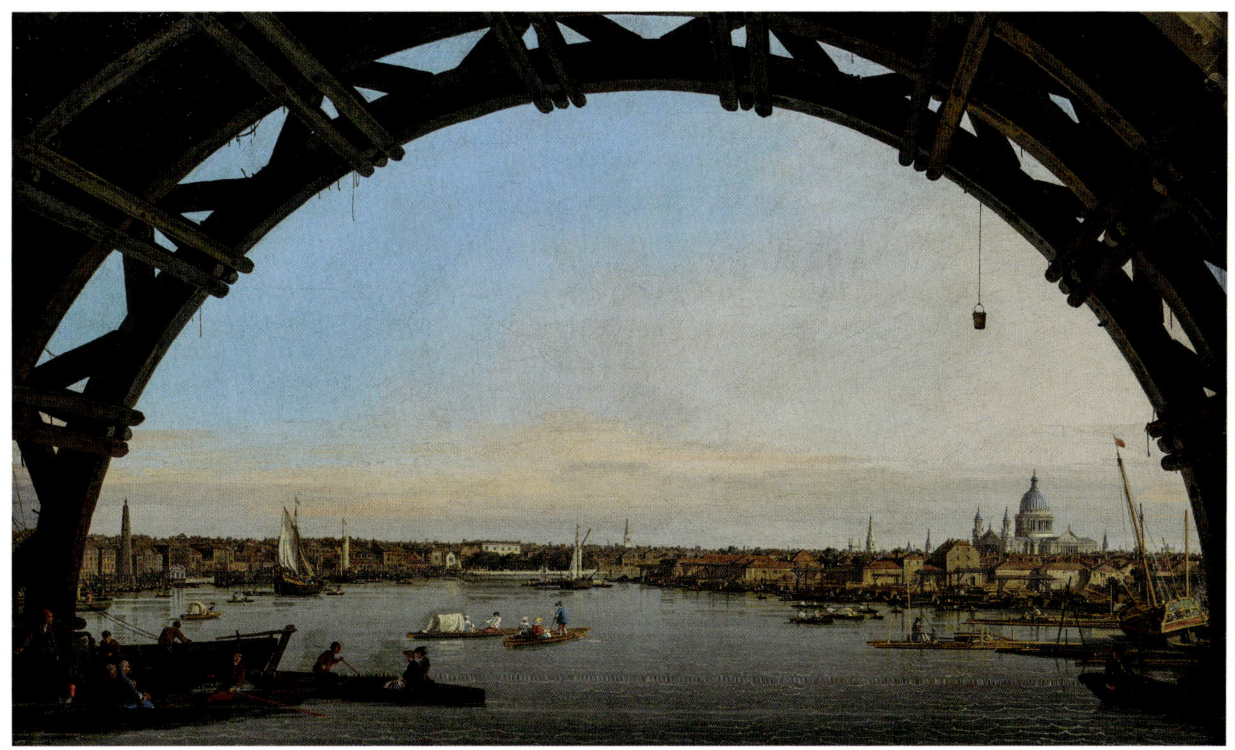

Fig. 24: Canaletto, *London Seen through an Arch of Westminster Bridge*, 1747, oil on canvas, 59.7 × 97.5 cm. Collection of the Duke of Northumberland, Alnwick Castle, Alnwick, Northumberland

elevated vantage typical of city views, Canaletto situates the viewer beneath the new span, looking eastward through the centering still in place. The picture celebrates its innovative straight-wedge design introduced by Labelye, which was more efficient and stable than traditional curved forms. A suspended bucket interrupts the symmetry, offering a discreet nod to the unseen laborers driving the project. Like a theatrical proscenium, the arch itself becomes a monumental viewing lens, directing the beholder's gaze toward London's receding skyline. There, to the left, rises the York Buildings Waterworks Tower, which supplied piped water to large sections of the city; at center, the spire of Wren's St. Clement Danes (1682); and to the right, St. Paul's Cathedral once again dominates the horizon with Imperial gravity. Across the foreground curves the Thames, swelling with ferrymen, cargo boats, and pleasure craft. Canaletto thus orchestrates a portrait of a city alive with movement and energy, a symbol at once of ancient grandeur and modern progress, where engineering, commerce, and labor converge.[86]

In doing so, Canaletto's treatment of the scene resonates with the poetic traditions of his time, particularly the eighteenth-century *georgic*—a form that celebrated labor, commerce, and national prosperity.[87] Modeled on Virgil's *Georgics* (37–30 BC), these poems elevated the details of British rural and civic life into reflections on trade, empire, and improvement. They praised the dignity of work, though often with little sympathy for its burdens. Within this literary imagination, the Thames was more than a working river: it was symbolic. Alexander Pope in *Windsor-Forest* (1720) hailed it as the "great Father of the British Floods," imagining its great bend as the meeting point of London's twin poles of power—Westminster, seat of monarchy and parliament, and the City, hub of commerce and finance. In the same poem, Pope envisioned London as a new "Augusta," her "glitt'ring spires" embodying the "beauteous works of Peace," a vision of harmonious prosperity.[88] Later visitors echoed this sense of vitality. Karl Philipp Moritz, writing in 1782, marveled that the "countless swarms of little boats" made the Thames "hardly less stir and bustle" than London's most crowded streets.[89] Canaletto's rendering of ferrymen, cargo vessels, and pleasure craft mirrors this energy, transfiguring the river into a layered social and economic stage where elite vision and working-class labor meet. Yet the painting, like the *georgic* mode itself, elides the harsher realities of urban life.

Indeed, the painting's apparent harmony is deceptive, for among the most vocal opponents of Westminster Bridge were the very watermen depicted in the foreground. For generations they had ferried passengers across the Thames; now, the new crossing threatened their trade. Their resistance was organized and fierce: they harassed masons on the scaffolding, rammed barges into the piers, and even sank boats in the working pits.[90] As the bridge also reshaped Westminster's banks it became the centerpiece of a broader campaign for gentrification: houses were demolished, residents displaced, and the surrounding streets recast as broad

Fig. 25: Canaletto, *London: The Old Horse Guards from St. James's Park*, c.1749, oil on canvas, 117.2 × 236.1 cm, detail on pp. 66–67. Tate, lent by the Andrew Lloyd Webber Foundation, UK

avenues lined with grand residences, turning the area into a landscape of elite display. Resistance by watermen, local residents, and vested interests in the City accordingly delayed construction for years. Canaletto registers none of this agitation directly, but instead subtly foreshadows this tension. In a quiet metaphor for their impending obsolescence, his watermen are absorbed in their tasks, seemingly indifferent to the monument already casting its shadow over them.[91] In this way, the painting transforms the Thames into both a site of civic ambition and a contested social space, where Enlightenment ideals of progress collide with the realities of economic displacement.

Canaletto was attentive to London's social mix in other canvases, too, even as he subordinated his staffage figures to an idealizing gaze. His c. 1749 *The Old Horse Guards from St. James's Park* (fig. 25), for instance, records not only a building on the brink of demolition but also London's populace. The canvas centers on the Stuart-era Horse Guards, the brick-built

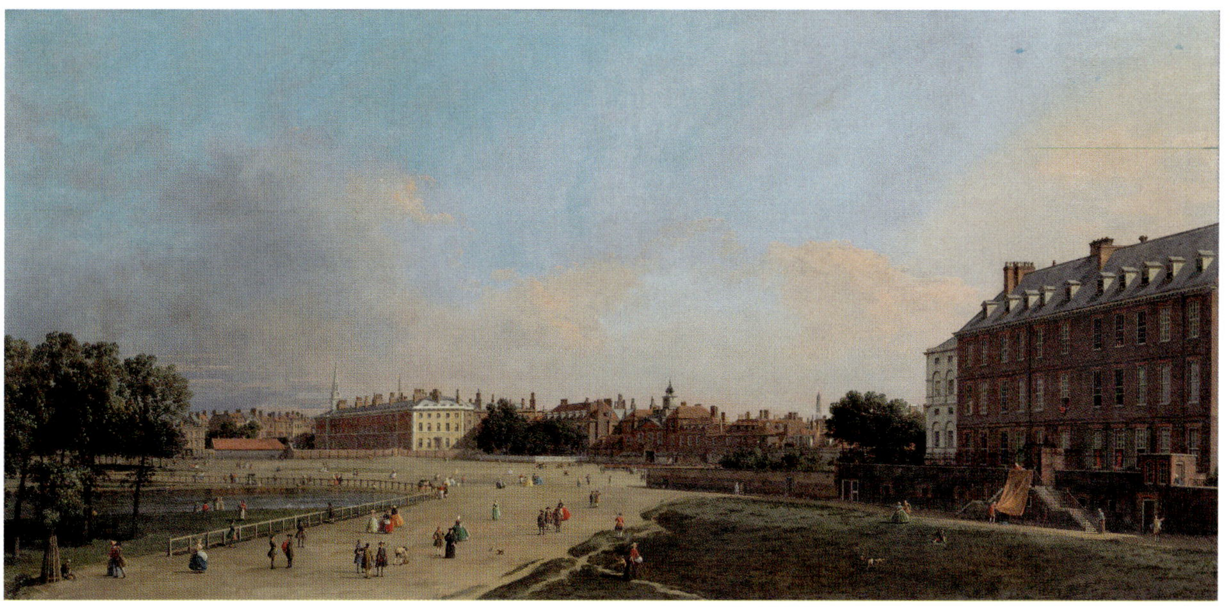

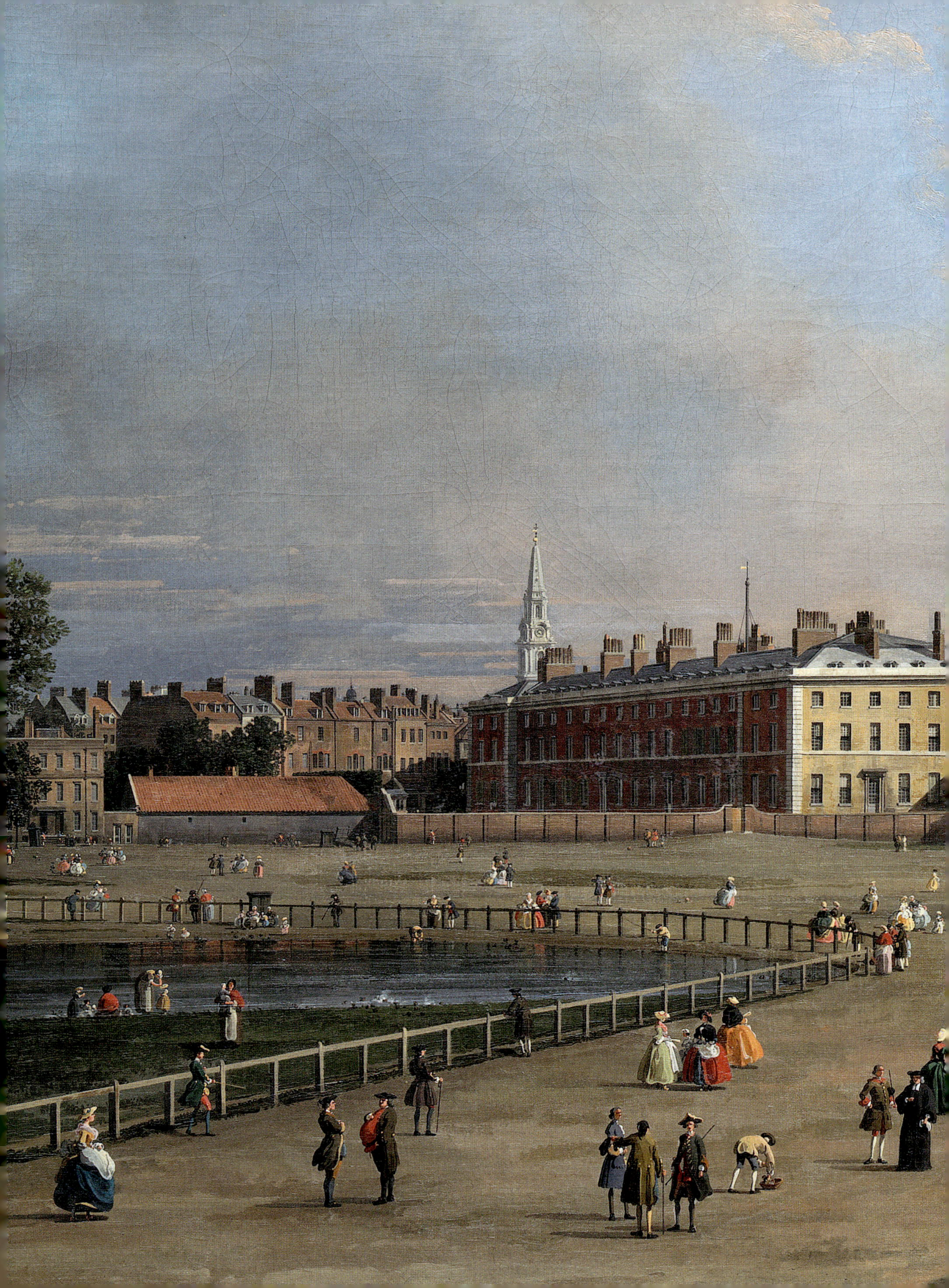

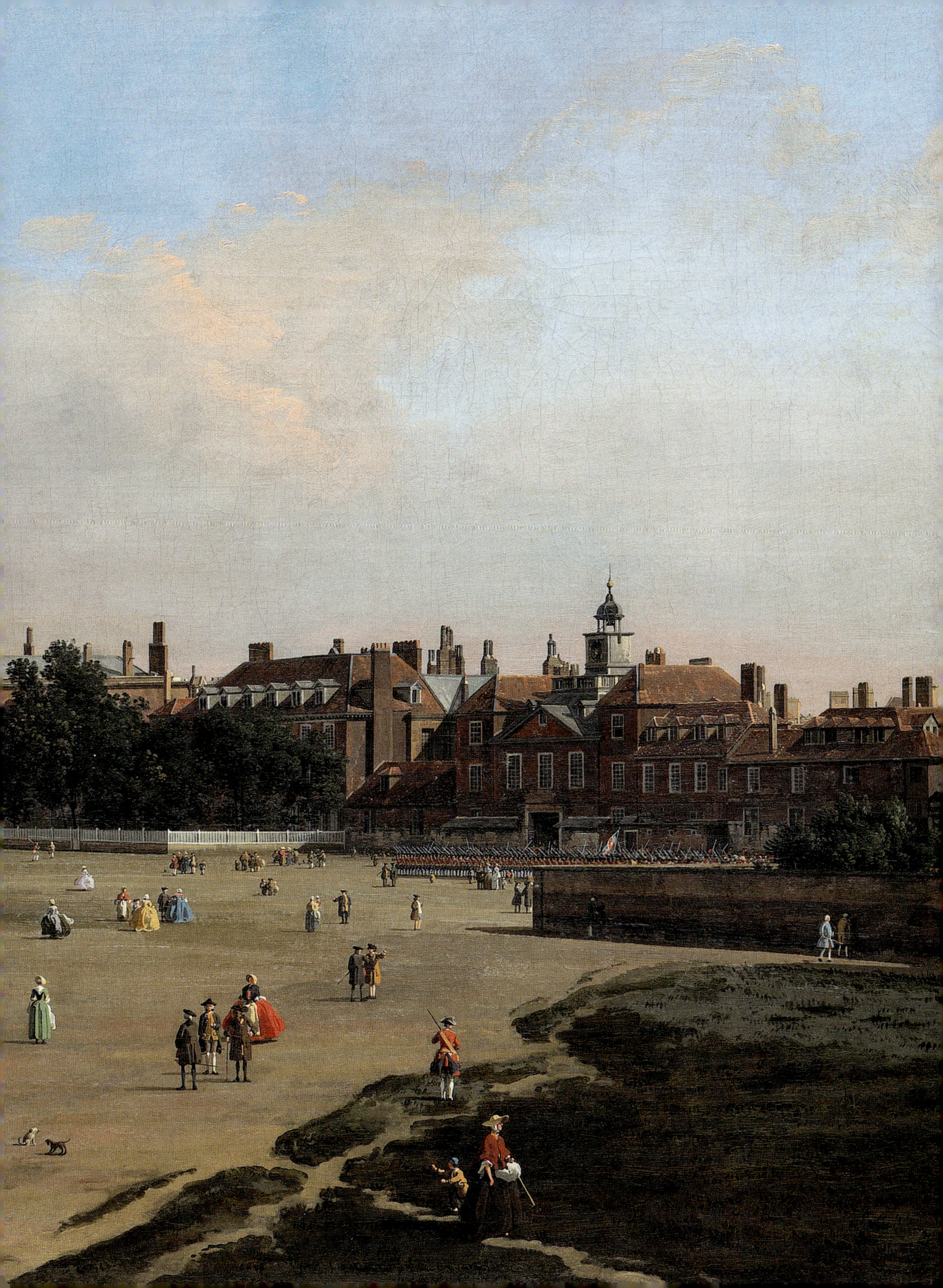

headquarters of the Commander-in-Chief of the Army. By the time Canaletto painted it, the structure—erected only in 1663–65—was already in disrepair and soon demolished to make way for William Kent's new white-stone Horse Guards, completed in 1753.[92] As with his views of Old London Bridge, Canaletto appears keenly aware of capturing a site on the verge of disappearance. Around this crumbling remnant, he assembles the confident architecture of Georgian London: to the left, partly screened by trees, stands the Office of the Paymaster General (1732–33); at center the bright façade of the Admiralty (1722–26), with the spire of Gibbs's St. Martin-in-the-Fields (1722–26) rising behind it. To the right, the York Buildings Waterworks Tower pierces the skyline, while in the foreground appear Kent's recently completed Treasury (1733–36) and the brick houses at No. 1 and No. 2 Downing Street. At the lower left, Canaletto includes the tip of the long canal laid out by Charles II in the 1660s.

The elevated viewpoint and panoramic composition along the park edge give the picture a striking sense of space and light rarely seen in London views before Canaletto's arrival. He may have hoped this novelty would attract a buyer on the open market, for he appears to have painted the work speculatively: In July 1749, he placed a notice in the *Daily Advertiser* inviting "any Gentleman" to view a new picture of St. James's Park at his Soho lodgings—a rare glimpse into Canaletto's entrepreneurial strategies.[93] Prominently featured on the right is Sir Watkin Williams-Wynn's house at No. 1 Downing Street. Perhaps Canaletto hoped to secure this wealthy landowner's patronage. Fate, however, intervened: Williams-Wynn's death from a riding accident in September 1749 thwarted any chance of a sale. The painting eventually passed to John Robartes, 4th Earl of Radnor, who acquired it sometime before 1756 and later praised it enthusiastically as "the most capital picture I ever saw of that master."[94]

Close examination reveals that the painting, capturing a diverse stratum of Londoners, is as much about architecture as it is about the life of St. James's Park. Soldiers drill before the Horse Guards, while nursemaids, servants, and fashionable pedestrians mingle across the open space. Children play, a man relieves himself against the Treasury wall, and servants beat a carpet in front of No. 1 Downing Street. In the left corner, a beggar rests under a tree, while nearby a woman lifts her skirts to reveal a flash of red heel—perhaps hinting at one of the Park's infamous prostitutes. These vivid details break the monotony of the topographic view and emphasize the park's status as a public space open to all classes. Contemporary accounts confirm this unruly mix: genteel promenaders shared the avenues with indecorous behavior and illicit encounters. In 1763, Casanova reported seeing "six or seven people" relieving themselves in the bushes, while James Boswell recorded his own casual sexual encounter there for sixpence.[95] Canaletto's inclusion of urinating figures and the ambiguous red-heeled woman thus underscores the park's dual identity as both a stage for polite society as well as moral ambivalence.

Alongside St. James's Park, Vauxhall Gardens and Ranelagh Gardens were London's most renowned pleasure grounds. These venues fostered sociability across classes, staging leisure as regulated performance. Canaletto captured both in *The Grand Walk, Vauxhall Gardens* (fig. 26) and *The Interior of the Rotunda, Ranelagh* (fig. 27). With these canvases—the only oil paintings of the venues—Canaletto transplanted his Venetian eye for ceremonial space to the heart of Georgian leisure culture, balancing documentary precision with the heightened drama of stage-like composition.

Vauxhall Gardens was situated on the south bank of the Thames in Kennington. Jonathan Tyers, who took over the lease in 1728, relaunched the grounds with an admission price of only a shilling, ensuring sustained prosperity under the patronage of Frederick, Prince of Wales. He regularized the layout: paths were straightened, the wilderness reduced to geometric plots, offering a visual metaphor of order. Canaletto's painting captures the vista that greeted visitors on entry: the broad Grand Walk, lined to the left with supper boxes, and to the right the octagonal orchestra pavilion (opened in 1735), the organ house (1737), and the so-called Turkish Tent (completed before 1744).[96] At the far end we see a gilded statue of Aurora, goddess of the dawn. Canaletto exaggerated the avenue's width and the scale of its

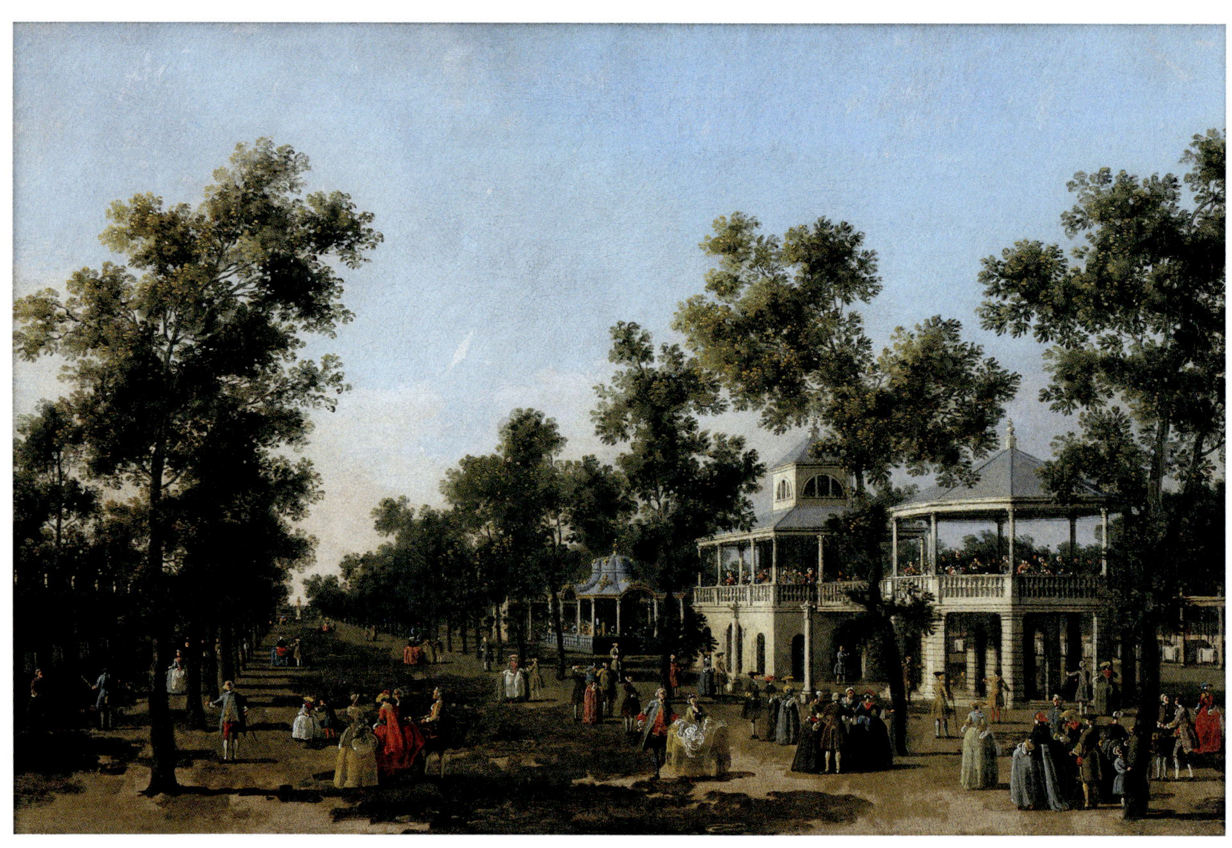

structures, heightening the sense of festivity and animation. Visitors typically arrived in late afternoon and stayed into the evening, promenading, dining, and enjoying music under the glow of 1,500 oil-lamps. Before Westminster Bridge opened in 1750, the journey itself was part of the spectacle, as Londoners braved the surly watermen who ferried them across the river. Musical performances were a major draw—most famously Handel's *Music for the Royal Fireworks*, whose 1749 rehearsal attracted more than 12,000 people and left Old London Bridge impassable for three hours. Aristocrats, artists, and ordinary citizens mingled here in great numbers until well after dawn, but Canaletto's genteel, tranquil, and somewhat stilted crowd and

Fig. 26: Canaletto, *The Grand Walk, Vauxhall Gardens*, c.1751, oil on canvas, 70 × 96 cm. Compton Verney, UK, inv. 0355.S

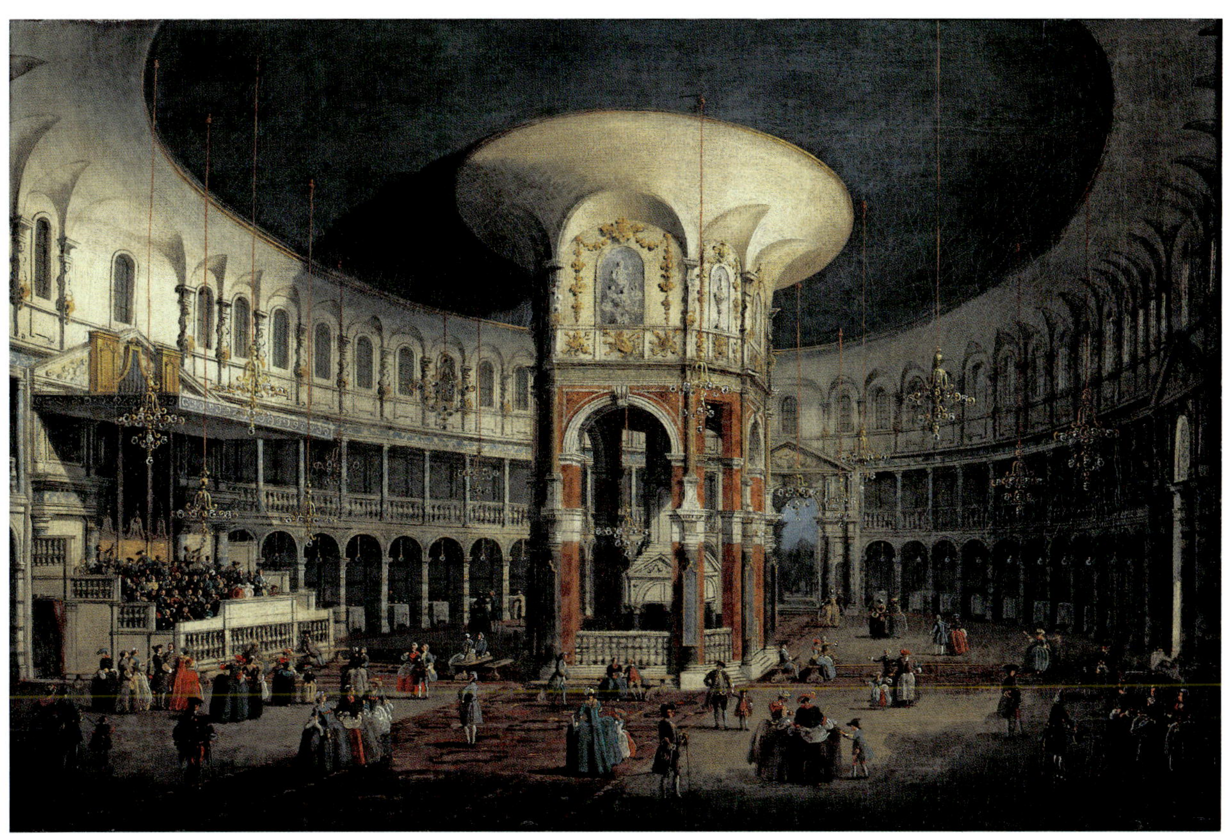

Fig. 27: Canaletto, *The Interior of the Rotunda, Ranelagh*, c.1751, oil on canvas, 70 × 96 cm. Compton Verney, UK, inv. 0356.S

warm daylight belie the chaotic and nocturnal reality described in contemporary accounts.[97]

Though similar to Vauxhall, Ranelagh served a more exclusive crowd, with admission costing several times Vauxhall's price (and including tea, coffee, bread, and butter). Established on the grounds of Ranelagh House in Chelsea, southwest of Westminster, the gardens were dominated by an extraordinary rotunda, completed in 1742. This vast timber structure, c. 46 meters wide, became one of London's architectural marvels. Inside, orchestras and choirs performed from raised stands, while two tiers of 52 boxes encircled a central column enclosing a fireplace. A weather-proof alternative to open-air gardens, the

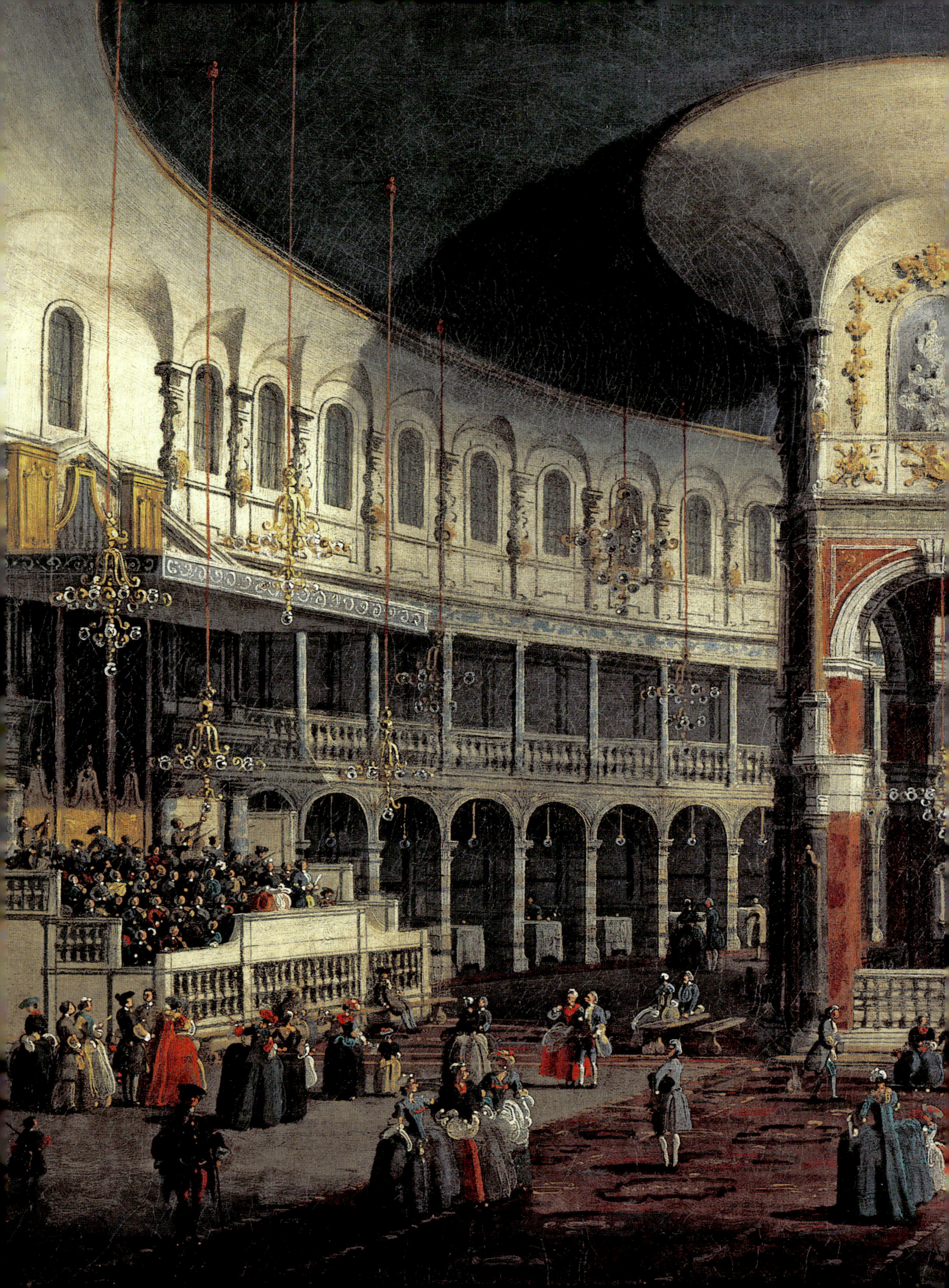

rotunda hosted masquerades, balls, and concerts — even the eight-year-old Mozart performed there in 1764 — and contemporaries praised its impact. Horace Walpole, on his first visit in May 1742, admired "a vast amphitheatre, finely gilt, painted and illuminated; into which everybody who loves eating, drinking, staring or crowding, is admitted for twelve pence."[98] Two years later, he noted Ranelagh had "totally beat Vauxhall," so popular amongst the elite that "you can't set your foot without treading on a Prince."[99] Canaletto's picture depicts this vast space from above, emphasizing the sweeping colonnade, the curved architectural surfaces lit in dramatic contrast, and the flow of elegantly dressed visitors.[100] To the left, an orchestra plays upon a raised platform, attracting a small audience, while others take refreshments beneath the arcades or stroll around the central column, richly adorned with Rococo motifs. Canaletto's treatment of light heightens the sense of spectacle, presenting another spotlighted, albeit ordered, view of London's society.

While Canaletto mostly painted lively city scenes, he occasionally turned his gaze to aristocratic estates in the countryside, including Windsor, Badminton, Syon, and Alnwick. However, no single subject in England (with the exception of the River Thames at Westminster) received as much attention from Canaletto as Warwick Castle, of which five paintings and three drawings are known.[101] Dramatically sited on a sandstone bluff above a bend in the River Avon, the castle had been founded by William the Conqueror in 1068 and continuously reshaped across the centuries. By the mid-eighteenth century it belonged to Francis Greville, 8th Baron Brooke, who not only inherited the estate upon coming of age in 1740, but was also created Earl Brooke in 1746 and later 1st Earl of Warwick in 1759. A seasoned Grand Tourist and already a collector of Canaletto's Venetian views, Greville was eager both to proclaim his lineage and to display the modern improvements he was making to Warwick. He had begun employing Lancelot "Capability" Brown in 1748 as architect and landscape gardener, setting in motion a long program that would transform both the castle and its grounds. It was in this context of renewal and aggrandizement that Greville commissioned Canaletto to record his ancestral seat. Between 1748

Detail of fig. 27

and 1752, several payments are recorded at Hoare's Bank, attesting to the artist's production of his views and the renumeration he received.[102]

Fig. 28: Canaletto, *The South Façade of Warwick Castle*, 1748, oil on canvas, 75 × 120.5 cm. Museo Nacional Thyssen-Bornemisza, Madrid, inv. 78 (1978.13)

Among the five paintings, three depict the south front from Castle Park across the Avon, while two focus on the east side. Perhaps the most imposing of the south-front views is the canvas now in Madrid (fig. 28). Painted in 1748, it shows the castle's residential wing looming above the river, its medieval towers integrated into the tree-lined landscape, with the town pressing in from the right behind the old bridge. Canaletto heightens the drama by including the summit of Guy's Tower projecting above the building's center, even though it is not visible from this actual viewpoint. To the left rises the Watch Tower Mount with its spiraling, tree-lined path. It is instructive to compare this with the painting at the Yale Center for British Art (fig. 29), of similar date, where the castle mill and weir are still visible to the right, and groups of workmen shift earth and stone as Brooke's improvements begin at the foot of the Mount. Alongside them, polite figures promenade by the river, pausing to admire the new walks and altered façade, where two freshly installed Gothic-style windows gleam conspicuously against the older masonry. In contrast, the Madrid version omits the mill and laborers; the Cedar Room's windows appear softer, their whiteness subdued. Painted while work was ongoing, this canvas seems to anticipate the finished transformation—an idealized vision of the castle, with onlookers enjoying the view from the windows. The foreground is sparsely populated: two men converse beside a dog, a gentleman approaches toward us, a fisherman tries his luck, and a couple picnics by the river. A gondola-like craft enlivens the water, perhaps recording the "pleasure boat" mentioned in castle accounts.[103] These details recall Canaletto's Venetian idiom while casting Warwick as a setting of aristocratic politeness and sociability, imbuing it with the cultivated elegance of Georgian refinement.[104]

Fig. 29: Canaletto, *Warwick Castle*, 1748/49, oil on canvas, 72.4 × 119.9 cm. Yale Center for British Art, New Haven, Paul Mellon Collection, inv. B1994.18.2

After nearly a decade in England, Canaletto, then approaching sixty, returned to Venice around 1755. During his English sojourn he had attracted distinguished patrons, including the Duke of Richmond, Sir Hugh Smithson, the Dean of

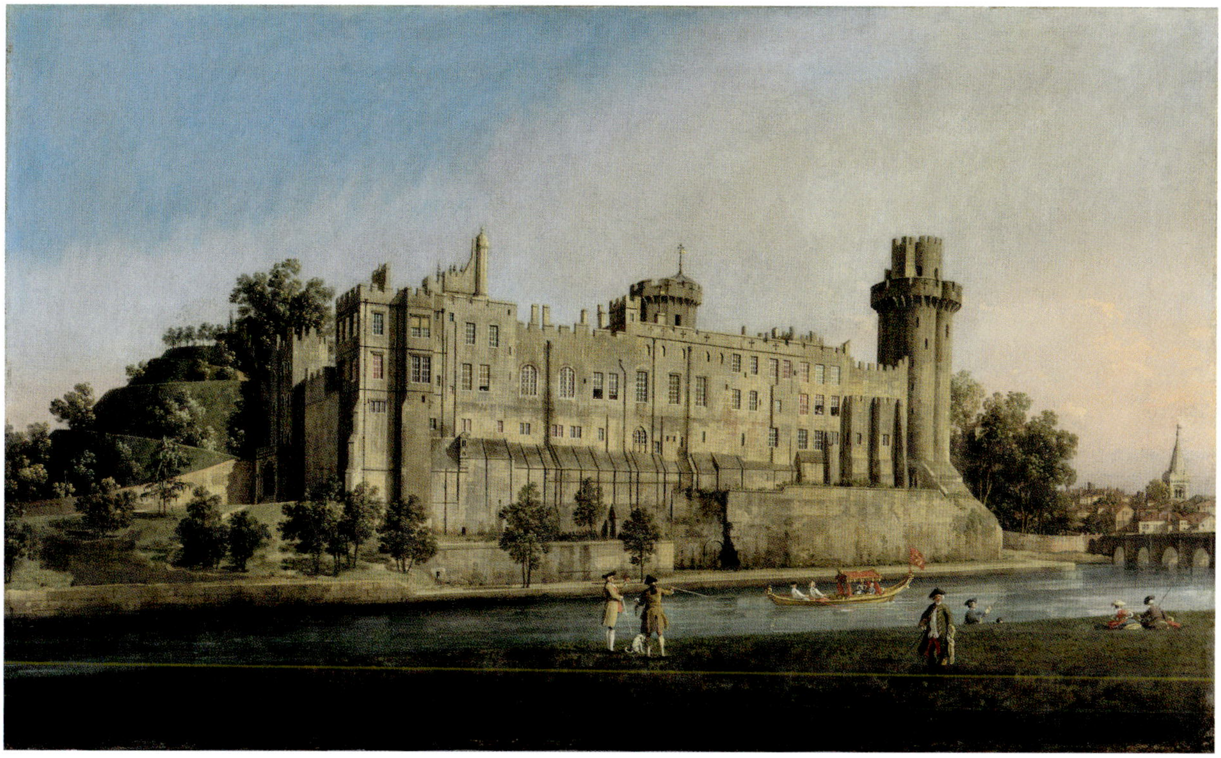

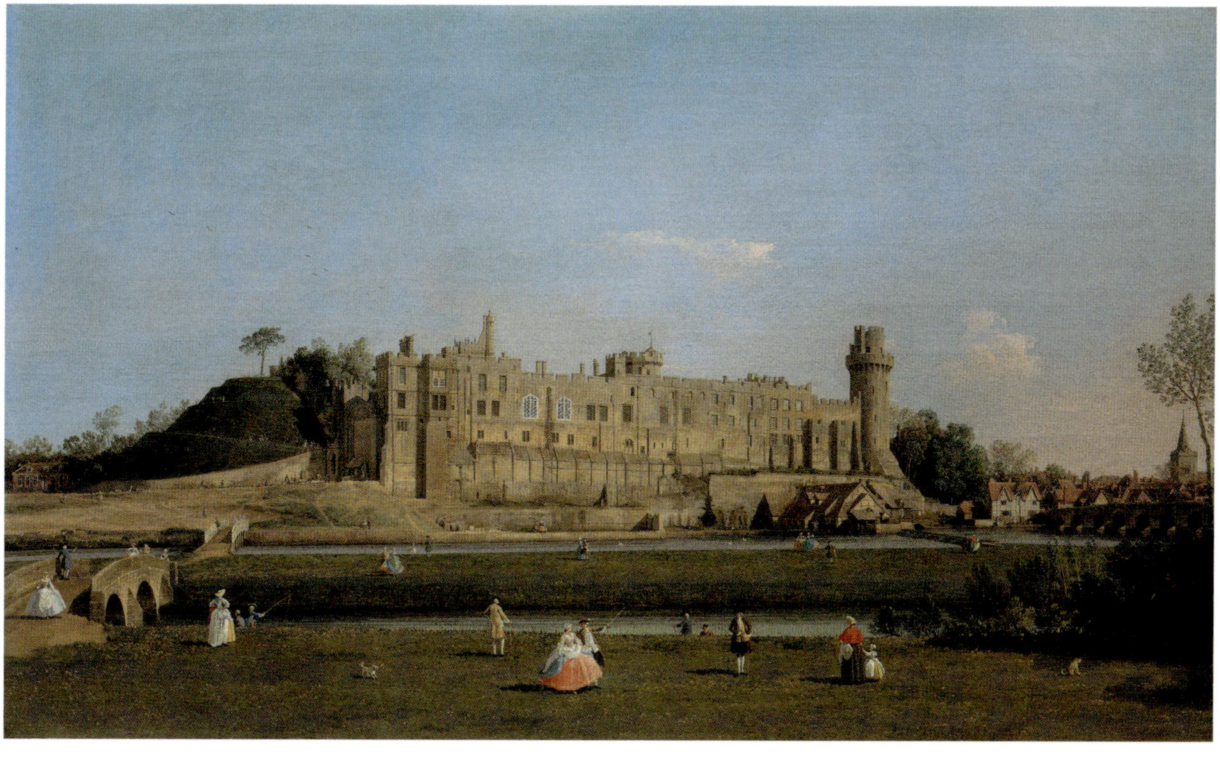

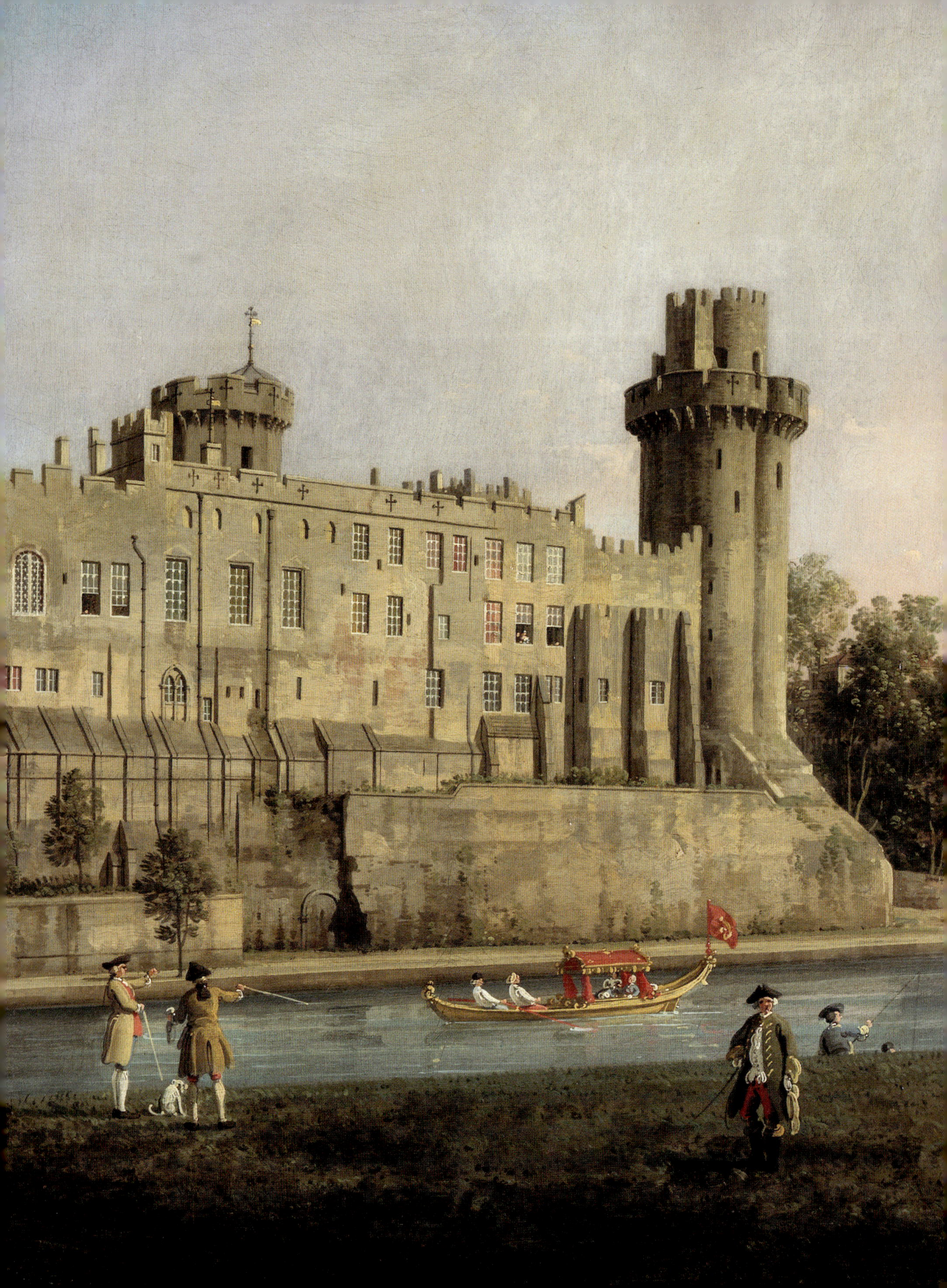

Westminster, Prince Lobkowicz, and Lord Brooke.[105] Yet not all of his English ventures were successful. Alongside commissions, he also painted works for speculative sale, with mixed results as we have seen with his view of St. James's Park. In 1751 he advertised another large view, *Chelsea College with Ranelagh Gardens*, but George Vertue judged it inferior to his earlier Venetian works, remarking that English painters could now produce equally good or better pictures.[106] Vertue's dismissal also reflects a London where artists like Hogarth defended native talent, and fears of foreign competition bred rivalry that often verged on xenophobia; thus it was hard for Canaletto to thrive.[107] The view of Chelsea College failed to sell and was eventually cut into two halves, perhaps to ease its marketability. A similarly ambitious *View of Whitehall and the Privy Garden*—an expanded version of the Richmond composition—likewise found no buyer in London. Canaletto thus carried it back to Venice, where it remained in his studio until John Crewe acquired it in 1761.[108] Such setbacks were not merely the result of nationalism but, as Brian Allen has observed, they were also structural: topographical painting ranked low in the hierarchy of genres, and while Venetian *vedute* carried the Grand Tour's associations of elegance and learning, London scenes offered little such cachet.[109]

Yet Canaletto's English views achieved more than topographical record: they projected urban order onto an unruly and rapidly changing place. His luminous depictions highlighted grand architecture, broad streets, and carefully choreographed public spaces, presenting London as a model city of harmony and civic virtue tied to notions of good governance that was at odds with more critical contemporary accounts. In this sense he was not merely a topographer but, as in his Venetian *vedute*, an interpreter who selected, idealized, and reframed the city before him. Nevertheless, the broader market could not sustain him. Back in Venice, his career entered a quieter phase. Commissions dwindled, and he turned increasingly to *capricci* and to drawings for publishers. Recognition came late: not until 1763, at sixty-six, was he admitted to the Venetian Academy—a belated honor that affirmed, at last, the artistic seriousness he had long claimed for his work. Still proud of his impeccable vision, both artistic and

Detail of fig. 28

literal, he remarked on his last drawing—an interior of the Basilica of San Marco (1766)—that he had rendered it without spectacles.[110] But his final years brought little financial reward. At his death in April 1768, his estate, which, as a lifelong bachelor, he left his three sisters, was modest: a small sum of cash, some silver and jewelry, a few furnishings, and investments offset by debts and obligations.[111] Despite decades of acclaim, his was the precarious life of a freelance *vedutista*, reliant on ever-changing demand and aristocratic favor. He never enjoyed the security of a salaried court position. This honor was reserved for another artist: his nephew, Bernardo Bellotto.

BELLOTTO IN SAXONY

In 1747, a year after his uncle left for England, Bellotto also departed Venice. It remains unclear whether this decision was influenced by his uncle's absence or by the decline in foreign visitors, for Bellotto had already begun building a reputation as an independent artist, notably through commissions from Charles Emmanuel III of Savoy.[112] Unlike Canaletto, who navigated the uncertainties of the open market, Bellotto seems to have aspired to a more stable, institutional route. He moved to Dresden to accept a salaried position as court painter to the Elector of Saxony and King of Poland, and over the next decade produced some of his most celebrated city views. In doing so, he carried the Venetian *veduta* beyond its place of origin, adapting its vocabulary to the political and cultural ambitions of new courts and cities.

Bellotto's move to Dresden was presumably aided by his Venetian connections. One key figure was Bonomo Algarotti, a witness at Bellotto's marriage to Maria Elisabetta Pizzorno on 5 November 1741, who may have facilitated contact with the Dresden court through his brother, Francesco Algarotti. Between 1742 and 1747, Francesco advised Augustus III and acquired artworks for the Saxon royal collection. As noted earlier, he knew Canaletto and thus was likely aware of Bellotto's talent. Support may also have come from Pietro Maria Guarienti, inspector of the Dresden gallery and godfather to Bellotto's daughter Francesca

Detail of fig. 30

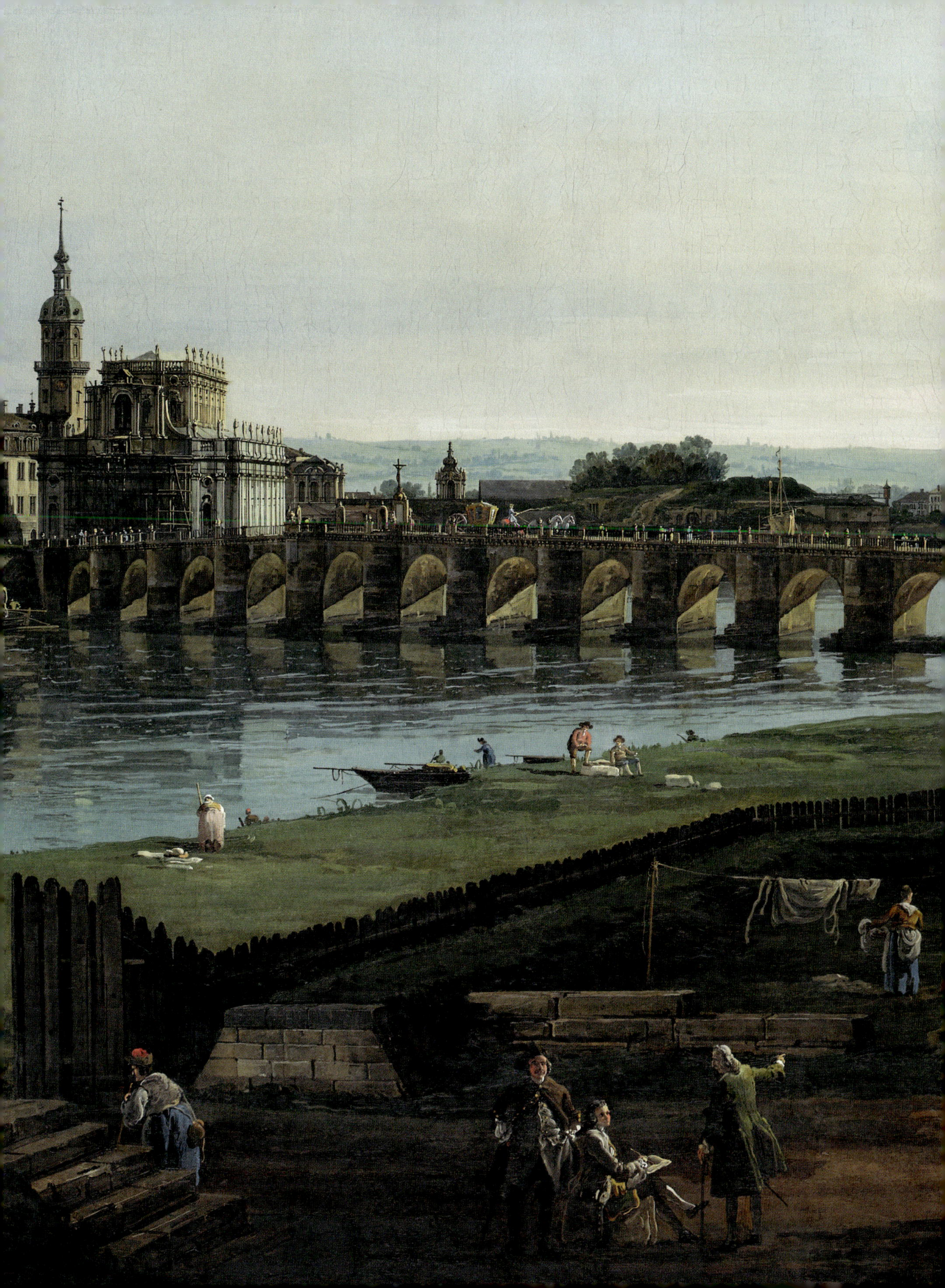

Elisabetta, who died at the age of two. There is also speculation about a link with the future Elector Frederick Christian, who, as previously noted, spent several months in Venice during his Grand Tour. However the introduction occurred, Bellotto—accompanied by his wife, his son Lorenzo, and a servant named Francesco—set out from Venice for the Saxon capital.[113]

Though modest in size at about 55,000 inhabitants, mid-eighteenth-century Dresden was at its cultural peak under Augustus III and his consort, Maria Josepha of Austria. The Zwinger, the Frauenkirche, and the Augustus Bridge defined its baroque cityscape, while the royal collection ranked among Europe's finest. The Saxon court prided itself on attracting international artistic and scholarly talent and, in appointing a painter visibly in Canaletto's lineage, made a clear statement of cosmopolitan ambition. Bellotto received a generous annual salary of 1,750 thalers, and the furnishing of his spacious Dresden apartment—with an art collection and a library—reflected his elevated status and intellectual outlook.[114] His position stood in sharp contrast to that of his uncle in London, who had to lodge with a cabinetmaker.

During his eleven years in Dresden, Bellotto produced a substantial body of work, ranging from large-scale views of the city and of nearby Pirna with its fortress Sonnenstein, to grand renderings of the fortress Königstein further east. Using optical aids like the camera obscura, Bellotto pursued unprecedented precision in recording monuments, streets, and riverbanks. Yet his realism was never mere transcription. Like his uncle, Bellotto refined the raw images produced by the camera to craft an idealized vision. He merged multiple viewpoints, heightened contrasts of light and shadow, and carefully arranged staffage figures, ensuring that topographical accuracy was always balanced with dramatic composition.[115]

When Bellotto arrived in Dresden, one of his first paintings was *Dresden from the Right Bank of the Elbe, above the Augustus Bridge* (fig. 30), where he inscribed on a stone fragment in the foreground: "BERNARDO BELLOTTO / DETTO CANALETO." This self-conscious signature is echoed by the presence of a draughtsman in the center—generally read as Bellotto—gazing

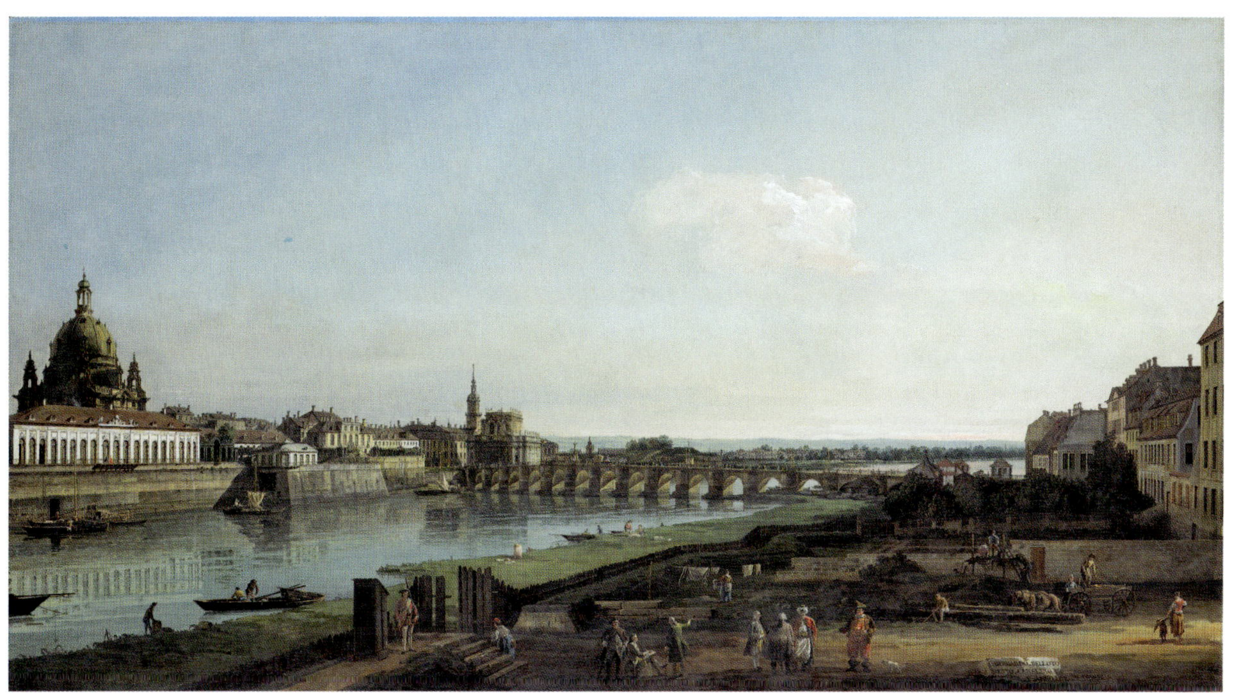

Fig. 30: Bernardo Bellotto, *Dresden from the Right Bank of the Elbe, above the Augustus Bridge*, 1747, oil on canvas, 133.3 × 238 cm. Gemäldegalerie Alte Meister, Dresden, inv. 602

toward an older man often identified as court painter Johann Alexander Thiele. Around him stand further figures traditionally linked to Dresden's artistic and courtly circles: possibly the painter Christian Wilhelm Ernst Dietrich behind the seated figure, and, to the right, the court jester Joseph Fröhlich in Tyrolean costume, and the Queen's physician, Filippo di Violante.[116] Though the likenesses are not precise, their dress and bearing suggest intended recognition. The message is clear: as a newcomer, Bellotto modestly positions himself within Dresden's established hierarchy, aligning with influential figures while marking his presence. The view itself is equally ambitious. The Elbe cuts diagonally through the canvas, guiding the eye across a cityscape that dramatizes Dresden's emergence as a cultural capital. Two churches dominate the skyline: to the left, the stately dome of George Bähr's Protestant *Frauenkirche* (1726–43); to its right, Gaetano Chiaveri's still-unfinished Catholic *Hofkirche* (1739–55). In front rises the

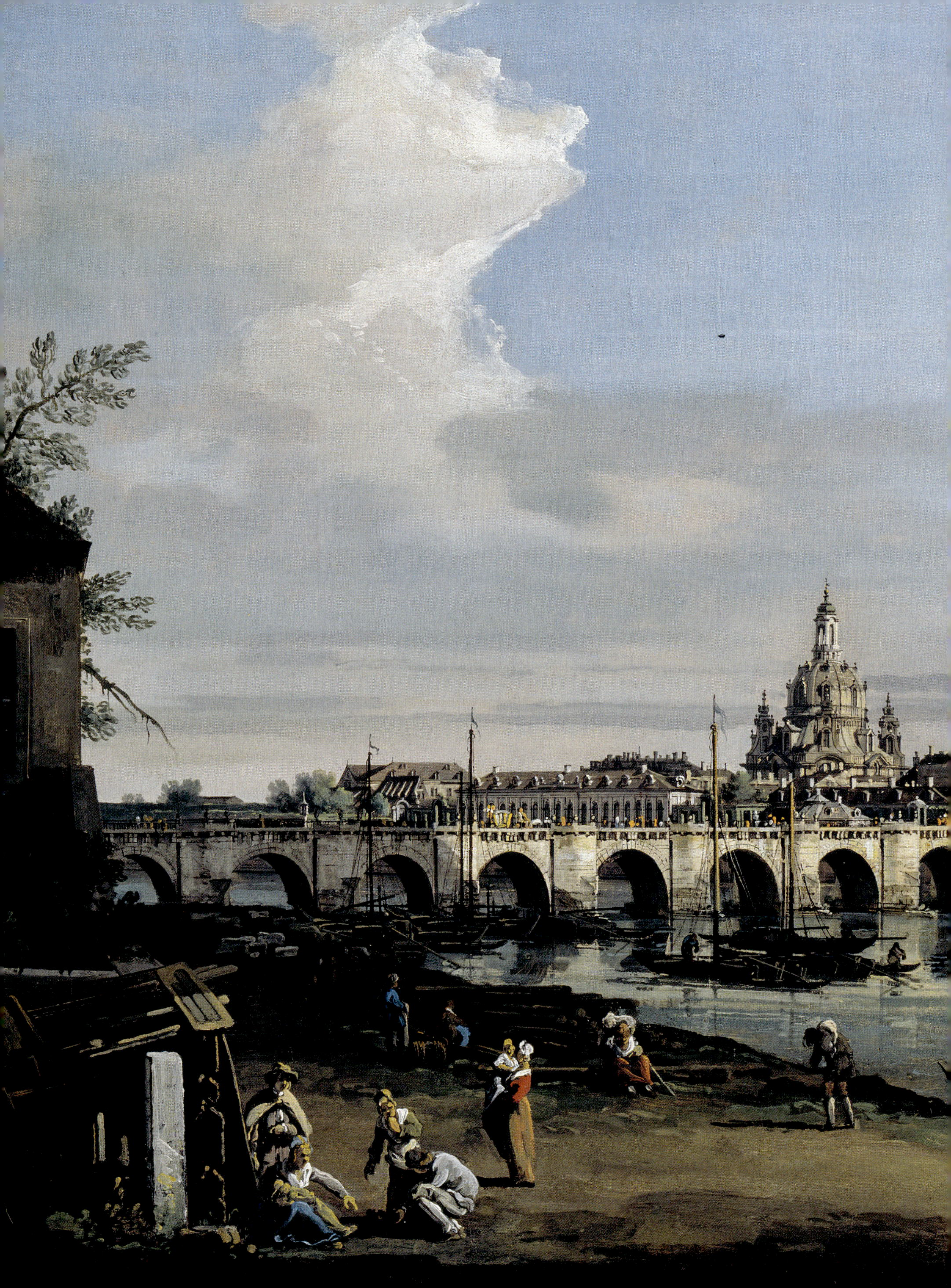

Brühl Terrace, elevated in 1739 atop old fortifications and, between 1740 and 1744, topped with a gallery, library, and palace of Saxony's powerful chancellor, Count Heinrich von Brühl. Anchoring the composition is the Augustus Bridge, rebuilt by Matthäus Daniel Pöppelmann under Augustus the Strong between 1727 and 1731—then the only bridge uniting Dresden's old and new towns. Similar to Westminster Bridge, it clearly signaled Dresden's aspiration to embrace a classicizing idiom.

Already with this first Dresden *veduta*, Bellotto adopted a working method that would define much of his Saxon output: producing multiple versions of the same composition, tailored to different patrons. The version just discussed was made for the royal collection, while a nearly identical replica—with simplified staffage and without the artist's self-portrait—was produced for Count Brühl (Raleigh, North Carolina Museum of Art). Further versions followed. Among the smaller-format replicas is the painting now in Dublin (see cat. 17), offering yet another iteration of the same iconic view. Like the Brühl version, the Dublin painting simplifies the foreground figures and omits self-representation, marking a shift from personal expression to a more neutral depiction of the city aimed at appealing to buyers beyond courtly circles.[117]

Bellotto produced a counterpart view captured from downstream—a composition now commonly referred to as Dresden's "Canaletto View," offering a commanding perspective from the riverbank, with the Elbe reflecting the city's distinctive skyline. In 1748, he first painted a large version for the royal collection, followed around 1750 by a smaller one now in Dublin (fig. 31). Central to Bellotto's visual strategy here is his manipulation of scale and perspective: although the Protestant Frauenkirche remains prominent, its true dimensions are shrunk and it is visually outshone by the Catholic Hofkirche, whose soaring tower dominates the scene. Notably, the tower had not yet been built—the actual construction occurred between 1752 and 1755—but Bellotto depicts it as already complete, most likely using architectural plans or a scale model.[118] He employed a similar tactic in the other Dublin canvas (cat. 17), but here the gesture carries added ideological weight: in the foreground,

Detail of fig. 31

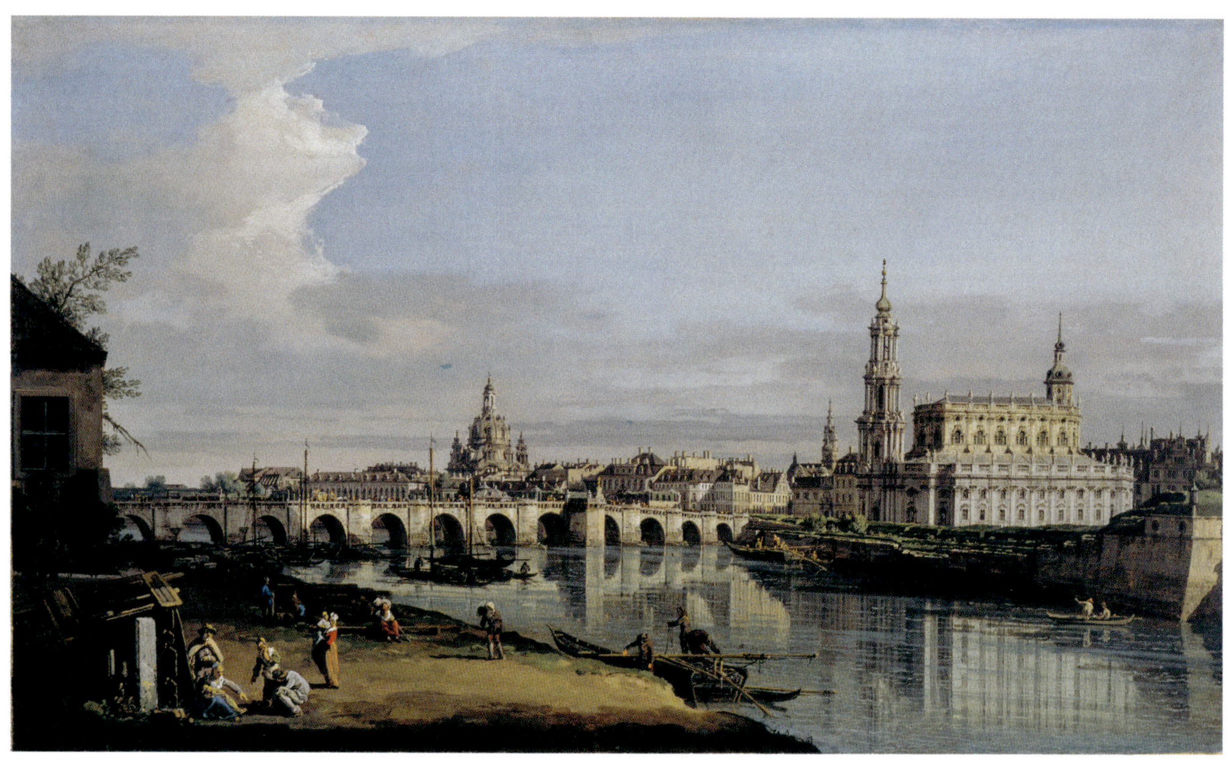

Fig. 31: Bernardo Bellotto, *Dresden from the Right Bank of the Elbe, below the Augustus Bridge*, c.1750, oil on canvas, 51.5 × 84 cm. National Gallery of Ireland, Dublin, inv. 182

a seated woman in Marian blue, a child, and a standing man evoke traditional imagery of the Holy Family. This pastoral vignette, set against a city rendered in gleaming light, reflects the broader Rococo ideal of cultivated idyll and the *georgic* we encountered above. But more importantly, scholars link this trio to the Hofkirche's inner program, initiated by Augustus III and Maria Josepha, whose church featured side altars to their personal patrons, Mary and Joseph. By echoing this iconography in the cityscape, Bellotto forges a symbolic link between Dresden and the court's Catholic identity. The depiction of a fully realized Hofkirche in a largely Protestant city thus serves a religious agenda, projecting Catholic aspirations onto Dresden's physical and spiritual landscape.[119]

It would take too long to enumerate all the splendid works, expertly examined elsewhere, Bellotto produced in Saxony.[120] What is important here is that Bellotto's successful Dresden period overlapped with his uncle's stay in England, before coming to an abrupt halt with the outbreak of the Seven Years' War (1756 – 63). In August 1756, Prussian forces under Frederick the Great, without a formal declaration of war, invaded Saxony and occupied Dresden. Augustus III retreated to the fortress of Königstein, hoping in vain for Austrian support, before fleeing to Warsaw with Count Brühl, leaving Queen Maria Josepha behind in the embattled city, where she died in late 1757. The conflict severely damaged Dresden: by November 1758, the Pirna suburb was devastated by fire, and in 1760 the city's historic center suffered from heavy canon fire. Amid this turmoil and the suspension of royal patronage, Bellotto's prospects grew increasingly uncertain. On December 5, 1758, he requested and received a passport to leave Dresden, traveling first to Bayreuth—possibly a brief stop or an attempt to secure commissions, perhaps encouraged by theater designer Giuseppe Galli Bibiena, who had ties to both cities.[121] Bellotto may also have considered returning to Venice, though his uncle's recent return there may have discouraged him. Ultimately, he relocated with his son Lorenzo to Vienna, arriving in January 1759 and staying until early 1761. Though perchance motivated by hopes of a new court appointment, this aspiration remained unfulfilled. Even so, the Viennese interlude proved a pivotal and strikingly productive phase in Bellotto's career.

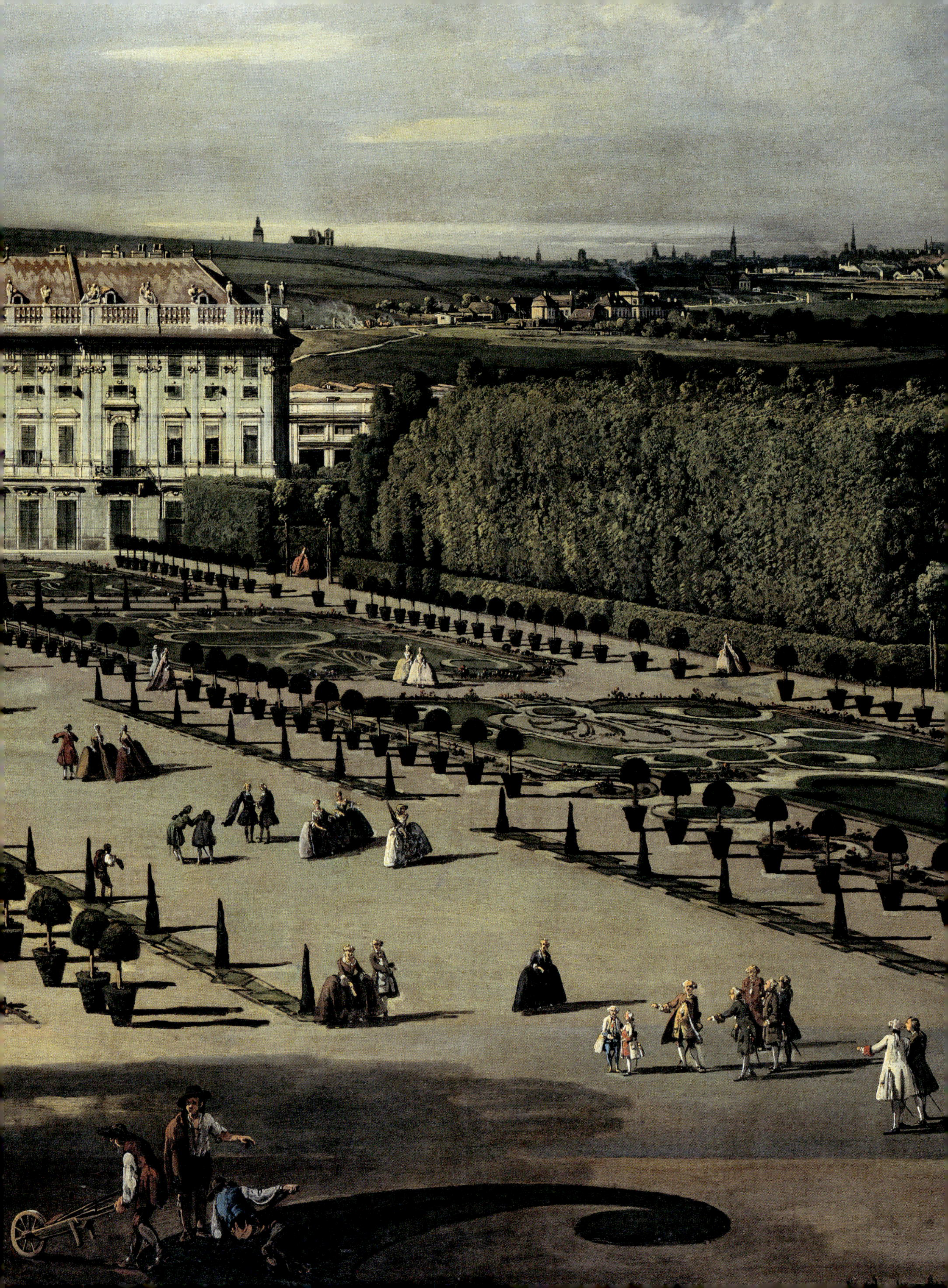

Bellotto in Vienna

Mid-eighteenth-century Vienna was the political and cultural heart of the Habsburg monarchy, a city of some 175,000 inhabitants whose fortunes were shaped by empire, reform, and war. Its setting on the Danube plain, ringed by hills and vineyards, made it a natural crossroads between Western and Eastern Europe—at once a cosmopolitan hub and a bulwark against Ottoman expansion. From here, the Imperial couple Maria Theresa and Francis Stephen projected an image of dynastic continuity and baroque magnificence, even as the War of the Austrian Succession and the Seven Years' War strained the couple's resources. Their artistic commissions drew heavily on baroque opulence but also classical idioms: their prominent 1750 portrait busts by Matthäus Donner, for instance, evoke ancient prototypes (see cats. 19, 20). Vienna herself—successor to the Roman camp of Vindobona—increasingly fused baroque splendor with classical ideals, as exemplified by the Karlskirche, completed in 1739. Meanwhile, political figures such as Chancellor Wenzel Anton von Kaunitz promoted reforms in administration, education, and culture that turned the city into a laboratory of Enlightenment governance.

After the dispersal of the Ottoman siege in 1683, the city experienced an unprecedented building boom. While imposing fortifications still curtailed the Inner City, aristocratic palaces and gardens now flourished in the suburbs, many designed by leading architects such as Johann Bernhard Fischer von Erlach and Johann Lucas von Hildebrandt. The Imperial court as well invested heavily: Maria Theresa's remodeling of Schönbrunn Palace on the city's outskirts gave visible form to Imperial grandeur. Palaces, churches, and civic buildings sprang up across the Inner City, too, even as the narrow, twisting streets rarely offered grand vistas. The result was an urban fabric simultaneously crowded and fortified as well as rationalized and magnificent. It was into this climate that Bellotto arrived in early 1759 and stayed until early 1761.

Although Bellotto remained in Vienna for only two years, he produced a substantial corpus: extant are ten larger canvases of palaces, castles, and gardens, and six smaller-format views of city squares and streets (presumably conceived as pairs). Earlier topographical views of Vienna had been largely confined to prints, such as those by Joseph Emanuel Fischer von Erlach and Johann Adam Delsenbach, and Salomon Kleiner, and while Bellotto often drew on these precedents, he endowed his subjects with a new painterly authority and compositional grandeur. Just as Canaletto had adapted his Venetian idiom to capture the rising aspirations of London, so Bellotto transplanted the *veduta* tradition into the Habsburg realm, rendering Vienna at once topographically precise and ideologically charged.

VIA PRIVATE PATRONS TO THE COURT

Bellotto's entry into Viennese circles was likely facilitated by Count Brühl, whose long-standing political ties with Kaunitz may have proved decisive.[122] The two first met in Dresden in 1731, and after having been appointed Chancellor in 1753, Kaunitz oversaw Habsburg relations with the Saxon court. A figure of considerable political weight and a passionate collector, Kaunitz may well have

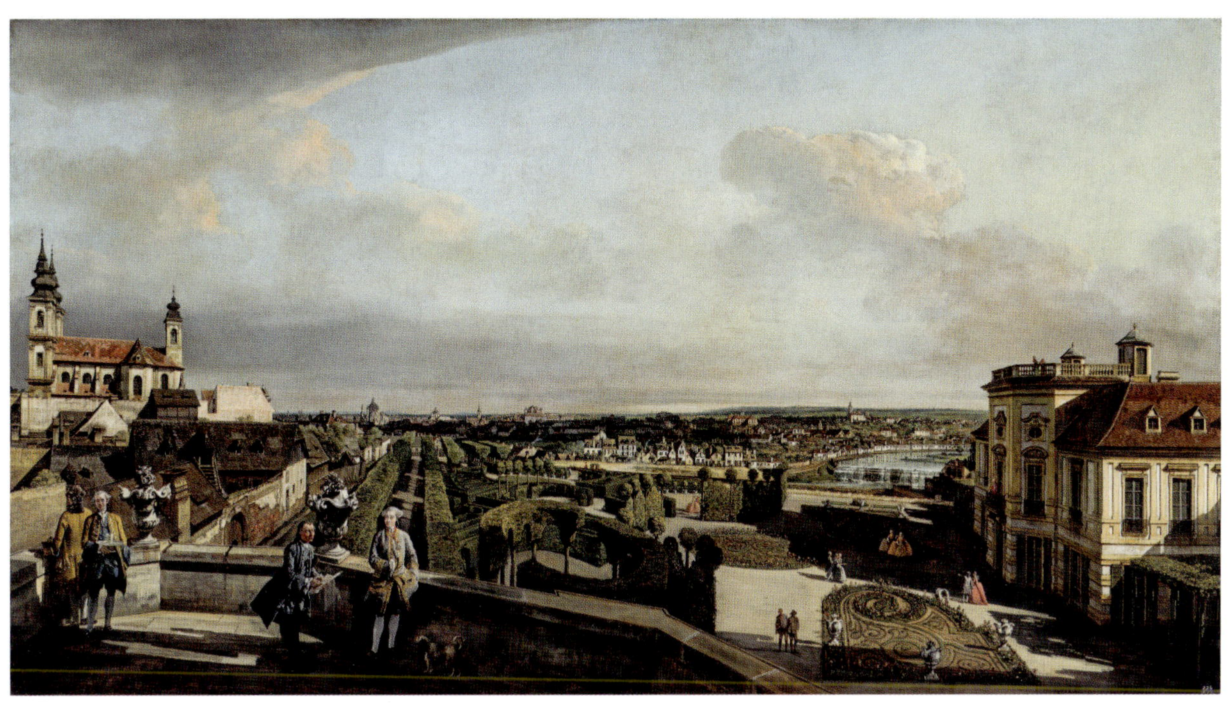

Fig. 32: Bernardo Bellotto, *The Kaunitz Palace and its Garden in Vienna*, 1759/60, oil on canvas, 134 × 237 cm. Szépművészeti Múzeum, Budapest, inv. 52.207

introduced Bellotto to Vienna's elite, but not without first employing the artist himself. Thus Bellotto's earliest commissions in the city appear to have been private: indeed his access to the Imperial house was only possible through such aristocratic networks. If this hypothesis is correct, Bellotto's first Viennese canvas was a view of the Palais Kaunitz in the suburb of Mariahilf (fig. 32). Originally a late seventeenth-century pleasure villa, the property was remodeled in baroque style after Kaunitz acquired it in 1753. Bellotto's large painting shows the residence from a side terrace overlooking geometrically ordered gardens — roughly corresponding to today's Esterházypark. From this elevated vantage, the view extends across the suburb: to the left rises the Mariahilfer Kirche (1714–26), to the right stretches the palace, and in between Vienna's skyline unfolds — from the dome of the Karlskirche and the tower of the Paulanerkirche (1717), to the dome of the Salesian Church (1717–30), and the Belvedere Palace on its hill, built by Johann Lukas von Hildebrandt for Prince Eugene of Savoy between 1717 and 1723 and acquired by Maria Theresa in 1752. Yet the real innovation lies in the depiction of the staffage. Dominating the foreground, an aristocratic figure, almost certainly Kaunitz, leans against the balustrade, hand in waistcoat, as a secretary presents a document while another servant waits with a glass of water. This is the first instance in Bellotto's oeuvre where a patron is so prominently depicted. Though the portrait likeness is limited, Kaunitz's pose, attire, and setting transform the *veduta* into an act of political image making. Indeed, he is presented as enlightened statesman and arbiter of taste, an image consistent with both his reputation for brilliance and the vanity for which he was often criticized.[123]

Fig. 33: Bernardo Bellotto, *The Liechtenstein Garden Palace in Vienna, seen from the East*, 1759/60, oil on canvas, 99.7 × 159.6 cm. LIECHTENSTEIN. The Princely Collections, Vaduz–Vienna, inv. GE 887

Bellotto applied a similar formula in his two views of the Liechtenstein Garden Palace, an early residence built in the suburban Rossau district after the siege of 1683. The Liechtenstein family had begun acquiring land in 1687, and the next year Johann Bernhard Fischer von Erlach built a "Belvedere" terminating the garden axis, as later engraved by Salomon Kleiner in 1737 (see cat. 21). The palace itself was constructed between 1692 and 1706 to plans by Domenico Egidio Rossi and Domenico Martinelli, resulting in a monumental H-shaped block with vast gardens extending toward Fischer's structure.[124] It quickly became a Viennese landmark, celebrated in the engraving series by Fischer the Younger and Delsenbach, after which, in 1747, the English publisher John Bowles issued another print (see cat. 22), further circulating the palace's image across Europe. Bellotto's two views of the palace were commissioned by Prince Joseph Wenzel of Liechtenstein, a distinguished statesman and art patron who, among other achievements, served as Imperial Ambassador to Paris (1738–41). A renowned military commander and discerning connoisseur, he transformed his family's residences into showcases of modern taste, commissioning artists like Bellotto who reflected his cosmopolitan outlook.

Fig. 34: Bernardo Bellotto, *The Liechtenstein Garden Palace in Vienna, seen from the Belvedere*, 1759/60, oil on canvas, 99.8 × 158.5 cm. LIECHTENSTEIN. The Princely Collections, Vaduz–Vienna, inv. GE 889

In both of his Liechtenstein paintings, Bellotto again adopts terrace viewpoints, transforming the foreground into a stage for aristocratic display. One canvas shows the palace obliquely from

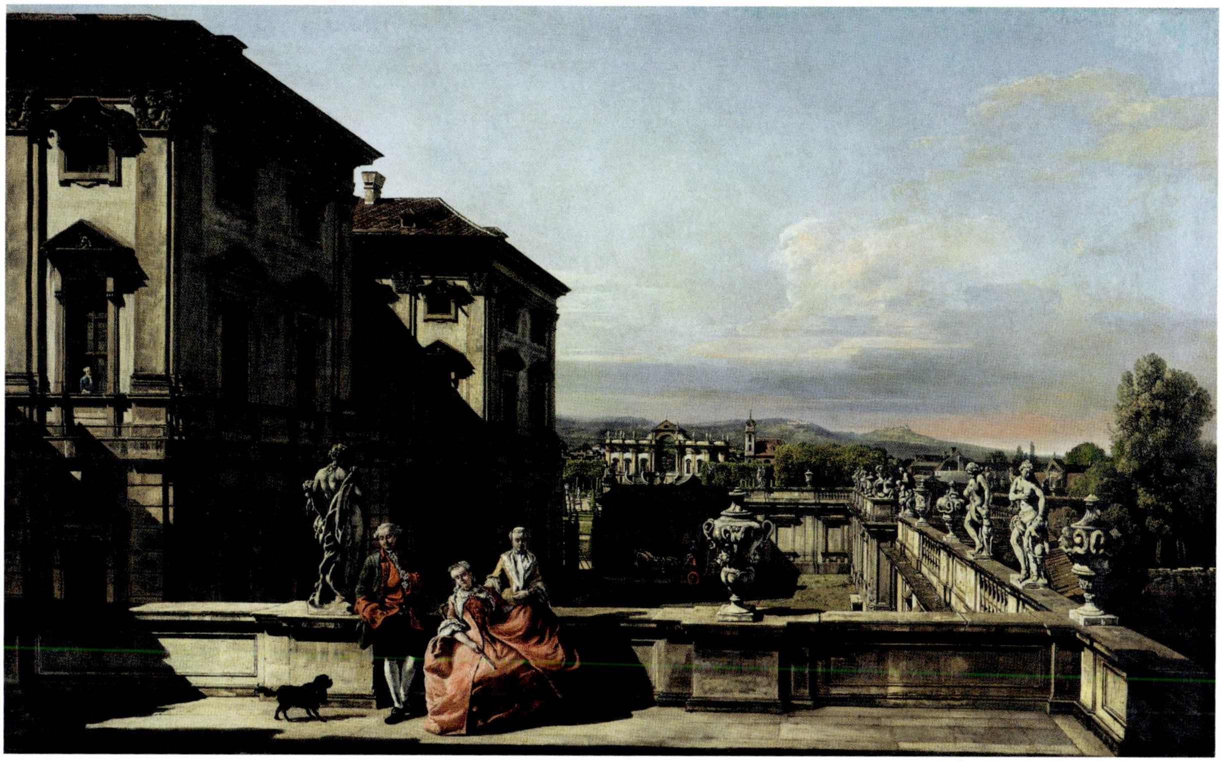

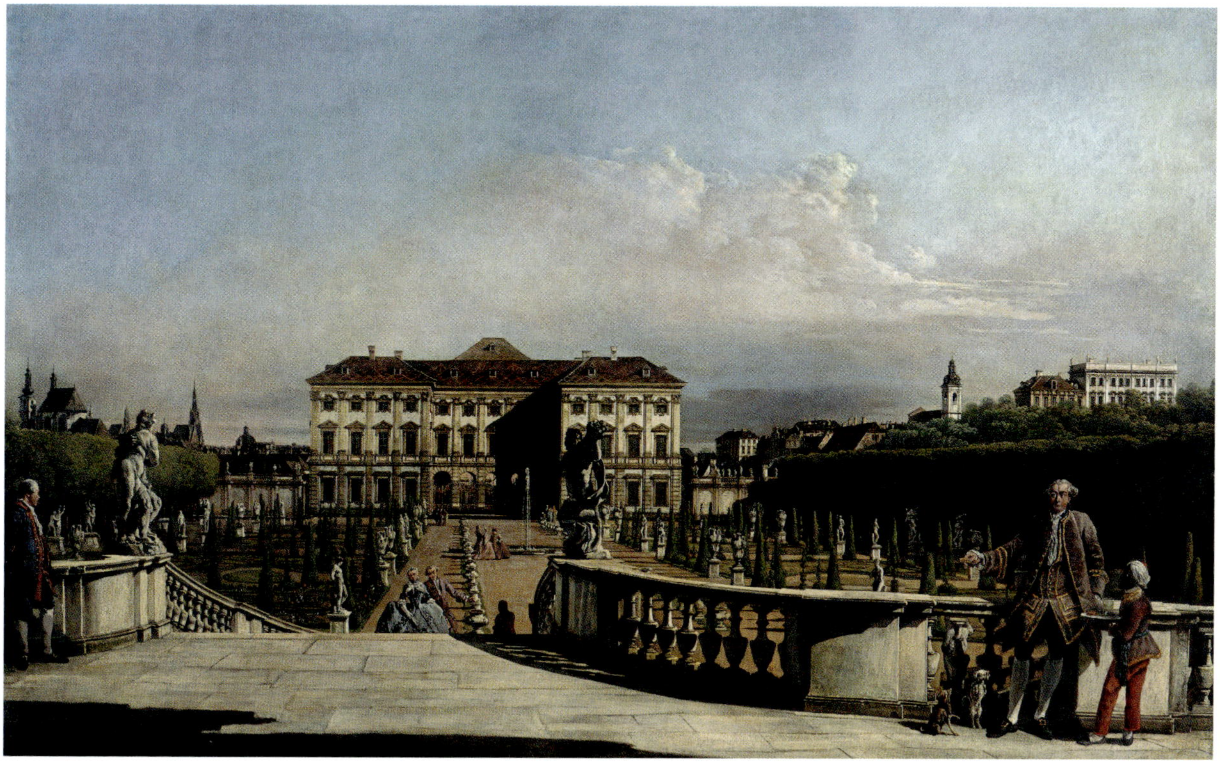

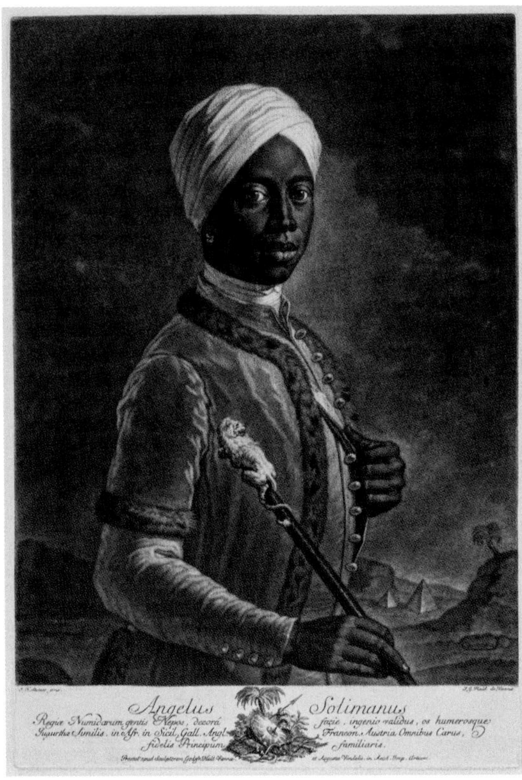

Fig. 35: Johann Gottfried Haid after Johann Nepomuk Steiner, *Angelus Solimanus*, 1760/65, mezzotint, 500 × 370 mm. LIECHTENSTEIN. The Princely Collections, Vaduz–Vienna, inv. GR 715

the side, leading the eye across the parterre toward Fischer's Belvedere (fig. 33). Beyond, the vista extends to the new suburb of Liechtental with its church (1712–30), and further still to the Kahlenberg—the iconic hill from which Polish troops under King Jan III Sobieski descended upon Ottoman troops in 1683. On the terrace in the foreground, a seated, unidentified lady in pink is attended by her maid, accompanied by a young man who tucks his hand into his waistcoat. This gesture was, by Bellotto's time, a well-established marker of authority, composure, and refined masculinity. Its origins can be traced back to ancient Greece, where orators, such as Aeschines, believed that speaking with one's arm outside the toga was improper and undisciplined.[125] Revived during the Enlightenment, it was widely promoted in conduct literature, including *The Rudiments of Genteel Behavior* (1737) by the French dance master François Nivelon, who emphasized posture and controlled gestures as key to "distinguish the polite gentleman from the rude rustick."[126] In portraiture, it became a visual shorthand for intelligence, leadership, and self-command—and understandably popular among aristocrats, military commanders, and statesmen. Bellotto's decision to depict Kaunitz *and* the unidentified man in the Liechtenstein picture in this pose thus aligns them with contemporary ideals of enlightened governance and personal cultivation, reinforcing the self-fashioning agendas already evident in the architectural and pictorial settings.

The companion picture reverses the perspective (fig. 34), depicting the palace's garden façade from the raised terrace of Fischer's Belvedere.[127] Against the bright sunlit architecture and parterre with its statues, offset by Bellotto's characteristically deep shadows, the skyline of Vienna unfolds behind the palace: to the left rise the twin towers of the Servite Church (1651–70), the Gothic spires of Maria am Gestade and St. Stephen's Cathedral (both completed c. 1430), and the dome of Hildebrandt's St. Peter's (1733). To the right, we see the 1749 tower of Our Lady of Montserrat and, high on its hill, the Strudelhof, former residence of the painter Peter Strudel. In the foreground stands a fashionably dressed aristocrat, plausibly Prince Liechtenstein himself, attended by a Black page.

The Black page signals not only an "exotic" marker within such aristocratic display but also the real presence of abducted Africans in Viennese elite society. Joseph Wenzel of Liechtenstein is known to have employed Angelo Soliman, who, born in Africa around 1721, was sold as a child into slavery in Sicily before entering aristocratic service.[128] After rising to the position of valet, soldier, and trusted companion to Field Marshal Georg Christian Prince Lobkowicz—an uncle of Ferdinand Philipp, 6th Prince of Lobkowicz, whom we encountered in the previous chapter—Soliman joined the Liechtenstein household in 1755, where he served as chamberlain and tutor to the princely children, and was portrayed around 1760/65 (fig. 35). Though the prince disapproved, Soliman secretly married a Viennese woman and briefly lived outside the noble household, likely in precarious conditions that later forced his return. Celebrated for his erudition, he became an active Freemason and moved in Enlightenment circles, reportedly associating with Mozart and leading scientists. Yet his refinement stood in tension with his forced role as an "exotic" emblem: after his death in 1796, Imperial authorities appropriated his body, embalmed and displayed it in the Natural History Cabinet as a semi-nude "savage" adorned with feathers and shells. His presence in Liechtenstein's milieu thus adds depth to Bellotto's picture, where the Black page, dressed in orientalizing garb, reflects conventions of aristocratic representation as well as Vienna's entanglement with the atrocities of slavery.

While the Kaunitz and Liechtenstein pictures underscore the performative nature of aristocratic identity, which relied both on refinement and subjugation, they also secured Bellotto's place within Vienna's highest social circles. It was ostensibly through patrons such as Kaunitz and Liechtenstein that he was introduced to the Imperial couple, Maria Theresa and Francis Stephen.[129] It was probably for them that he produced two monumental views of Schönbrunn Palace, a sequence of six cityscapes, and depictions of Schloss Hof. Although the exact circumstances of these commissions remain unclear, their ambitious scale and compositional structure clearly affirmed Vienna's status as a political, cultural, and scientific capital.[130]

Court life alternated between the Hofburg in the Inner City and Schönbrunn, the suburban summer residence fully realized under Maria Theresa. Beginning in 1743, her favored architect Nicolò Pacassi transformed the structure into a coherent ensemble, inserting a mezzanine above the main floor, adding exterior staircases, and remodeling much of the interior. Pacassi linked the service wings to the palace with arcaded corridors, creating a unified representational forecourt—precisely the remodeled complex Bellotto captured in his large paintings.

One canvas (fig. 36) captures the forecourt from an upper window of the northern service wing. Rather than a frontal view, Bellotto chose a diagonal vantage that enlivens the scene, using two subtly offset vanishing points to draw the eye along the side wings toward the central block. The forecourt bustles with

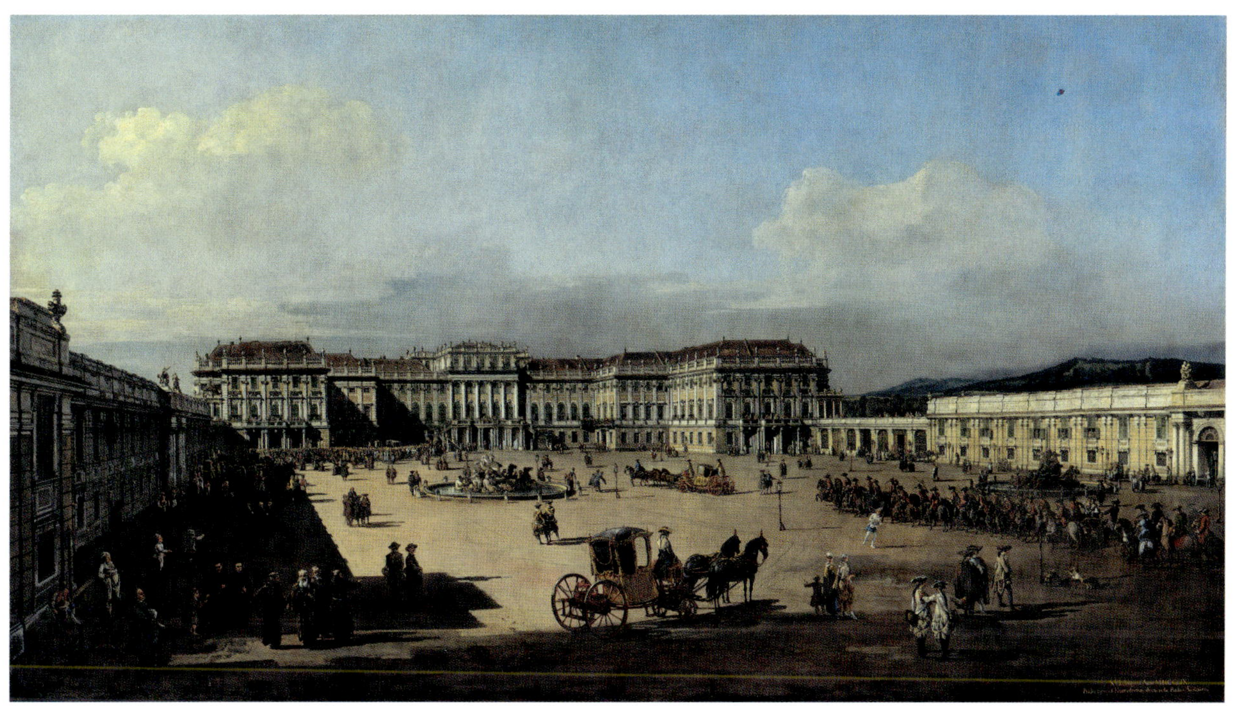

Fig. 36: Bernardo Bellotto, *View of Schönbrunn from the Forecourt*, 1759/60, oil on canvas, 135 × 235 cm, detail on pp. 96–97. Kunsthistorisches Museum, Vienna, Picture Gallery, inv. 1666

activity, and a Latin inscription at lower right provides context: "On the 16th of August, in the year 1759, the Prussian [army] was defeated at Frankfurt by the Russo-Austrian army."[131] Although the allied victory at Kunersdorf actually occurred on August 12, the painting commemorates the official news reaching the Imperial court. In the middle ground, Count Franz Joseph Kinsky arrives in a carriage drawn by four horses, leading twenty postillions and four senior postal officials, about to deliver the long-awaited news of Frederick the Great's defeat. While Maria Theresa had received word of the victory the day before from a courier dispatched by Field Marshal Daun, Bellotto emphasizes the ceremonial delivery by the official messenger on August 16.[132]

Among the many figures animating the forecourt, Bellotto includes courtiers, soldiers, and riders, but also a beggar seated in

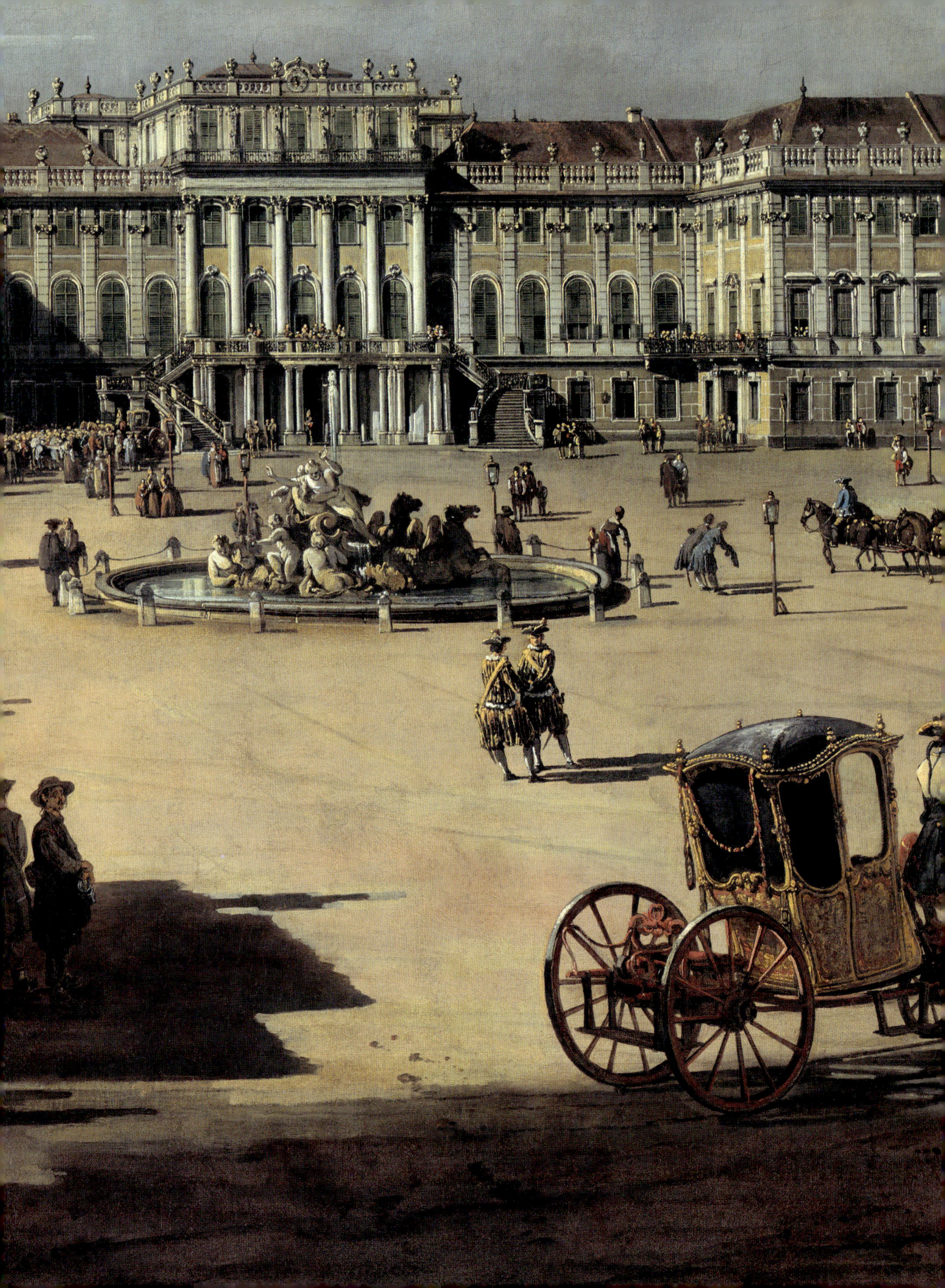

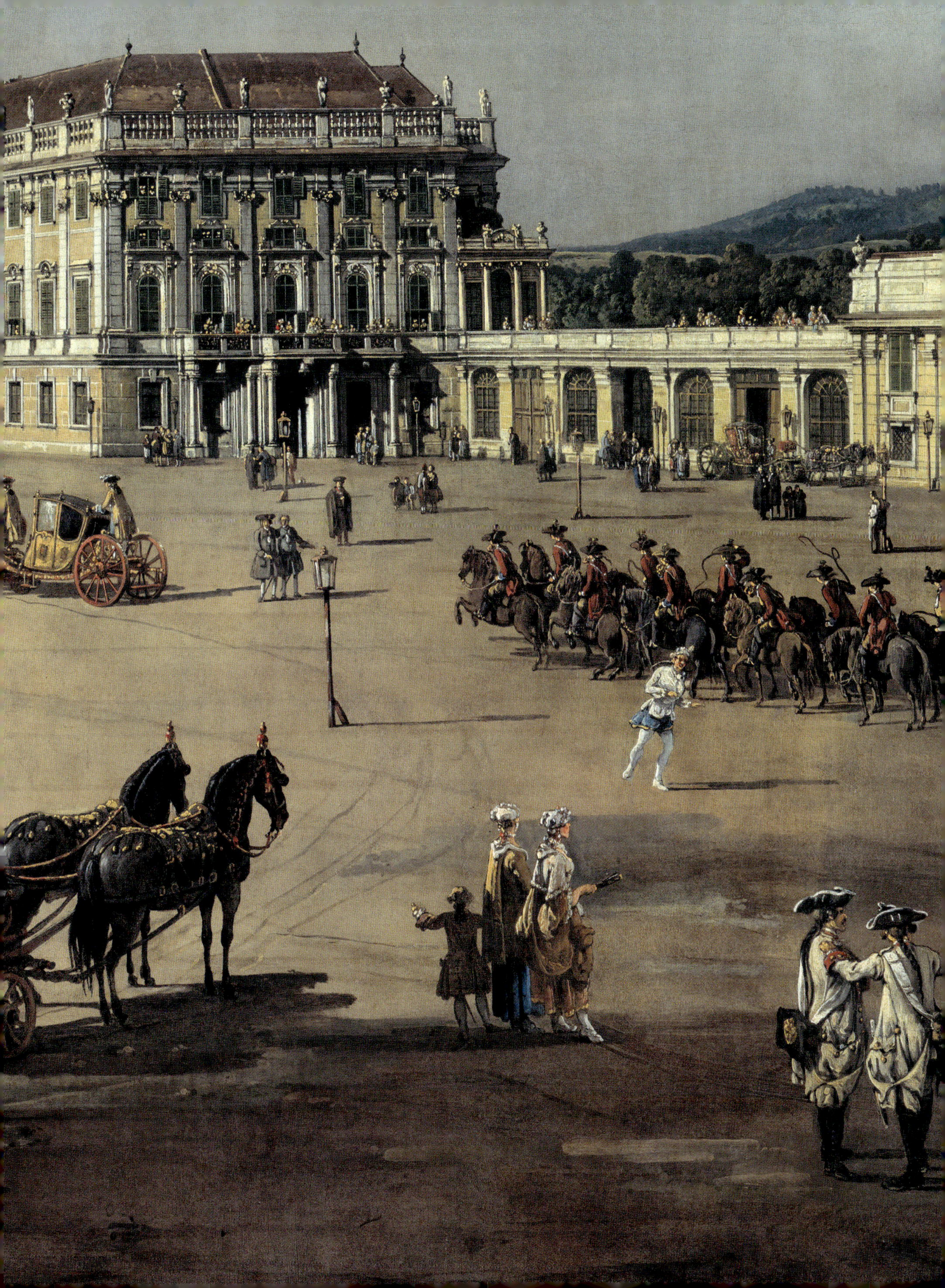

the shade at far left, and three cooks—two of whom rush toward the center. The gentleman in green at lower left, hand tucked into his waistcoat and holding a scroll, remains unidentified, though his prominent placement suggests intentional portrayal. Beside him stand two Jesuits, one offering alms to a poor child, followed by four Capuchins, one pointing toward the scene's center. Such a gesture may imply a link between Roman Catholic sanctity and victory over Protestant Prussia.[133] Also notable is the white-clad runner (*Läufer*) before the postillions, one of the professional court footmen tasked with clearing roads for carriages and swiftly relaying information.[134] In the painting, he may be connected to the second carriage in the foreground, whose owner is unknown; some propose it belonged to the Empress, as a similar coach recurs throughout Bellotto's Viennese canvases.[135] The Empress herself is often thought to appear on the eastern pavilion's balcony, surrounded by members of her court, while a dense crowd fills the courtyard below.[136] Yet Bellotto renders these figures in cursory strokes and their faces in simple dots, making individual identification impossible. The canvas ultimately emerges as a hybrid of *veduta* and history painting, or an architectural portrait that simultaneously stages a moment of political import.[137] Painted at a time when the Seven Years' War weighed heavily on the Viennese court—and when Bellotto's own family faced peril in besieged Dresden—it stands among the most significant of his Viennese *vedute*.

The companion piece (fig. 37) turns to the palace's opposite façade. Painted on an equally monumental scale from the slope of Schönbrunn hill, the elevated vantage point aligns the palace's long roofline with the horizontal silhouette of the hills stretching northward and gently descending east. To the left of the palace lies the so-called Lothringerhaus amid a small cluster of buildings, with the Kahlenberg and Leopoldsberg rising in the far distance. To the right, Bellotto opens a sweeping panorama across the still largely undeveloped suburban landscape toward Vienna. Just right of center, partly obscured by a hill, appears the Piarist Church (1750s); further on, beyond the city wall, stands the dark silhouettes of the Minorite Church and St. Stephen's Cathedral. Diagonally in front stands the Mariahilferkirche—already

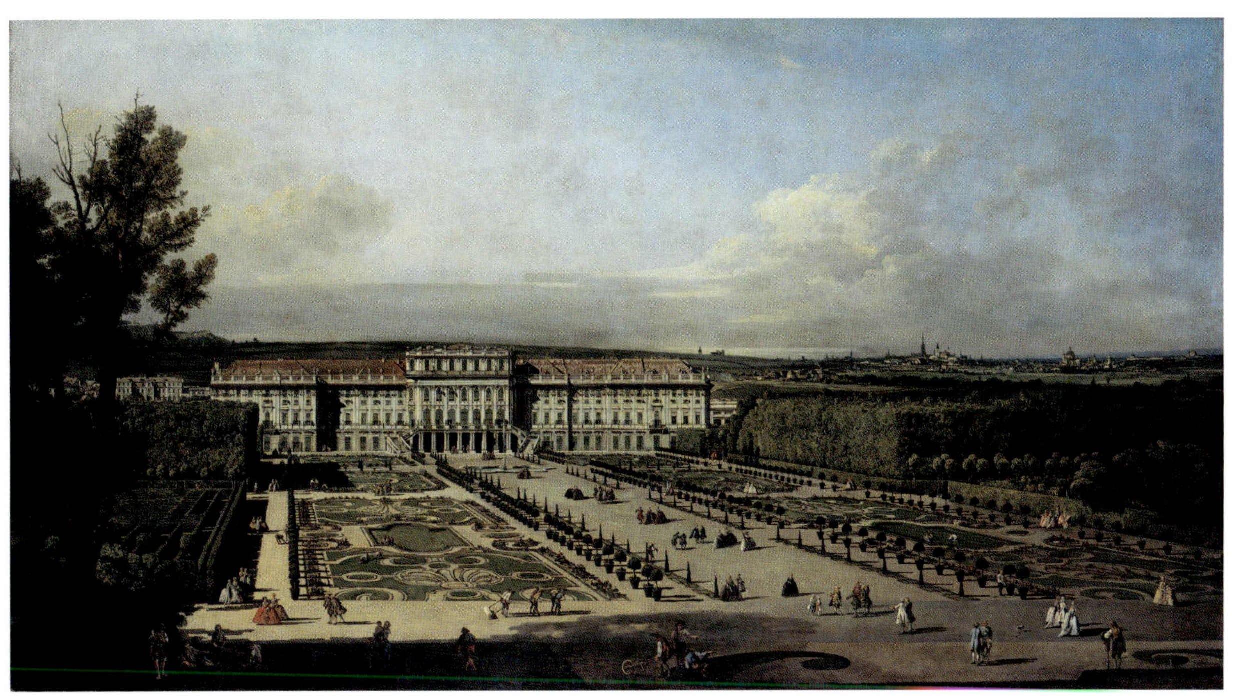

Fig. 37: Bernardo Bellotto, *View of Schönbrunn from the Gardens*, 1759/60, oil on canvas, 134 × 238 cm. Kunsthistorisches Museum, Vienna, Picture Gallery, inv. 1667

familiar from Bellotto's view of Kaunitz's palace—anchoring the suburban belt, where the prominent dome of the Karlskirche also comes into view. At the far edge of the horizon emerges once again the Belvedere Palace (acquired by the Empress in 1752).[138]

In the foreground, the broad parterre of the Imperial gardens dominates the scene. Bellotto depicts it as redesigned in the 1750s under Francis Stephen, involving architect Jean Nicolas Jadot, engineer Jean-Baptiste Brequin de Demenge, and gardener Louis Gervais. In the center stretch the so-called *parterres à l'angloise*, where grass panels are cut through with ornamental gravel paths edged with box hedges that create geometric patterns both ordered and playful.[139] At the centers of the southern parterres lie recessed lawns known as *boulingrins*. Rows of spherical and conical trees line the paths, along which aristocratic figures

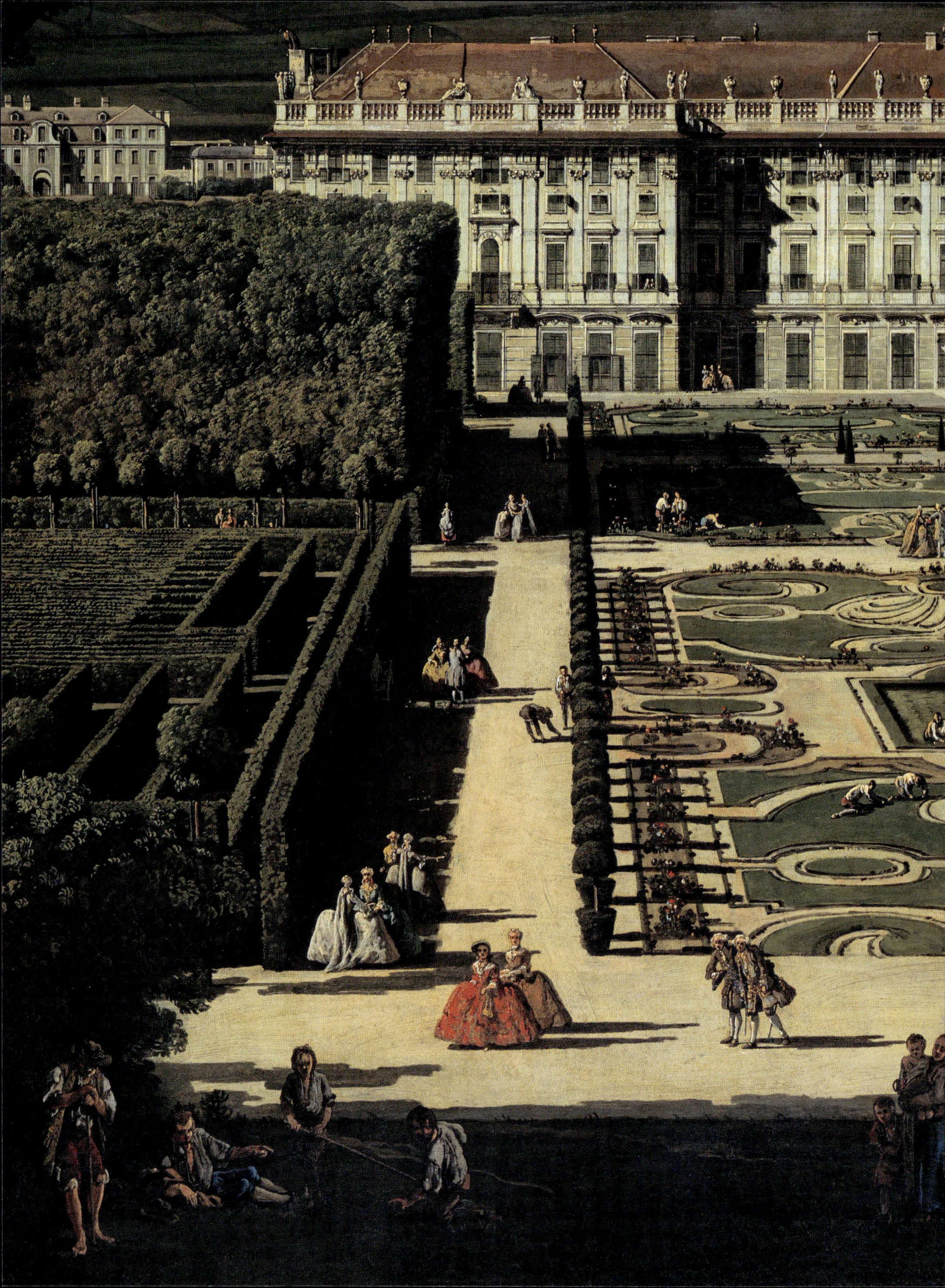

Detail of fig. 37

stroll, pausing to converse, exchange bows, or admire the view from a bench. Maximilian Maurer has suggested that some of these elite figures may allude directly to the Imperial family: the woman in red at lower left, who recurs throughout the Vienna series, could represent Maria Theresa, while the two boys in white at center may be read as her young sons, Archdukes Ferdinand Karl Anton and Maximilian Franz—an interpretation reinforced by the pointing gestures of nearby figures.[140] Dressed in *robes à la française* and waistcoats, these figures transform the parterre into a stage of polite cordiality, where displays of rank and refinement mirror the setting's geometry.

Similar to Canaletto, who in his *Whitehall and the Privy Garden* (fig. 17), captured gardeners at work, Bellotto was also attentive to the horticultural labor sustaining an aristocratic landscape. Gardeners appear throughout: at right, one trims a clipped tree along the parterre, while behind him, three figures tend the *boulingrin*. Along the main path, another gardener carries a sack, while in the left parterre, more men work the grass and flowerbeds. In the foreground, gardeners heave a large roller across the path to level the ground, while in the shaded lower left, four gardeners (one barefoot) pause from their labor. Beside them, a woman with two children supplements the presence of a humbler social stratum within this cultivated space. To their right, another worker leans over the lawn with a long metal tool, perhaps for cutting weeds, and at center, a small group maneuvers a wheelbarrow. Bellotto's meticulous rendering of a landscape disciplined into symmetrical order by human labor reflects broader eighteenth-century ideals of refinement and regulation, a civilizing process controlling both environment and social conduct.[141] Reflecting this process, Bellotto—much as his uncle Canaletto had idealized London—exalts modern architecture and horticultural achievement, yet pushes humbler figures to the margins, often casting them in shadow while bathing the aristocratic staffage in sunlight. The parterre thus becomes a stage where geometry, horticultural labor, and Imperial authority converge in a vision of ordered society.

If the Kaunitz, Liechtenstein, and Schönbrunn views framed aristocratic and dynastic representation within suburban settings, Bellotto's panoramic *View of Vienna from the Belvedere* (fig. 38) turns to Vienna's center.[142] With a vantage point from an upper window of the northwest pavilion of Prince Eugene's Belvedere Palace providing an elevated perspective, the viewer is guided across the formal terraces, reflective pools, and ornamental parterres of the Belvedere gardens and the adjacent grounds of the Palais Schwarzenberg—ultimately reaching the densely built Inner City and the distant hills of the Wienerwald, including the Kahlenberg and Leopoldsberg. In the foreground, Bellotto carefully renders the designs of both gardens—conceived, respectively, in the 1710s and 1720s, by Dominique Girard and Jean Trehet, pupils of the French court gardener André Le Nôtre—and dramatizes their spatial depth through carefully modulated contrasts of light and shadow.[143] Particularly striking is the shadowed diagonal line of trees slicing through the foreground, dividing the canvas into two zones and guiding the gaze into the panorama's deep recesses.

At the far end of the gardens, key architectural landmarks define the vista's middle ground. From left to right in the front row are the Karlskirche, the Palais Schwarzenberg (completed 1728), the Belvedere with its Orangery (both completed in 1717), and the Salesian Church. Beyond lies the Glacis, the open defensive belt before the city's fortifications that was later erased by the nineteenth-century Ringstrasse developments. In the second row, far left, rises the district of Josefstadt, with the façade of the Palais Auersperg facing the Glacis and the Piarist Church behind. Moving inward across the city walls, one can identify a dense array of landmarks: the Imperial Hofburg with its Leopoldine Wing, Schweizerhof, and Court Chapel tower, along with the monumental Court Library (1722–26); then the towers of the Minorite and Augustinian churches (the latter still crowned by its baroque spire); the roof of the Bürgerspital Church (demolished 1784); the tower of St. Michael's; and the Dorotheer Church (demolished in the 1780s). Further right are the bell tower of the Schottenkirche, the tower of St. Anna's, and the baroque dome of St. Peter's, followed by the Church of St. Agnes (since demolished) and the Gothic spire of Maria am Gestade, nestled beside the city's dominant landmark, St. Stephen's Cathedral. Continuing right, we see the Franciscan Church; the university's 1755 astronomical observatory; the Jesuit Church's seventeenth-century twin towers, the order's 1733 observatory; and the gleaming white twin towers of the seventeenth-century Dominican Church. Beyond the walls, in Leopoldstadt, rise the towers of the seventeenth-century Carmelite Church and the Brothers of Mercy (rebuilt in the 1730s), followed by a watery stretch indicating the Danube and its forested wetlands. At the far right, on the Landstrasse, the tower of St. Elisabeth's (completed 1749) marks the panorama's edge.

Fig. 38: Bernardo Bellotto, *View of Vienna from the Belvedere*, 1759/60, oil on canvas, 135 × 213 cm. Kunsthistorisches Museum, Vienna, Picture Gallery, inv. 1669

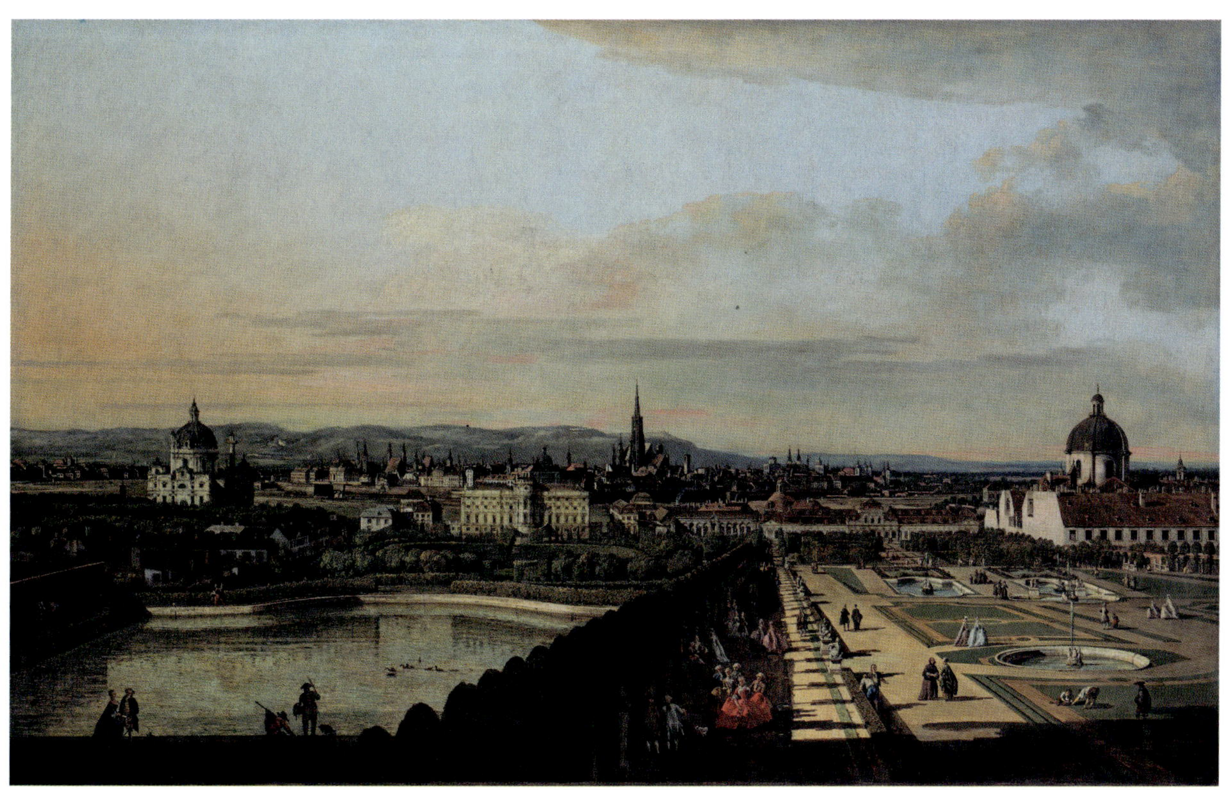

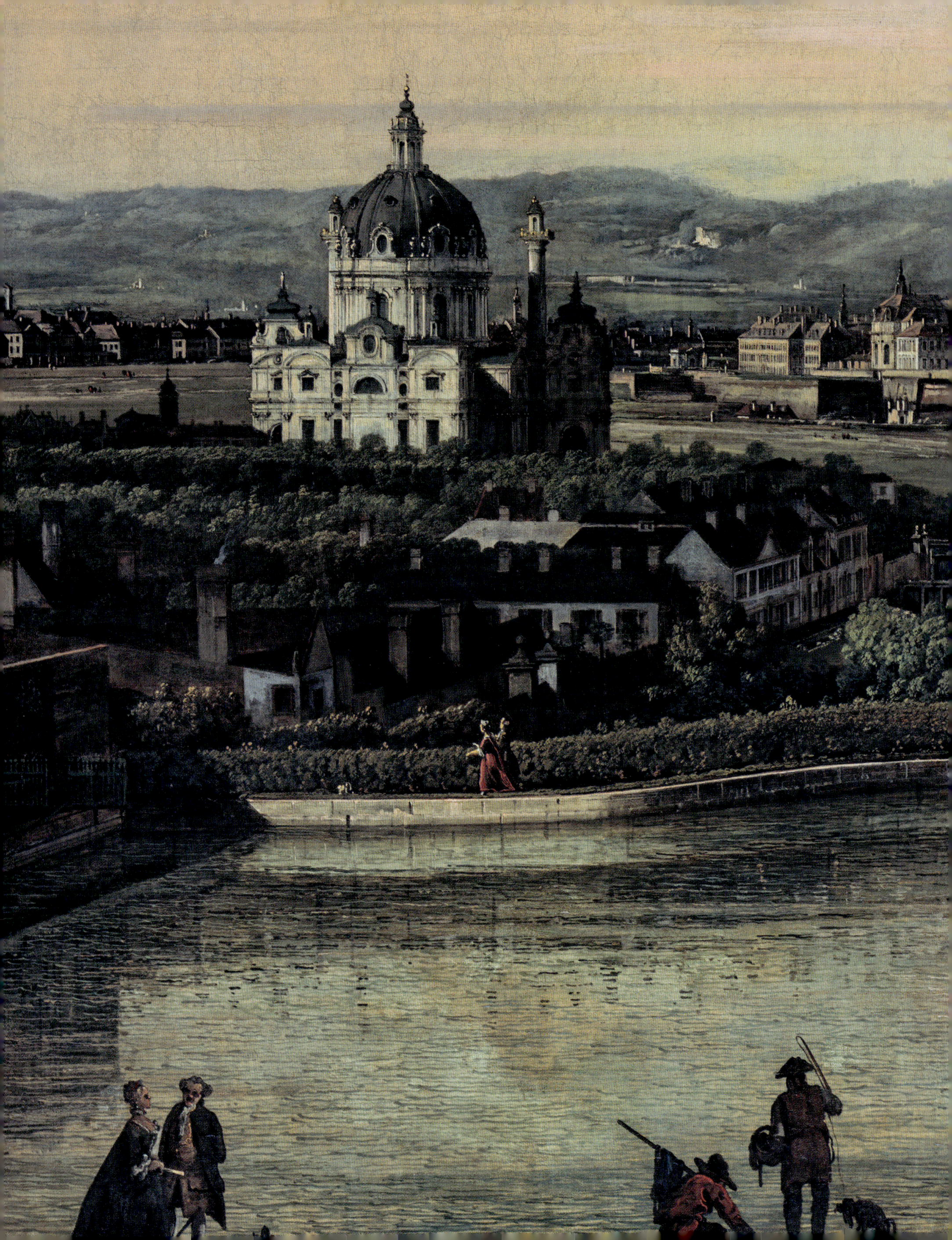

Executed in 1759/60, the view documents a city skyline in the midst of transformation, marked by a succession of medieval structures and newly completed baroque landmarks. In its sweep from palaces and gardens to parish churches, from monastic spires to modern observatories, Bellotto's panorama encapsulates the full range of Vienna's civic, religious, and scientific life.

However, like his uncle Canaletto, Bellotto, for dramatic effect, introduced subtle but deliberate distortions in scale and proportion . Most notably, he compressed Vienna's skyline: towers and domes are drawn closer together, their verticality exaggerated so that the city appears denser and more monumental. The Karlskirche and Salesian Church are shown in closer proximity, their domes effectively framing the composition. The Palais Schwarzenberg is rendered taller and narrower than its true form. And St. Stephen's is depicted on an exaggerated scale, its steep

Details of fig. 38

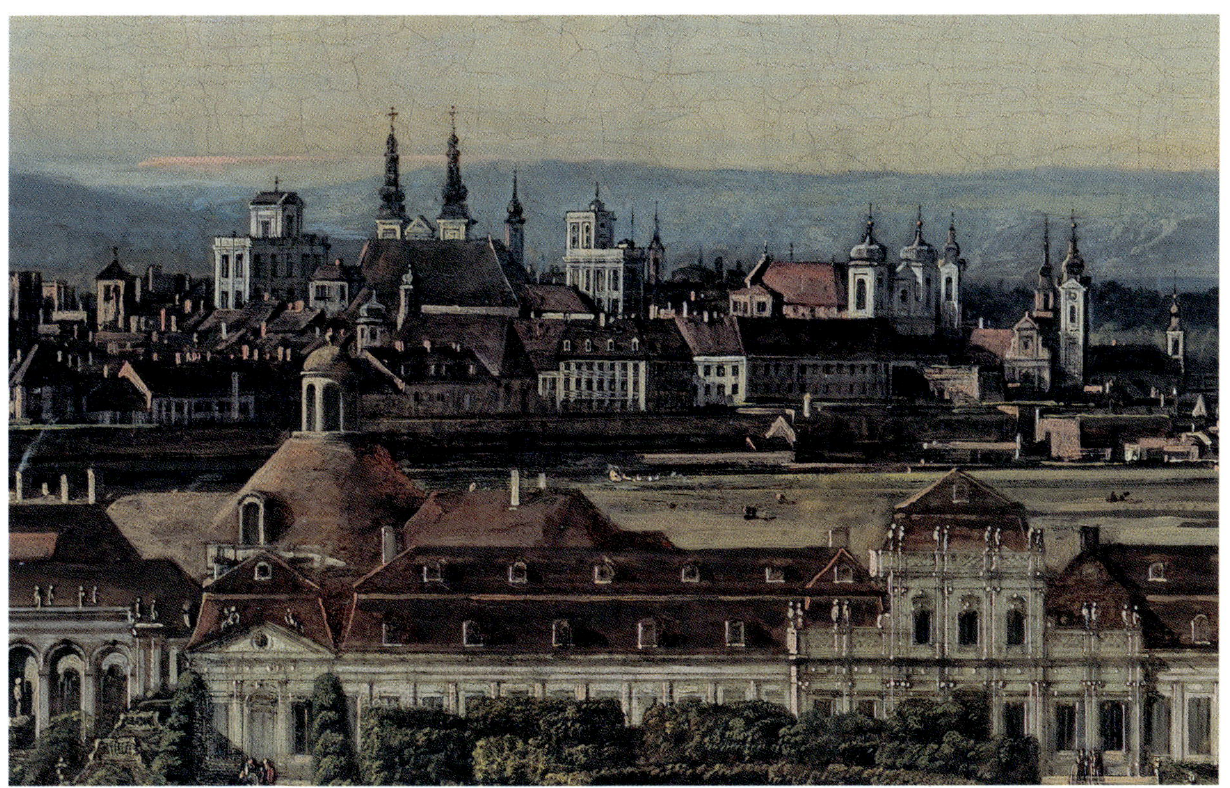

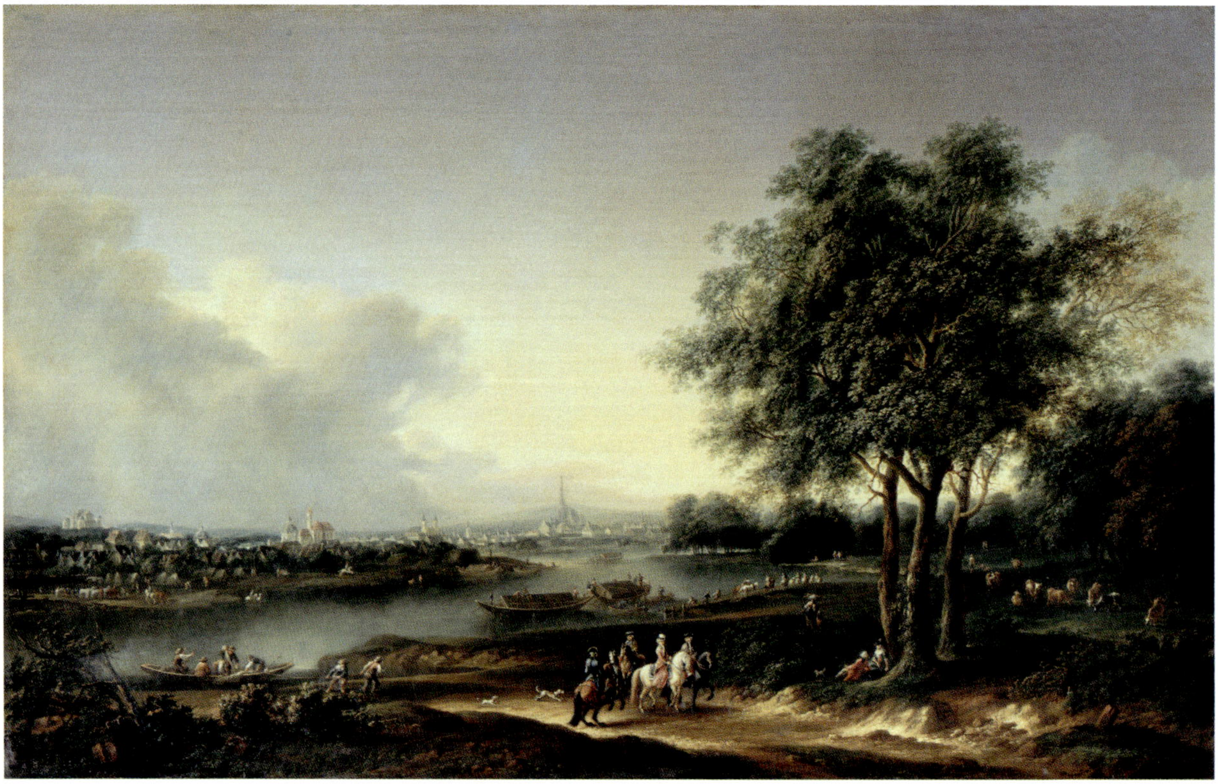

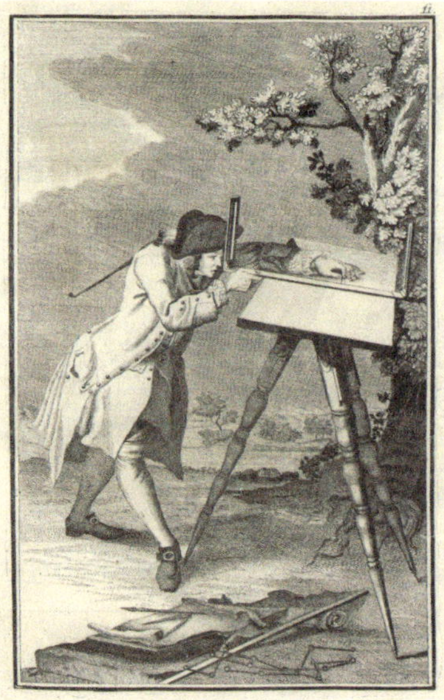

Fig. 40: Giovanni Jacopo de Marinoni, *De re ichnographica* (Vienna, 1751). Austrian National Library, Vienna, 568.676-C, engraving on p. 11

Fig. 41: Unidentified Italian artist, *Sketchbook on military art, including geometry, fortifications, artillery, mechanics, and pyrotechnics*, 17th century, pen and ink, 120 × 160 mm. Library of Congress, Washington D.C., inv. Rosenwald Coll. ms. no. 27

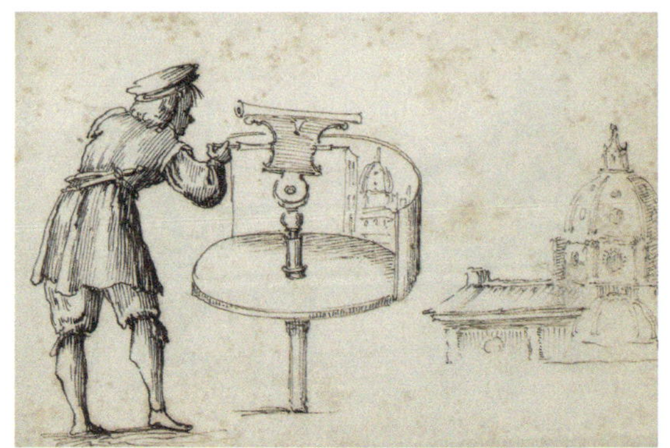

Fig. 39: Josef Heideloff, *View of Vienna from the Prater*, c.1781, oil on canvas, 85.6 × 134.6 cm. Academy of Fine Arts, Vienna, Picture Gallery, inv. 152

Gothic roof and soaring spire dominating the horizon. In concentrating the skyline's rooftops and towers, these adjustments narrow the visual field, and draw the gaze upward, transforming the distant city into an imposing, monumental presence, characterized by palaces and church spires.[144] More than a neutral record, the panorama presents Vienna as an idealized capital, a "Canaletto view," whose persuasive power shaped cultural memory well beyond the eighteenth century—resonating even in modern debates over Vienna's UNESCO World Heritage status.[145]

Nevertheless, Bellotto's overall precision reveals his close study of Viennese topography, a quality that stands in striking contrast to other artists, such as Josef Heideloff, who trained at Vienna's Academy of Fine Arts. In his 1781 *View of Vienna from the Prater* (fig. 39), Heideloff devotes the foreground to a romanticized, pastoral vision of the park across the Danube, animated by hunters, strollers, and rustic figures, while the city herself recedes into a hazy middle ground. From left to right are faintly suggested the Belvedere's side façade, the domes of the Salesian Church and the Karlskirche, an invented church rising improbably on a hill, St. Roch's on the Landstraße (completed 1721), and, in the far distance, St. Stephen's Cathedral—but their forms and details are generalized and barely legible. Rather than being elegantly compressed into a unit, the city's skyline fizzles out along the horizon and is filtered through the Prater's landscape in the foreground, where aristocratic leisure culture (hunting parties, a couple resting against a tree) mingles with pastoral and *georgic* motifs (watermen at work, a woman with child, cattle grazing). In Heideloff's hands, Vienna becomes an Arcadian adjunct to nature. Bellotto's panorama, by contrast, resists such pastoral mediation. His insistence on clarity renders the Habsburg capital as a sharply defined urban organism.

Such empirical precision inevitably raises questions of method. Just as with his uncle Canaletto, the exactitude of Bellotto's *vedute* has long suggested the use of optical devices such as the camera obscura, which, we have seen, he also employed during his Dresden years. In Vienna, too, he will have worked with such an apparatus. In including Vienna's surrounding landscape, Bellotto's elevated panoramas further resonate with the techniques of contemporary cartographers, who likewise relied on high vantage points when applying the method of intersection, targeting distant landmarks — most often church spires — and registering their positions with graphometers (see cat. 30).[146] In his 1751 *De re ichnographica*, the Imperial mathematician, astronomer, and geodetic surveyor, Giovanni Jacopo de Marinoni, described another type of surveying device that Bellotto may have known: a leveled drawing board equipped with a sighting ruler (fig. 40).[147] This apparatus allowed practitioners to register the precise directional bearings of buildings and transfer them directly onto paper, creating a fixed framework that could then be elaborated with more detailed studies of individual monuments. Similar techniques appear in earlier sources: a seventeenth-century anonymous manuscript, for example, shows a draughtsman depicting a domed church using a device (fig. 41) resembling one conceived by Baldassare Lanci, a sixteenth-century military engineer from Urbino — demonstrating how readily tools of cartographic measurement could be adapted to pictorial ends.[148]

By Bellotto's time, measurement practices had become integral to a broader empirical culture. In Saxony, Augustus the Strong ordered a systematic mapping of his territories, while his son, Augustus III, arguably extended this ambition by commissioning Bellotto to transpose the logic of survey into paint.[149] In Vienna, Maria Theresa's reign fostered a similar cartographic ethos, advanced by Marinoni and the Jesuit mathematician Joseph Liesganig, both of whom undertook pioneering geodetic research. Around 1760, for example, Liesganig mapped Vienna's environs (see cat. 32), including floorplans of the Imperial palaces of Schönbrunn and Laxenburg, laying the groundwork for the Josephinian Land Survey — the first systematic mapping of the Habsburg lands, conducted between 1763 and 1787.[150] The same empirical spirit informed the ambitious bird's-eye view of Vienna by military cartographer Joseph Daniel von Huber, presented to Maria Theresa in 1773 and published in 1778.[151] As well, the numerous eighteenth-century guidebooks on Vienna's history and topography, including Mathias Fuhrmann's *Alt- und Neues Wien* (1738/39), can be understood before the same background.[152] Within this context,

Bellotto's *vedute* emerge as artworks also functioning as measured visual documentation of the Imperial city.

Bellotto's immersion in a culture of empirical observation certainly began in Venice. As seen in Chapter One, Venetian optical innovation and pictorial practice were closely linked: the city's glass industry, famed for producing flawlessly curved, blemish-free glass, supplied lenses for spectacles, microscopes, telescopes, and camera obscuras—tools that nourished the visual language of Canaletto and prompted Algarotti to encourage artists to use camera obscuras like scientists used microscopes and telescopes. Within this network, nearby Padua—then under Venetian rule—forms a direct link to Vienna. In 1739, the aforementioned Imperial mathematician Giovanni Jacopo de Marinoni corresponded with the Paduan professor of experimental philosophy, Giovanni Poleni, seeking advice about the telescopes made by the Selva family.[153] Marinoni's inquiry related to the private observatory he had built in 1730 atop his Mölkerbastei residence (with Emperor Charles VI's approval) visible in the background in one of Bellotto's Vienna views to which we shall return later (fig. 49). Marinoni not only conducted observations but also designed and built his own instruments—including quadrants, micrometers, and telescopes—some of which, together with his observatory, he proudly illustrated in a 1745 publication dedicated to his former student, Maria Theresa (fig. 42), whom he had instructed in astronomy and cartography.[154] His exchange with Poleni highlights how Venice and Vienna shared an enlightened culture of empirical observation, a *zeitgeist* also materializing in Bellotto's canvases.

Indeed, by the 1760s, Vienna had become a major center of scientific inquiry. The newly restructured university, with Jesuit-led initiatives in mathematics and astronomy, along with medical reforms, fostered an atmosphere of intellectual ferment; and where empirical methods were increasingly institutionalized and optical instruments, including microscopes and telescopes, widely used (see cats. 33, 34). Francis Stephen himself had a marked interest in the natural sciences—an attitude memorably captured in Johann Zoffany's posthumous portrait of 1776/77 (fig. 43), showing him surrounded by scientific instruments (such as a

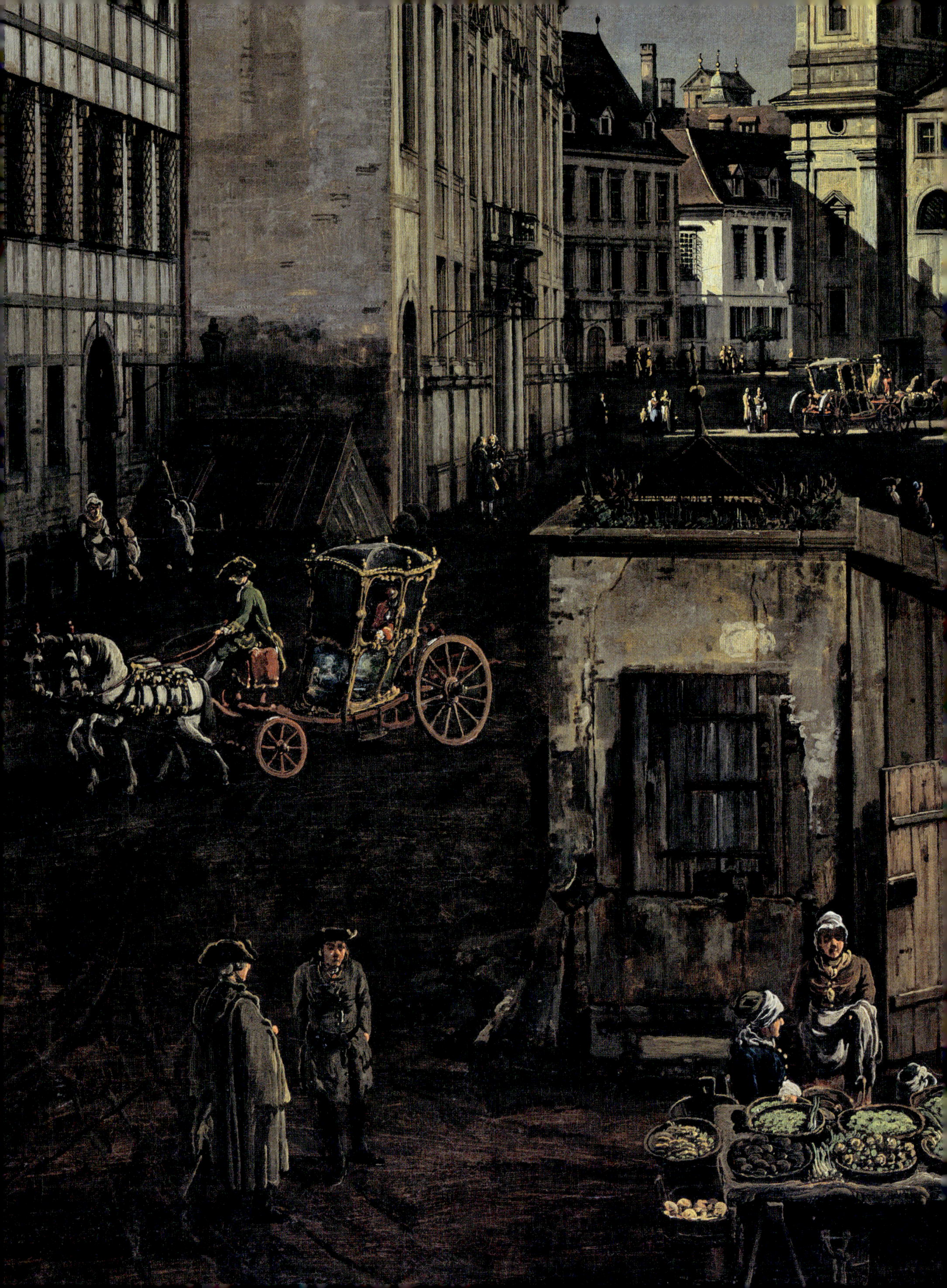

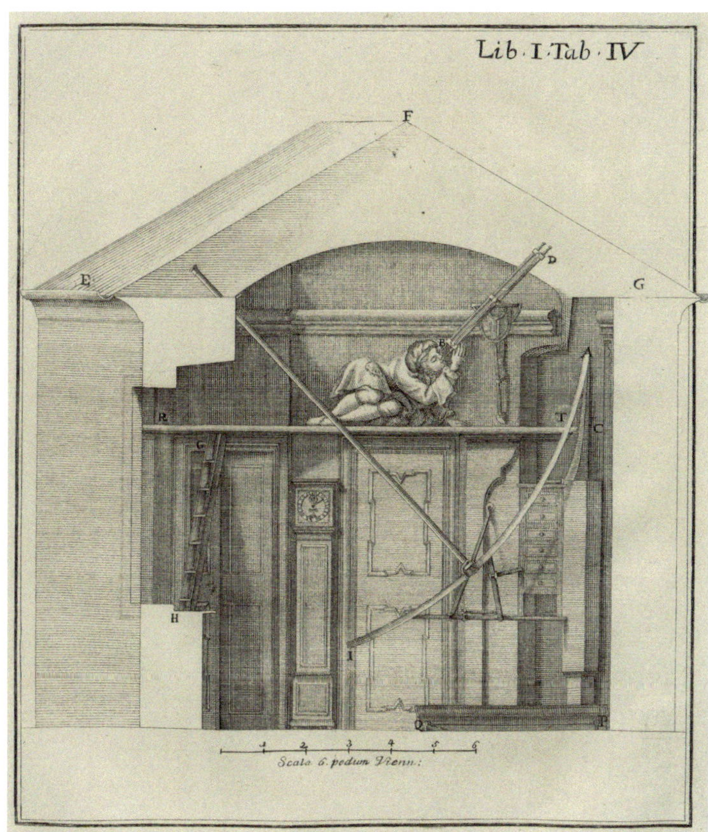

Fig. 42: Giovanni Jacopo de Marinoni, *De astronomica specula domestica et organico apparatu astronomico libri duo* (Vienna, 1745). Austrian National Library, Vienna, 72.C.57, Lib.1, Tab. IV

telescope and an armillary sphere) alongside coins and naturalia. Similarly, Anton von Maron's 1773 portrait of Maria Theresa (fig. 44) presents her gesturing toward a map with a bird's-eye view of Schönbrunn. Such imagery reveals how Imperial self-fashioning itself drew upon the visual language of empirical observation and cartographic order. Bellotto's detailed pictorial practice, therefore, mirrors the epistemic ambitions of the Viennese court.

Bellotto focused on sites directly tied to scientific inquiry in two of his Viennese *vedute*. The first (fig. 45) depicts a seemingly inconspicuous corner of the university district. From an elevated position, it looks southward along the Postgasse in Vienna's Inner City.[155] To the left is the dramatically foreshortened façade of the Dominican Church (1631–75); the right half is dominated by

Detail of fig. 49

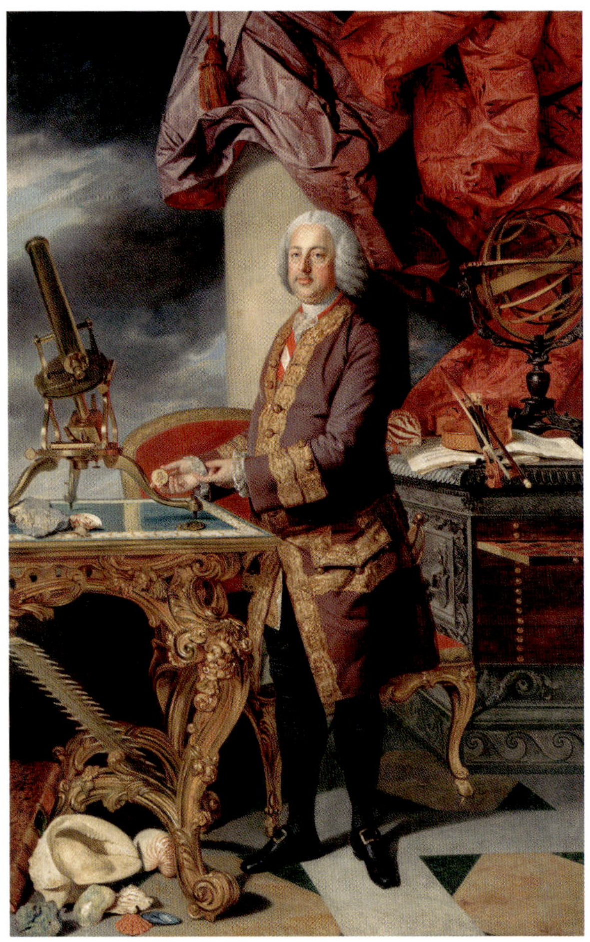

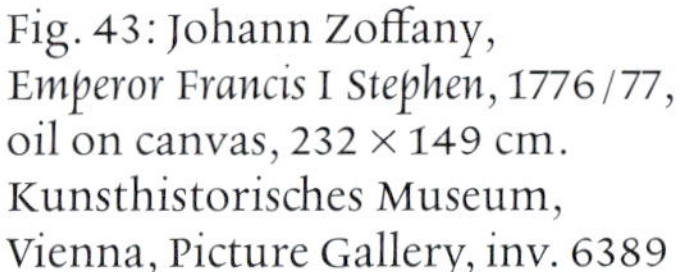

Fig. 43: Johann Zoffany, *Emperor Francis I Stephen*, 1776/77, oil on canvas, 232 × 149 cm. Kunsthistorisches Museum, Vienna, Picture Gallery, inv. 6389

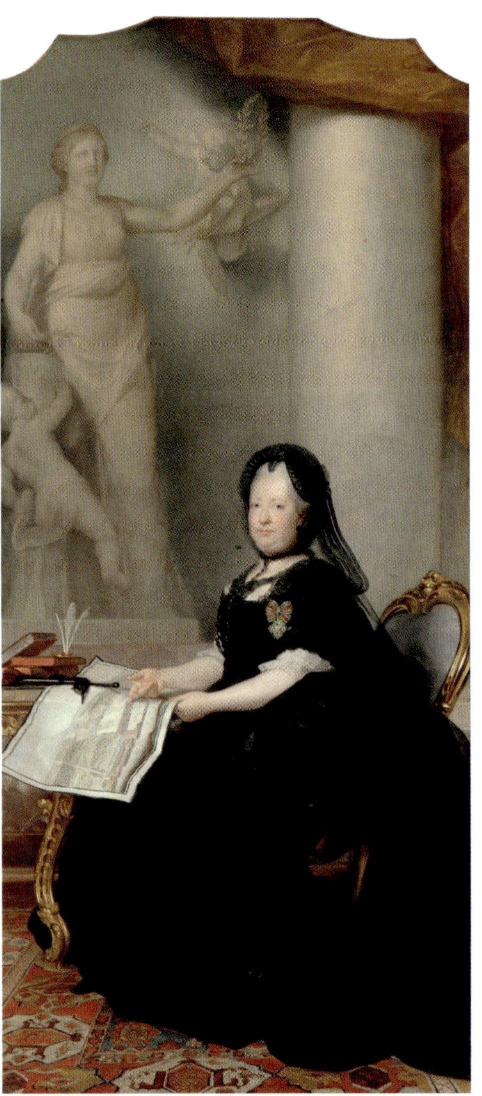

Fig. 44: Anton von Maron, *Empress Maria Theresia*, 1773, oil on canvas, 287 × 125 cm. Kunsthistorisches Museum, Vienna, Picture Gallery, inv. 6201

the sunlit rear of the Jesuit College, a vast complex with a long, sober façade built after Emperor Ferdinand II entrusted the Jesuits with reorganizing Vienna's medieval university in 1623. Bellotto's viewpoint follows a 1737 engraving by Salomon Kleiner (fig. 46), though Kleiner's closer vantage only captures the lower segment of the church's façade. Bellotto expands the street into a legible urban volume, likely blending multiple camera obscura views into a coherent perspective. His composition is enlivened by dramatic chiaroscuro: the sharply cast shadow of the church projects its silhouette across the Jesuit College, underscoring spatial depth. At the street's end stands the aforementioned Jesuit observatory tower, built in 1733. Although astronomy had long been taught at the University of Vienna, the tower—apart from private observatories like Marinoni's—was the first permanent institutional facility.[156] Originally 45 meters high and crowned by an armillary sphere, as seen in Kleiner's print, the tower appears truncated in Bellotto's view. Yet by placing it at the vanishing point, he emphasizes a landmark of Jesuit astronomical research, embedding his *veduta* within Vienna's broader culture of scientific observation.

The second canvas (fig. 47) shifts to the opposite side of the Jesuit College, looking onto what is now Dr-Ignaz-Seipel-Platz.[157] While rendering the soaring twin-towered Jesuit Church (1624–31) at right, and the recessing Bäckerstrasse at left, it centers on the new university aula, built by Jean Nicolas Jadot between 1753 and 1755. This structure, with its lecture halls, anatomical theater, and rooftop observatory, embodied the university's transformation during a pivotal moment of Enlightenment reform. After arriving in Vienna in 1745, Maria Theresa's court physician, Gerard van Swieten—later portrayed by Franz Xaver Messerschmidt around 1770/72 (see cat. 37)—led a sweeping modernization program that reshaped the Faculty of Medicine and the university's broader institutional framework, including the commissioning of Jadot's aula.[158]

In composing the scene, Bellotto appears to have once again merged two slightly offset viewpoints to enhance architectural clarity: the foreshortened Jesuit Church follows the actual angle of view from one of the windows of the old university, while the

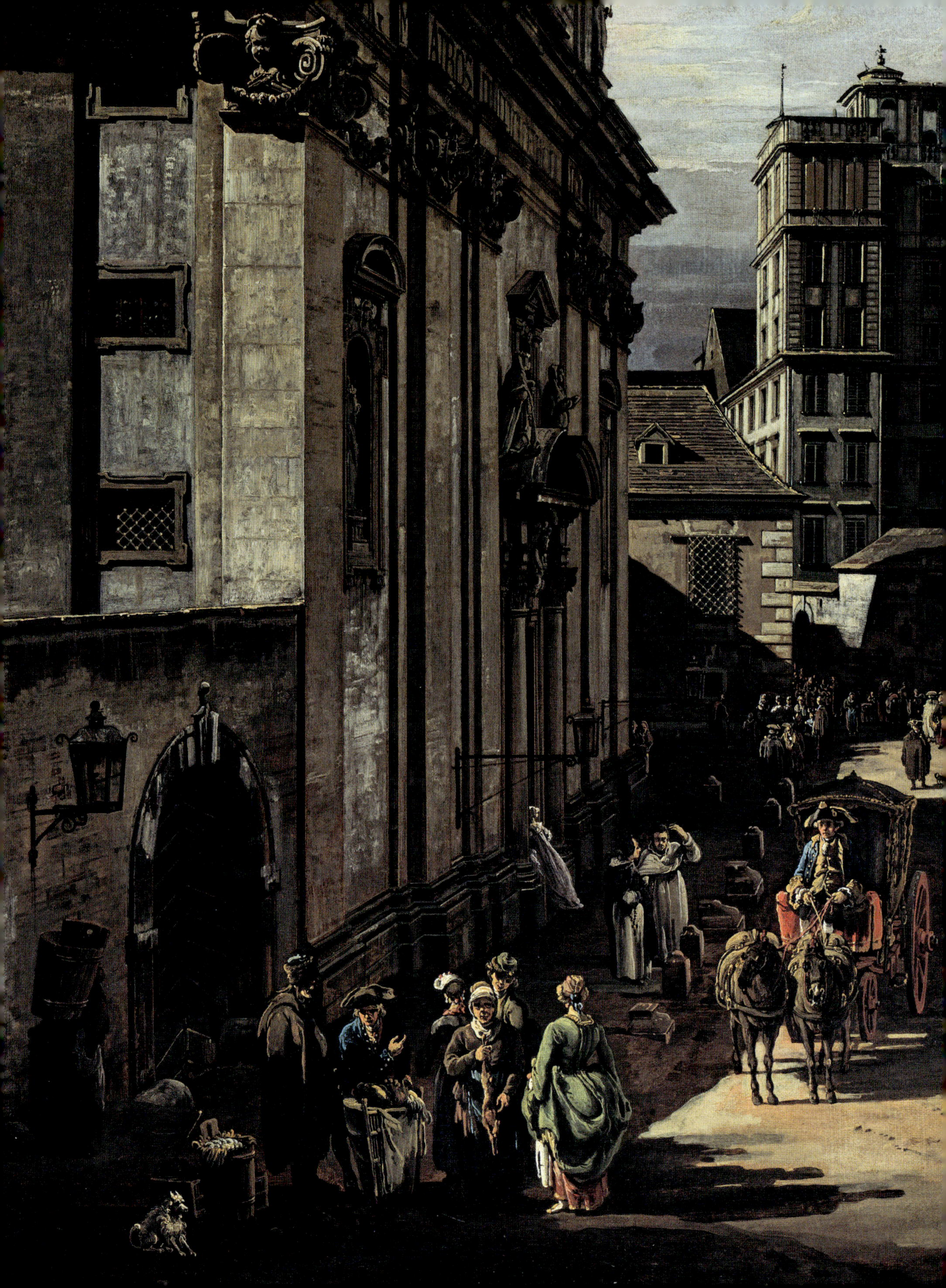

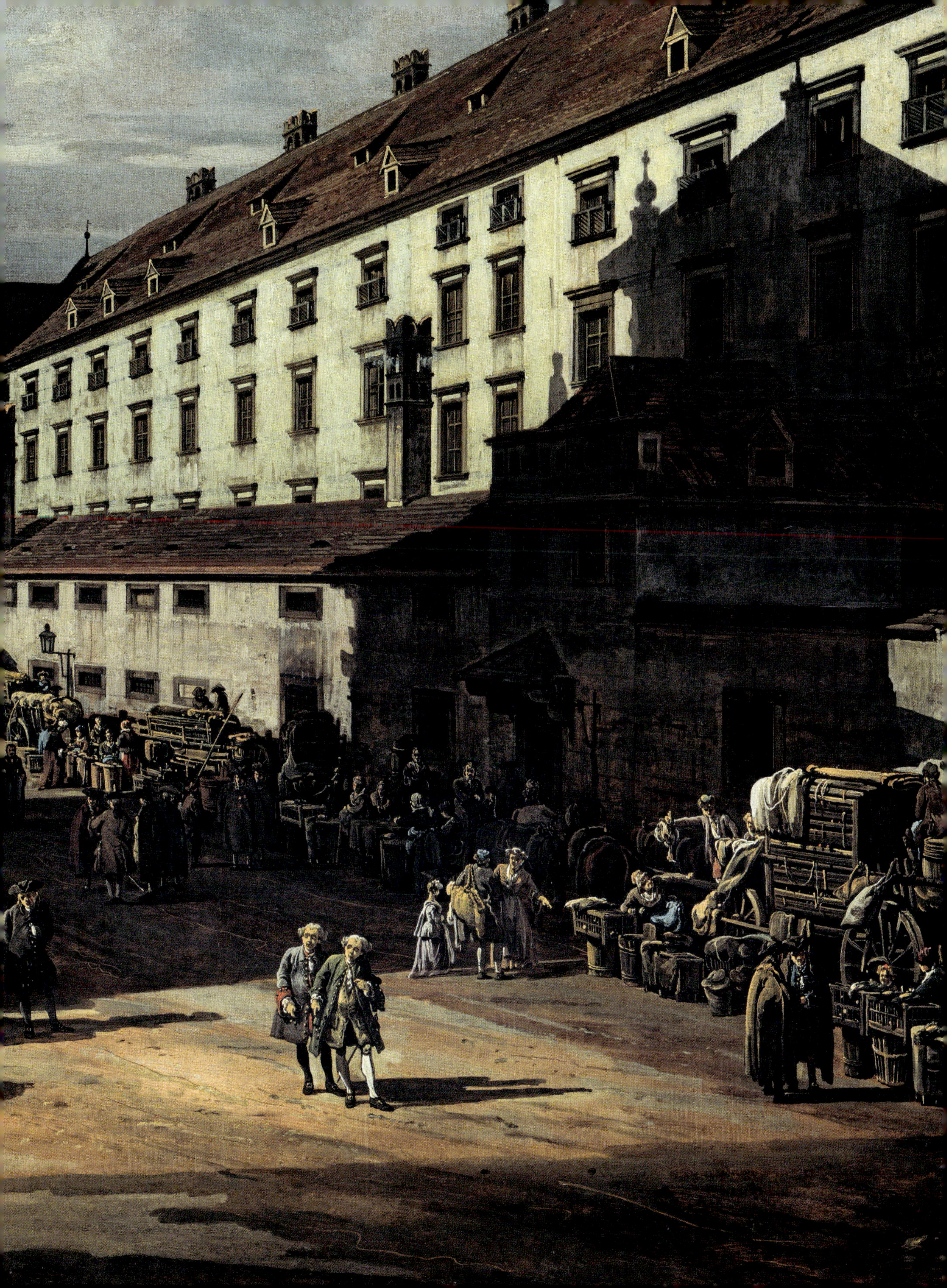

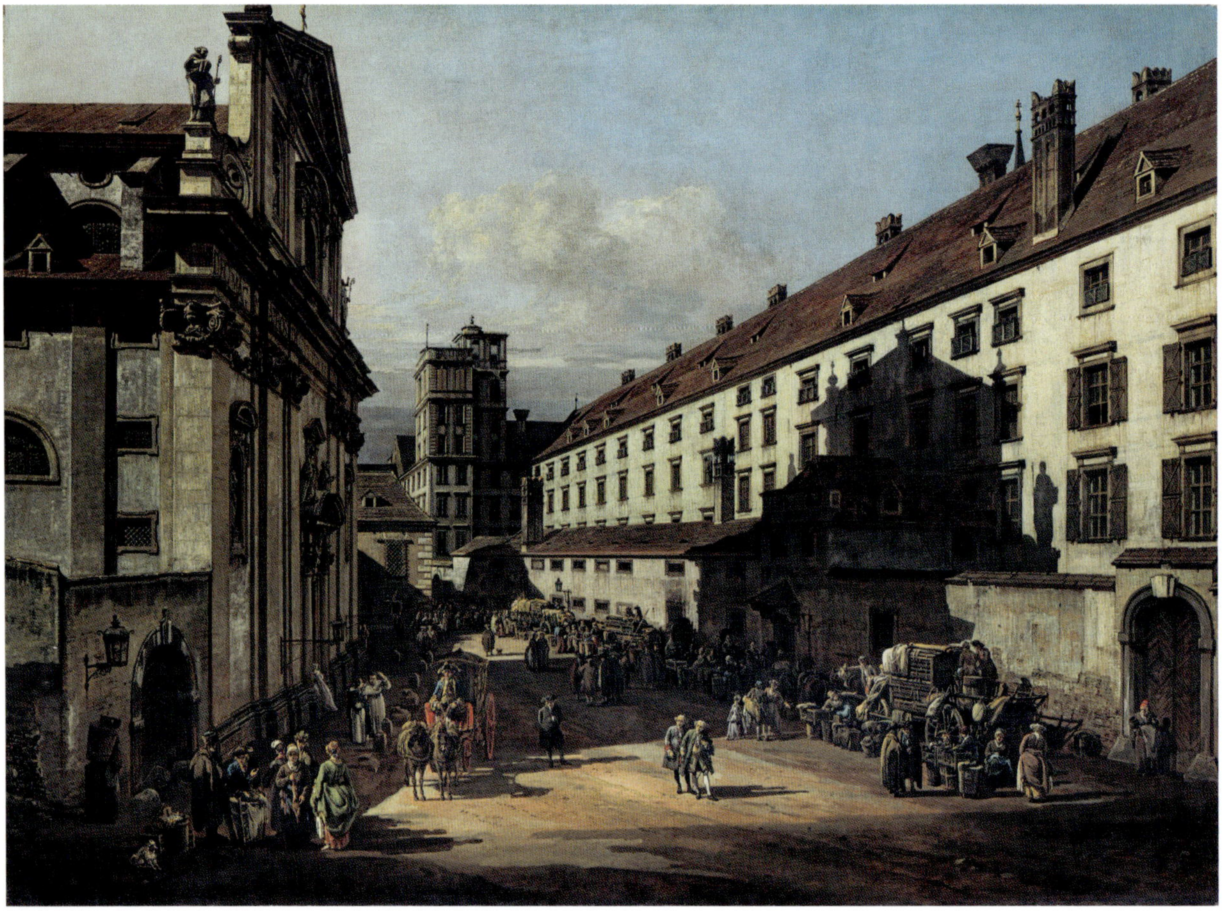

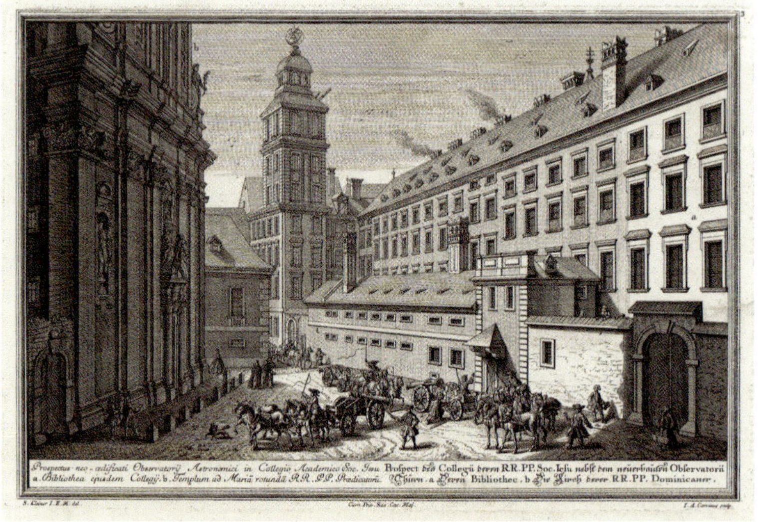

Fig. 45: Bernardo Bellotto, *The Dominican Church in Vienna*, 1759/60, oil on canvas, 115 × 155.5 cm, detail on pp. 114–15. Kunsthistorisches Museum, Vienna, Picture Gallery, inv. 1672

Fig. 46: Salomon Kleiner, *The Dominican Church and Observatory in Vienna*, 1737, engraving, 310 × 445 mm. Wien Museum, Vienna, inv. 105765/109

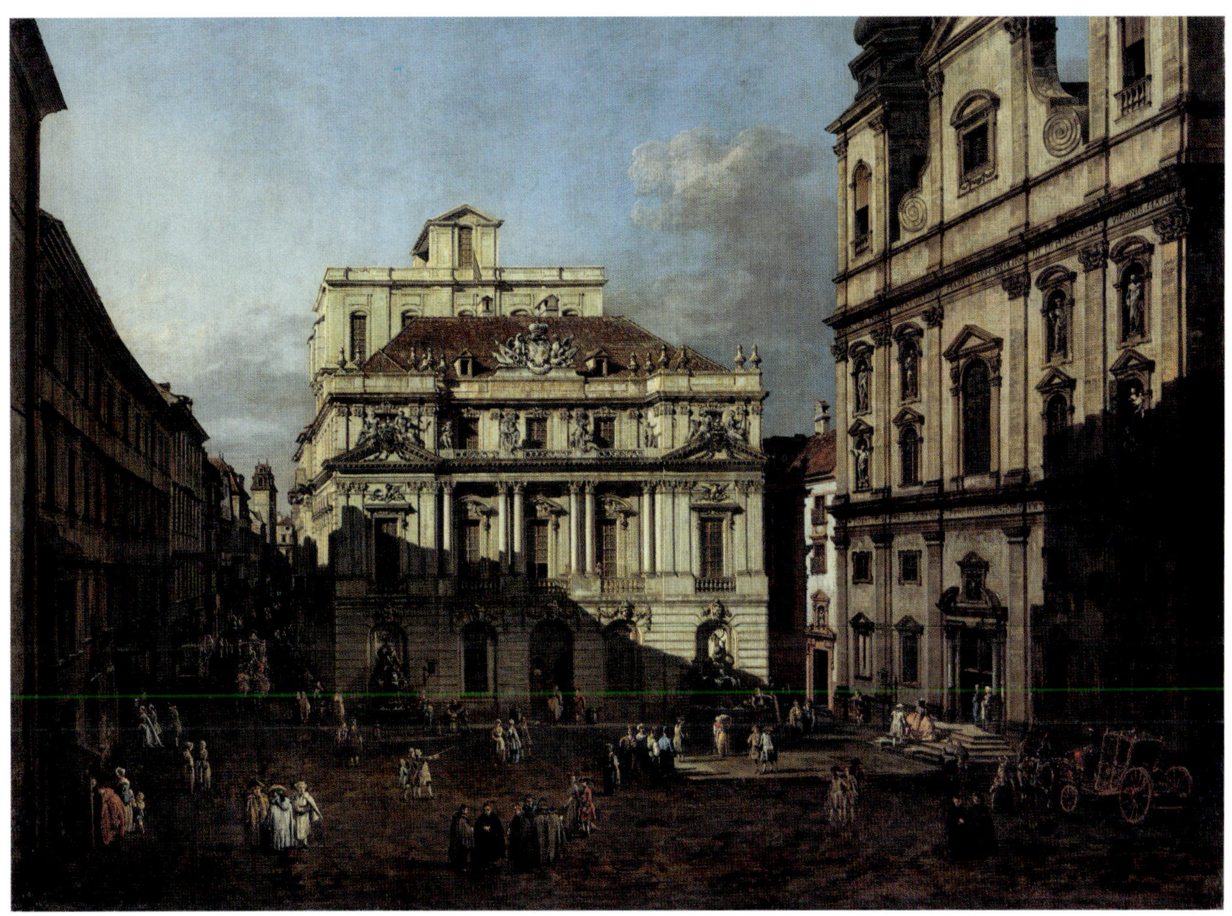

Fig. 47: Bernardo Bellotto, *The University Square in Vienna*, 1759/60, oil on canvas, 115.5 × 155.5 cm. Kunsthistorisches Museum, Vienna, Picture Gallery, inv. 1670

aula's façade is rendered frontally, even though it would appear, in reality, more steeply angled.[159] In addition to the diagonal fall of light from the left—casting the aula's ornamented façade in sharp sculptural relief—this manipulation emphasizes the building's prominence, distinguished within late Viennese baroque architecture by its French classicist forms. By carefully rendering the new observatory on this building's roof, Bellotto pays tribute to a further turning point in the institutionalization of astronomy in Vienna. Upon Marinoni's death in 1755, his instruments were bequeathed to the Crown, and Maria Theresa moved them to the newly built aula, prompting the addition of the observatory on top. Under its first director, the Jesuit Maximilian Hell, the facility soon gained international standing, especially tied to his observations of the transit of Venus.[160] Even though the observatory's wooden structure proved ill-suited to the demands of precise measurement, being vulnerable to wind and street traffic, its pioneering efforts secured Vienna's key role in Enlightenment astronomy.[161]

In this light, Bellotto's recurring observatory towers were no incidental detail—they served as emblems of a civic and dynastic identity grounded in scientific prestige. Indeed, at left of *View of the University Square*, the foreshortened and deeply shadowed row of houses in Bäckerstraße offers another view of Bellotto's interest in such structures. For, at the far end rises the observatory tower of the so-called Großer Federlhof, long tied to scientific inquiry. Around 1630, Italian astronomer Andrea Argoli had established an observatory there, and from 1713–1714 the polymath Gottfried Wilhelm Leibniz lodged in the same building.[162] Against the intellectual backdrop of Leibniz's debates on vision and knowledge, Bellotto's Viennese *vedute* particularly emerge as rather complex images. In his 1714 *Monadology*, Leibniz likened a city viewed from different angles to the multiplicity of perspectives within a single universe, each "monad" offering its own partial but valid apprehension of the whole.[163] Bellotto's views of Vienna embody precisely such a logic, presenting the capital not as a single synoptic totality but rather, a composite of diverse vantage points, each yielding a different but related facet of the city. Taken together, these vantage points resonate with mid-eighteenth-century epistemologies that privileged the accumulation of partial, situated observations. After all, also Diderot insisted in his writings on natural philosophy that truth could be derived from the variability of appearances, so long as they were systematically ordered—a project epitomized by his *Encyclopédie*, which also featured the camera obscura (fig. 8). Bellotto's panoramic sequences similarly transform empirical observation into a coherent tableau, employing multiple vantage points to mediate the complexity of Vienna's identity: as Imperial capital, scientific hub, religious center, and commercial crossroads.[164]

With this spirit, Bellotto's depiction of the Schottenkirche (fig. 48) also captures elements of urban life—ceremonial, spiritual, and commercial—that were central to the identity of the Viennese court. As elsewhere, he combines two distinct vantage points, again prioritizing artistic effect over strict fidelity: the frontal view of the abbey church is taken from the first floor of a corner building at Schottengasse and Teinfaltstrasse (then owned by the Kinsky family), while the view of the Freyung to the right derives from a more oblique angle further southeast.[165] The left half is dominated by the façade of the Schottenkirche and the adjoining Schottenhof, shown here before Joseph Kornhäusel's major alterations of 1826–32. A dramatic interplay of light and shadow defines this area: sunlight from the upper left shades the Schottenhof, casting Bellotto's characteristic triangular shadow across the church's front. To the right, the viewer's gaze moves into the broad expanse of the Freyung, its market stalls largely in shadow. The square is framed by buildings from different periods, from modest two-story houses of the sixteenth century to the taller baroque edifices of the seventeenth and eighteenth centuries—regarded in Bellotto's time as symbols of urban progress.[166] Among the most notable are, from left to right: Fischer von Erlach's Palais Batthyány-Schönborn (partially obscured by the church); the multi-storied "Schmiedisch Haus," where court farrier Johann Christof Schillinger ran a forge (probably established soon after 1721), its covered portal sheltering a wagon under repair; the smaller sixteenth-century inn, "Zum goldenen Straußen," in front of which barrels are being handled; and "Zum roten Mandl," then housing a spice business.[167] Further right stands the eighteenth-century Heilig-Geist-Haus across from a townhouse with a distinctive bay window—Bellotto's likely vantage point for the painting's counterpart (fig. 49). At the far right, the view concludes with Palais Harrach and its now-lost 1721 garden pavilion by Johann Lucas von Hildebrandt.

In the shaded foreground before the church, a solemn procession unfolds. At its head walk elegant noblemen and courtiers bearing long candles; at the center are clerics in albs, one carrying a golden, circular object beneath a processional

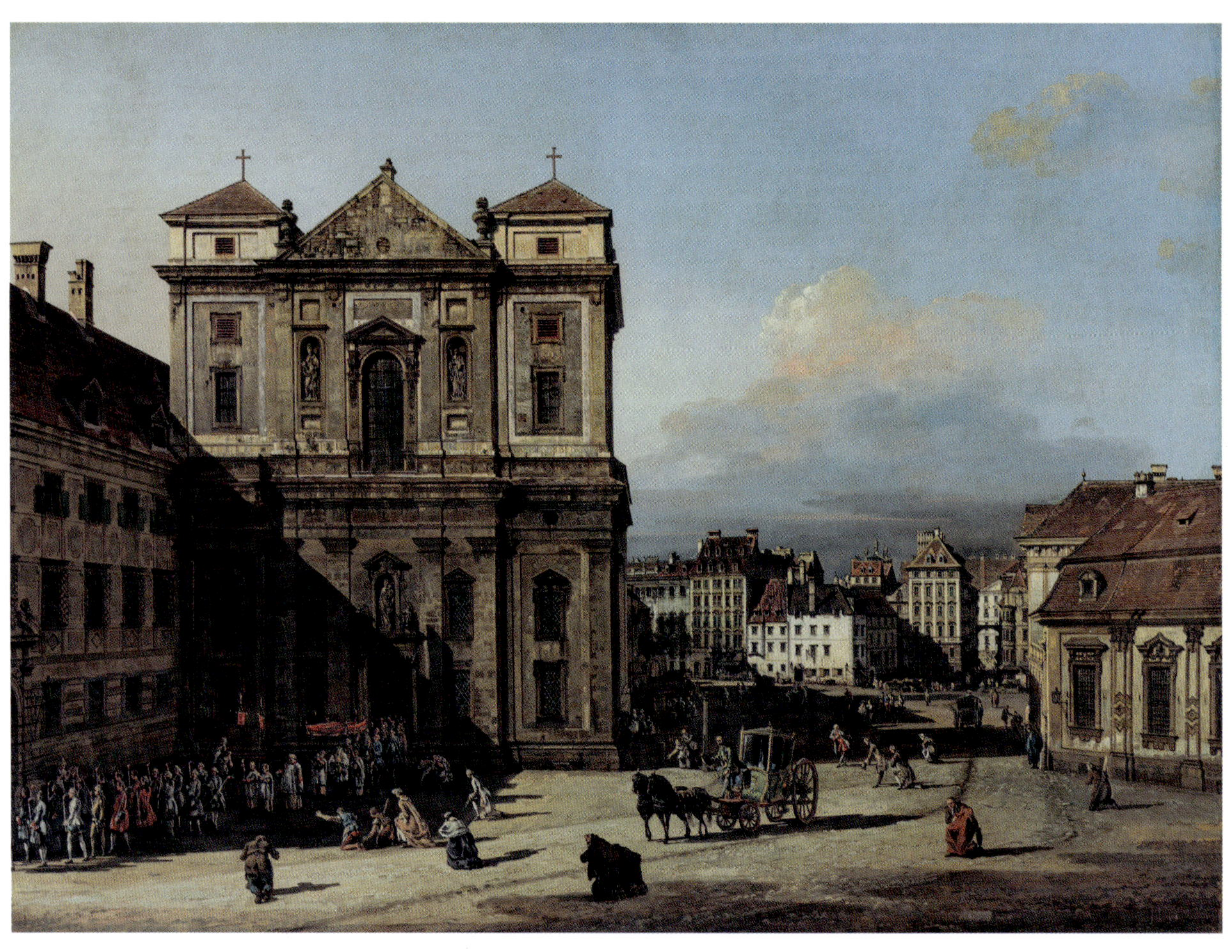

canopy. Though its precise identity remains uncertain, earlier writers labeled the scene a Corpus Christi procession.[168] If so, it would require a monstrance displaying the consecrated Host, such as the radiant *Strahlenmonstranz* donated to the Schottenstift by Maria Hirschkorn in 1761 (see cat. 39).[169] Yet the compact, round form of Bellotto's object does not convincingly match such a monstrance. It more likely represents a reliquary, perhaps tied to a confraternity linked to the abbey—especially the *Sebastiani-Bruderschaft*, which annually displayed relics of Saint Sebastian and included aristocratic, courtly, and burgher patrons. Other abbey sodalities also held processions that Bellotto may have captured here.[170] Whatever the specific rite, the canopy and the attitudes

Fig. 48: Bernardo Bellotto, *The Freyung in Vienna, View from Northwest*, 1759/60, oil on canvas, 116 × 152 cm. Kunsthistorisches Museum, Vienna, Picture Gallery, inv. 1652

Detail of fig. 48

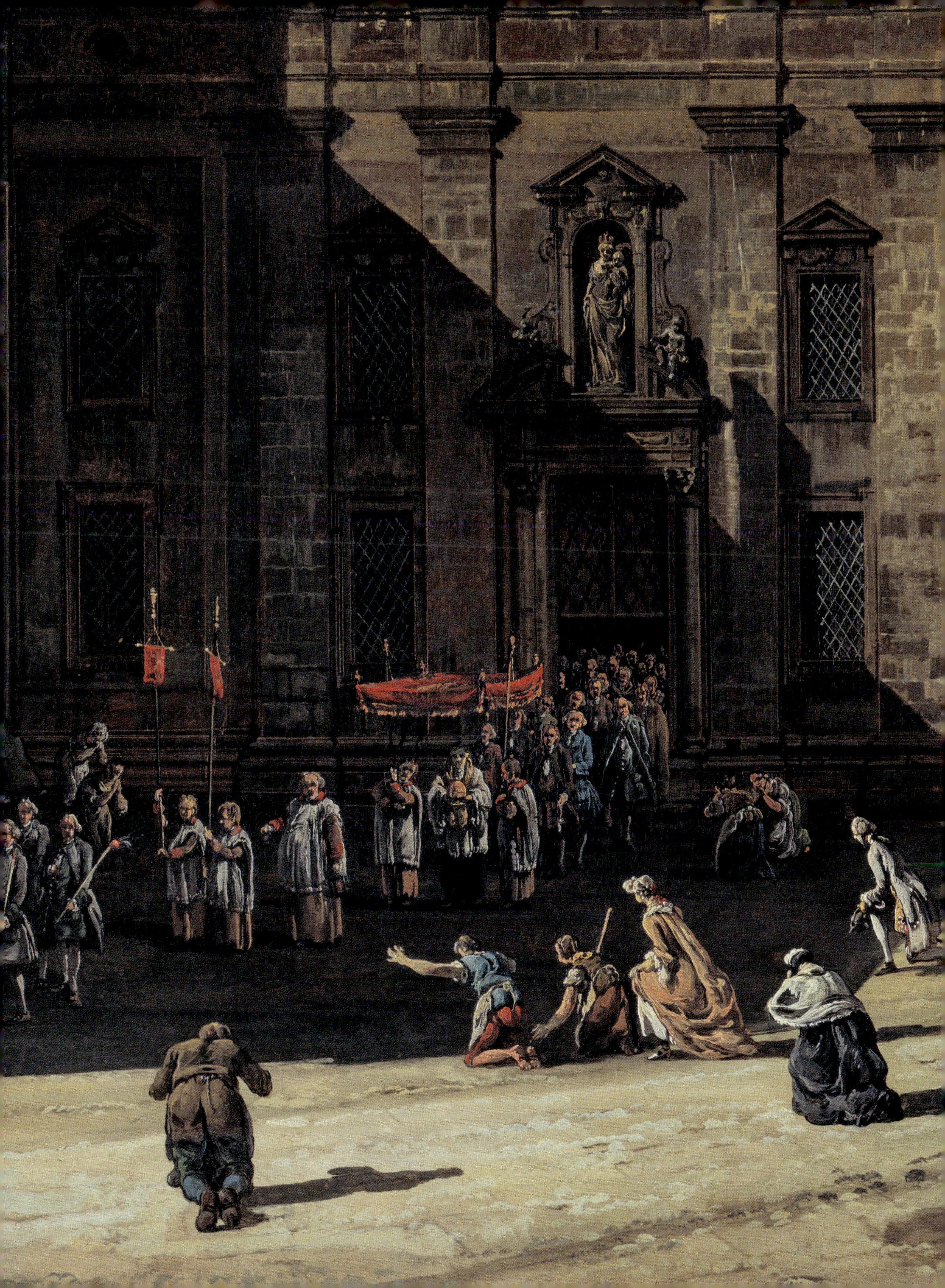

of deference—noblemen, noblewomen, monks, servants, even a coachman bowing in unison—center attention on the sacred nucleus. This coherence of action is striking in Bellotto's oeuvre. Whereas in most *vedute* his figures appear loosely scattered and absorbed in separate tasks, here they unite in a shared act of worship—akin to Canaletto's depiction of processing knights at Westminster Abbey—lending the painting unusual narrative intensity and transforming the Freyung into a stage of communal piety.

Bellotto's pendant view of the Freyung from the southeast (fig. 49) shifts focus from religious ritual to the square's commercial character. Taken from the corner house mentioned earlier, the scene unfolds across the gently rising triangular square toward the Schottenkirche. At left, rendered in steep foreshortening, stand the Kaunitz and Abensperg-Traun residences, followed by the elongated frontage of Palais Harrach. Behind them appear two houses at the entrance to Teinfaltstrasse, the right of which is the same wherefrom Bellotto conceived his complementary view from the northwest. Over the rooftops rise the small turret of the Melkerhof chapel and, farther off, the astronomical tower of Marinoni's residence on the Mölkerbastei, already noted in our earlier discussion of Jesuit astronomy. At center, the Schottenkirche's elevation, built between 1638 and 1648 by Antonio Carlone and Andrea Allio the Elder, commands attention. The twin towers initially planned for the church were never fully realized; instead, they were topped off with short upper storeys in 1732. Behind the choir rises the abbey's tall church tower, while to its right the monastic wall encloses trees from the abbey's former cemetery, abandoned in 1751. At far right, the view ends with the houses "Zum goldenen Straußen" and "Zum roten Mandl," both aglow in afternoon sun.

Bellotto devotes the foreground to the Freyung's longstanding role as a market, its uneven surface animated by rows of mostly wooden stalls shaded with makeshift awnings. Women predominantly display herbs and produce from shallow baskets, while burghers, servants, and soldiers mingle among their booths. Notably, in the lower right, three figures in red liveries, blue stockings, and golden hat bands are identifiable as sedan chair

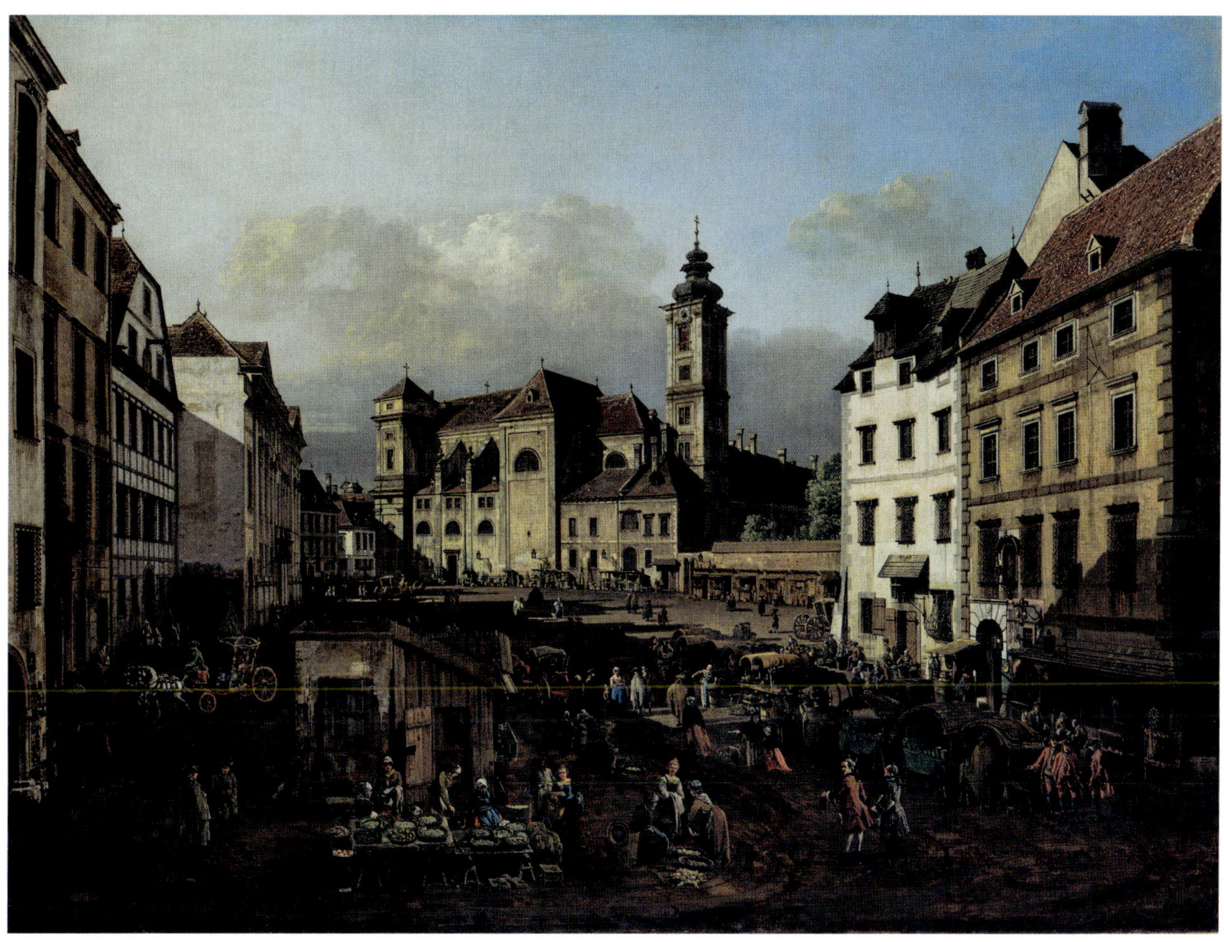

Fig. 49: Bernardo Bellotto, *The Freyung in Vienna, View from Southeast*, 1759/60, oil on canvas, 119 × 153 cm. Kunsthistorisches Museum, Vienna, Picture Gallery, inv. 1654

bearers—standing apart from their three black sedans, partially obscured by a stall in front of the inn "Zum goldenen Straußen."[171]

The true protagonists of the composition remain the many vendors populating the square. The picture thus reflects the Freyung's centuries-old identity as a commercial hub. Since the abbey's foundation in the twelfth century, the square had hosted herb and produce sellers. By the eighteenth century, this tradition had expanded into a marvel of both the abundance of goods and Vienna's unique rhythms of provisioning. Gardeners and farmers from the suburbs arrived at dawn with small carts or heavy *Butten*—wooden baskets carried on one's back—selling wholesale

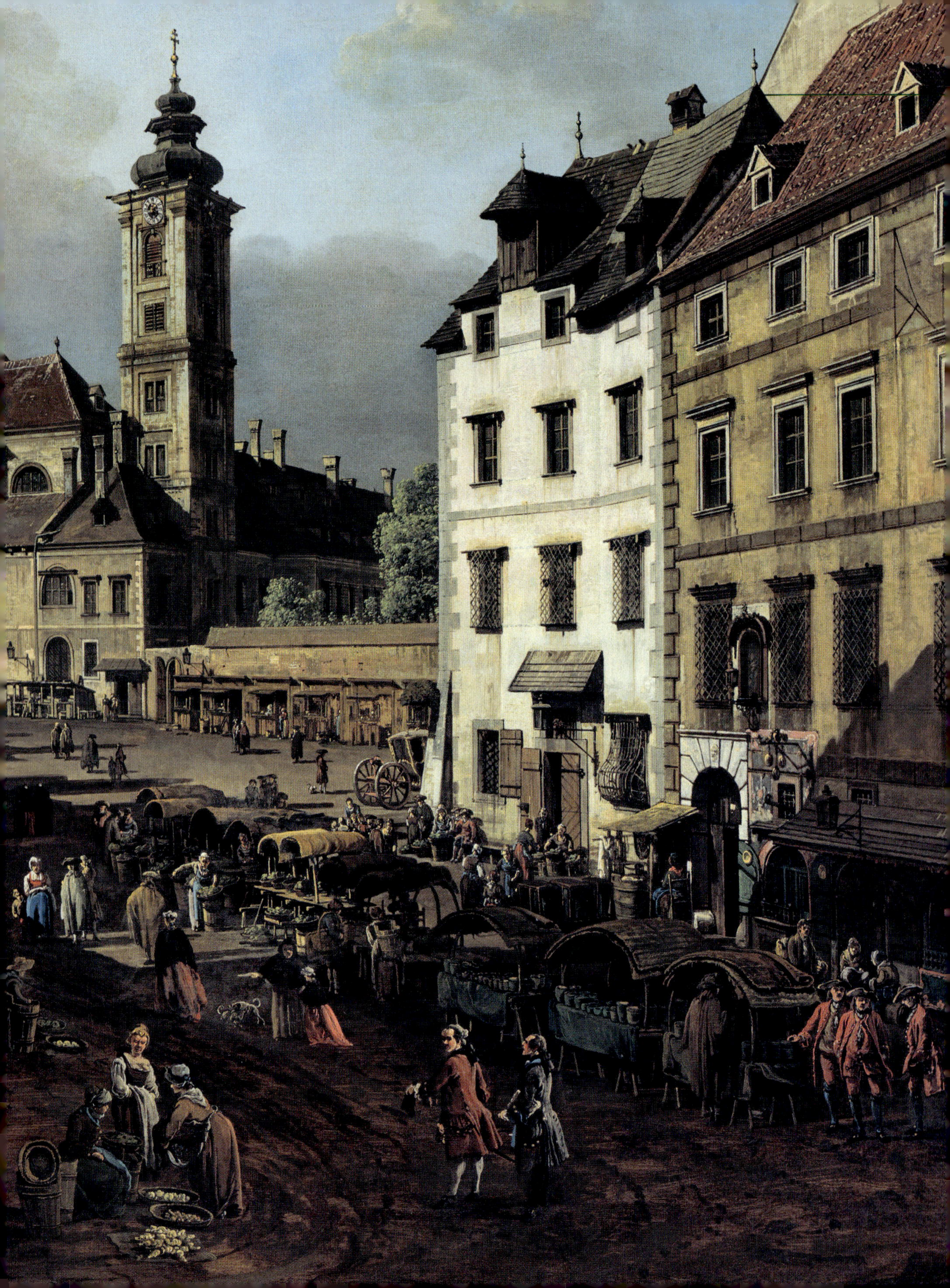

to larger dealers, who then supplied minor vendors and *Ständelweiber* at street corners. Maids and kitchen boys bought from them, passing goods on to their stewards and masters. As Friedrich Nicolai noted in 1781, "all food was bought fresh every day, and even in the grandest households one found neither eggs, nor flour, nor butter in storage."[172]

The plenitude became proverbial: in 1766, Mathias Fuhrmann described an ambassador who tried, jokingly, to buy all the vegetables in Vienna, only to see the markets instantly replenished.[173] In 1773, Charles Burney likewise observed that "in the inn where I lodged, there was literally a fair every day; merchants and hawkers seemed to sell nothing in shops, but carried their goods from house to house like peddlers."[174] Bellotto condenses such testimony into a vivid tableau of abundance and social commotion that sustained its markets, even as famines often plagued the Habsburg lands.

This attentiveness to street life is one of the most striking features of Bellotto's Viennese oeuvre, setting him apart also from the more formulaic figures in many of his uncle's pictures. In emphasizing the everyday activity of townspeople, Bellotto's *vedute* anticipate Johann Christian Brand's *Wiener Kaufruf* (*Vienna Street Cries*) of 1775, a series of etchings depicting Vienna's street vendors. Brand's plates cover a wide range of occupations: food sellers; hawkers of textiles and household goods; and service providers like day laborers, maids, and knife-grinders. Each figure was marked by a distinctive cry, often sung to a set melody, giving the series its title. Belonging to the pastoral tradition, these prints, though illustrating the common people of Vienna, targeted an aristocratic audience. As a result, they signaled Vienna's claim to metropolitan status, just as similar works portrayed the commoners of London and Paris.[175]

Bellotto's paintings of Vienna affirm the same urban ecology, embedding figures that directly correspond to Brand's etched types. In his *View of the University Square*, for example, staffage includes burghers strolling, Jesuits and students before the aula, as well as Greek merchants and washerwomen at the fountains (fig. 47). Both the Greek merchant and the laundress appear in Brand's *Kaufruf* (figs. 50, 51).[176] In the *View of the Dominican Church*,

Detail of fig. 49

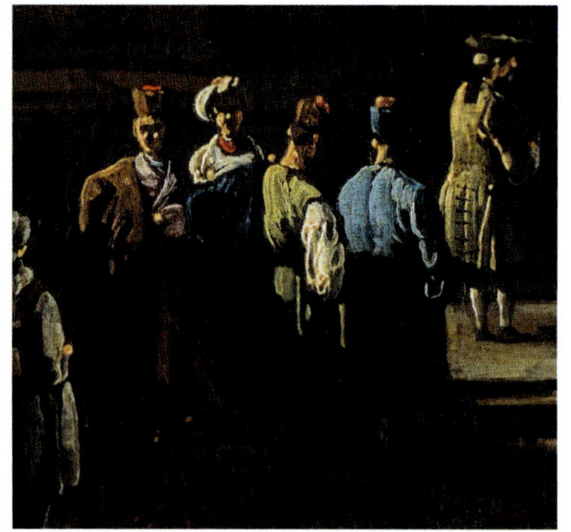

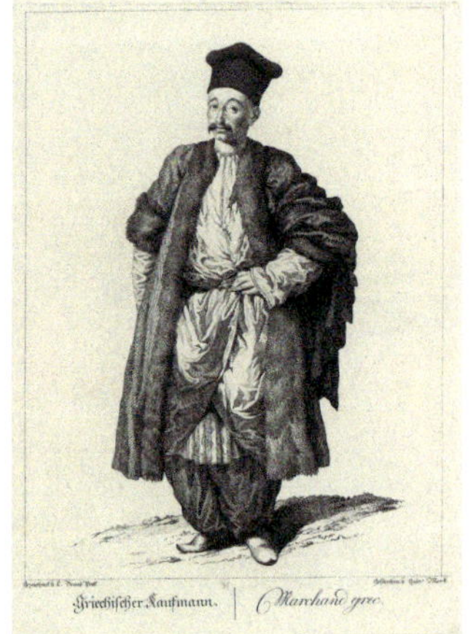

Detail of fig. 47

Fig. 50: Johann Christian Brand, "Greek Merchant" from *Drawings of the Common People, especially Street Cries, in Vienna*, 1775, engraving, 443 × 314 mm. Wien Museum, Vienna, inv. 95836/31

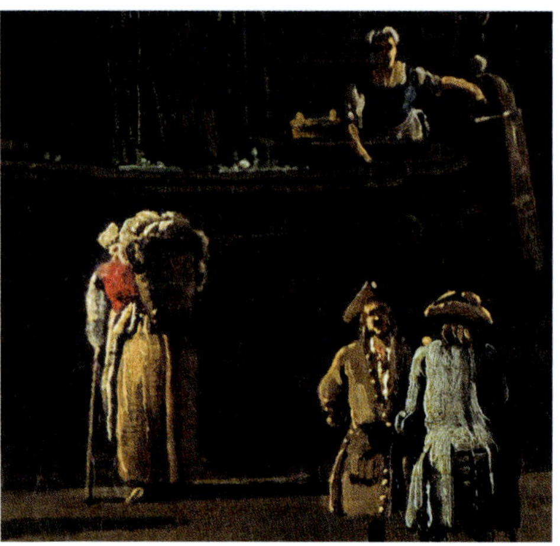

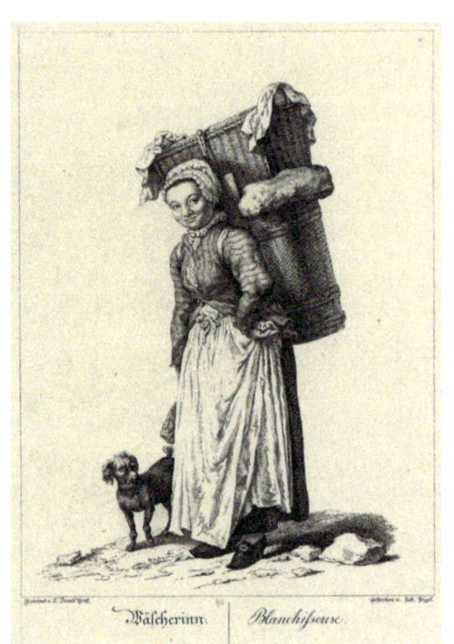

Detail of fig. 47

Fig. 51: Johann Christian Brand, "Washerwoman" from *Drawings of the Common People, especially Street Cries, in Vienna*, 1775, engraving, 443 × 314 cm. Wien Museum, Vienna, inv. 95836/38

the city's commercial character becomes even more vivid (fig. 45). At left, an elderly woman with an empty basket passes a man selling eggs; nearby, a man leans over a basket of chickens beside a woman trying to sell a hare to a lady in green. Opposite, a poultry seller lifts a chicken toward a woman in yellow and her daughter, accompanied by a kitchen boy bearing a large woven basket. Wagons, vendors, and couriers further underscore Postgasse's role as a commercial artery. The hare vendor, poultry seller, and kitchen boy all echo Brand's etched figures (figs. 52, 53, 54); two kitchen boys also appear in Bellotto's *Freyung* (fig. 49). In this way, Bellotto's *vedute* resonate not only with empirical culture's

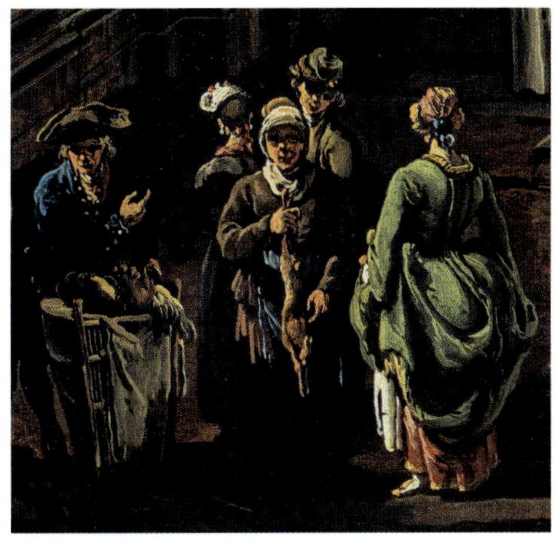

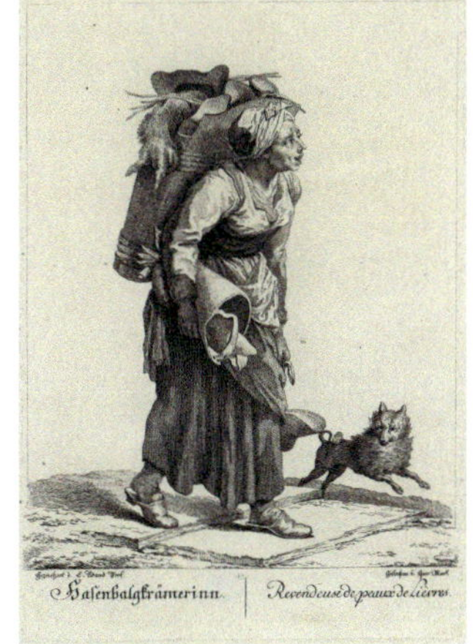

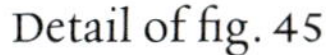

Detail of fig. 45

Fig. 52: Johann Christian Brand, "Hare-Skin Seller" from *Drawings of the Common People, especially Street Cries, in Vienna*, 1775, engraving, 443 × 314 mm. Wien Museum, Vienna, inv. 95836/13

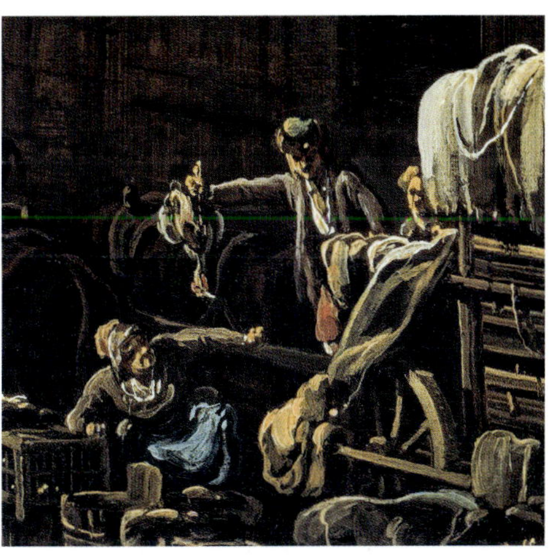

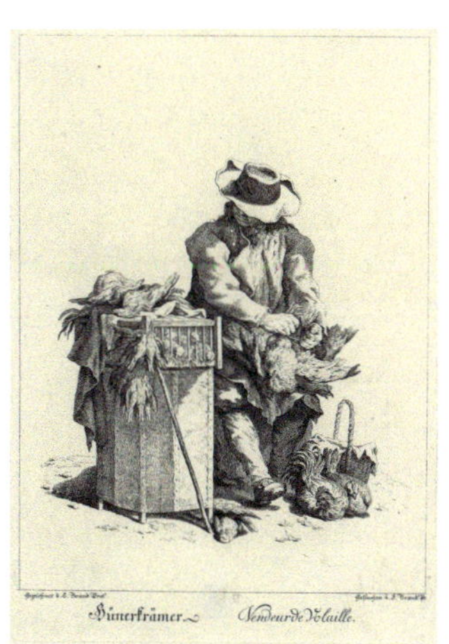

Detail of fig. 45

Fig. 53: Johann Christian Brand, "Poultry Seller" from *Drawings of the Common People, especially Street Cries, in Vienna*, 1775, engraving, 443 × 314 mm. Wien Museum, Vienna, inv. 95836/27

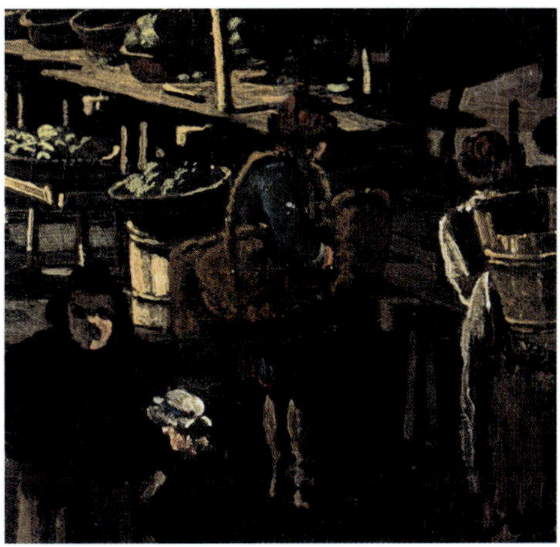

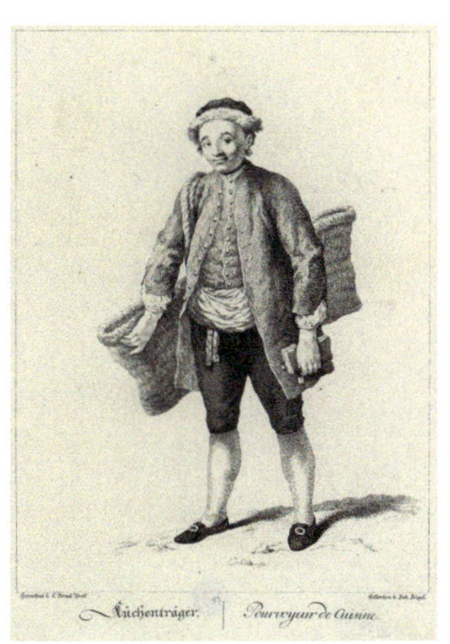

Detail of fig. 49

Fig. 54: Johann Christian Brand, "Kitchen Porter" from *Drawings of the Common People, especially Street Cries, in Vienna*, 1775, engraving, 443 × 314 mm. Wien Museum, Vienna, inv. 95836/17

cartographic precision but also with the ethnographic eye of contemporaries like Brand, capturing Vienna as measured city as well as lived social space.

VIENNA AS A STAGE

Even as Bellotto's *vedute* impress with empirical clarity, they are equally theatrical. As we have seen, he often composed views from multiple vantage points, manipulating perspective to increase legibility and arranging scenes like stage sets. Architecture forms a backdrop, the foreground often becomes a proscenium where staffage figures appear as actors in deliberate groupings, while light dramatizes some zones and obscures others. In the Kaunitz and Liechtstein canvases we observed aristocratic self-display on terraces, while in the Schottenkirche view, nobles, clerics, and burghers joined in a solemn processional movement. Even in more quotidian sites like the Postgasse or Freyung, space is carefully orchestrated. Carriages pivot at compositional nodes,

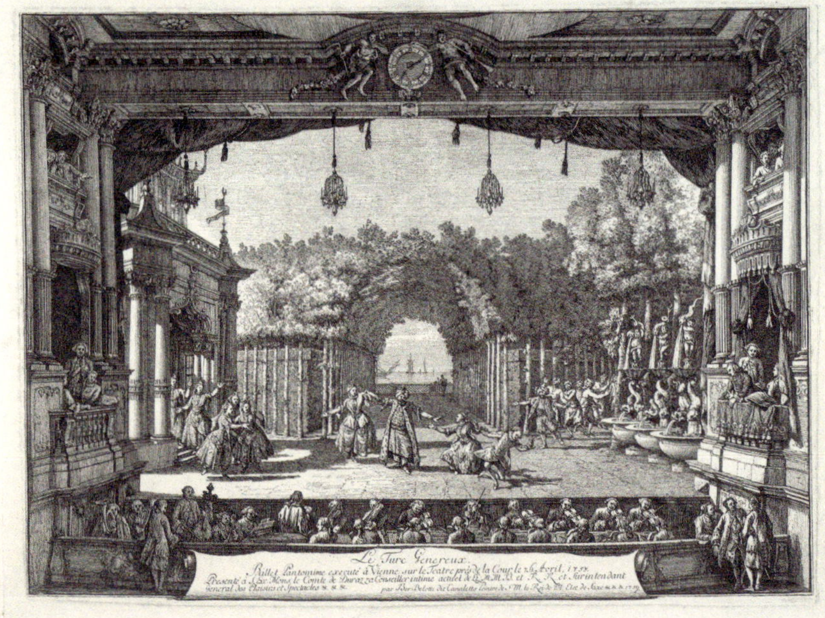

Fig. 55: Bernardo Bellotto, *Scene from "Le Turc Généreux" at the Hofburgtheater*, 1759, etching, 510 × 670 mm. ALBERTINA, Vienna, inv. DG2005/10286

Detail of fig. 38

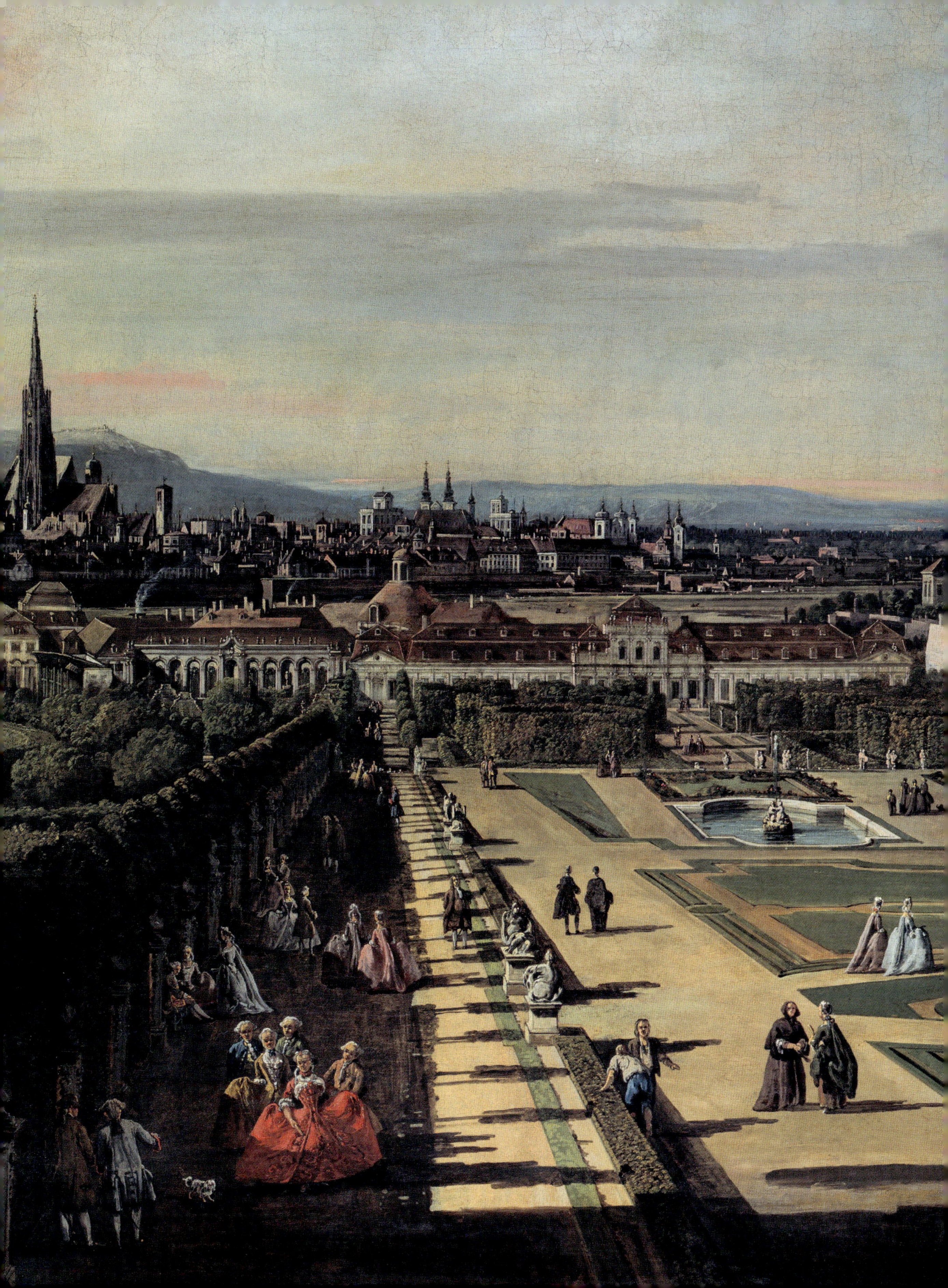

merchants and vendors form balanced clusters. In the garden views, finally, aristocrats adopt polite gestures that echo courtly spectacle.

Similar to Canaletto, such artifice reflects Bellotto's sensitivity to theater—an inheritance from his grandfather Bernardo Canal, a set designer, and from his exposure to the scenographic innovations of Ferdinando Galli Bibiena, whose treatise he owned. Bellotto's only surviving Viennese print, a 1759 etching of the ballet-pantomime *Le Turc Généreux*, makes this theatrical link explicit (fig. 55).[177] Premiered in 1758 at the Hoftheater to honor the Ottoman envoy Rasmi Ahmed Efendi, the work was part of Jean-Philippe Rameau's *Les Indes galantes*, adapted in Vienna by choreographer Franz Anton Hilverding. The plot, which centers on the jealous Pasha Osman, the lovers Emilie and Valère, and a final act of magnanimity, was staged as a ballet of gestures. Bellotto's etching captures its climax: the Pasha raising his dagger in fury, only to be restrained. An oriental pavilion, fountains, and seascape set the scene, while the diagonal grouping of figures heightens the tension. Exceptional within his graphic œuvre that otherwise shows city views, this print demonstrates how readily Bellotto translated theatrical spectacle into pictorial form. His *vedute*, though ostensibly urban records, follow the same principle: transforming the city into a stage, where movement, gesture, and setting unite in harmonious performance.

This sense of staging is particularly evident in the *View of Vienna from the Belvedere*, where promenading visitors and gardeners animate the parterres (fig. 38). Their bright costumes enliven the gardens' geometry, while their social range—from aristocrats to humble workers—appears less as casual observation than as a carefully composed tableau. This staged quality later fascinated writers like Hugo von Hofmannsthal. In the 1892 prologue to *Anatol*, inspired by Bellotto's painting, Hofmannsthal, imagining the city as a stage where men and women performed the comedy of life, conjured "das Wien des Canaletto" as a theater of gallant gardens, marble basins, and strolling couples.[178] For Hofmannsthal and the *Jung-Wien* circle, Bellotto's view epitomized a Vienna of spectacle and artifice, where social life merged with theatrical self-presentation. Such response reveals what was already latent in Bellotto's work: his canvases did not merely depict urban reality, they staged it.

Yet staging also entails selection and idealization. Bellotto's staffage favors elegance, refinement, and social harmony: aristocrats promenade in fine robes; processions advance in perfect order; markets bustle without descending into disorder. While poverty and hardship are not absent — kitchen boys, washerwomen, barefoot gardeners, and even beggars appear at the margins — the overall view remains picturesque, subsumed by the architectural frame and compositional whole. Other contemporaries, by contrast, could be unsparing about the lived realities in Vienna. A satirical *Quodlibet über Wien* of 1751 defined the city as "a clump of houses and palaces, / full of vermin, full of strangers ... / stench and filth in every street."[179] The Freyung, which Bellotto depicts as abundant, was in reality the subject of frequent complaints from the Schottenstift, which protested the herb sellers' makeshift stalls along its cemetery wall, noting that refuse accumulated between the huts and the wall, while abandoned

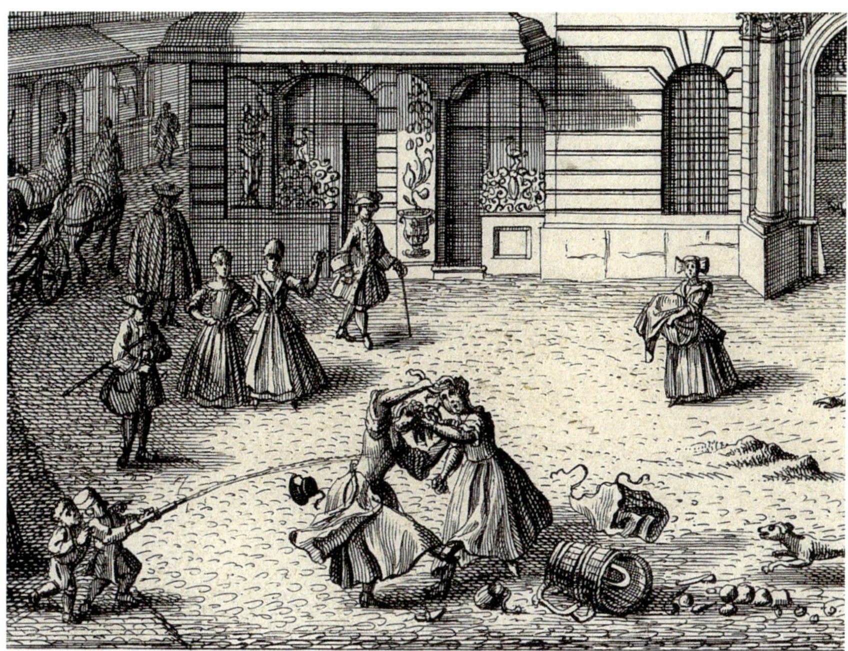

Fig. 56: Salomon Kleiner, *View of the Visendisches Haus under the Tuchlauben* (detail), 1733, engraving, 308 × 439 mm. Wien Museum, Vienna, inv. 105437

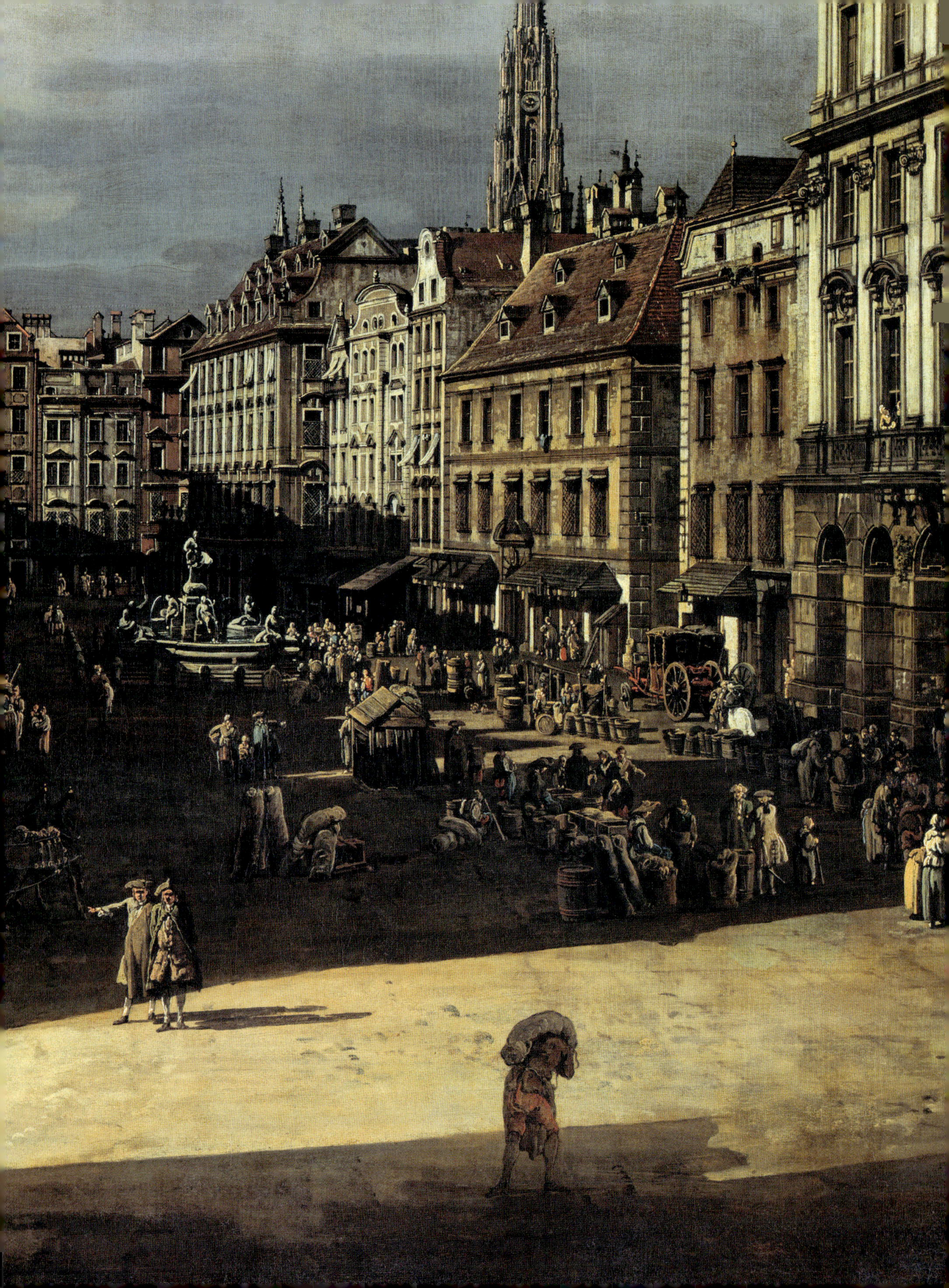

infants were sometimes left there at night.[180] Even Salomon Kleiner, in a 1733 engraving of the Tuchlauben, shows two women tearing at each other's hair (fig. 56). Of course, much more serious crime than the one Kleiner showed inflicted Vienna on a daily basis, and authorities draconically tried to keep it in check. Maria Theresa, who is often mythologized as an enlightened reformer and lauded for initiatives in education, finance, and social policy, and purported abolition of torture, in fact codified the latter's use in judicial procedure in the *Constitutio Criminalis Theresiana* of 1768 (see cat. 46).[181]

Seemingly none of this enters Bellotto's view. What was permissible to depict in print and prose directly was out of place in a painted *veduta* destined for Imperial display. His canvases smooth harsh realities into order and apparent contentment. From today's perspective, such staged harmony captures the era's duality: a city bathed in sunlit clarity, measured and disciplined, even as labor, coercion, and poverty persisted in the shadows. For Bellotto's aristocratic patrons, these images affirmed not just urban grandeur but the values of public duty and elite legitimacy. The marginalization (rather than complete erasure) of the poor, the unruly, and the immoral renders the vision persuasive.[182] Hence the city appears as a stage where the Habsburg monarchy could see itself reflected: luminous, orderly, and controlled.

BETWEEN SPLENDOR AND HARDSHIP

In the shaded foreground of Bellotto's view of the Mehlmarkt (fig. 57), a solitary figure bends beneath the weight of a flour sack—a striking reminder that the city's daily sustenance depended on individual labor.[183] His posture anchors the canvas, drawing the viewer into a square named for the grain trade that once defined it. Laid out in the thirteenth century as the "New Market," by the eighteenth century it was known as the Mehlmarkt, the main site of grain exchange. The elongated square unfolds from Bellotto's vantage in the now-lost Palais Schwarzenberg at its southern end. Characteristically, he dramatizes the scene with late-afternoon light: most of the

Detail of fig. 57

square lies in shadow. At the left edge stands the Capuchin Church, founded in 1618 by Empress Anna and later expanded as the Habsburgs' dynastic burial place. Its plain façade is abruptly cropped, but the 1760 portal and fresco of St. Francis before Christ secure the canvas in time. Emerging from its doorway, an aristocratic lady—sometimes identified as Maria Theresa, who had a mausoleum for herself and her husband erected in this church's crypt in 1753/54—heads toward her carriage.[184] On the steps to her right, a humble woman sits, underscoring the coexistence of social extremes.

From this sacred threshold, the eye is drawn into the square, where Georg Raphael Donner's Providentia Fountain (1737–39) forms the compositional and symbolic center. Around it, the Mehlmarkt is framed by seventeenth- and eighteenth-century façades (most medieval buildings having been replaced or refronted in Baroque style by Bellotto's time). Next to the Capuchin Church stretches a continuous row of townhouses, ending with the richly ornamented *Hatschierenhaus* "Zu den sieben Säulen," rebuilt around 1735 for Heinrich Ernst Rauchmüller, master of the sedan-chair trade.[185] The northern end closes with several houses featuring seventeenth-century façades, forming a compact backdrop. On the right, narrow multi-storied Bürgerhäuser alternate with larger dwellings like the Bauer house with its projecting arcade. Above their roofs rise the Gothic spire of St. Stephen's Cathedral and the tips of its Romanesque Heidentürme. Anchoring the right foreground is the vast bulk of the Mehlgrube, whose breadth and height dominate the square.

The Mehlgrube was erected by Johann Bernhard Fischer von Erlach between 1697/98 and c. 1703.[186] Its peculiar name recalled its fifteenth-century role as a municipal flour depot. In Fischer's redesign, the late-medieval storehouse became a palatial edifice: the cellars remained for flour storage, while the upper floors were repurposed as tavern, lodging, and above all, a venue for splendid balls, staples of the city's social calendar by the 1720s. A print by Fischer von Erlach the Younger and Delsenbach makes this function explicit (fig. 58), showing dancers, musicians, and elegant guests in the open windows, with others on the rooftop terrace. In 1761, Johann Peter Willebrandt and other contemporaries

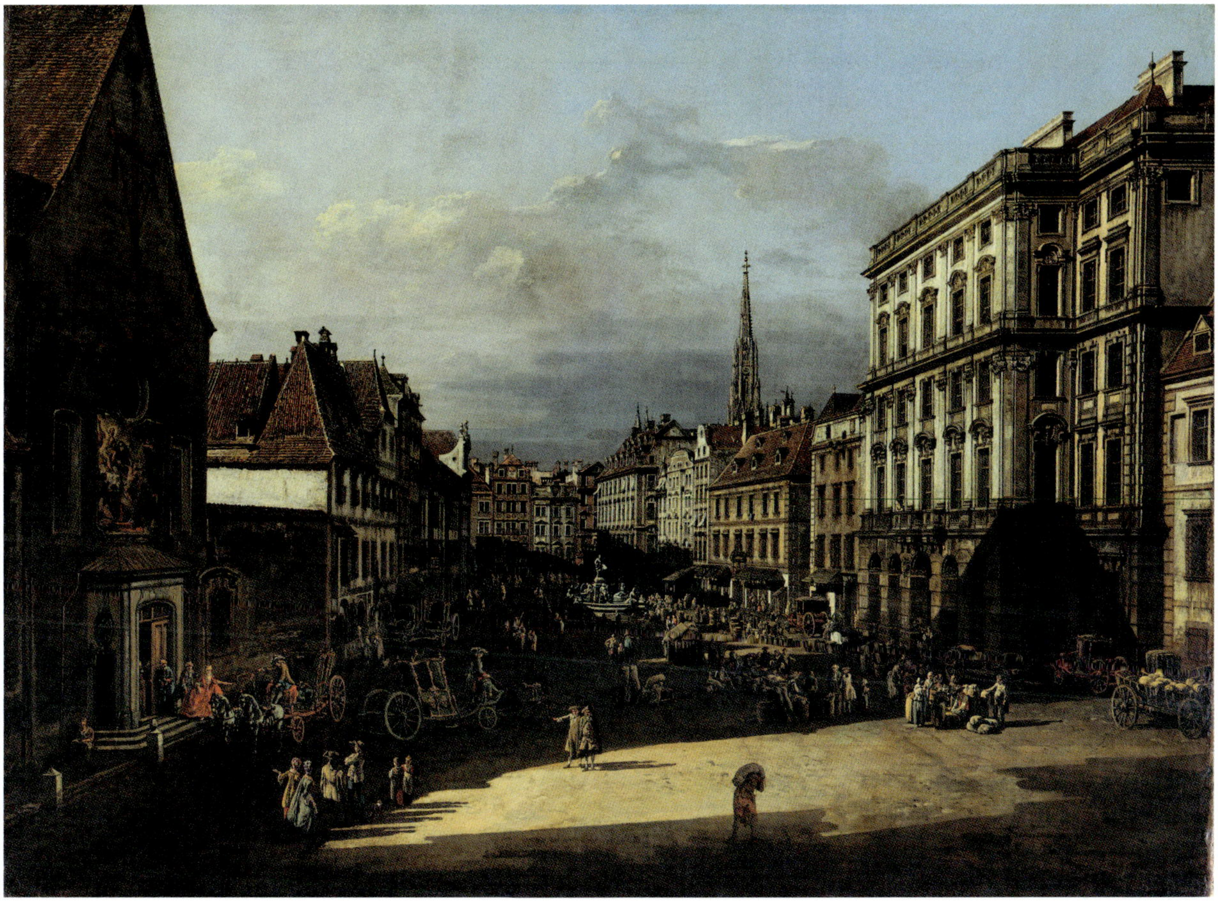

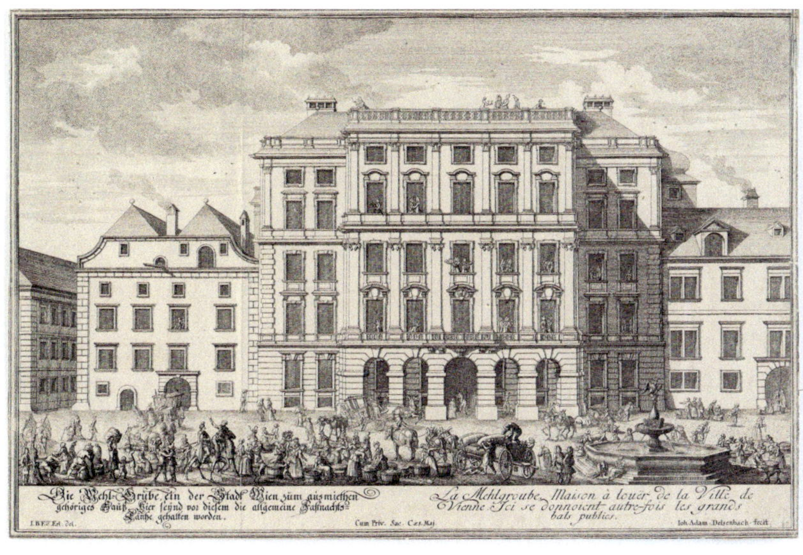

Fig. 57: Bernardo Bellotto, *The Mehlmarkt in Vienna*, 1759/60, oil on canvas, 116 × 155 cm. Kunsthistorisches Museum, Vienna, Picture Gallery, inv. 1668

Fig. 58: Johann Adam Delsenbach after Joseph Emanuel Fischer von Erlach, *The Mehl-Grube*, 1719, engraving, 223 × 330 mm. Wien Museum, Vienna, inv. 28805

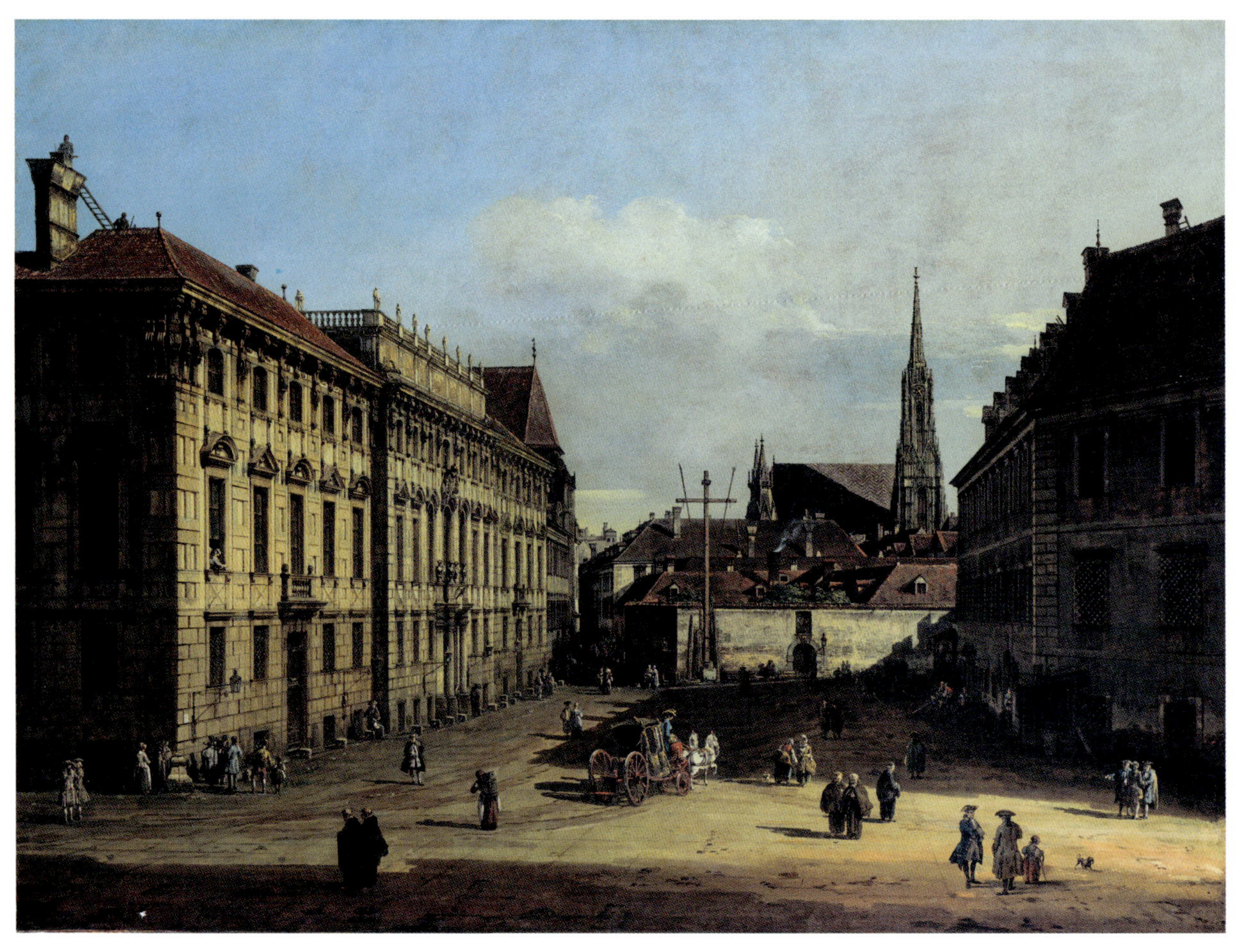

Fig. 59: Bernardo Bellotto, *The Lobkowitz Square in Vienna*, 1759/60, oil on canvas, 114.5 × 151 cm. Kunsthistorisches Museum, Vienna, Picture Gallery, inv. 1671

distinguished between the court balls at the Hofburg and the "city Redouten" in the Mehlgrube, which drew a wide cross-section of nobility eager to see and be seen.[187] Later, the same hall hosted concerts, including several of Mozart's academies in the 1780s. Yet in Bellotto's canvas, none of this revelry appears. The façade stands mute, its associations with spectacle eclipsed by the prosaic rhythms of daily life across the square. What emerges is a scene both ordinary and emblematic: a stage where laborers, worshippers, and revelers would move within the same urban space, their differences leveled by Bellotto's unifying brush.

Bellotto's view of the Lobkowitz Square (fig. 59) offers another pointed meditation on contrast. From the first-floor windows of the Augustinian monastery, Bellotto looked northeast across the narrow square and subtly reworked the scene for clarity, combining two vantage points into a single, legible whole. He also widened the square, shifted St. Stephen's Cathedral leftward so that it crowns the horizon, and treated the light—falling from the upper right—according to an internal aesthetic logic rather than natural sunlight.[188] At left stands the Lobkowitz Palace, begun in 1687 for Count Philipp Sigmund Dietrichstein, remodeled around 1694 by Johann Bernhard Fischer von Erlach, and owned by the Lobkowitz family since 1745.[189] Bellotto adjusted its broad façade, straightening its natural convexity. Opposite stretches the vast Bürgerspital, a medieval foundation repurposed in 1530 that by the eighteenth century housed up to three thousand poor, elderly, and infirm residents.[190] Since 1754, it also contained the *medicinisch-praktische Lehrschule*, which—established under Gerard van Swieten and directed by Anton de Haen—pioneered clinical bedside teaching. Between palace and hospital runs the Capuchins' garden wall, marked by a tall wooden mission cross bearing the *Arma Christi* (the instruments of Christ's suffering). The juxtaposition is eloquent: the sunlit palace and the shadowed Bürgerspital, bespeaking the vulnerability of thousands dependent on charity, confront each other across the square, framed by St. Stephen's and the Capuchin's mission cross, adding registers of piety and mortality. Together they bind the city's splendor and fragility into a single image.

Staffage figures reinforce the polarity. A finely dressed man leans from a palace window; above him, two sweeps tend the rooftop chimney with a ladder. At the center of the square, an aristocrat's sunlit carriage moves toward the city center, surrounded by loosely grouped, more anonymous pedestrians: working figures, monks, and conversing men in waistcoats and tricorns. In the shaded areas near the Bürgerspital appear two men in black, one supporting his lame friend, and a small girl on a crutch. Such figures recall contemporary studies of illness and deformity like Jakob Matthias Schmutzer's drawing of a frail boy leaning on a stick, his head wrapped in bandages (fig. 60). Yet while Schmutzer isolated his subject, evoking sympathy, Bellotto

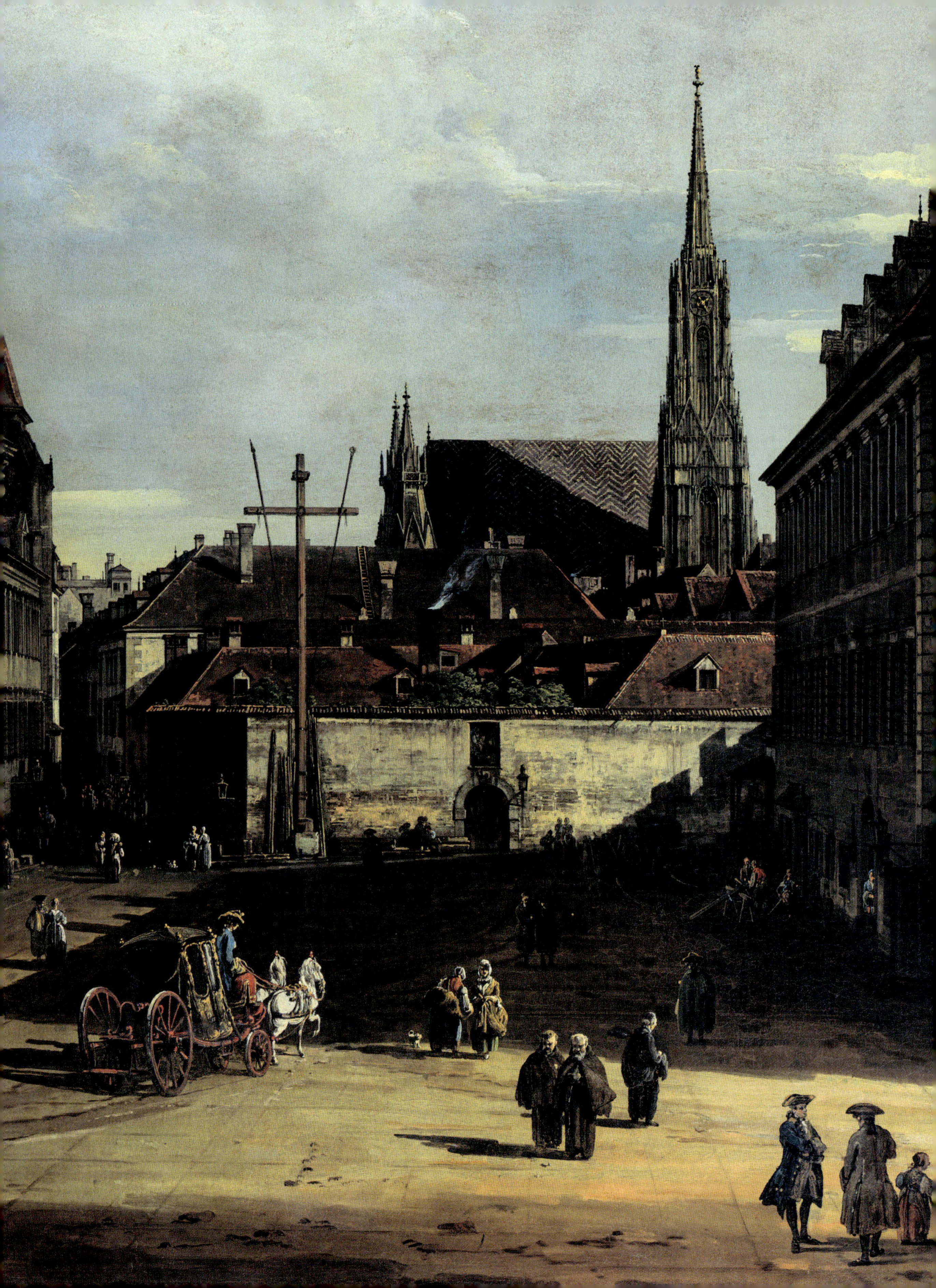

disperses his invalids into the bustle of the street, subordinated to the architectural frame and holistic image. Hardship is acknowledged but subdued, absorbed into a compositional order that reassures the viewer of Vienna's stability.

This interplay of splendor and hardship is not confined to Vienna's inner squares. Bellotto extended it to the countryside as well when he turned his attention (at an undefined point during his Viennese interlude) to Schloss Hof on the March River, east of the city. Originally a seventeenth-century fortified complex, Schloss Hof was transformed between 1725 and 1729 by Johann Lucas von Hildebrandt for Prince Eugene of Savoy, who also commissioned ambitious terraced gardens completed in 1732 under Dominique Girard. Hundreds of craftsmen, gardeners, and day-laborers worked on the site, part of Eugene's expressed intention to provide work for the local population and his returning soldiers.[191] After his death in 1736, the estate passed to his niece Victoria of Savoy, Princess of Saxe-Hildburghausen, before being purchased by Francis Stephen and Maria Theresa in 1755. Thereafter, Schloss Hof became their favored hunting lodge

Detail of fig. 59

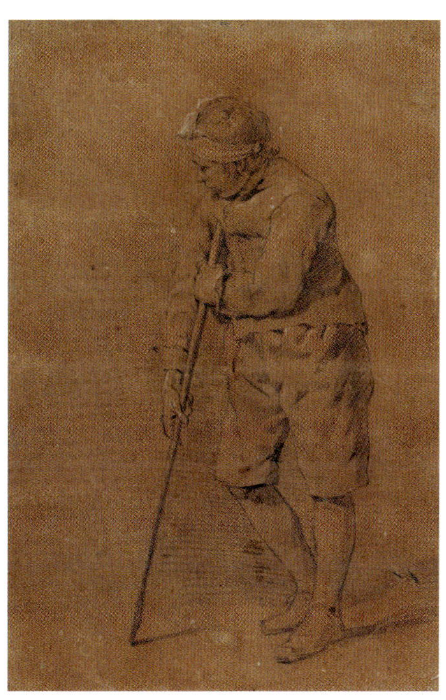

Fig. 60: Jakob Matthias Schmutzer, *Peasant Boy Leaning on a Staff with Bandaged Head*, 1770/90, chalk on paper, 400 × 264 mm. Academy of Fine Arts, Vienna, Kupferstichkabinett, inv. HZ-12436

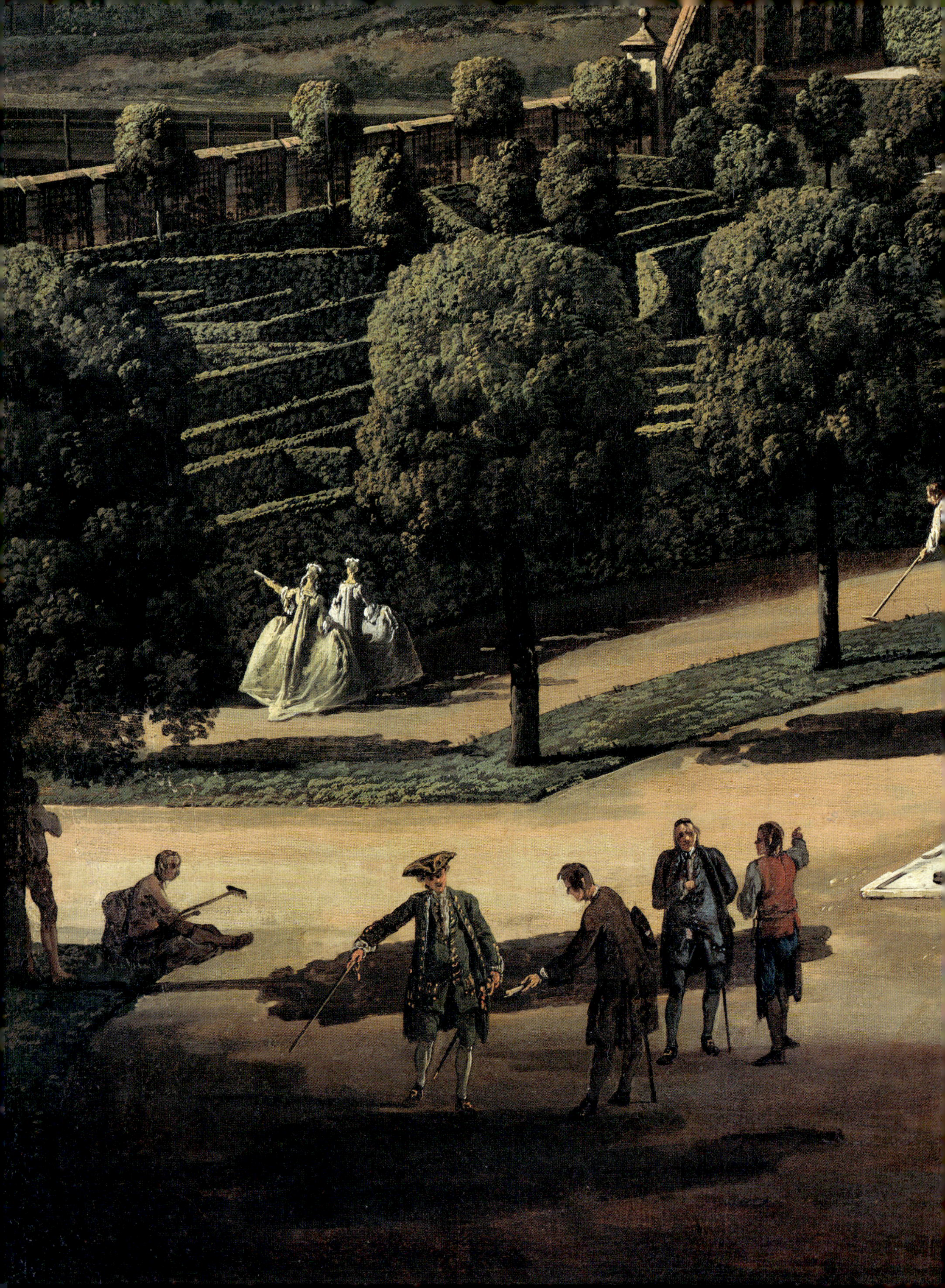

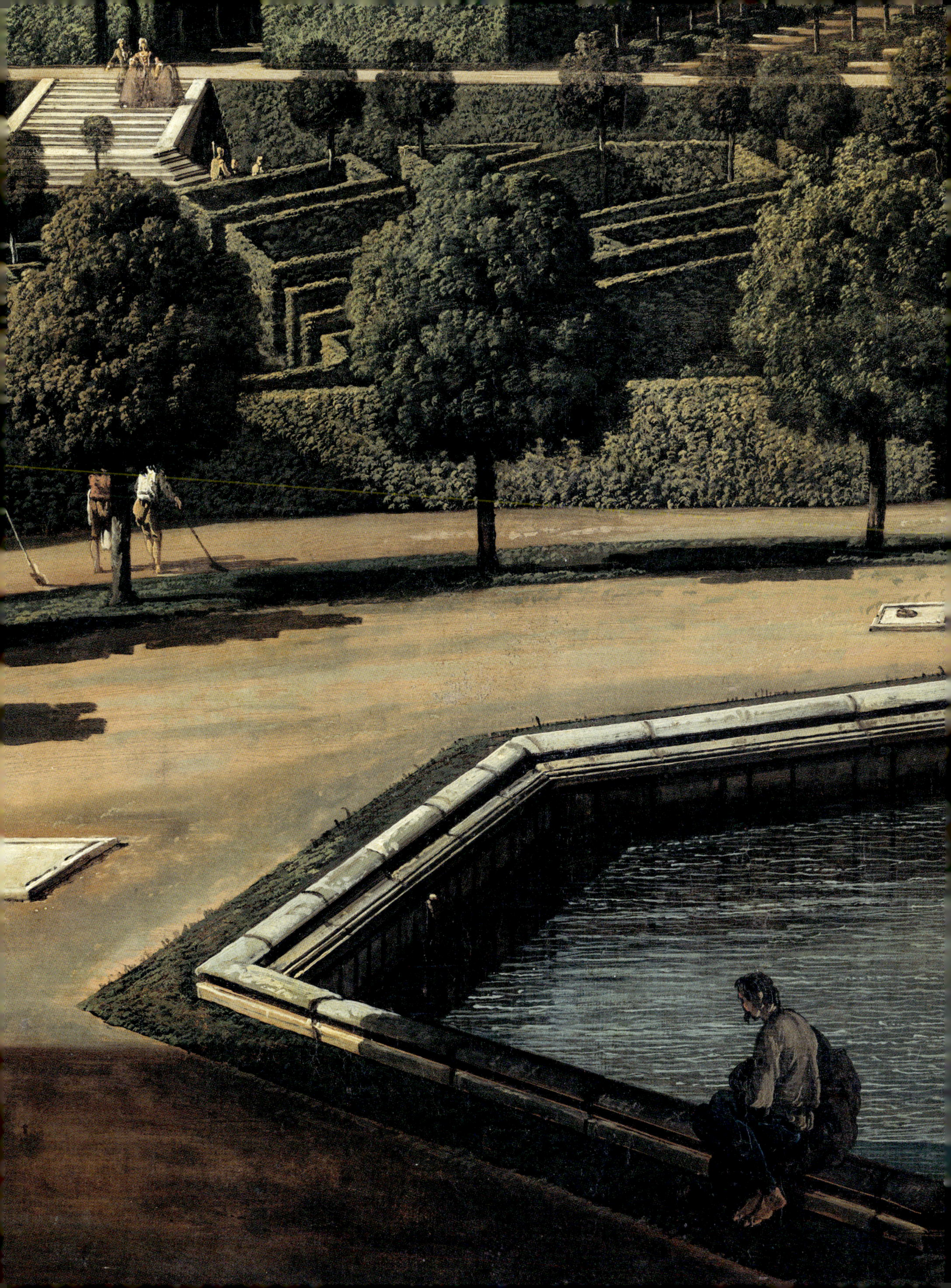

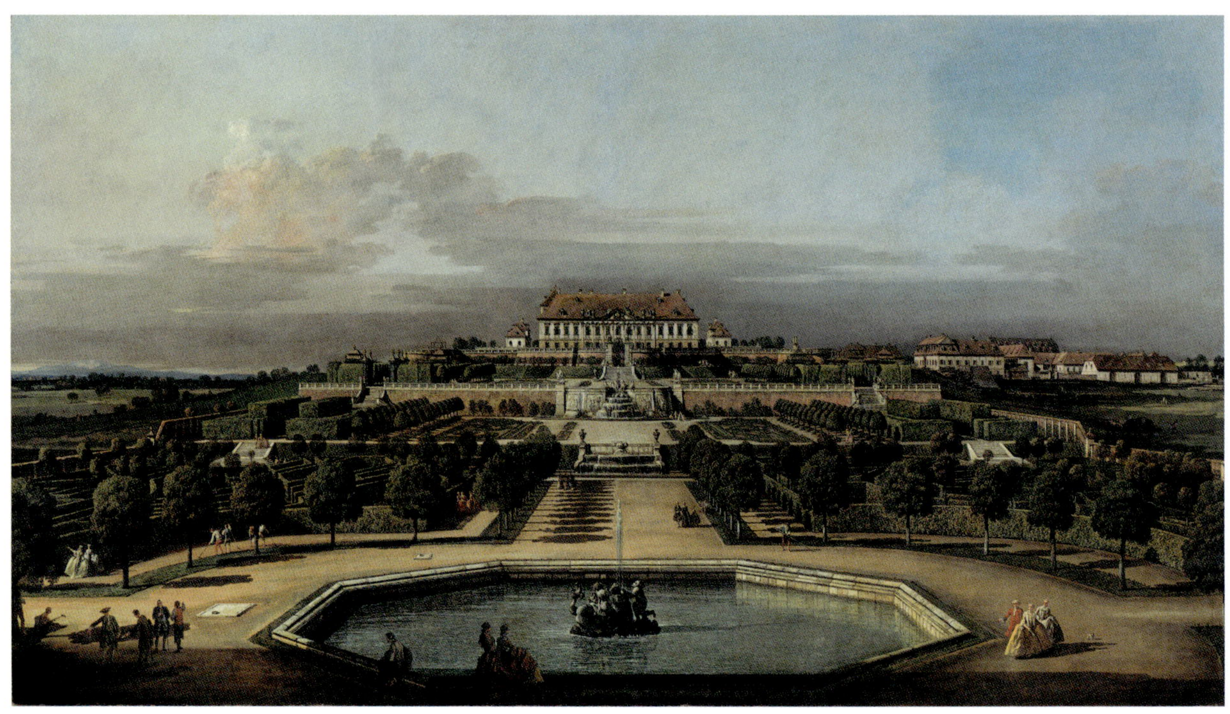

Fig. 61: Bernardo Bellotto, *View of Schloss Hof from the Gardens*, 1759/60, oil on canvas, 136 × 216 cm, detail on pp. 140–41. Kunsthistorisches Museum, Vienna, Picture Gallery, inv. 1674

and, after Francis Stephen's death in 1765, Maria Theresa's widow's residence. It also hosted major dynastic events, including the 1766 wedding of her favorite daughter, Archduchess Marie Christine, to Duke Albert of Saxe-Teschen. Bellotto painted three large canvases of similar format, recording the complex before the alterations of the 1760s and 1770s that added another story and re-clad the façades in early neoclassical style. His three works show, respectively, the garden, forecourt, and northern flank of the palace; in a fourth canvas he depicted the nearby ruins of the fortress Theben/Devín near Bratislava, long tied to the frontier once contested in wars with the Ottoman Empire, whose border had been pushed back through Prince Eugene's victories.

Arguably the grandest of Bellotto's Schloss Hof canvases is the view of the garden side (fig. 61).[192] From a vantage above the hexagonal basin, the canvas surveys the garden's five terraces, rhythmical and foreshortened so that all vanishing points converge on the palace block crowning the axis. To the right, low-lying service buildings nestle into the landscape; to the left, the vista opens across the Marchfeld plain. The garden unfolds with cascades, fountains, grottos, bosquets, rows of orange trees, espaliered fruit, arbors, hedge mazes, and vaulted pavilions, animated by staffage figures: At lower right, a noblewoman in a yellow *robe à la française* appears with a lady in white, a gentleman in red, and a lapdog. At center, an aristocratic couple admires the view beyond the basin, at whose edge rests a disheveled barefoot man. To the left, a small group of men confer as one delivers a message to the figure in green; nearby, two gardeners rest in the shade, while two ladies, one gesturing with her fan, discuss the garden's splendor. Further right, gardeners tend the semicircular path. More genteel figures appear promenading throughout the garden, though another shabby man seated under the main path's trees again interrupts the social coherence. At the far right beyond the garden walls, rustic laborers work around the service buildings, including a horse-and-ox cart hauling a barrel. Bellotto's emphasis on order and monumental scale subordinates these figures to the garden's near-abstract geometry—a vision of nature once again disciplined into artifice. Comparable to Schönbrunn, the garden here becomes an emblem of control, abundance, and authority, rising triumphantly from the Marchfeld plain.

If the garden view emphasizes abstraction and symbolic grandeur, Bellotto's rendering of the forecourt introduces a livelier interplay of architecture and human presence (fig. 62).[193] It depicts the western approach, where Hildebrandt extended the older rectangular core with projecting wings and corner pavilions embracing a spacious forecourt. At its center stands the Neptune fountain, framed by semicircular ramps and balustrades adorned with sculptural groups of Hercules and Antaeus and pairs of lions, evoking Prince Eugene's military triumphs. Behind, the palace rises in clear axial symmetry—its clock set to forty minutes before midday—while to the right the eye extends into the Marchfeld valley toward the distant ruin of Theben / Devín.

Bellotto's two Schloss Hof pictures also reveal how, in some pictures, his artistic process diverged from his uncle's. While he, too, employed the camera obscura, he built his compositions

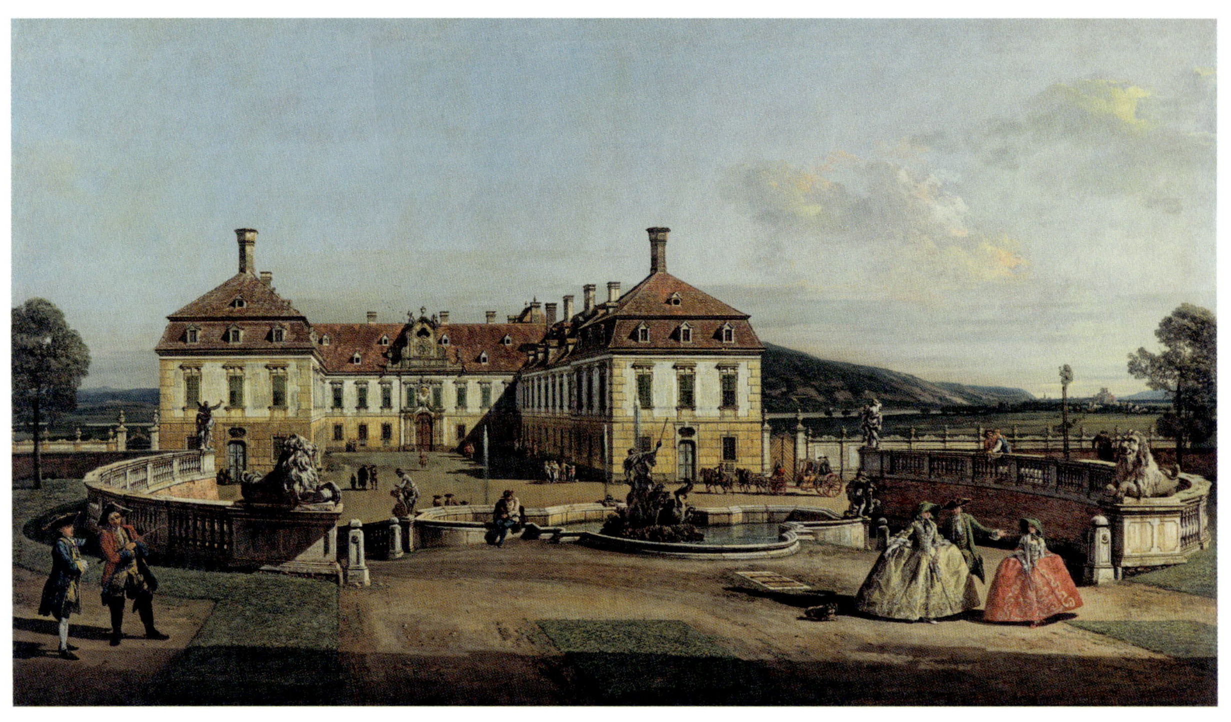

Fig. 62: Bernardo Bellotto, *View of Schloss Hof from the Forecourt*, 1759/60, oil on canvas, 138 × 237 cm, detail on pp. 146–47. Kuntsthistorisches Museum, Vienna, Picture Gallery, inv. 1673

through rigorous perspectival construction. For the garden view he adopted a fictive elevated vantage and, unlike Canaletto, strict central perspective, manipulating angles and proportions to dramatize the palace's height. The forecourt picture also presents a constructed, slightly elevated view, with continuous horizontal lines showing through the paint between windows—evidence that details were aligned along carefully ruled marks. His working method was otherwise as systematic as his teacher's: Bellotto too sometimes incised lines into wet paint with a stylus, their ridges catching light to accentuate architectural details. After merging viewpoints and fixing perspectival scaffolds, he painted skies and landscape, then architecture, foliage in layers, and finally staffage—sometimes so thinly applied that over time earlier layers became visible, for instance underneath the figures standing or sitting at the palace's basins. Bellotto thus turned observed reality into calculated compositions, empirically

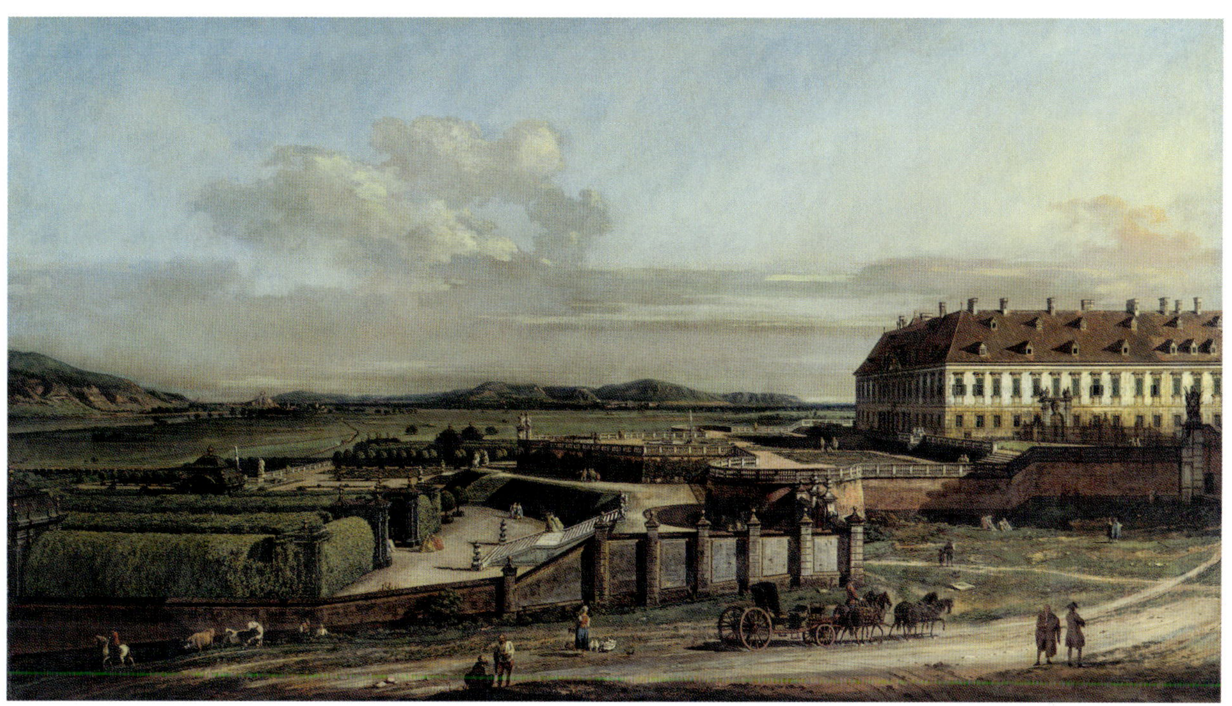

Fig. 63 : Bernardo Bellotto, *View of Schloss Hof from the North*, 1759/60, oil on canvas, 136 × 238 cm. Kunsthistorisches Museum, Vienna, Picture Gallery, inv. 1675

grounded yet staged, in tune with the Enlightenment culture of observation and calculation that would have resonated in elite circles.[194]

In the courtyard view, the staffage is unusually prominent. At right, in the foreground, stand two noblewomen and a cavalier, rendered almost portrait-like, though their identities remain uncertain. Their presence sets a courtly tone, counterbalanced by humbler figures: at far left a coachman and a man in blue, hand tucked into his waistcoat; at the fountain's edge a seated vagrant; on the balustrade to the right a rustic couple looking on. Close to the palace a four-horse carriage rolls in, while nearby a group of cooks have gathered. Along the remaining façade, other domestic workers converse or work, while before the main entrance a gentleman in brown leans nattily on his cane. Once again, without disturbing the harmony of the scene, the upper classes, servants, and commoners intermingle. The result is a

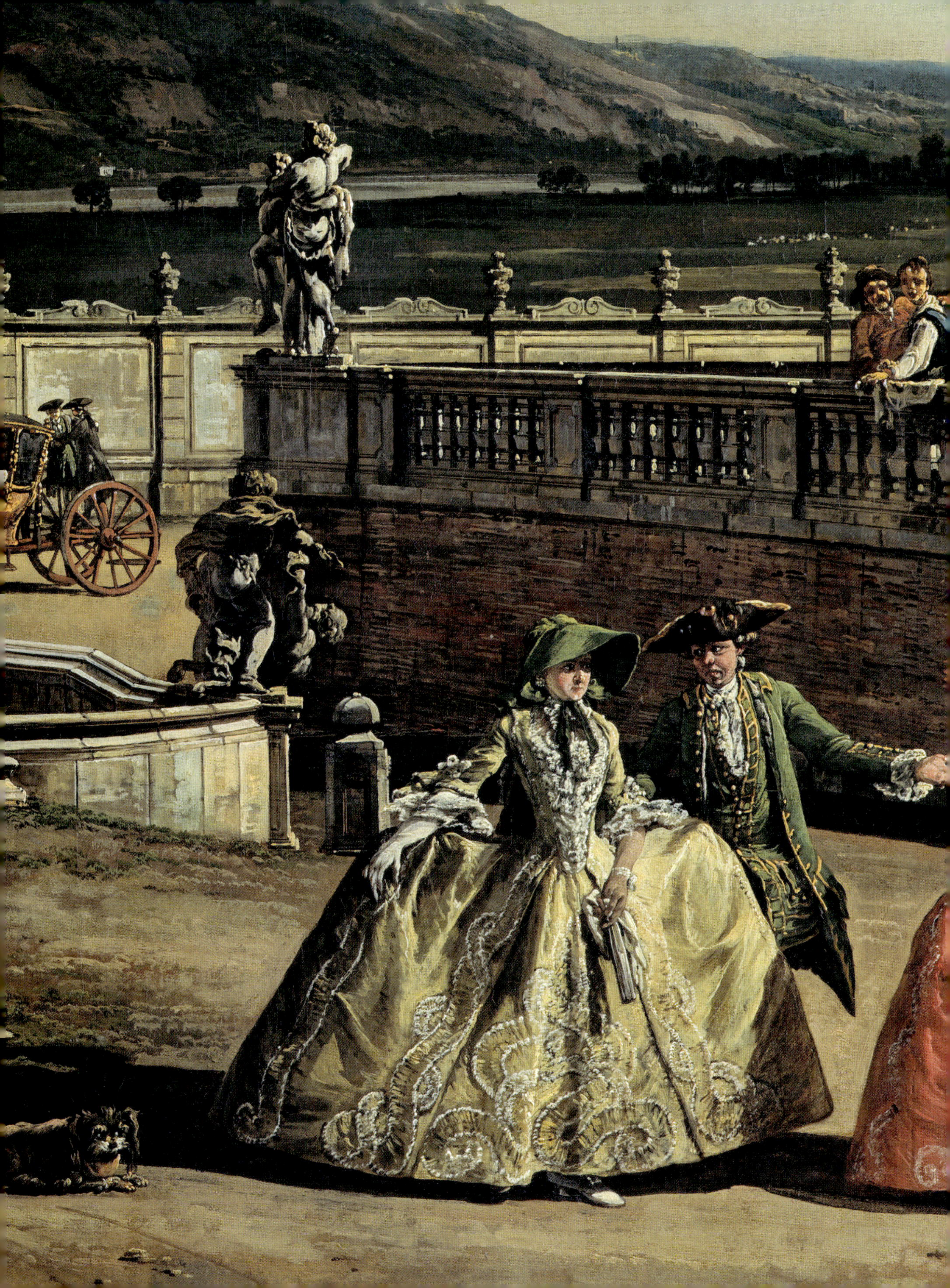

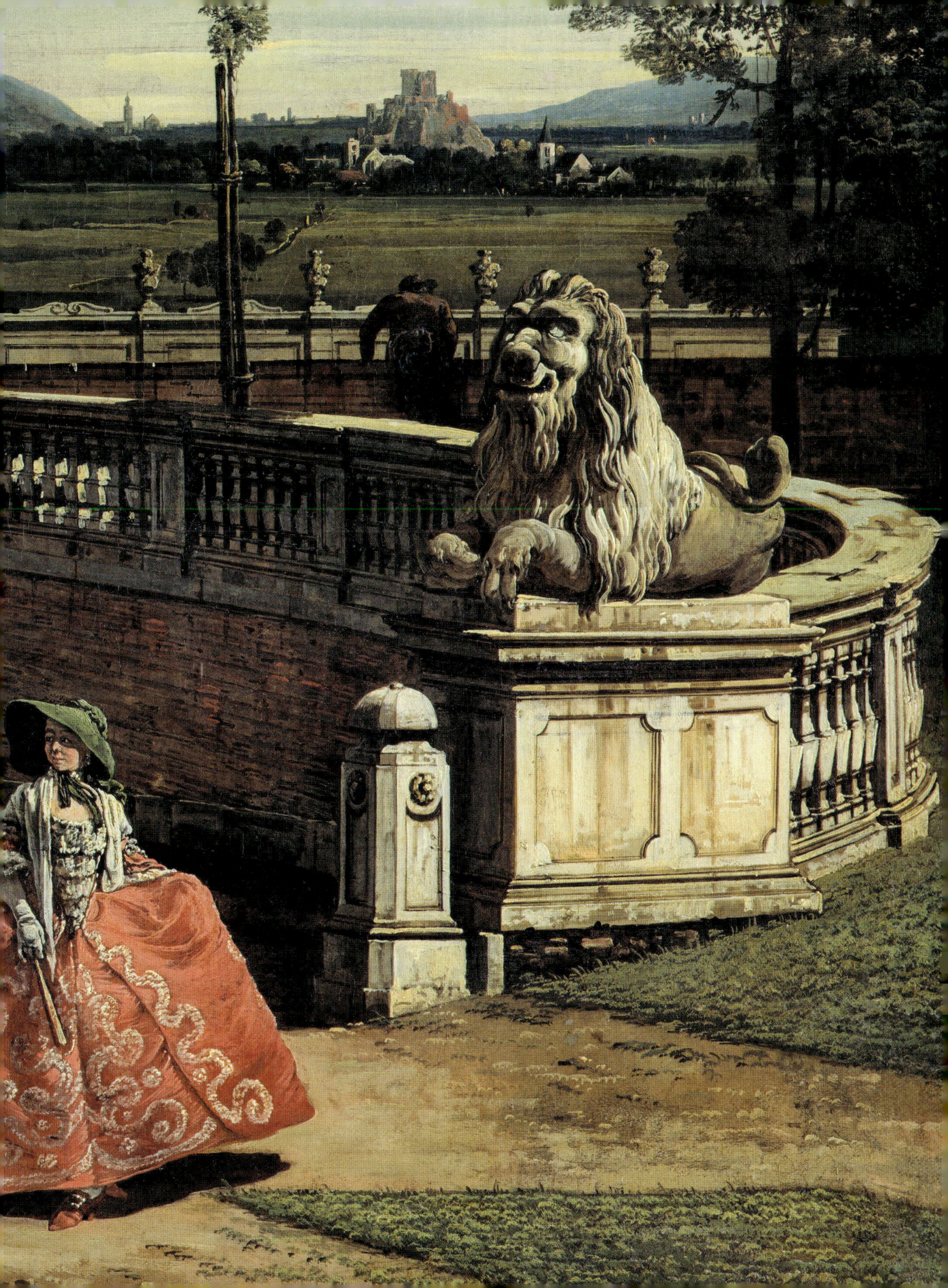

carefully calibrated equilibrium between aristocratic magnificence and the everyday.

By contrast, Bellotto's rendering of the palace's northern prospect turns away from courtly display to reveal the site's fortified mass against the Marchfeld plain (fig. 63). The canvas adopts a vantage from the upper stories of the service buildings outside the garden walls, looking across the gardens toward the south, the palace itself pushed to the picture's right edge. In the foreground, agricultural and domestic laborers appear: women spread laundry to dry, another feeds geese and chickens, peasants stand beside cattle, and a four-horse carriage moves toward the side gate. Two impoverished figures—one seated, one standing—appear closest to the viewer, in stark contrast to the handful of fashionably dressed aristocrats and working gardeners glimpsed beyond the garden wall. The background opens onto the plain of the March and Danube, with Hainburg and its hilltop castle faintly visible at center and the ruins of Theben/Devín to the left. Compared with the dynamic composition of the garden view, the palace here seems austere and isolated, its terraces functioning less as ornament than as ramparts, evoking a citadel. This martial quality was deliberate: Hildebrandt wrote to Count Aloys Thomas Harrach, then Viceroy of Naples, that he had shaped the terraces "to be secure in case of attack."[195] Bellotto's rendering crystallizes this dual identity—Schloss Hof as cultivated palace and frontier fortress, symbol of both retreat and vigilance on the Imperial borderlands.[196]

The series culminates with the *View of the Ruins of Theben/Devín*, conceived as a counterpart to the northern prospect of Schloss Hof but slightly smaller (fig. 64). Unlike the palatial views, it centers on a medieval fortress above the confluence of the March and Danube rivers, marking the former western border of the Hungarian kingdom. First established as a border fort before the year 1000, Devín came into Hungarian possession in 1414 and was expanded in the sixteenth and seventeenth centuries. Though besieged by the Ottomans in 1683, it held out, only to be blown up by French troops in 1809. The composition recalls Bellotto's Dresden landscapes, especially the views of Königstein, where a fortress likewise crowns a river valley beneath shifting skies.[197]

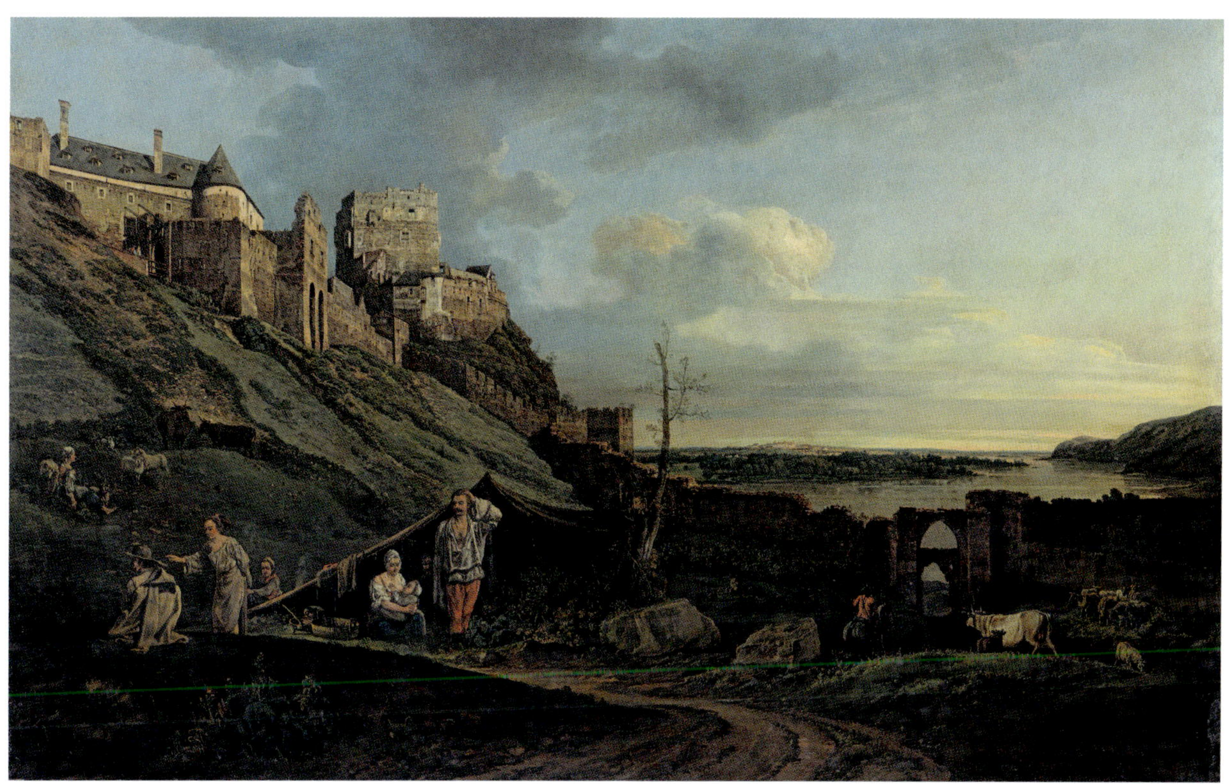

Fig. 64: Bernardo Bellotto, *View of the Ruins of Theben / Devín*, 1759 / 60, oil on canvas, 136 × 214 cm. Kunsthistorisches Museum, Vienna, Picture Gallery, inv. 1676

A diagonal rhythm organizes the Vienna canvas, punctuated by a bare central tree whose decrepit form echoes the ruin itself. The castle walls stretch along the ridge at left, their illuminated masonry silhouetted against storm clouds, while to the right the atmosphere clears over the plain. On the horizon, Schloss Hof reappears, reduced to a speck across the river.[198]

The foreground is animated by a destitute family before a makeshift tent, their figures prominently silhouetted against the dark ground. Earlier artists such as Nicolaes Berchem and Francesco Zuccarelli had shaped the convention of showing rustic families as carefree pastoral shepherds and peasants in their traditional *georgic* prints — cast in an idyllic, Arcadian light.[199] And while Bellotto appears to have copied the cow with calf from one of Zuccarelli's prints, his human group has none of the elegance or charm of Zuccarelli's figures.[200] Their block-like

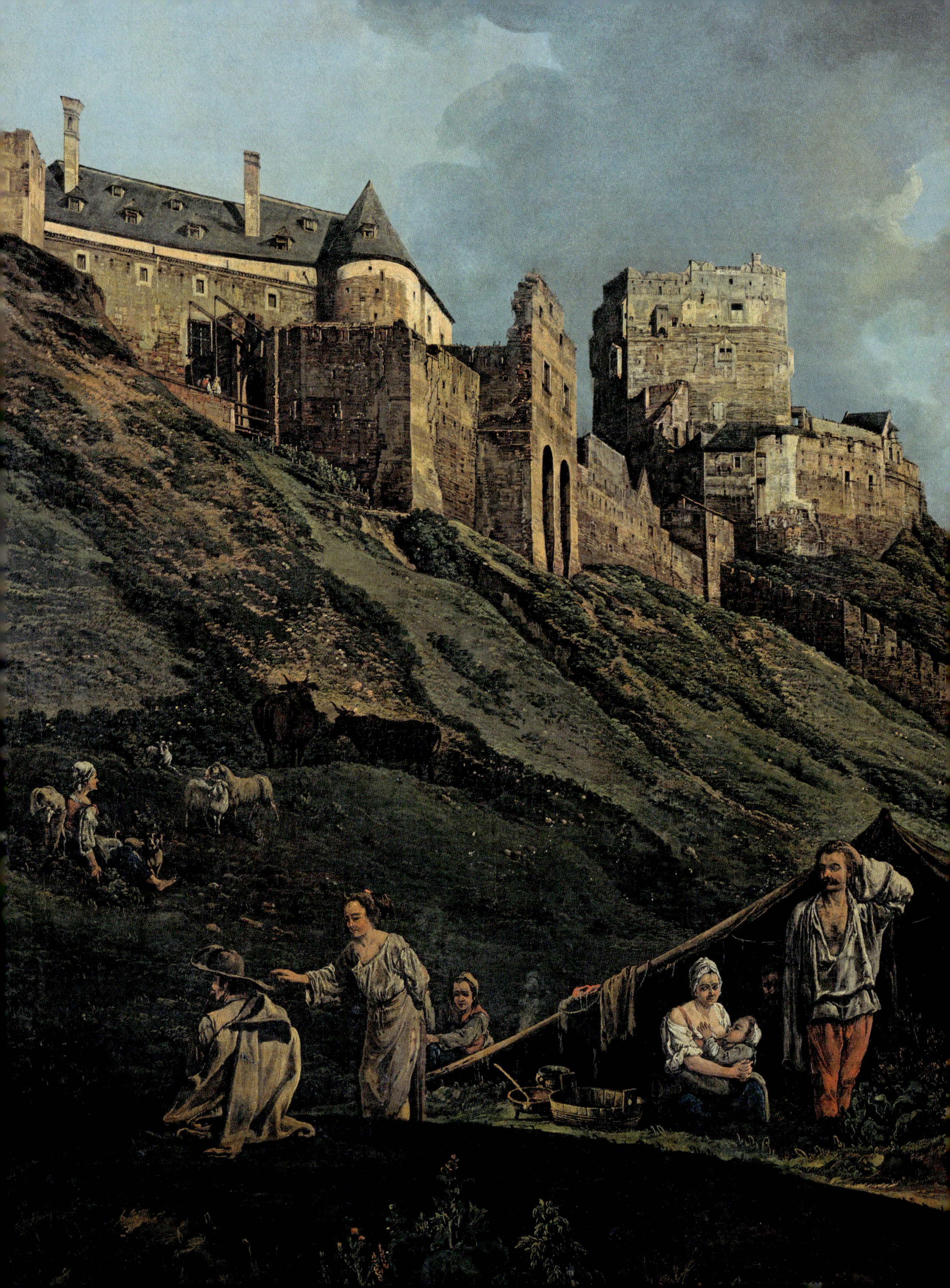

rendering and rough presence suggest direct observation, in line with the more realist detail he increasingly brought to his Viennese scenes, from busy marketplaces to aristocratic forecourts. Yet, unlike the typified staffage of Bellotto's urban *vedute*, these figures' scale and proximity command unusual presence. Scholars have long noted how, together with the dark tonality of the landscape, they contribute to the painting's melancholic effect, but have tended to interpret the group simply as "gypsies."[201] However, the man's body adds an unsettling detail: his right arm, hidden beneath his shirt, seems truncated. Might he perhaps be a disabled veteran; an oblique reminder of many a soldier's unemployment and poverty that Prince Eugene had once sought to mitigate by employing them on his estates? Whether or not Bellotto intended such a moralistic allusion directly, war, hardship, and suffering surely were on his mind when painting this picture.

Indeed, war had driven Bellotto from Dresden to Vienna. His family remained behind, his Saxon court income vanished, and he no doubt arrived in Vienna hoping for a court appointment—ultimately in vain. Despite the cycle's significance, its precise genesis remains unclear. The paintings were first securely documented only in 1781, in an inventory of Bratislava Castle, where Archduchess Marie Christine and Duke Albert of Saxe-Teschen resided as governors of Hungary before moving to Brussels.[202] This archival gap invites speculation. Perhaps Bellotto executed the cycle on direct commission from the Imperial couple, as is often assumed, though no contract survives. Perhaps he painted it speculatively as a gift for Maria Theresa, hoping to secure the coveted position of court painter. It is equally possible that intermediaries such as Kaunitz, Liechtenstein, or others acted as patrons and presented the works to the court. Whatever their precise origins, the canvases came to embody a curated vision of Vienna as "eternally prosperous and safe," to quote Martina Frank, as well as indelibly tied to the Habsburgs.[203] Yet, despite their importance, Bellotto failed to secure the position he sought, leaving him financially precarious, likely fearing a fate like the destitute family he placed before Devín.

Detail of fig. 64

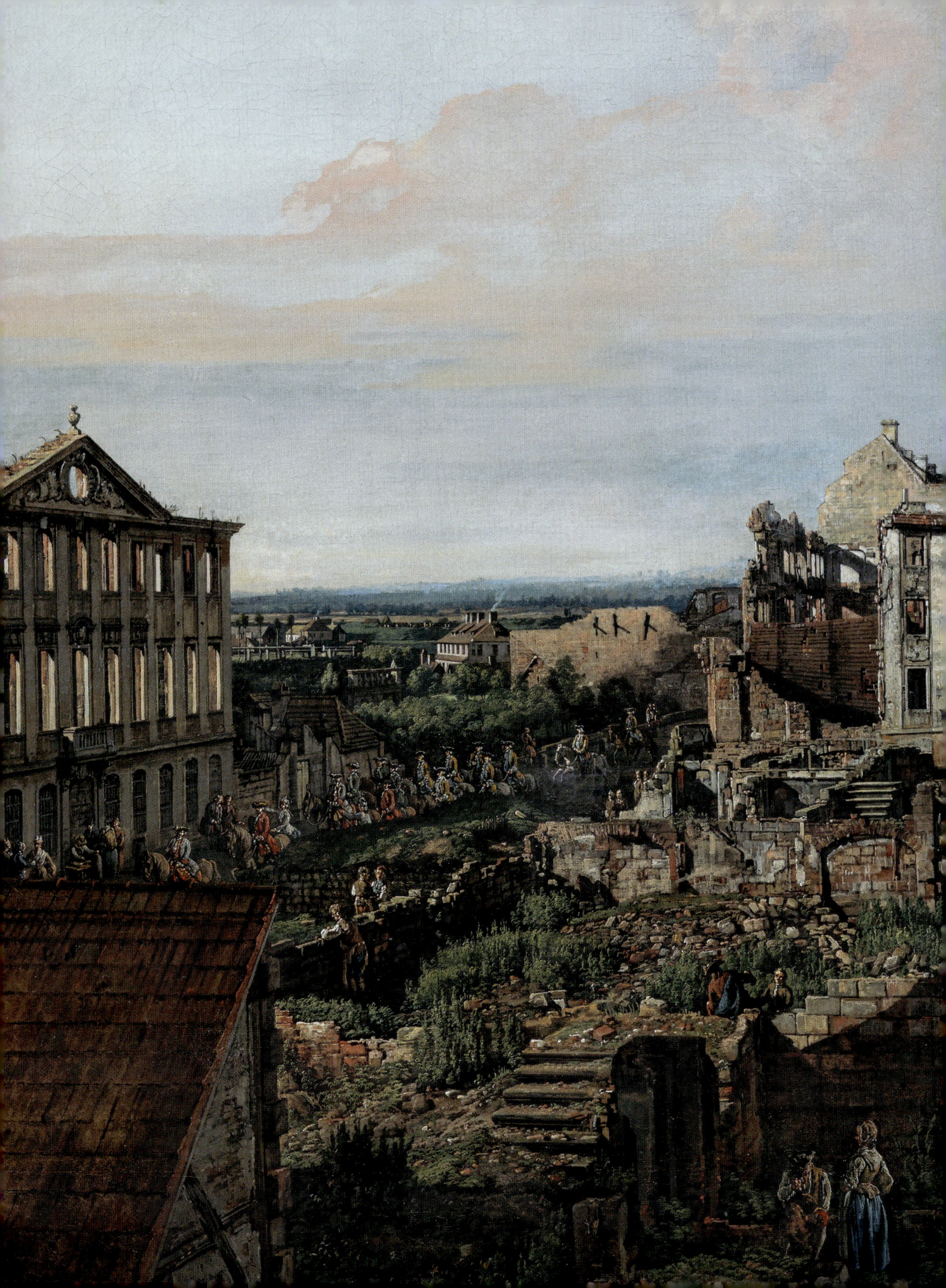

Postscript: Aftermath of War

In early 1761, Bellotto, realizing that his hopes for a salaried position in Vienna were futile, left for Munich. The Empress mentioned him only briefly—and somewhat laconically—in a letter to her cousin's daughter, Princess Maria Antonia of Bavaria (fig. 65): "Madam, my dear cousin, I could not let Canaletti [=Bellotto] leave without entrusting him with these few lines and recommending him to you; he behaved very well here and provided us with several pieces of his work, which are very beautiful. I envy him for getting to see you—perhaps eight months before I do."[204] The letter then turns to New Year's wishes and updates about Saxon relatives at the Viennese court, so that Bellotto appears almost in passing—less as a formal endorsement than as a polite aside. Married to Friedrich Christian of Saxony, Maria Antonia had relocated from Dresden to Munich in 1759, where, during the war, she and her husband found refuge at the court of her brother, Elector Maximilian III Joseph. As mentioned, Bellotto may have known Friedrich Christian since his Grand Tour and probably hoped this connection might lead to commissions at

Maximilian's court. Although he did indeed paint three canvases, his Munich stay was short-lived: by the end of 1761 or early 1762, he departed once more for Dresden, returning to a city severely scarred by the Seven Years' War.[205]

In Dresden, while reunited with his family in good health, Bellotto confronted devastation. In a 1762 inventory, listing the contents of his residence in the Salzgasse (his furnishings, library, and artworks, as well as his portable artistic equipment such as prints, copperplates, and accumulated drawings), he recorded losses estimated at 50,000 thalers.[206] Having packed these belongings into crates before leaving in 1758 and entrusting them to neighbors, he found them destroyed upon his return. Beyond material loss, Bellotto faced profound professional uncertainty. The situation worsened with the deaths, in 1763, of his principal

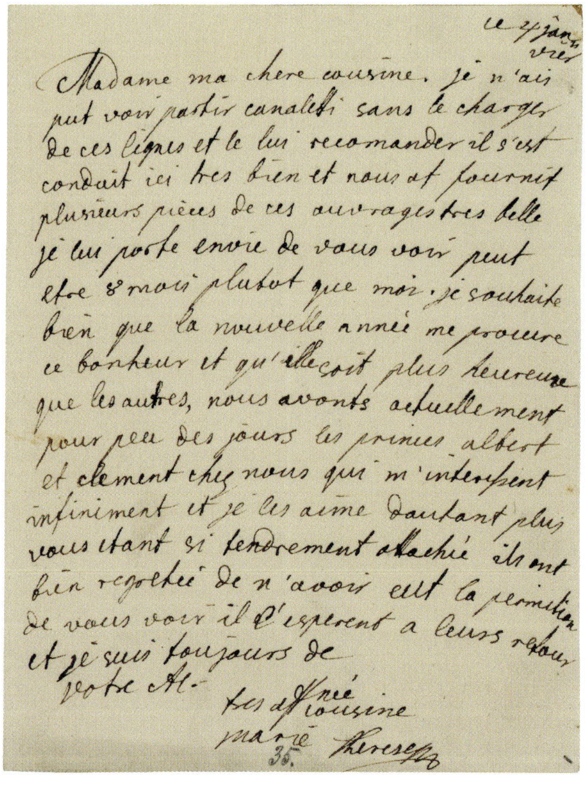

Fig. 65: Empress Maria Theresia to Maria Antonia of Bavaria, Electoral Princess of Saxony, on 4 January 1761, pen and ink on paper, 149 × 197 mm. Sächsisches Staatsarchiv, Hauptstaatsarchiv Dresden, 12528 Estate of Maria Antonia, Electress of Saxony, No. 104, letter No. 35

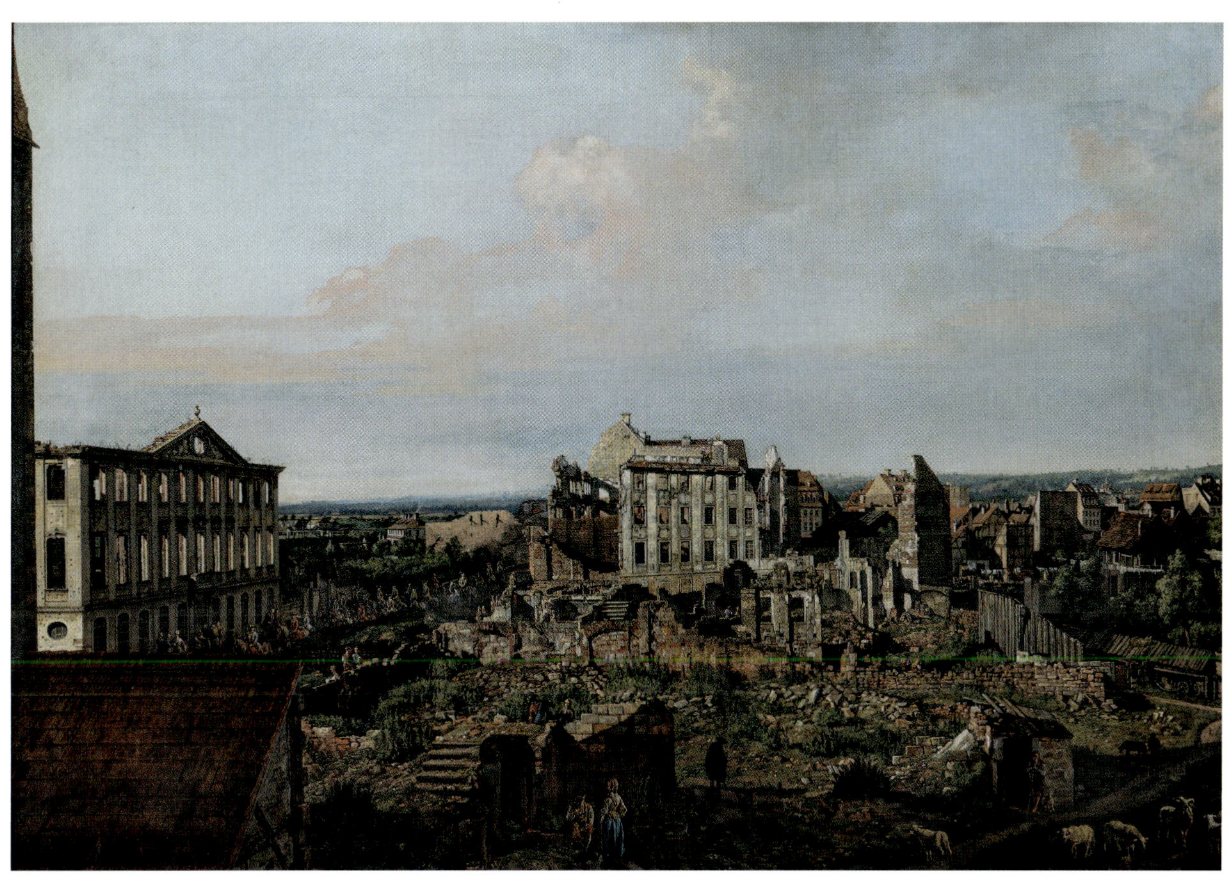

Fig. 66: Bernardo Bellotto, *The Ruins of the Pirna Suburb in Dresden*, 1762/67, oil on canvas, 80.5 × 113 cm. Musée des Beaux-Arts et d'Archéologie, Troyes, inv. 850.1.4

patrons King Augustus III and Count Brühl, followed by the death of the new elector, Friedrich Christian. Friedrich Christian's widow, Maria Antonia of Bavaria, and his brother Franz Xavier took over regency on behalf of the minor heir Friedrich Augustus III. The regents instituted drastic economies across all areas of court and state administration, a climate that, despite the peace treaty of Hubertusburg of February 1763, left the electorate economically depleted, with little scope for lavish artistic patronage.[207]

Despite (or perhaps because of) such hardship, Bellotto produced an unorthodox *veduta* of the ruined city—widely read as a personal response to wartime catastrophe: *The Ruins of the Pirna Suburb in Dresden* (fig. 66). Painted sometime between 1762

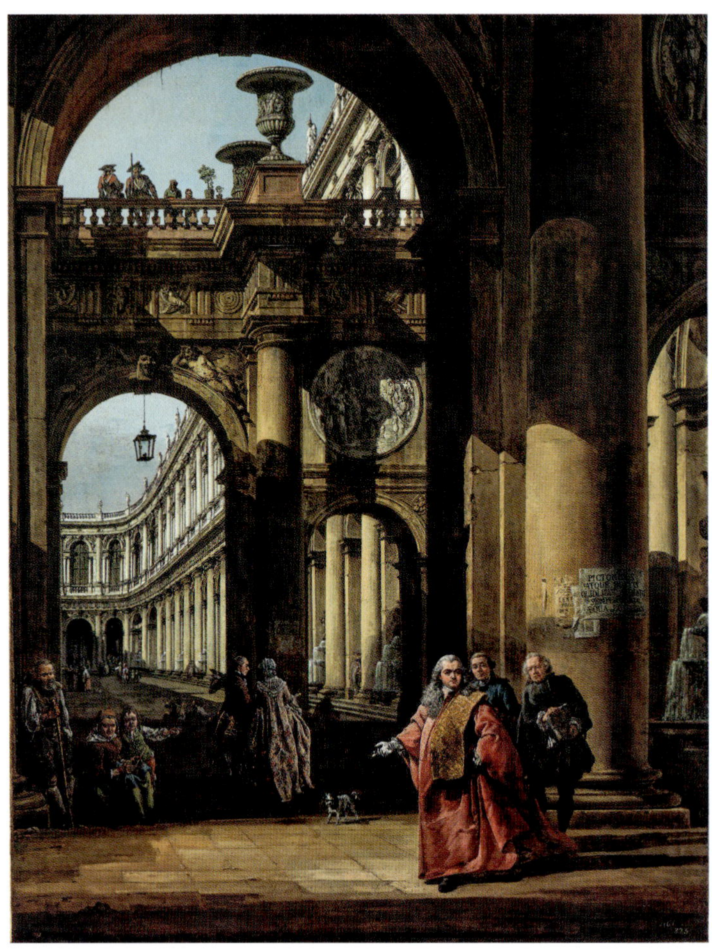

Fig. 67: Bernardo Bellotto, *Architectural Capriccio with Self-Portrait of the Artist in the Robes of a Venetian Nobleman*, c.1765, oil on canvas, 153 × 114 cm. The Royal Castle in Warsaw – Museum, inv. ZKW 3537

and 1767, the painting conveys not only the physical destruction wrought by Prussian canons, but also devastating emotional and cultural loss.[208] At left, the charred façade of the Fürstenhof palace looms over a district reduced to rubble, while unsettling notes of pastoral calm — overgrown vegetation, grazing sheep, and a shepherd in the foreground — suggest nature's quiet persistence amidst human catastrophe. A formally dressed equestrian group to the left, presumably representing the regents Maria Antonia and Franz Xavier, surveys the scene, highlighting Dresden's monumental task of rebuilding. At once a personal reckoning and a reflection on the wider toll of war, Bellotto's composition transcends documentation, transforming destruction into a meditation on resilience, renewal, and the passage of time.

Yet even as Bellotto transformed destruction into artistic reflection, institutional developments compounded his difficulties. In 1764, the directorship of Dresden's newly founded Academy of Arts passed to Christian Ludwig von Hagedorn. As a close associate of Johann Joachim Winckelmann and champion of classicist ideals, Hagedorn not only openly favored native-born artists over foreign painters but also dismissed Bellotto's *vedute* as decorative furnishings, unworthy of the gallery's collection.[209] Bellotto, despite his reputation, was relegated to teaching introductory courses in perspective, with his annual salary reduced to 600 thalers, barely a third of what he had once earned at court. Financial strain was heightened by creditors' demands, leaving the former court painter dependent on private commissions and teaching. His son Lorenzo assisted him as interpreter in the classroom, since Bellotto spoke no German, but soon caused embarrassment: accused of an affair with the daughter of an electoral forester, Lorenzo left his father legally bound to pay alimony for an illegitimate child.[210]

Amidst such ruin, Bellotto painted an architectural fantasy with a Venetian nobleman (fig. 67). Made around 1765, it is one of his most enigmatic capriccios. At once a technical tour de force and a declaration of artistic independence, it fuses imagined architecture with striking perspectival rigor, transforming imagined arcades into a vast stage. At the center, a red-cloaked figure in the ceremonial robes of a Venetian *procuratore* gestures leftward. Though this figure has often been identified as Bellotto himself, such claims remain uncertain. The robes marked one of the Republic's most prestigious offices, second only to the Doge, and it seems improbable that Bellotto would be so audacious. More plausibly, the figure functions as an *alter ego*: just as the *procuratori de supra* oversaw the built fabric of Venice, Bellotto asserts mastery over the architecture of his imagination.[211]

Theatricality underscores this claim. The elegant, foreshortened architecture resembles a stage set, dramatized by sharp contrasts of light and shadow, with its columns plastered with playbills. On one, Bellotto inscribed a line from Horace's

Ars poetica: "Pictoribus atque poetis quidlibet audendi semper fuit aequa potestas," or "Painters and poets have always enjoyed an equal freedom to dare anything." In Dresden, where Hagedorn had demoted him to teaching perspective and dismissed his *vedute* as decorative trifles, this citation reads as defiance. Perspective, reduced by Hagedorn to a mechanical drill, here becomes scaffolding for invention. Essentially, Bellotto presents himself not as a craftsman bound to accuracy, but as an artist free to imagine. He thus seems to address the old prejudice we already encountered when discussing Zanetti's caricature of Marieschi (fig. 12).

Detail of fig. 67

Bellotto's painting also anticipates a new chapter. At the end of 1766, he requested leave to travel to St. Petersburg, but instead disembarked in Warsaw in early 1767 at the court of Stanisław II August Poniatowski, last monarch of the Polish–Lithuanian Commonwealth.[212] By 1768 he had entered the king's service as court painter and settled permanently in Warsaw with his family. He likely took *Architectural Capriccio*, of which three versions in the same format exist, with him to Poland, perhaps intended as a demonstration piece for the royal gallery. More than a display of virtuosity, the work articulates a claim to artistic autonomy at a moment of personal and professional precarity. In this sense, it forms an apt epilogue to Bellotto's hardship years — transforming the constraints of an itinerant *vedutista* into an affirmation of invention, pointing toward the new opportunities that awaited him in Warsaw, where he would once again become court painter and devote the remainder of his career to painting the city's urban fabric until his death in 1780.[213]

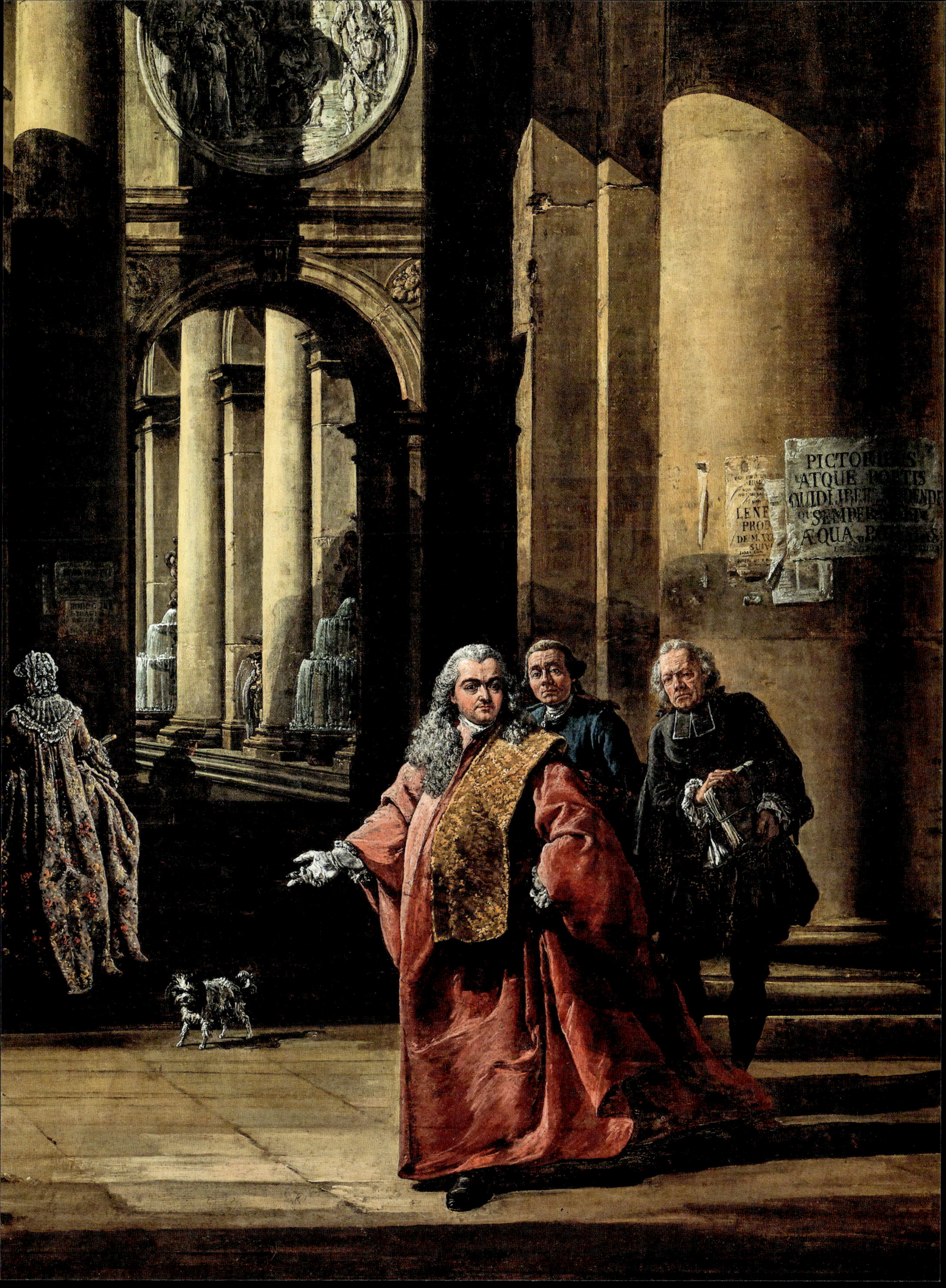
ATQUE
SEMPER
ÆQUA

List of Works

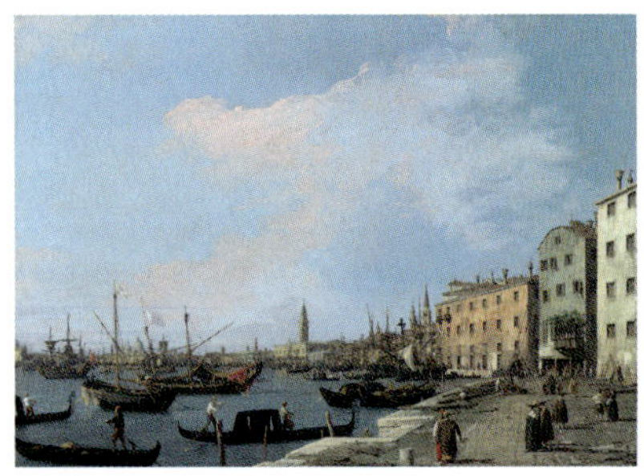

Cat. 1 | Fig. 1

Canaletto
The Riva degli Schiavoni in Venice
c.1730

Oil on canvas, 46 × 63 cm
Kunsthistorisches Museum, Vienna, Picture Gallery, inv. 6332
Provenance: Earlier suggestions localizing the painting in the collections of Consul Joseph Smith (c.1682–1770), the Princes of Liechtenstein, or Girolamo Manfrin (1742–1801) remain unverified. By 1859 in the collection of Count Sámuel Festetics de Tolna (1806–1862), Vienna; 1859–1872 in the collection of Friedrich Jakob Gsell (1812–1871), Vienna; auctioned at Georg Plach, Vienna, 1872, lot. 146b; by 1902 with Josefine Brüll (1839–1926), Vienna; in 1918 acquired from the collection of Stefan Auspitz von Artenegg (1869–1945) for the Imperial Gallery

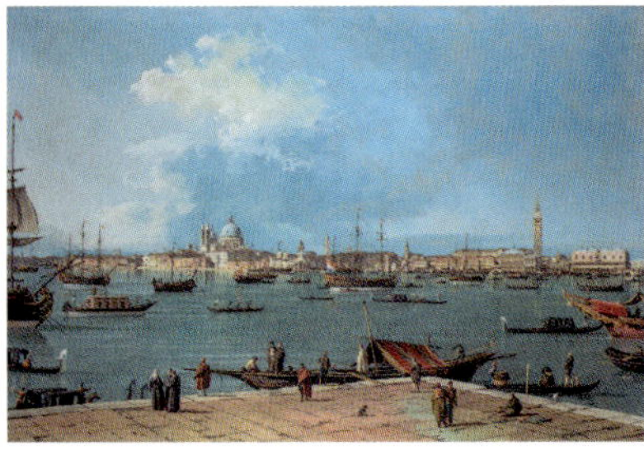

Cat. 2 | Fig. 4

Canaletto
Venice: The Bacino di San Marco from San Giorgio Maggiore
1735/44

Oil on canvas, 129,2 × 188,9 cm
The Wallace Collection, London, inv. P497
Provenance: Presumably commissioned by Francis Seymour-Conway, 1st Marquess of Hertford (1719–1794), during his Grand Tour 1737–1740; by descent to Francis Ingram Seymour-Conway, 2nd Marquess of Hertford (1743–1822); by descent to Francis Charles Seymour-Conway, 3rd Marquess of Hertford (1777–1842); by descent to Richard Seymour-Conway, 4th Marquess of Hertford (1800–1870); by descent to Sir Richard Wallace, 1st Baronet (1818–1890); by descent to his wife Julie Amélie Charlotte Castelnau, Lady Wallace (1819–1897); 1897 bequeathed to the British nation

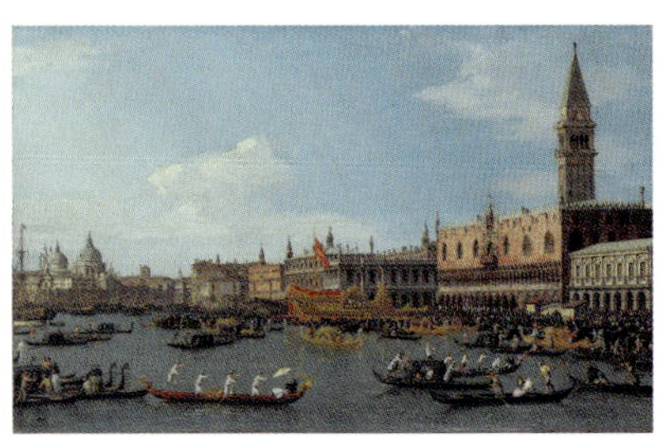

Cat. 3 | Fig. 5

Canaletto
The Bucintoro
1745/50

Oil on canvas, 57 × 93 cm
Museu Nacional d'Art de Catalunya, Barcelona (Thyssen-Bornemisza Collection on deposit at the MNAC, 2004), inv. 212851
Provenance: Probably in the collection of Henry Reveley (c.1788–1875), Bryn, Wales (?); by 1876 in the collection of Hugh John Reveley (1812–1889), Wales; later with Mrs A. L. Snapper, London; auctioned at Sotheby's, London, 14 June 1961, lot 52; on the market with Agnew's, London; 1962 in the Thyssen-Bornemisza Collection, Lugano; 1992 on deposit at the Museo Nacional Thyssen-Bornemisza, Madrid; acquired by the Museo Nacional Thyssen-Bornemisza, Madrid, in 1993

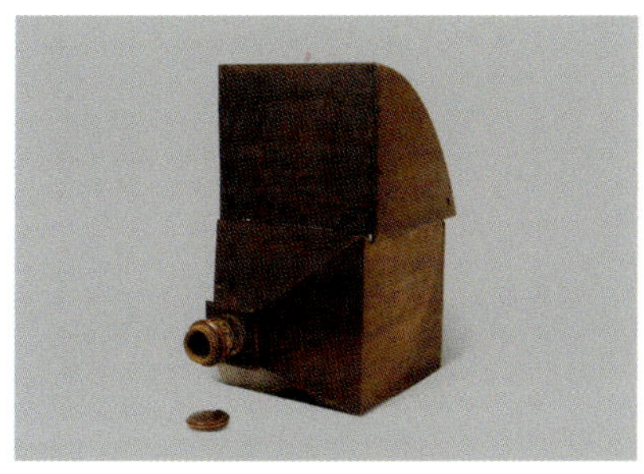

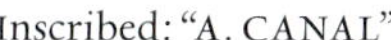

Cat. 4

Canaletto
Camera obscura
18th century

Inscribed: "A. CANAL"
Scientific instrument in wood, glass, and mirror, opened: 40 × 22,5 × 40 cm; closed: 22,5 × 22,5 × 40 cm
Fondazione Musei Civici di Venezia, Museo Correr, Venice, inv. CI. XXIX s.n. 30
Provenance: Donated by Luigi Vason to the Museo Correr in 1901

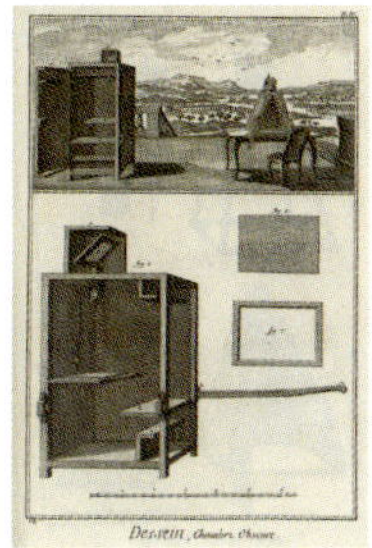

Cat. 5 | Fig. 8

Denis Diderot
Encyclopédie, ou dictionnaire raisonné des sciences, des arts et des métiers
Paris, 1770/79

Austrian National Library, Vienna, 56.Q.1.(Vol.Planches,3), Pl. 4, Dessein, Chambre Obscure

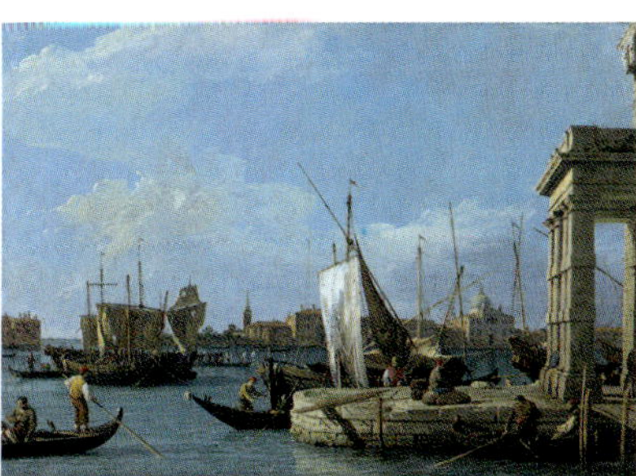

Cat. 6 | Fig. 10

Canaletto
The Dogana in Venice
c.1730

Oil on canvas, 45,8 × 63,4 cm
Kunsthistorisches Museum, Vienna, Picture Gallery, inv. 6331
Provenance: Earlier suggestions localizing the painting in the collections of Consul Joseph Smith (c.1682–1770), the Princes of Liechtenstein, or Girolamo Manfrin (1742–1801) remain unverified. By 1859 in the collection of Count Sámuel Festetics de Tolna (1806–1862), Vienna; 1859–1872 in the collection of Friedrich Jakob Gsell (1812–1871), Vienna; auctioned at Georg Plach, Vienna, 1872, lot. 146a; by 1902 with Josefine Brüll (1839–1926), Vienna; in 1918 acquired from the collection of Stefan Auspitz von Artenegg (1869–1945) for the Imperial Gallery

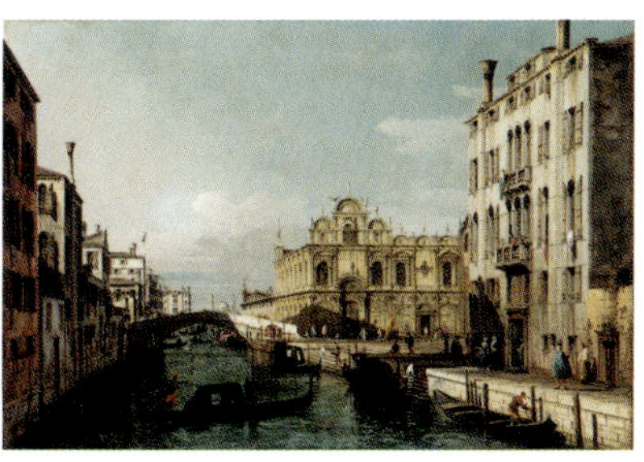

Cat. 7 | Fig. 14

Bellotto
The Rio dei Mendicanti and the Scuola di San Marco
c.1740

Oil on canvas, 41 × 59 cm
Gallerie dell'Accademia, Venice, inv. 494
Provenance: Before 1794 in the collection of Girolamo Manfrin (1742–1801), Venice; by descent to his son Pietro Manfrin († 1833); by descent to his sister Giulia Angela Giovanna Manfrin († 1848); by descent to her children Antonio Maria and Bortolina Plattis; acquired by the Gallerie dell'Accademia, Venice, in 1856

Cat. 8 | Fig. 15

Bellotto
View of the Grand Canal with the Palazzi Foscari and Moro Lin
c.1740

Oil on canvas, 101 × 162 cm
Nationalmuseum, Stockholm, inv. NM 49
Provenance: By 1792 in the collection of King Gustav III (1746–1792); transferred to the Royal Museum (today the Nationalmuseum), Stockholm, in 1865

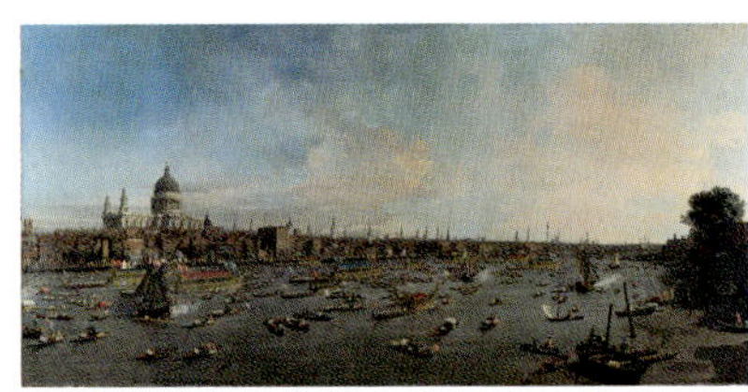

Cat. 9 | Fig. 18

Canaletto
London: The River Thames on Lord Mayor's Day
c.1748

Oil on canvas, 118,5 × 237,5 cm
The Lobkowicz Collections, Prague
Provenance: Believed to have been acquired sometime after 1745 by Ferdinand Philip, 6th Prince Lobkowicz (1724–1784), during or following his visit to England; recorded at Roudnice Castle in 1752; by descent to the present owner

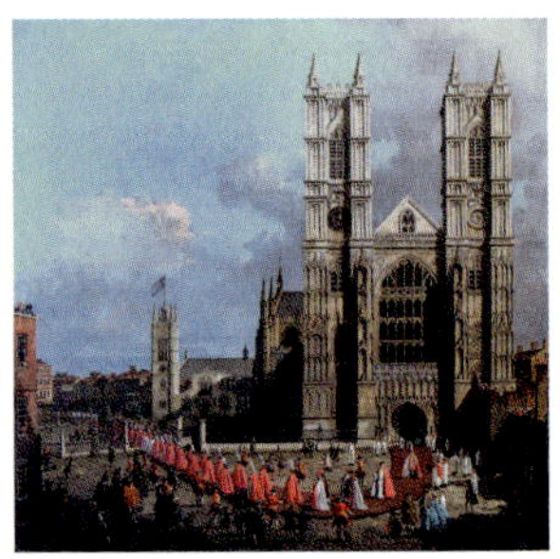

Cat. 10 | Fig. 19

Canaletto
Westminster Abbey with a Procession of the Knights of the Bath
1749

Oil on canvas, 99 × 101.5 cm
The Dean and Chapter of Westminster, London
Provenance: Probably commissioned by Joseph Wilcocks (1673–1756), Dean of Westminster 1731–1756; by descent to his son Joseph Wilcocks jun. (1724–1791); by whom bequeathed to Westminster Abbey in 1791

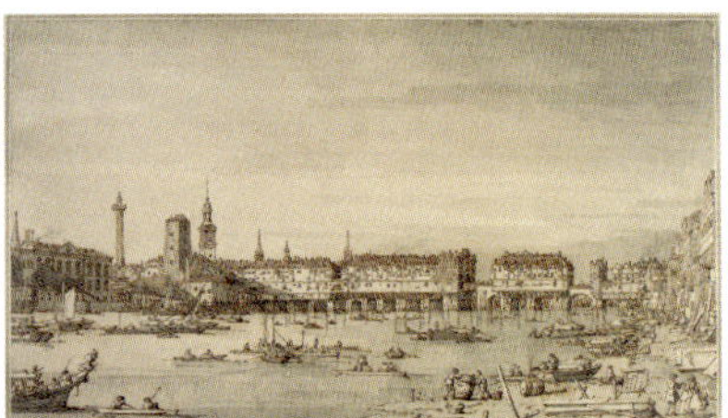

Cat. 11 | Fig. 21

Canaletto
Old London Bridge
1746/52

Pen and brown ink, with grey wash, over ruled black chalk lines, 307 × 539 mm
The British Museum, London, inv. 1909,0406.4
Provenance: (Possibly) sale of 1766 (sold for 3 guineas); by the late nineteenth or early twentieth century in the collection of John Calthorpe Blofeld (1874–1920); acquired from him by the British Museum in 1909

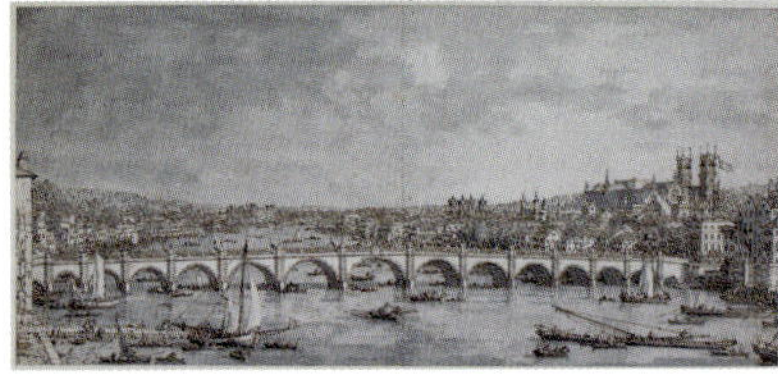

Cat. 12 | Fig. 23

Canaletto
View of the River Thames and Westminster Bridge from the North
c.1750

Pen and brown ink, with grey wash, over ruled black chalk lines, 345 × 738 mm
The British Museum, London, inv. 1868,0328.306
Provenance: With Colnaghi, London, from whom purchased by the British Museum in 1868

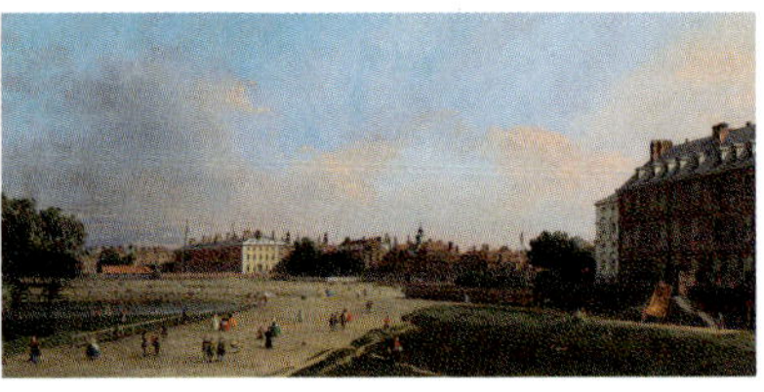

Cat. 13 | Fig. 25

Canaletto
London: The Old Horse Guards from St. James's Park
c.1749

Oil on canvas, 117.2 × 236.1 cm
Tate, lent by the Andrew Lloyd Webber Foundation, UK
Provenance: By 1756 in the collection of John Roberts, 4th Earl of Radnor, Cross Deep, Twickenham, Middlesex; bequeathed in 1757 to James Harris, MP; thereafter by descent in the family of the Earls of Malmesbury; acquired for the Andrew Lloyd Webber Foundation in 1992; on long-term loan to Tate since 2000

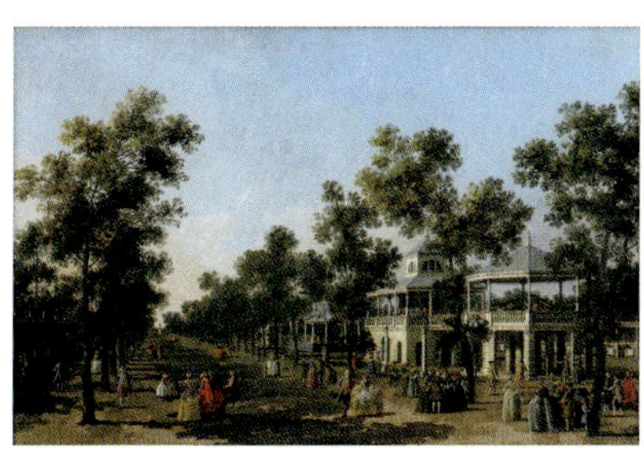

CAT. 14 | FIG. 26

CANALETTO
The Grand Walk, Vauxhall Gardens
c.1751

Oil on canvas, 70 × 96 cm
Compton Verney, UK, inv. 0355.S
Provenance: Believed originally in the collection of the Wellesley family; by descent to Charles Edward Hill-Trevor, 3rd Baron Trevor (1863–1950); by descent within the Trevor family; sold 9 July 1999, Christie's, London, lot 84, to David Robert Graham; donated 2006 to the Cable Trust; sold 8 June 2006 to the Peter Moores Foundation (subsequently Compton Verney Collections Settlement), Compton Verney, UK

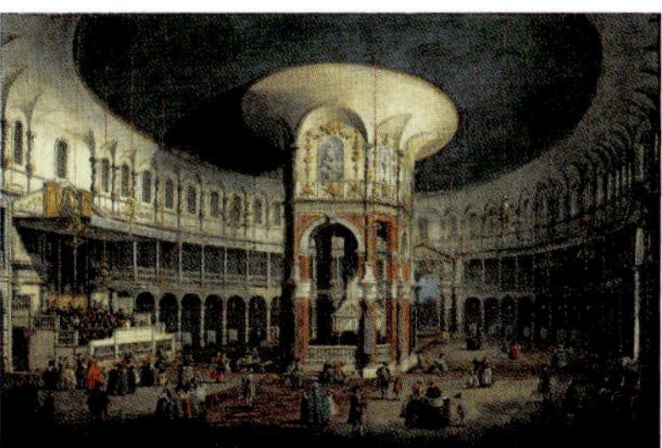

CAT. 15 | FIG. 27

CANALETTO
The Interior of the Rotunda, Ranelagh
c.1751

Oil on canvas, 70 × 96 cm
Compton Verney, UK, inv. 0356.S
Provenance: Believed originally in the collection of the Wellesley family; by descent to Charles Edward Hill-Trevor, 3rd Baron Trevor (1863–1950); by descent within the Trevor family; sold 9 July 1999, Christie's, London, lot 84, to David Robert Graham; donated 2006 to the Cable Trust; sold 8 June 2006 to the Peter Moores Foundation (subsequently Compton Verney Collections Settlement), Compton Verney, UK

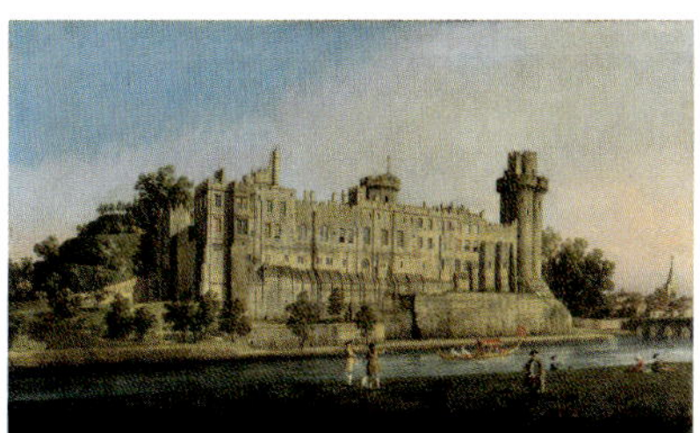

CAT. 16 | FIG. 28

CANALETTO
The South Façade of Warwick Castle
1748

Oil on canvas, 75 × 120,5 cm
Museo Nacional Thyssen-Bornemisza, Madrid, inv. 78 (1978.13)
Provenance: In the collection of Francis Greville, 1st Earl of Warwick (1719–1773), London; by descent to George Greville, 2nd Earl of Warwick (1746–1816), London; by descent to Henry Greville, 3rd Earl of Warwick (1779–1853), London; from 1846 in the Greville Collection, Warwick Castle; 1978 with Malborough, London; 1978 in the Thyssen-Bornemisza Collection, Lugano; 1992 on deposit at the MuseoNacional Thyssen-Bornemisza, Madrid; acquired by the Museo Nacional Thyssen-Bornemisza, Madrid, in 1993

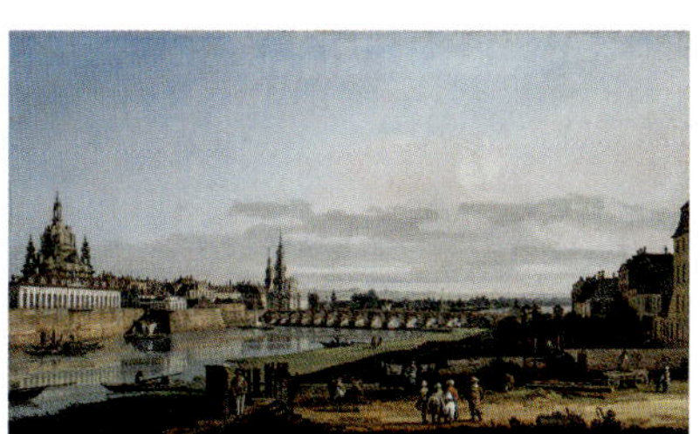

CAT. 17

BELLOTTO
Dresden from the Right Bank of the Elbe, above the Augustus Bridge
c.1750

Oil on canvas, 51.5 × 84 cm
National Gallery of Ireland, Dublin, inv. 181
Provenance: In the collection of M. B. Naryschkin; auctioned in Paris, 1883; acquired there by the National Gallery of Ireland, Dublin

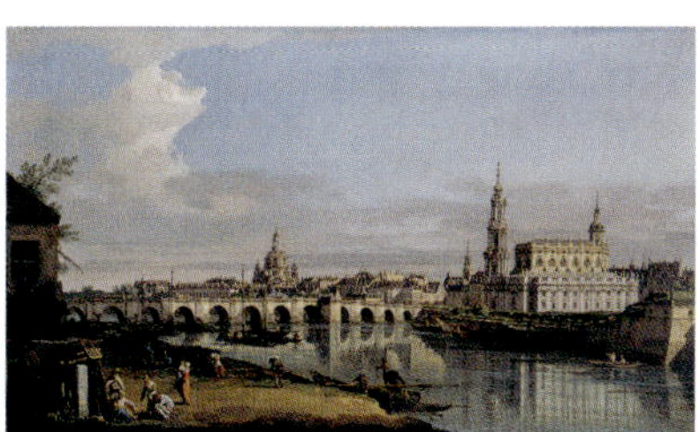

CAT. 18 | FIG. 31

BELLOTTO
Dresden from the Right Bank of the Elbe, below the Augustus Bridge
c.1750

Oil on canvas, 51,5 × 84 cm
National Gallery of Ireland, Dublin, inv. 182
Provenance: In the collection of M. B. Naryschkin; auctioned in Paris, 1883; acquired there by the National Gallery of Ireland, Dublin

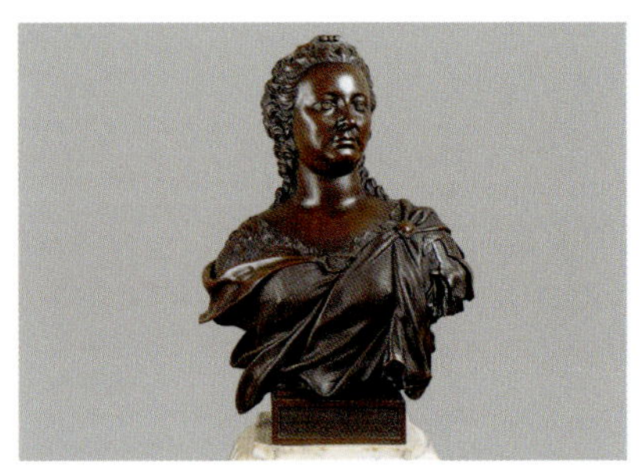

CAT. 19

MATTHÄUS DONNER
Empress
Maria Theresia
1750

Signed: "M. Donner, Fecit. 1750"
Inscription: "MAR(IA). THERESIA. AVSTR(IACA). REG(INA). AVG(VSTA). ANTIQVIT(ATIS). HONORE. REST(ITVTO). IVNO. MON(ETA)."
Bronze, H. 68 cm
Kunsthistorisches Museum, Vienna, Kunstkammer, inv. KK 6142
Provenance: Made for a cabinet of the Treasury in the Hofburg in 1750

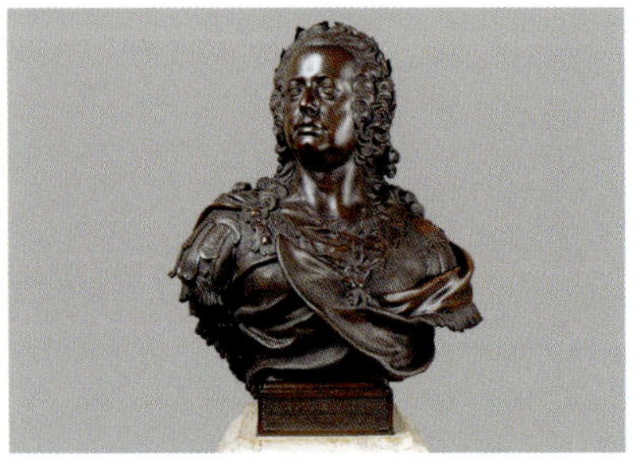

CAT. 20

MATTHÄUS DONNER
Emperor
Francis I Stephen
1750

Signed: "M. Donner, Fecit. 1750"
Inscription: "FRANCISCVS. LOTHARING(VS). IMP(ERATOR). P(IVS). F(ELIX). AVG(VSTVS). AMPLIATO. NVM(MORVM). THESAVRO. APOLLO. MON(ETARIVS)."
Bronze, H. 69 cm
Kunsthistorisches Museum, Vienna, Kunstkammer, inv. KK 6143
Provenance: Made for a cabinet of the Treasury in the Hofburg in 1750

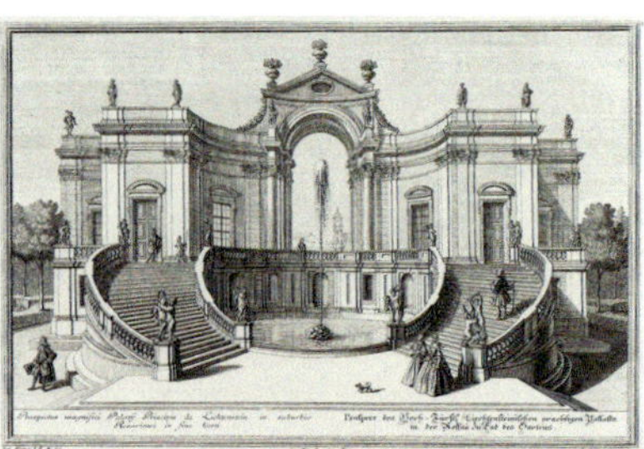

CAT. 21

SALOMON KLEINER
The Belvedere in the Gardens of the Liechtenstein Palace in the Rossau Quarter
1737

Engraving, 333 × 470 mm
LIECHTENSTEIN. The Princely Collections, Vaduz–Vienna, inv. GR 2194
Provenance: Acquired in 1982 by Prince Franz Josef II von und zu Liechtenstein (1906–1989)

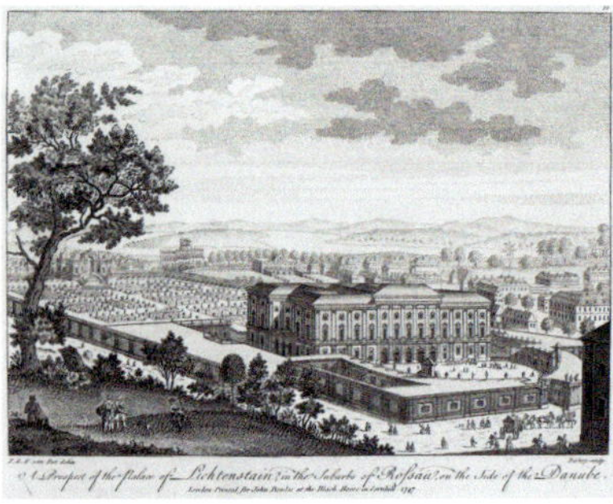

CAT. 22

BISHOP after JOSEPH EMANUEL FISCHER VON ERLACH
The Liechtenstein Garden Palace in the Rossau Quarter, with the Park and the Belvedere
1747

Engraving, 241 × 364 mm
LIECHTENSTEIN. The Princely Collections, Vaduz–Vienna, inv. GR 3167
Provenance: Historical family property

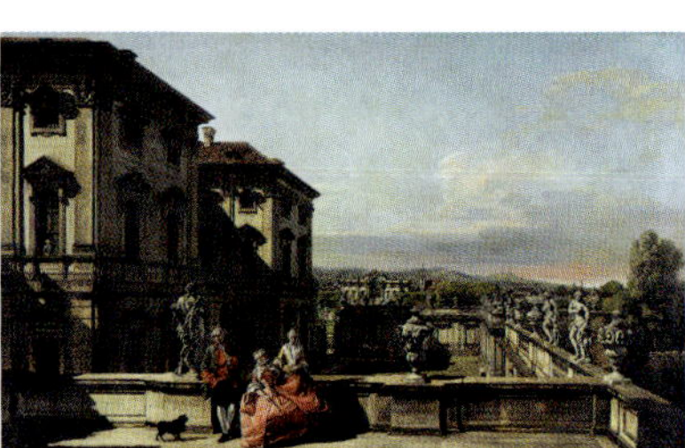

CAT. 23 | FIG. 33

BELLOTTO
The Liechtenstein Garden Palace in Vienna, seen from the East
1759/60

Oil on canvas, 99,7 × 159,6 cm
LIECHTENSTEIN. The Princely Collections, Vaduz–Vienna, inv. GE 887
Provenance: Acquired in 1759/60 by Prince Joseph Wenzel I von Liechtenstein (1696–1772) on commission from the artist

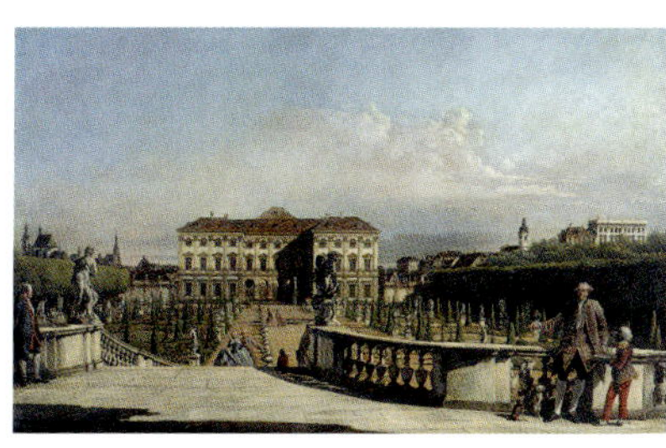

Cat. 24 | Fig. 34

Bellotto
The Liechtenstein Garden Palace in Vienna, seen from the Belvedere
1759/60

Oil on canvas, 99,8 × 158,5 cm
LIECHTENSTEIN. The Princely Collections, Vaduz–Vienna, inv. GE 889
Provenance: Acquired in 1759/60 by Prince Joseph Wenzel I von Liechtenstein (1696–1772) on commission from the artist

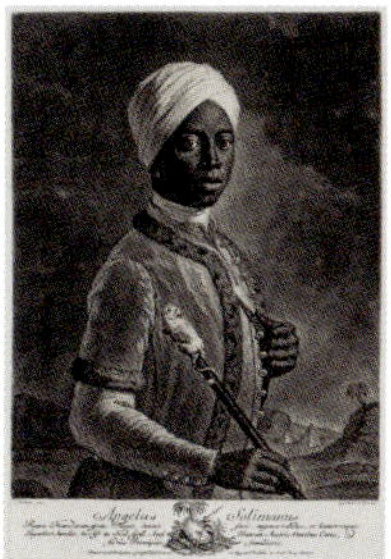

Cat. 25 | Fig. 35

Johann Gottfried Haid after Johann Nepomuk Steiner
Angelus Solimanus
1760/65

Mezzotint, 500 × 370 mm
LIECHTENSTEIN. The Princely Collections, Vaduz–Vienna, inv. GR 715
Provenance: Acquired in 1979 by Prince Hans-Adam II von und zu Liechtenstein (b. 1945)

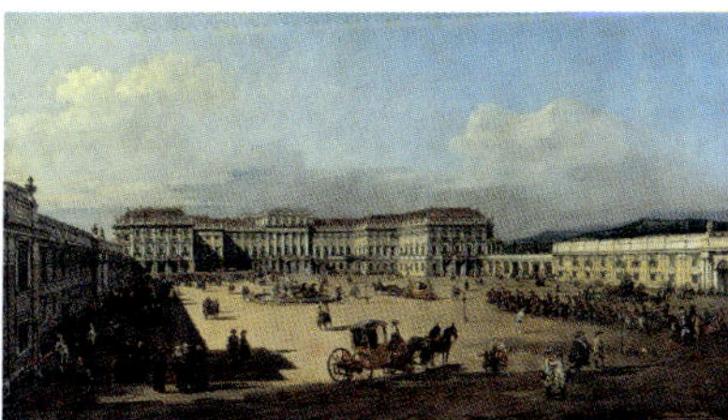

Cat. 26 | Fig. 36

Bellotto
View of Schönbrunn from the Forecourt
1759/60

Inscription: "XVI. Augusti. Anno M.D.C.C.LIX Prusso caeso ad Francofurtum ab exercitu Russo-Austriaco"
Oil on canvas, 135 × 235 cm
Kunsthistorisches Museum, Vienna, Picture Gallery, inv. 1666
Provenance: Recorded in the Pressburg inventory of 1781, No. 10 Billiard Zimmer, No. 42; since 1822 in Laxenburg Palace; by 1878 in the Hofburg, Vienna (Obersthofmeisteramt); on display in the Gemäldegalerie, Vienna, from 1891

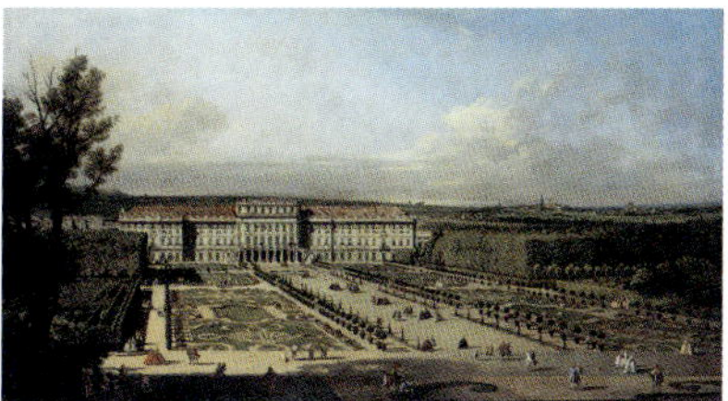

Cat. 27 | Fig. 37

Bellotto
View of Schönbrunn from the Gardens
1759/60

Oil on canvas, 134 × 238 cm
Kunsthistorisches Museum, Vienna, Picture Gallery, inv. 1667
Provenance: Recorded in the Pressburg inventory of 1781, No. 10 Billiard Zimmer, No. 43; since 1822 in Laxenburg Palace; by 1878 in the Hofburg, Vienna (Obersthofmeisteramt); on display in the Gemäldegalerie, Vienna, from 1891

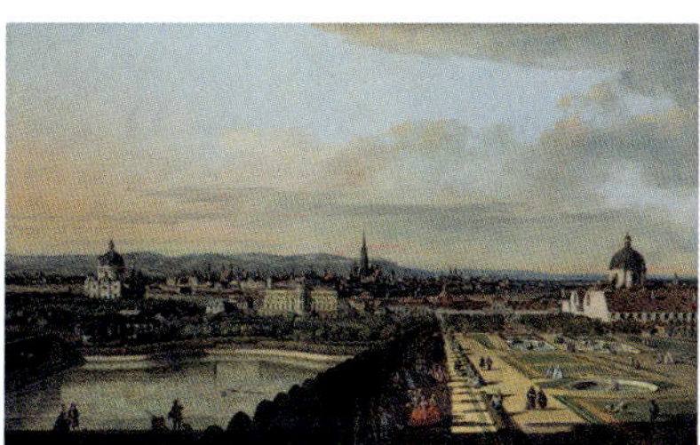

Cat. 28 | Fig. 38

Bellotto
View of Vienna from the Belvedere
1759/60

Oil on canvas, 135 × 213 cm
Kunsthistorisches Museum, Vienna, Picture Gallery, inv. 1669
Provenance: Recorded in the Pressburg inventory of 1781, No. 10 Billiard Zimmer, No. 41; since 1822 in Laxenburg Palace; by 1878 in the Hofburg, Vienna (Obersthofmeisteramt); on display in the Gemäldegalerie, Vienna, from 1891

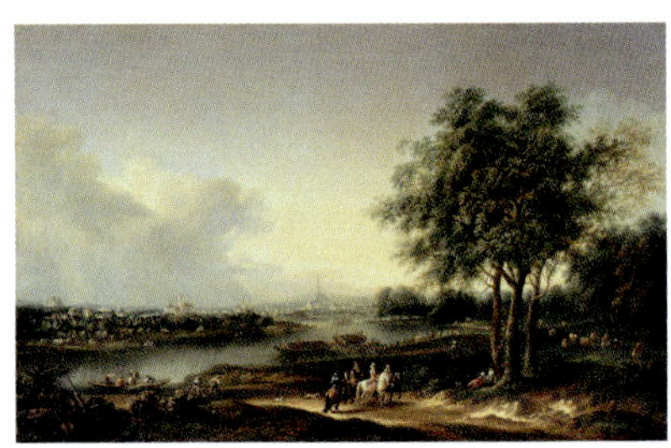

Cat. 29 | Fig. 39

Josef Heideloff
View of Vienna from the Prater
c.1781

Oil on canvas, 85.6 × 134.6 cm
Acadamy of Fine Arts, Vienna, Picture Gallery, inv. 152
Provenance: Admission Piece, 1801

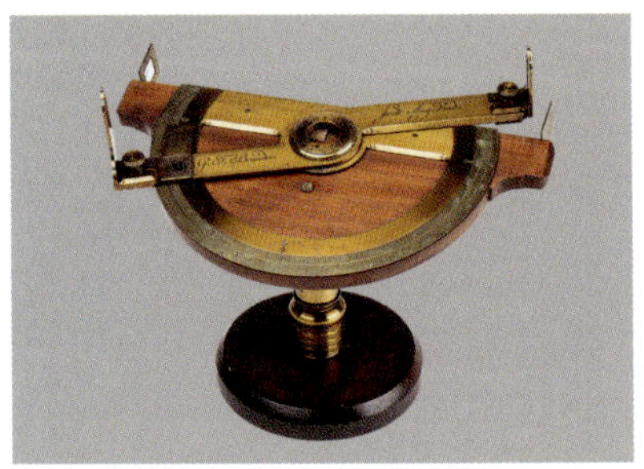

Cat. 30

Georg Friedrich Brander
Graphometer
Augsburg, 1750/80

Wood, brass, 25 × 23 × 20.5 cm
Technisches Museum Wien, inv. 18560
Provenance: Transferred in 1915 as a loan from the Imperial and Royal German Technical University in Prague to the Museum of Technology for Industry and Trade (today the Technisches Museum Wien)

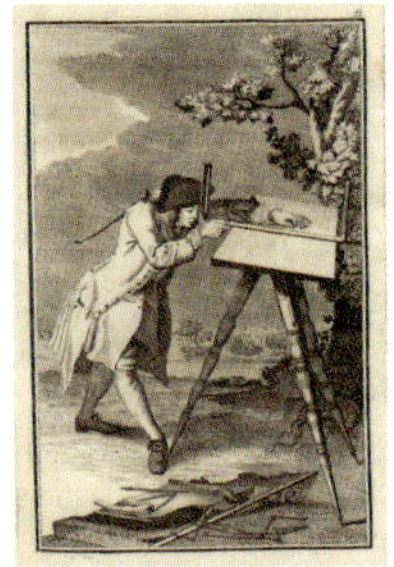

Cat. 31 | Fig. 40

Giovanni Jacopo de Marinoni
De re ichnographica, cujus hodierna praxis exponitur, et propriis exemplis pluribus illustrator
Vienna, 1751

Austrian National Library, Vienna, 568.676-C, engraving on p. 11

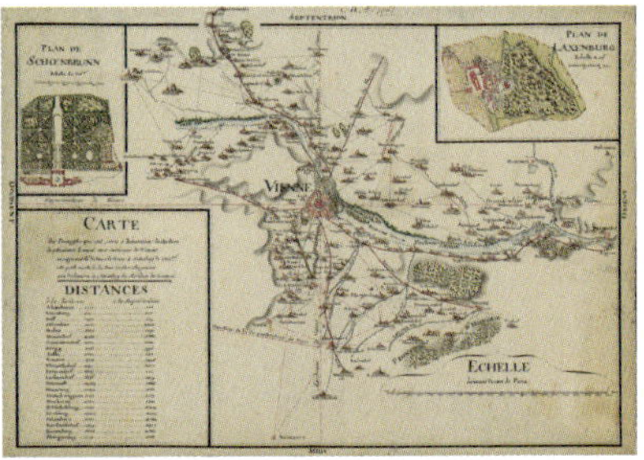

Cat. 32

Joseph Liesganig (attributed)
Carte des Triangles qui ont servis a déterminer la Position de plusieurs Lieux aux environs de Vienne
c.1761

Pen, ink and wash on paper, 670 × 470 mm
Austrian National Library, Vienna, KAR AB 7 B 1

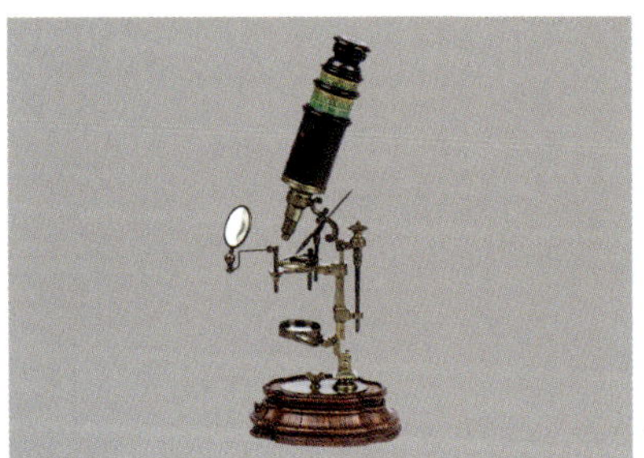

Cat. 33

Unidentified instrument maker
Microscope
Vienna, c.1750

Wood, brass, parchment, 13 × 17 × 41 cm
Leica Microsystems GmbH
Provenance: On loan from Leica Microsystems GmbH to the Technisches Museum Wien since 2000 (inv. no. 52734)

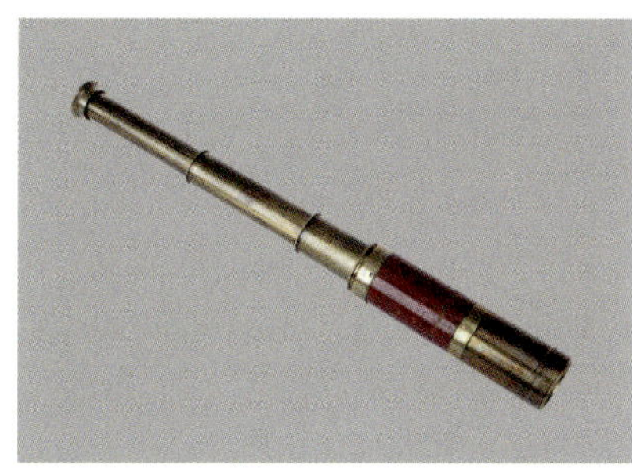

Cat. 34

Jesse Ramsden
Three-draw Telescope
London, 1760/90

Brass, mahogany wood, glass, 3.5 × 34.7 cm
Technisches Museum Wien, inv. 15745/4
Provenance: Donated in 1916 by the Imperial and Royal Ministry of War to the Museum of Technology for Industry and Trade (today the Technisches Museum Wien)

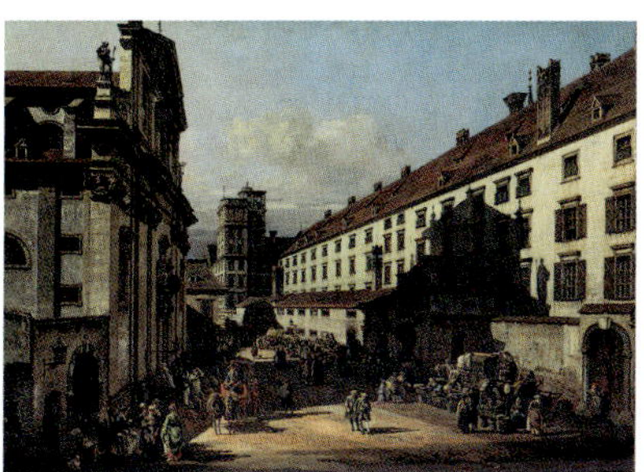

Cat. 35 | Fig. 45

Bellotto
The Dominican Church in Vienna
1759/60

Oil on canvas, 115 × 155.5 cm
Kunsthistorisches Museum, Vienna, Picture Gallery, inv. 1672
Provenance: Recorded in the Pressburg inventory of 1781, No. 10 Billiard Zimmer, No. 49; since 1822 in Laxenburg Palace; by 1878 in the Hofburg, Vienna (Obersthofmeisteramt); on display in the Gemäldegalerie, Vienna, from 1891

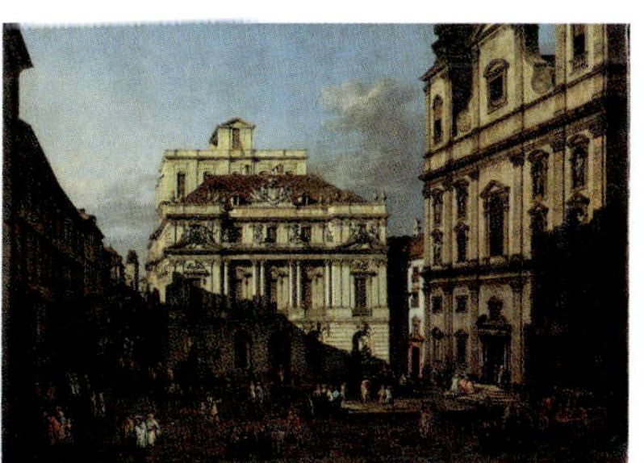

Cat. 36 | Fig. 47

Bellotto
The University Square in Vienna
1759/60

Oil on canvas, 115.5 × 155.5 cm
Kunsthistorisches Museum, Vienna, Picture Gallery, inv. 1670
Provenance: Recorded in the Pressburg inventory of 1781, No. 10 Billiard Zimmer, No. 48; since 1822 in Laxenburg Palace; by 1878 in the Hofburg, Vienna (Obersthofmeisteramt); on display in the Gemäldegalerie, Vienna, from 1891

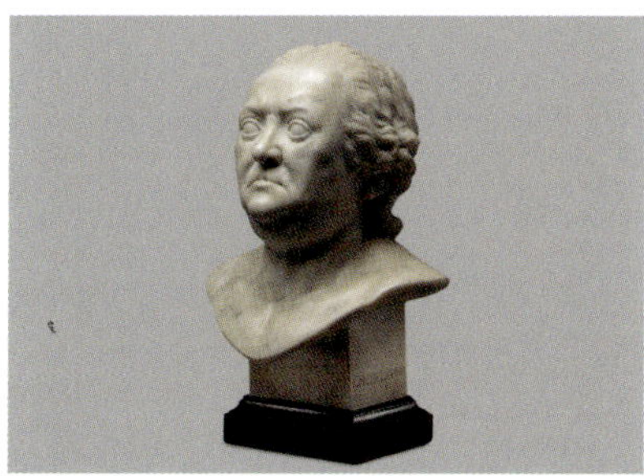

Cat. 37

Franz Xaver Messerschmidt
Gerard van Swieten
1770/72

Signed: „F. MESSERSCHMIDT"
Inscription: „GERARDVS L. B. VAN SWIETEN"
Marble, H. 47 cm
Kunsthistorisches Museum, Vienna, Kunstkammer, inv. KK 8921
Provenance: Until 1936 in the Austrian National Library, Vienna; thereafter transferred to the Kunsthistorisches Museum, Vienna

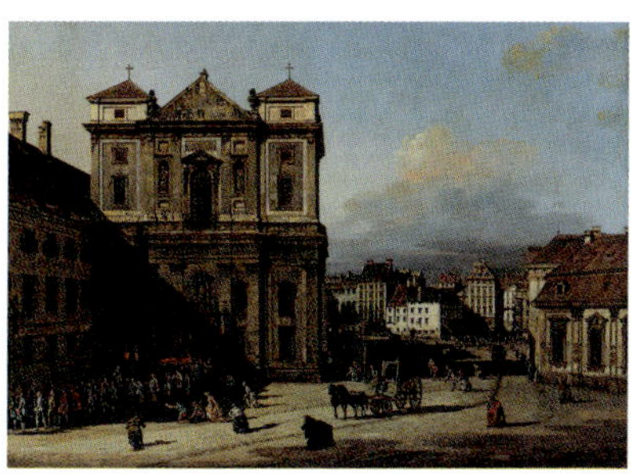

Cat. 38 | Fig. 48

Bellotto
The Freyung in Vienna, View from Northwest
1759/60

Oil on canvas, 116 × 152 cm
Kunsthistorisches Museum, Vienna, Picture Gallery, inv. 1652
Provenance: Recorded in the Pressburg inventory of 1781, No. 10 Billiard Zimmer, No. 45; in the early 19th century in the Hofburg, Vienna; 1849 in the Belvedere; transferred to the Kunsthistorisches Museum, Vienna, in 1891

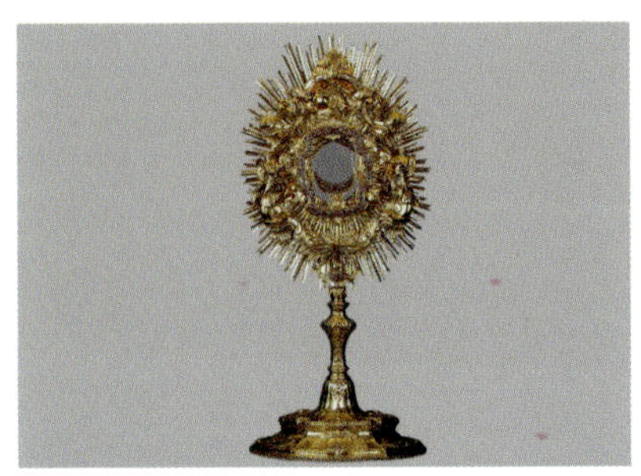

CAT. 39

UNIDENTIFIED GOLDSMITH
Monstrance
Vienna, 1761

Inscribed: "Legato Nob D Maria Anna Hirschkornin Hoc Tabernaculum Altissimo Surrexit 1761"
Gilded silver, set with rubies and diamonds, H. 73 cm
Schottenstift, Vienna
Provenance: Bequeathed by Maria Hirschorn, 1761

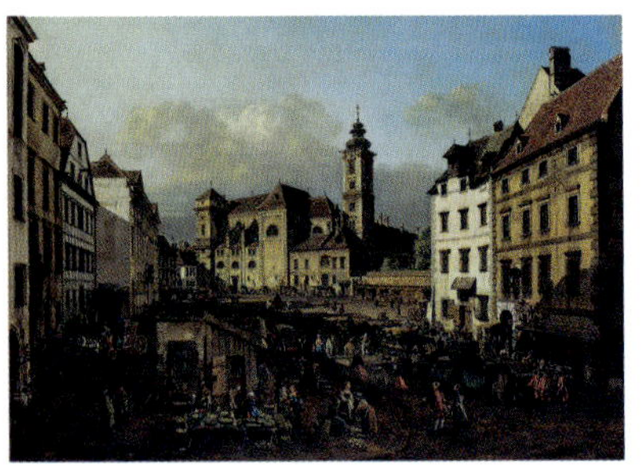

CAT. 40 | FIG. 49

BELLOTTO
The Freyung in Vienna, View from Southeast
1759/60

Oil on canvas, 119 × 153 cm
Kunsthistorisches Museum, Vienna, Picture Gallery, inv. 1654
Provenance: Recorded in the Pressburg inventory of 1781, No. 10 Billiard Zimmer, No. 44; in the early 19th century in the Hofburg, Vienna; 1849 in the Belvedere; transferred to the Kunsthistorisches Museum, Vienna, in 1891

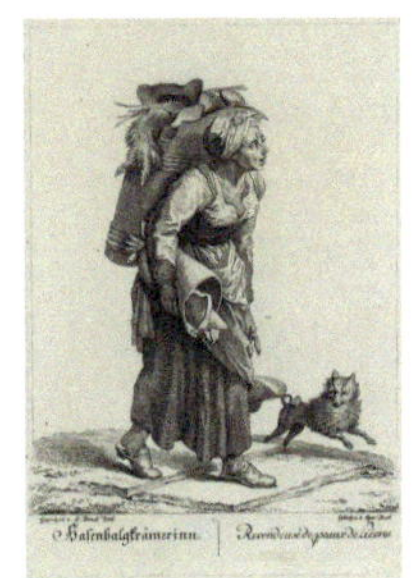

CAT. 41 | FIG. 52

JOHANN CHRISTIAN BRAND
"Hare-Skin Seller"
from: *"Drawings of the Common People, especially Street Cries, in Vienna"*
1775

Engraving, 443 × 314 mm
Wien Museum, Vienna, inv. 95836/13
Provenance: Acquired in 1961 at the 469th book auction at the Dorotheum, Vienna

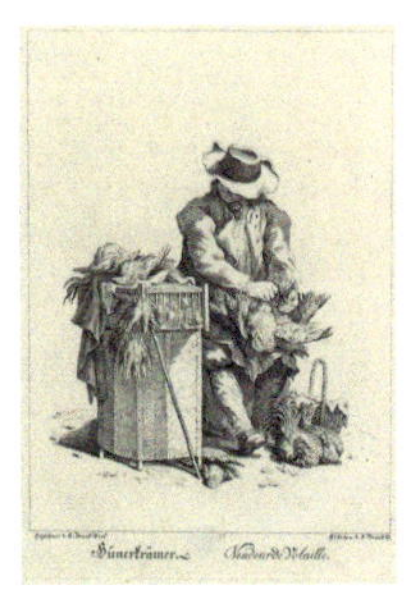

CAT. 42 | FIG. 53

JOHANN CHRISTIAN BRAND
"Poultry Seller"
from: *"Drawings of the Common People, especially Street Cries, in Vienna"*
1775

Engraving, 443 × 314 mm
Wien Museum, Vienna, inv. 95836/27
Provenance: Acquired in 1961 at the 469th book auction at the Dorotheum, Vienna

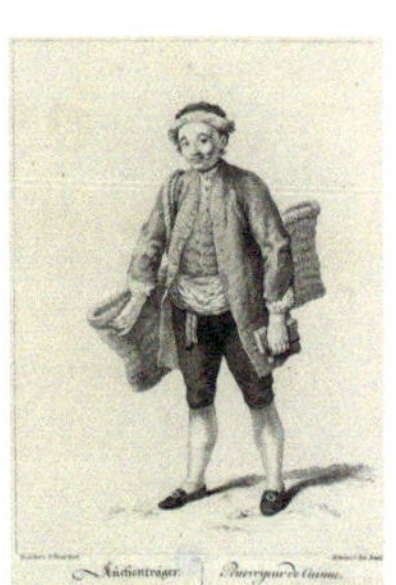

CAT. 43 | FIG. 54

JOHANN CHRISTIAN BRAND
"Kitchen Porter"
from *"Drawings of the Common People, especially Street Cries, in Vienna"*
1775

Engraving, 443 × 314 mm
Wien Museum, Vienna, inv. 95836/17
Provenance: Acquired in 1961 at the 469th book auction at the Dorotheum, Vienna

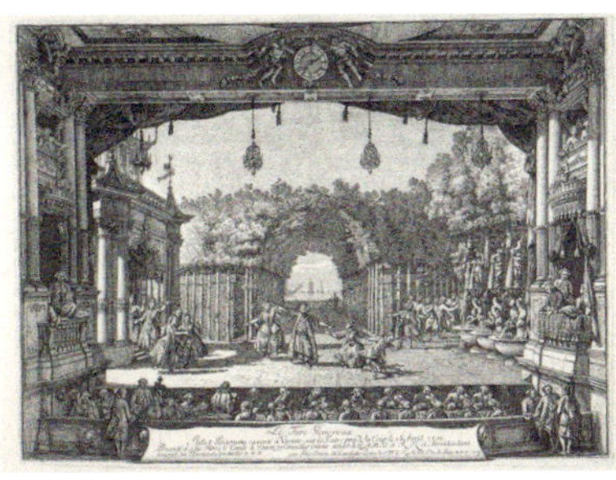

Cat. 44 | Fig. 55

Bellotto
Scene from "Le Turc Généreux" at the Hofburgtheater
1759

Inscribed: "Le Turc Genereux. / Ballet Pantomime executé à Vienne sur le Teatre près de la Cour, le 26. Avril, 1758. / Presenté à S. Exc. Mons. le Comte de Durazzo, Conseiller intime actuel de LL: M.M. I.I. et R.R. et Surintendant / Géneral des Plaisirs et Spectacles &.&.&. / par Ber: Belotti dit Canaletto Peintre des SM. Le Roi de Pol: Elec. de Saxe: &.&.&. 1759"
Etching, 510 × 670 mm
ALBERTINA, Vienna, inv. DG2005/10286

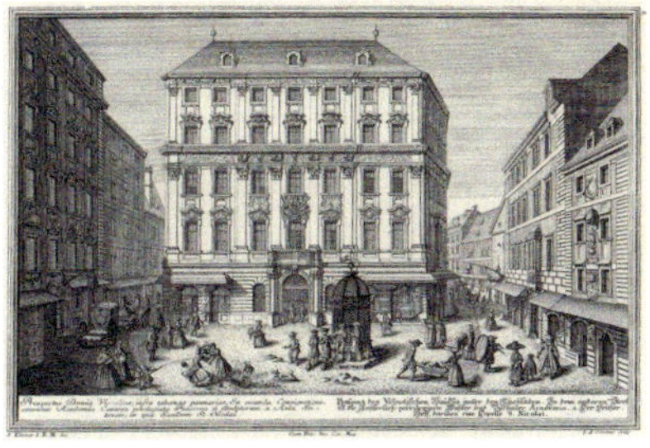

Cat. 45 | Fig. 56

Salomon Kleiner
View of the Visendisches Haus under the Tuchlauben
1733

Engraving, 308 × 439 mm
Wien Museum, Vienna, inv. 105437
Provenance: Purchased in 1956 from the antiquarian bookseller Heinrich Hinterberger, Vienna

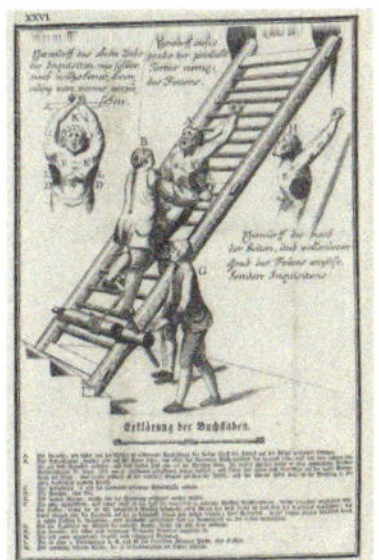

Cat. 46

Constitutio Criminalis Theresiana
Vienna, Johann Thomas Edlen von Trattnern, 1769

Austrian National Library, Vienna, 226.970-D, plate XXVI

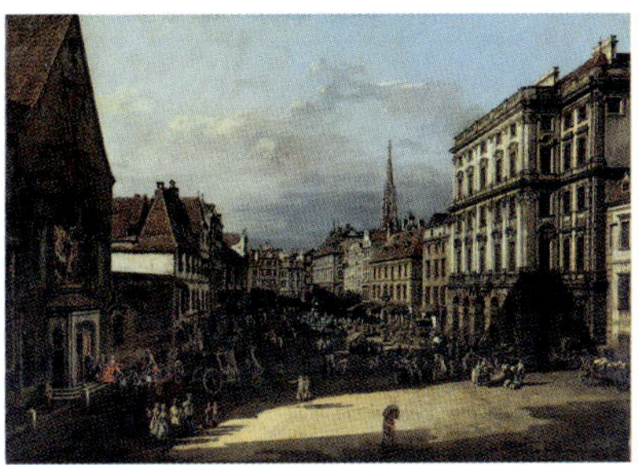

Cat. 47 | Fig. 57

Bellotto
The Mehlmarkt in Vienna
1759/60

Oil on canvas, 116 × 155 cm
Kunsthistorisches Museum, Vienna, Picture Gallery, inv. 1668
Provenance: Recorded in the Pressburg inventory of 1781, No. 10 Billiard Zimmer, No. 46; since 1822 in Laxenburg Palace; by 1878 in the Hofburg, Vienna (Obersthofmeisteramt); on display in the Gemäldegalerie, Vienna, from 1891

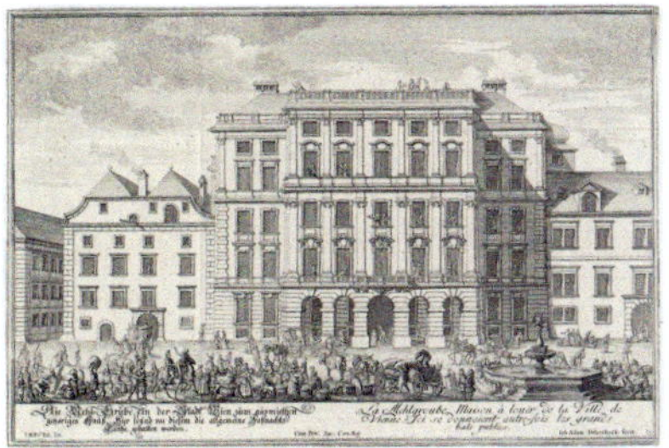

Cat. 48 | Fig. 58

Johann Adam Delsenbach after Joseph Emanuel Fischer von Erlach
The Mehl-Grube
1719

Engraving, 223 × 330 mm
Wien Museum, Vienna, inv. 28805
Provenance: Inventoried since 1901

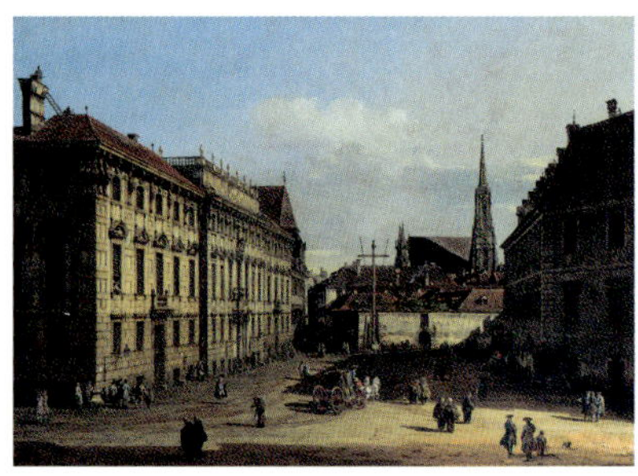

CAT. 49 | FIG. 59

BELLOTTO
The Lobkowitz Square in Vienna
1759/60

Oil on canvas, 114.5 × 151 cm
Kunsthistorisches Museum, Vienna, Picture Gallery, inv. 1671
Provenance: Recorded in the Pressburg inventory of 1781, No. 10 Billiard Zimmer, No. 47; since 1822 in Laxenburg Palace; by 1878 in the Hofburg, Vienna (Obersthofmeisteramt); on display in the Gemäldegalerie, Vienna, from 1891

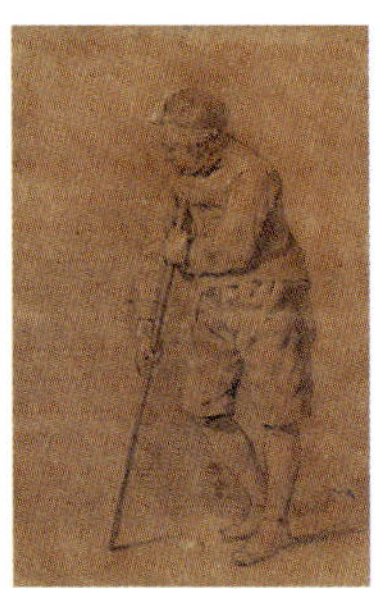

CAT. 50 | FIG. 60

JAKOB MATTHIAS SCHMUTZER
Peasant Boy Leaning on a Staff with Bandaged Head
1770/90

Chalk on paper, 400 × 264 mm
Academy of Fine Arts, Vienna, Kupferstichkabinett, inv. HZ-12436
Provenance: Acquired from Jakob Matthias Schmutzer, 1790

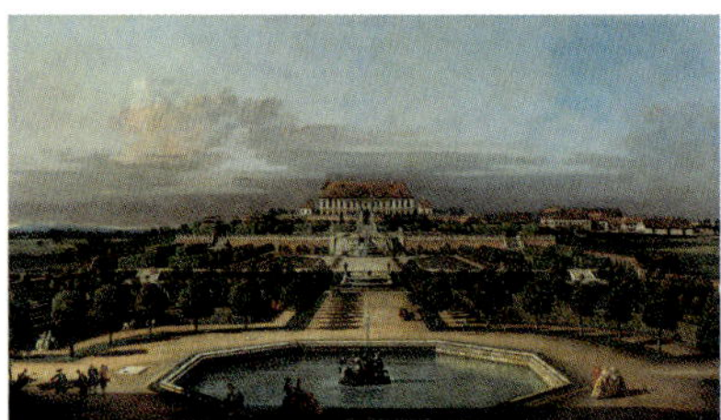

CAT. 51 | FIG. 61

BELLOTTO
View of Schloss Hof from the Gardens
1759/60

Oil on canvas, 136 × 216 cm
Kunsthistorisches Museum, Vienna, Picture Gallery, inv. 1674
Provenance: Recorded in the Pressburg inventory of 1781, No. 10 Billiard Zimmer, No. 38; since 1822 in Laxenburg Palace; by 1878 in the Hofburg, Vienna (Obersthofmeisteramt); on display in the Gemäldegalerie, Vienna, from 1891

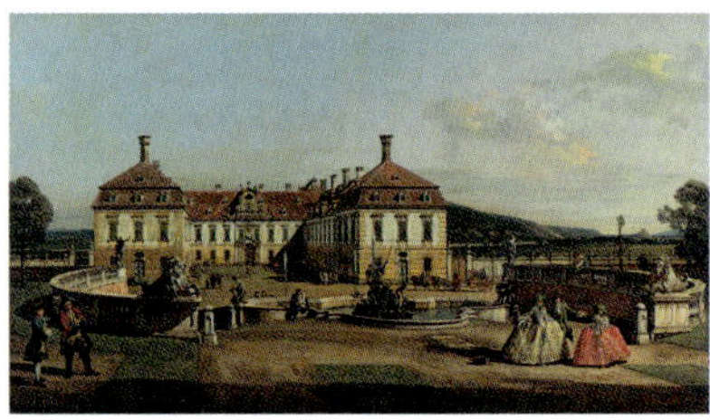

CAT. 52 | FIG. 62

BELLOTTO
View of Schloss Hof from the Forecourt
1759/60

Oil on canvas, 138 × 237 cm
Kunsthistorisches Museum, Vienna, Picture Gallery, inv. 1673
Provenance: Recorded in the Pressburg inventory of 1781, 2nd Antichambre (2nd floor), No. 197; since 1822 in Laxenburg Palace; by 1878 in the Hofburg, Vienna (Obersthofmeisteramt); on display in the Gemäldegalerie, Vienna, from 1891

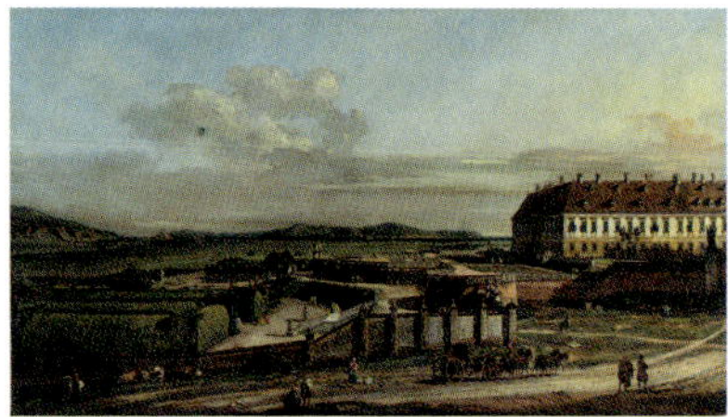

CAT. 53 | FIG. 63

BELLOTTO
View of Schloss Hof from the North
1759/60

Oil on canvas, 136 × 238 cm
Kunsthistorisches Museum, Vienna, Picture Gallery, inv. 1675
Provenance: Recorded in the Pressburg inventory of 1781, No. 10 Billiard Zimmer, No. 39; since 1822 in Laxenburg Palace; by 1878 in the Hofburg, Vienna (Obersthofmeisteramt); on display in the Gemäldegalerie, Vienna, from 1891

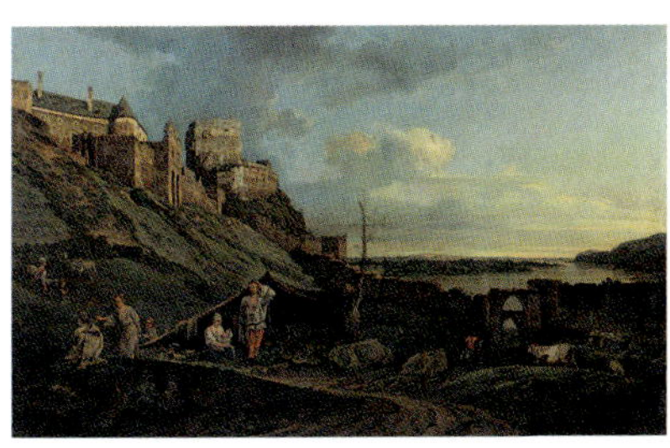

Cat. 54 | Fig. 64

Bellotto
View of the Ruins of Theben / Devín
1759 / 60

Oil on canvas, 136 × 214 cm
Kunsthistorisches Museum, Vienna, Picture Gallery, inv. 1676
Provenance: Recorded in the Pressburg inventory of 1781, No. 10 Billiard Zimmer, No. 40; since 1822 in Laxenburg Palace; by 1878 in the Hofburg, Vienna (Obersthofmeisteramt); on display in the Gemäldegalerie, Vienna, from 1891

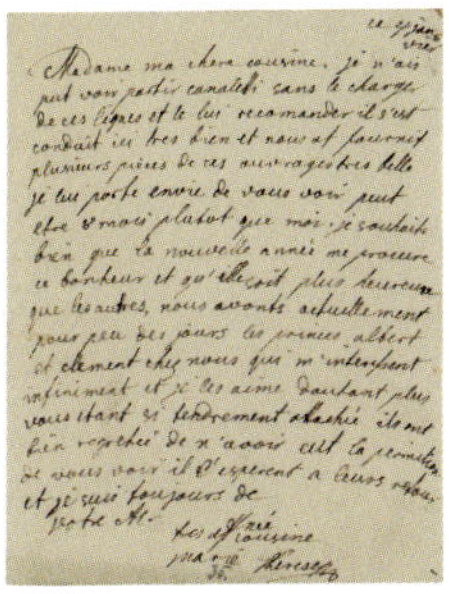

Cat. 55 | Fig. 65

Empress Maria Theresia to Maria Antonia of Bavaria, Electoral Princess of Saxony
4 January 1761

Pen and ink on paper, 149 × 197 mm
Sächsisches Staatsarchiv, Hauptstaatsarchiv Dresden, 12528 Estate of Maria Antonia, Electress of Saxony, No. 104, letter No. 35

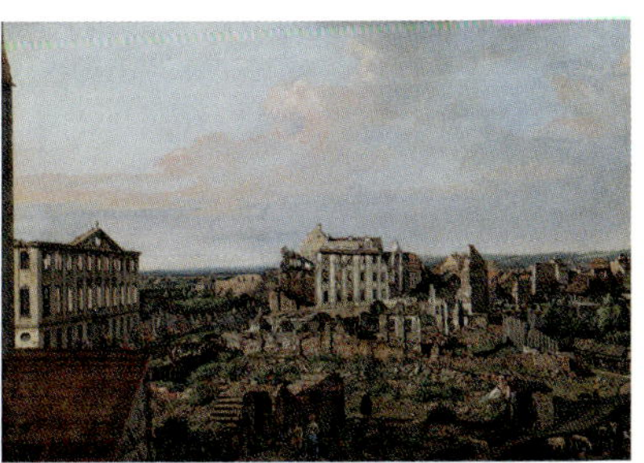

Cat. 56 | Fig. 66

Bellotto
The Ruins of the Pirna Suburb in Dresden
1762 / 67

Oil on canvas, 80,5 × 113 cm
Musée des Beaux-Arts et d'Archéologie, Troyes, inv. 850.1.4
Provenance: Believed to have been offered by the artist to Prince Xavier of Saxony (1730–1806); by 1768 in the collection of Prince Xavier of Saxony, transferred by him to the Château de Pont-sur-Seine following his settlement in France; seized there during the French Revolution in the early 1790s; entered the museum before 1850

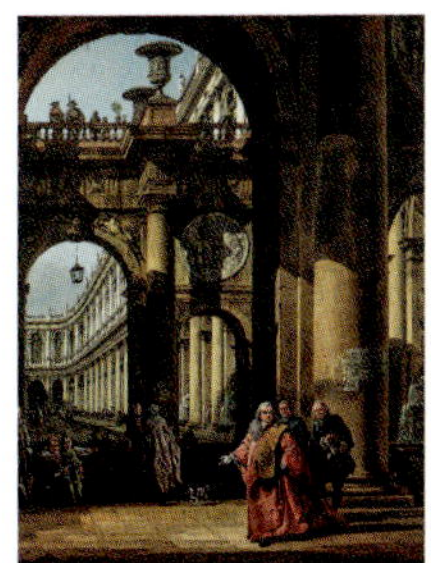

Cat. 57 | Fig. 67

Bellotto
Architectural Capriccio with Self-Portrait of the Artist in the Robes of a Venetian Nobleman
c.1765

Oil on canvas, 153 × 114 cm
The Royal Castle in Warsaw – Museum, inv. ZKW 3537
Provenance: Probably taken by the artist from Dresden to Warsaw in 1767, perhaps as a gift to King Stanisław II August Poniatowski (1732–1798); 1798 inherited by his nephew Prince Józef Poniatowski (1763–1813); 1813 inherited by the latter's sister, Countess Maria Teresa Tyszkiewicz (1760–1834); 1821 purchased by Antonio Fusi and taken by him to Russia (1821–1822); 1914 in the collection of A. A. Kosen, a lady of the court in St. Petersburg; after 1914 in the collection of Stanisław Krosnowski (1865–1933), St. Petersburg; 1922 transferred to the Royal Castle, Warsaw, Krosnowski Foundation, Polish State Collections; 1939 evacuated to the National Museum, Warsaw; 1939 removed by German occupying forces to Kraków; 1944 in Seichau (Sichów) near Legnica, Palace of Count Manfred von Richthofen; 1945 in Muhrau (Morawa) Castle, Lower Silesia; subsequently moved to Coburg, Callenberg Castle, and Munich, Central Art Collecting Point; 1946 found there by Karol Estreicher, Polish Restitution Commission; 1946 restituted to Poland, transferred to the National Museum, Warsaw; since 1994 property of the Royal Castle, Warsaw, on permanent loan to the National Museum, Warsaw

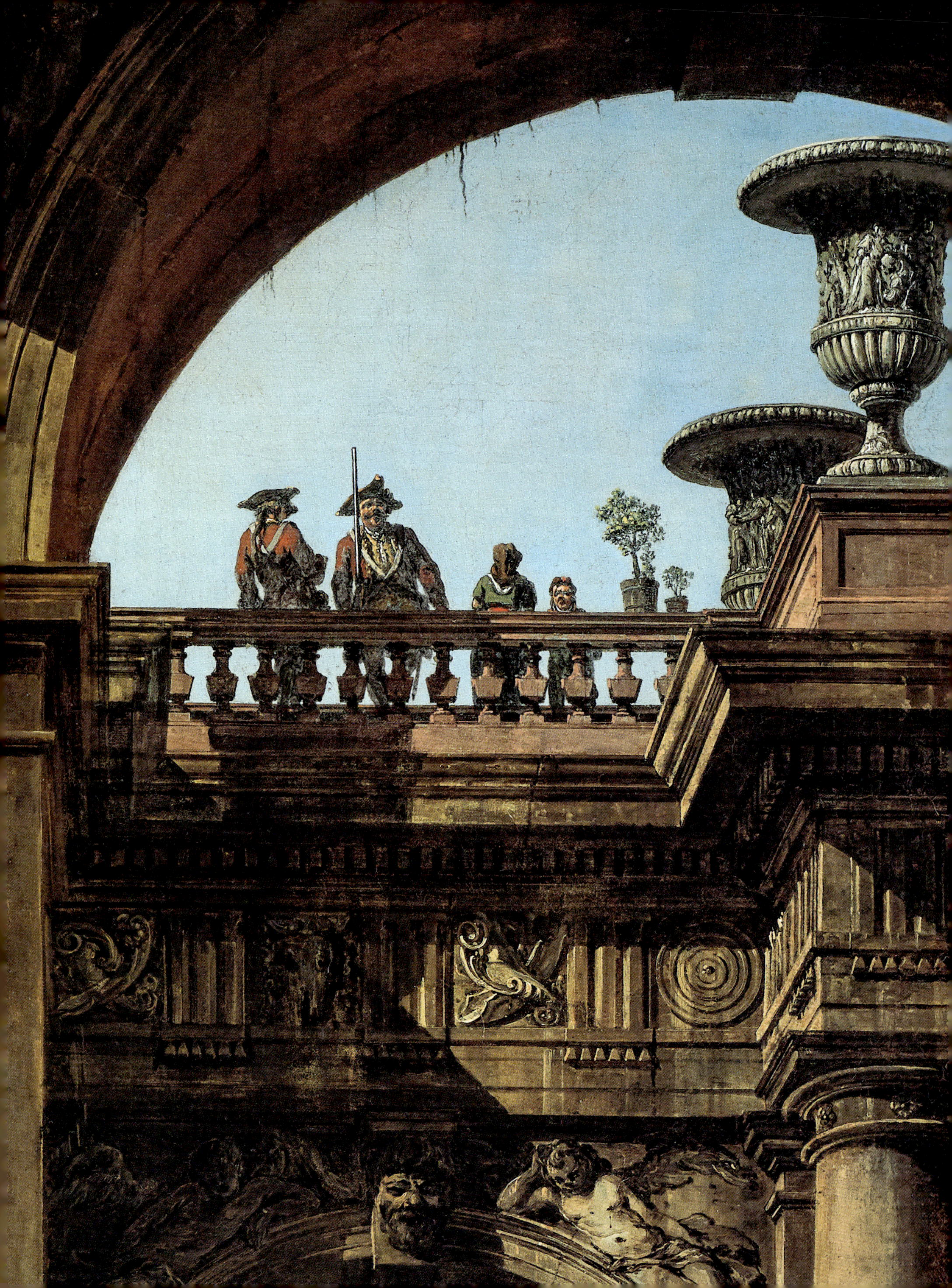

ENDNOTES

Director's foreword

1 Woolf 1928, 227.
2 Woolf 1928, 223–24.

Main Text

1 Cf. Constable 1989, vol. 2, 245, no. 121, vol. 3 (supplement), 12, no. 121.
2 Variants of the signature "Bernardo Bellotto detto Canaletto" appear on several works, including *The Old Bridge over the River Po in Turin* (1745, Turin, Galleria Sabauda, inv. 469) and *View of Dresden from the Right Bank of the Elbe, above the Augustus Bridge* (1747, Dresden, Gemäldegalerie Alte Meister, inv. 602). See Kozakiewicz 1972, vol. 2, nos. 93 and 140.
3 Already contemporaries confused the two. In 1749, the English antiquarian George Vertue noted: "Canali ... had a sister who had a son who having some genius was instructed by his uncle Cannali. and this young stripling by degrees came on forward in his proffession being taken notice of for his improvements he was called Cannaleti—the young. but in time getting some degree of merit. he being puffd up disobliged his uncle who turned him adrift. but well imitating his uncles manner of painting became reputed and the name of Cannaletti was indifferently used by both uncle and nephew." Vertue 1933–34, 149.
4 On Canaletto's life and work see especially exh. cat. New Haven and London 2006/07; Corboz 1985; Links 1982; and Constable 1962.
5 Cf. Magrini 2001, 221–45; Magrini 1998, 273–81; and Links 1982, 32.
6 "[Canaletto] il giorno di S. Rocco espose al pubblico una sua veduta di S. Gio. e Paolo che fece meravigliare tutti. L'Ambasciatore dell'Imperatore se la levò, e ne fece l'acquisto avendone un'altra di maggior grandezza, e li diè l'ordine d'accompagnarla." (On St Roch's Day, [Canaletto] exhibited to the public a view of Santi Giovanni e Paolo, which amazed everyone. The Emperor's Ambassador picked it up and bought it, having another larger version of it, and gave orders for it to be accompanied.) Alessandro Marchesini to Stefano Conti in August 1725. Cf. Bożena Anna Kowalczyk in exh. cat. Venice 2001, 150–51 and Haskell 1956, 298 (transl. David Graham).
7 "Intesi il bisogno di che V.S. Ill.ma desidera per li due accennati quadri da accompagnare gli altri che tiene dipinti dal Sig.r Lucca Carlevari. Ma adesso veram. te vive il Soggetto, se non fosse superato di maggior stima dal Sig.r Ant. Canale, che fa in questo paese stordire universalmente ognuno che vede Le sue opere, che consiste sul ordine dl Carlevari ma vi si vede Lucer entro il Sole, sicchè questo è mio amico che appoggerò le due opere." (I understand the need expressed by Your Most Illustrious Excellency for the two aforementioned paintings to accompany the others you have painted by Mr Lucca Carlevari. But now the subject really does come to life, were it not surpassed by the even greater esteem accorded to Signor Antonio Canale; Canale amazes everyone in this country who sees his works, working within Carlevari's style, but in which the very Sun shines, so this is my friend whose two works I recommend.) Alessandro Marchesini to Stefano Conti in July 1725. Cited after Haskell 1956, 297 (transl. David Graham).
8 "The fellow is whimsical and vary's his price every day: and he that has a mind to have any of his work, must not seem to be too fond of it, for he'l be ye worse treated for it, both in the price and in the painting too. He has more work than he can doe, in any reasonable time." Owen McSwiney to Lord March, Venice, 28 November 1727. Cited after Constable 1962, vol. 1, 174.
9 Redford 1996.
10 On Smith see Vivian 1971.
11 Cf. exh. cat. Bath 2021.
12 On Canaletto's early style see especially exh. cat. Venice 2001.
13 Other architectural features help date the picture to c. 1735–44, given that the twin towers on the horizon slightly left of center might be those of Angelo Raffaele or Santa Maria del Rosario (completed in 1735 and 1736), while the campanile of Santa Maria della Carità—visible behind the Dogana's golden globe—collapsed in March 1744. Cf. Packer and Beddington 2025, 27–28, 56–65, no. 2 and Duffy and Hedley 2004, 63.
14 On Canaletto's father see briefly Constable 1989, vol. 1, 7 and Delneri 2007, 315–21.
15 Serlio 1545; Sabbattini 1638; Pozzo 1693; and Bibiena 1711. See further Kemp 1990, 141–47.
16 On Canaletto's techniques see Sperber and Stenger 2016; Pemberton-Pigott 2001, 207–17; and Pemberton-Pigott 1989, 53–63.
17 Cf. Julia Thoma in exh. cat. Munich 2014/15, 150–53, nos. 1–2 and Constable 1962, 332–39, nos. 332–345.
18 Steadman 2025.
19 See Crary 2001, 25–66 and Kemp 1990, 188–203.
20 Newton 1704.

21 Nollet 1764, vol. 5, 480.

22 On the Correr camera see Steadman 2025, 26–29, 249–51 and Bożena Anna Kowalczyk in exh. cat. Milan 2016/17, 72–73, no. 11.

23 The *quaderno* contains some 140 pages with tracings of the Venetian skyline, often annotated with place names and color notes. See especially Nepi Scirè 1997.

24 Steadman 2025, 23–55.

25 Gravesande 1711, pl. 30; Savérien 1753, vol. 1, pl. XXIII; and Diderot 1772, pl. IV and pl. V.

26 A folded tent-like camera once owned by the painter Sir Joshua Reynolds survives at the Science Museum in London (inv. no. 1875-28).

27 Alongside several related sketches, this drawing may have also informed the large canvas showing the Riva now in the Sir John Soane's Museum. Cf. Links 2010, 26–28; Clayton 2006, 106–07, no. 25; Constable 1989, vol. 2, 245, no. 121, vol. 3 (supplement), 12, no. 121.

28 Cf. Constable 1989, vol. 2, 261, no. 156.

29 "Par le moyen de cet instrument, sur-tout s'il est construit conformément à la derniere des trois manieres de le construire dont on parlera plus bas, quelqu'un qui ne fait pas le dessein pourra néanmoins dessiner les objets avec la derniere justesse & la derniere exactitude; & celui qui sait dessiner ou même peindre pourra encore par ce même moyen se perfectionner dans son art." (With this instrument – especially if it is constructed following the last of the three methods described below – someone who does not know how to draw will nevertheless be able to draw things with the utmost precision and exactitude, and anyone who knows how to draw, and even paint, will be able to achieve perfection in his art.) Diderot 1753, 62 (transl. Imogen Taylor).

30 Cf. Schumacher 2014/15, 20–21 and Bettagno 1969, 107, no. 326.

31 Centuries later, Walter Benjamin famously argued that technological reproduction undermines the uniqueness or 'aura' of artworks, and transforms their social and political function. See Benjamin 1936, 40–66.

32 "Il avoit fait dans sa jeunesse le voyage de Rome, et, depuis qu'il eut abdiqué le théâtre, il ne s'occupa plus qu'à peindre des veues d'après nature, faisant usage de la chambre noire, dont il scavoit modérer le faux." (He had travelled to Rome in his youth and after turning his back on the theater, he devoted himself to painting scenes from nature, making use of the camera obscura, whose faults he was able to mitigate.) Mariette 1853, vol. 1, 298 (transl. Imogen Taylor).

33 "Insegnò il Canal con l'esempio il vero uso della camera ottica; e a conoscere i difetti che recar suole a una pittura, quando l'artefice interamente si fida della prospettiva che in essa camera vede, e delle tinte spezialmente della arie e no sa levar destramente quando può offendere il senso." Zanetti 1771, 463. See also Steadman 2025, 23.

34 "Canaletto. Douze vuës de Venise. Depuis Nro. 195 jusque au Nro. 206. Elles représentent les morceaux les plus remarquables de cette Ville. Les objets y sont rendus dans la plus grande vérité; et cet habile artiste doit s'être servi adroitement de la chambre obscure, qui rend les objets trop brillans et trop durs, si on ne sait pas en faire usage. Peints sur toile, hauts 18 pouces, sur 24 de largeur." (Canaletto. Twelve views of Venice. From No. 195 to No. 206. They represent the most remarkable buildings in the city. The objects are reproduced with the greatest veracity, and this skilled artist must have made shrewd use of the camera obscura, which can make objects too bright and harsh if not correctly used. Painted on canvas, 18 inches high, 24 inches wide.) Dallinger von Dalling 1780, 74 (transl. Imogen Taylor).

35 Steadman 2025, 14–19.

36 "If to a hole made in the window-shut of a darkned room, you apply a lens, and over-against this at a proper distance there be placed a sheet of white paper, you will see all the objects which are without the window (especially those which are directly opposite to the lens) inverted and painted upon the paper with a beauty, vivacity and softness of colours that would make a landskip drawn by Claude Lorrain, or a visto by Canaletto, appear faint and languid." Algarotti 1739, 131.

37 "S'adopri pure la camera ottica per far la perspettiva d'un canale di Venezia con le sue fabbriche: Il Canaletto per la sua sagacità potrà trasferire nella sua pittura più punti di un altro; ma non è possibile che mai tutti li trasferisca. Contuttociò i trasferiti da lui saranno un'impressione così viva nell'occhio, che vedendo il suo quadro a prima vista io farò persuaso di vedere l'oggetto stesso." Conti 1756, vol. 2, 250.

38 Corboz 1985, vol. 1, 171–74.

39 In his chapter on coloring, Algarotti further noted "It must likewise be of great service to a painter desirous to excell in colouring, to be well acquainted with that part of opticks, which has the nature of light and colours of its objects." Cf. Algarotti 1764, 60 and 66.

40 Cf. Pirenne 1970, 102–103 and Corboz 1985, vol. 1, 267. In his recent discussion, Philip Steadman remains skeptical as to this Newtonian definition of Canaletto's style: Steadman 2025, 18–19.

41 Owen McSwiney to Lord March, Venice, November 28, 1727. Cited after Constable 1962, vol. 1, 174.

42 Steadman 2025, 57–65.

43 Ibid.

44 See Selva 1761 and Burlini 1758.

45 Steadman 2025, 60.

46 Vertue 1933–34, 149.

47 Cf. Steadman 2025, 58–60.

48 Cf. Wagner 2022, 58–62. See also Liebsch 2022, 196–97.

49 Steadman 2025, 58–60.

50 Designs for such adaptations of the camera obscura appear as early as 1686 and were further developed throughout the eighteenth century. See Steadman 2025, 155–62. On Canaletto's technique see Sperber and Stenger 2016; Pemberton-Pigott 2001, 207–17; and Pemberton-Pigott 1989, 53–63.

51 On the pantograph see Kemp 1990, 180 and Steadman 2025, 161–62.

52 Cf. Sperber and Stenger 2016; Pemberton-Pigott 2001, 207–17; and Pemberton-Pigott 1989, 53–63.

53 My sincere thanks to Eva Götz and Flaminia Rukavina Vidovgrad for patiently discussing their observations with me during their treatment of the two pictures at the KHM's conservation studio.

54 On Bellotto's life and work see especially Kozakiewicz 1972. For more recent studies see exh. cat. Dresden 2022; exh. cat. Warsaw 2022; exh. cat. Darmstadt 2022/23; exh. cat. London 2021; exh. cat. Milan 2016/17; exh. cat. Munich 2014/15; exh. cat. Vienna 2005; and exh. cat. Houston 2001.

55 Cf. Kowalczyk 2016/17, 15–37 and Kowalczyk 2001, 3–13.

56 Cf. exh. cat. Warsaw 2022, 119–23, no. 3; Julia Thoma in exh. cat. Munich 2014/15, 168–69, no. 9; Gerlinde Gruber in exh. cat. Vienna 2005, 72–74, no. 2; and Bożena Anna

Kowalczyk in exh. cat. Houston 2001, 56–57, no. 5.

57 Cf. Badach 2022, 94; Gruber 2005, 66; Kowalczyk 2001, 4; Kowalczyk 1999, 200; and Constable 1989, vol. 1, lviii.

58 On the prince see especially Cassidy-Geiger 2018 and Cassidy-Geiger 2007/08, 208–55.

59 "I suppose you know he has been lame from his birth, and is carried about in a chair, though a beautiful person from the waist upwards: it is said his family design him for the Church, he having four brothers who are fine children." Lady Mary Wortley Montagu to Mr. Wortley Montagu, Venice, 29 March 1740. Cited after Wortley Montagu 1861, 58.

60 Vertue 1933–34, 132.

61 This period was pivotal especially for Bellotto's formation, as he traveled across Italy—first with his uncle along the Brenta Canal, then alone to Florence, Rome, Turin, and Verona. Cf. Badach 2022, 89–105; Kowalczyk 2012, 24–31; Succi 2011/12, 18–51; and Gruber 2005, 61–69.

62 "Latter end of May. came to London from Venice the famous painter of views Cannalletti ... of Venice. the multitude of his works done abroad for the English nobleman & gentleman has procured him great reputation & his great merit & excellence in that way, he is much esteemed and no doubt but what views and works he doth here, will give the same satisfaction." Vertue 1933–34, 130.

63 On Canaletto's English years see especially Beddington 2006/07, 8–29; Russell 2006/07, 38–47; and Liversidge 1993, 10–29.

64 "Tis time therefore for us to look about us too, and endeavour to vie with our neighbours in politeness, as well as power and empire.... No nation can reproach us for want of expence in our publick buildings, but all nations may for our want of elegance and discernment in the execution." Anonymous 1734, 2–5.

65 "In the same proportion as publick magnificence increases, in the same proportion will a love of elegance increase among all ranks and degrees of people, and that refinement of taste, which in a nobleman produces true magnificence and elegance, will in a mechanic produce at least cleanliness and decorum." Gwynn 1766, 1.

66 "The only news I know to tell you, is what I had this day from Swiney at the Duke of Montagu's House, where we dined, & he, I think got almost drunk. Canales, alias Canaletti, is come over with a letter of recommendation from our old acquaintance the consul of Venice to Mac in order to his introduction to your Grace, as a patron of the politer arts, or what the Italians understand by the name of virtù. I told him the best service I thought you could do him wd be to let him draw a view of the river from yr dining-room which in my opinion would gain him as much reputation as any of his Venetian prospects." Thomas Hill to the Duke of Richmond, 20 May 1746. Cited after Liversidge 1993, 16.

67 Cf. Jane Farrington in exh. cat. Birmingham 1993, 68–71, nos. 9, 12 and Constable 1962, vol. 2, 385–86, 395, nos. 424 and 438.

68 Hallett 1993, 51–52.

69 On the ways in which English painters idealized the poor in landscape painting see especially Barrell 1980, 1–33.

70 Lobkowicz had visited Goodwood House and was rumored to be enamored of the Duke of Richmond's daughter while also flirting with the Venetian ambassador's wife; perhaps he learned of Canaletto through these circles. See Russell 2006/07, 42. See further Kerber 2017, 126–28 and Constable 1962, vol. 2, 386, no. 425.

71 Cf. Campbell 2007, 21, 130.

72 Gwynn 1766, xv.

73 On the Rome pictures see Lloyd 2015, 85–93.

74 Cf. Redford 1996, 76. Later artists, such as William Marlow in the 1790s, would make this analogy between London and Venice even more explicit in works like *Capriccio: St. Paul's and a Venetian Canal* (London, Tate, inv. no. N06213). See Michael Liversidge in exh. cat. Birmingham 1993, 146–47, no. 76 and Links 1982, 179–80.

75 Cf. Charles Beddington in exh. cat. New Haven and London 2006/07, 92–93, no. 19 and Jane Farrington in exh. cat. Birmingham 1993, 88, no. 27.

76 Cf. Charles Beddington in exh. cat. New Haven and London 2006/07, 92–93, no. 19; Jane Farrington in exh. cat. Birmingham 1993, 88, no. 27; and Saussure 1902, 97–106. Directly before them stand two rows of plume-less figures: in the front, the Order's recorder, secretary, and gentleman usher; behind them, the First and Second Kings-at-Arms, accompanied by the genealogist.

77 "You cannot imagine the quantity of people at the windows, balconies, and in the streets to see the pageant pass. The populace on that day is particularly insolent and rowdy ... it is almost dangerous for an honest man, and more particularly for a foreigner, to walk in the streets ... he runs a great risk of being jeered at, bespattered with mud, or even pelted with dead dogs and cats." Saussure 1902, 111–12.

78 Anonymous 1744, 1.

79 For an overview of Hogarth's work see Hallett 2000.

80 *The Guardian*, no. 22 (6 April 1713).

81 Cf. Charles Beddington in exh. cat. New Haven and London 2006/07, 56–57, no. 3.

82 Cf. Kerber 2017, 121–32; Solkin 2015, 114–21; Ellis 2012, 152–73; O'Byrne 2008, 243–70; Charles Beddington in exh. cat. New Haven and London 2006/07, 100–15, nos. 23–30; and Hallett 1993, 47–54.

83 Cf. Kerber 2017, 125–26; Beddington 2006/07, 14; Russell 2006/07, 42; Constable 1962, vol. 2, 386, no. 425.

84 Charles Beddington in exh. cat. New Haven and London 2006/07, 112–13, no. 28.

85 Charles Beddington in exh. cat. New Haven and London 2006/07, 103–07, nos. 24–25.

86 Cf. Solkin 2015, 119 and Hallett 1993, 47–54.

87 O'Byrne 2008, 243–70.

88 "Thou too, great father of the British floods! With joyful pride survey our lofty woods; Where tow'ring Oaks their spreading honours rear, And future Navies on thy banks appear.... Behold! Augusta's glitt'ring spires increase, And temples rise, the beauteous works of Peace. I see, I see where two fair cities bend Their ample bow, a new White-hall ascend!" Pope 1720, 19, 29.

89 "On the Thames itself are countless swarms of little boats passing and repassing, many with one mast and one sail, and many with none, in which persons of all ranks are carried over. Thus there is hardly less stir and bustle on this river, than there is in some of its own London's crowded streets." Moritz 1886, 16.

90 Cf. Ellis 2012, 152–73 and Hallett 1993, 47–54.

91 Hallett 1993, 49.

92 Cf. Charles Beddington in exh. cat. New Haven and London 2006/07, 86–89, no. 17 and Jane Farrington in

exh. cat. Birmingham 1993, 80–81, no. 19.

93 "Signor Canaleto hereby invites any Gentleman that will be pleased to come to his house to see a picture done by him being a View of St. James's Park, which he hopes may in some manner deserve approbation any morning or afternoon at his lodgings Mr. Wiggan Cabinet maker in Silver street Golden Square." Vertue 1933–34, 151.

94 Cited after Charles Beddington in exh. cat. New Haven and London 2006/07, 86–89, no. 17.

95 Casanova wrote to Lord Pembroke of "six or seven people shitting in the bushes with their hinder parts turned towards the Publick," while Boswell noted on 24 June 1763: "I went into St. James's Park and picked up a young Brimstone… I agreed with her for Six Pence: we went to the bottom of the park arm in arm… I dipped my Machine in the Canal and then perform'd most manfully…" Both citations after Burford 1988, 47–48.

96 On Canaletto's painting see especially Charles Beddington in exh. cat. New Haven and London 2006/07, 116–19, no. 31 and Jane Farrington in exh. cat. Birmingham 1993, 89–90, no. 28.

97 Cf. Coke and Borg 2011; Bolla 1995, 282–95; and Hallett 1993, 53–54.

98 Cited after Wroth 1896, 200.

99 "Mr. Walpole goes every night constantly to Ranelagh, which has totally beat Vauxhall. … The floor is all of beaten princes; you can't set your foot without treading on a Prince or Duke of Cumberland." Cited after Wroth 1896, 200.

100 On Canaletto's painting see especially Charles Beddington in exh. cat. New Haven and London 2006/07, 116–19, no. 32 and Jane Farrington in exh. cat. Birmingham 1993, 91, no. 29.

101 Cf. Charles Beddington in exh. cat. New Haven and London 2006/07, 143–51, nos. 44–48; Jane Farrington in exh. cat. Birmingham 1993, 82–86, nos. 21–25; and Buttery 1987, 427–45.

102 Buttery 1987, 439.

103 Buttery 1987, 441.

104 With regard to eighteenth-century Britain, *politeness* and *sociability* are scholarly terms referring to the ideals and practices of refined interaction that structured public life—from conversation, correspondence, and club culture to shared leisure and artistic patronage. Cf. Capdeville and Kerhervé 2019; Klein 2002, 869–98.

105 See esp. Russell 2006/07, 38–47.

106 "Lately … Canaletto. painter has painting a large picture a view on the River Thames. of Chelsea College. Ranelagh gardens &c. and parts adjacent. with barges & boats figures—this he exposd to publick view at his lodgings—being a work lately done to shew his skill—this valud at 60. or 70 pounds. haveing made a tour to his own country at Venice for some affairs—in 8 months going and comeing. it is thot that this view is not so well as some works of Canaletti formerly brought into England. nor does it appear to be better than some painters in England can do." Vertue 1933–34, 158. On the painting see Charles Beddington in exh. cat. New Haven and London 2006/07, 16, 122–25, no. 34.

107 "… the picture dealing tribe carried their assurance so far, as to deny that Canaletti was the person who painted his pictures at Venice, that is, on his arrival in London; and when, by provocation, he was tempted to sit down, and produce some, to convince the public, they still persisted that the pieces now produced were not in the same style; an assertion which materially injured him for a time, and made him almost frantic. By this scheme they hoped to drive him from the country, and thereby prevent him from detecting the copies they had made from his works, which were in great repute." Bradley 1805, 322.

108 See Beddington 2006/07, 16–17.

109 Allen 1987, 29–48.

110 "Io Zuane Antonio da Canal. Hò fatto il presente disegno delli Musici che canta nella Chiesa Ducale di San Marco in Venezia in età de anni 68 cenzza Ochiali. Lanno 1766." (I, Zuane Antonio da Canal, made this drawing of the musicians who sing in the Ducal Church of San Marco in Venice, at the age of 68, without glasses. In the year 1766.) See Constable 1962, 453–54, no. 558.

111 See Constable 1989, vol. 1, 43–48.

112 Cf. Badach 2022, 89–105; Succi 2011/12, 18–51; and Gruber 2005, 61–69.

113 Especially Rottermund has emphasized that Bellotto secured his family's standing through his choice of wedding witnesses and his children's godparents. See Rottermund 2021, 215–54.

114 Cf. Manikowska 2022, 65–77; Marinelli 2016/17, 39–49; Manikowska 2014; and Manikowska 2012, 32–36.

115 Weddigen 2008, 28–41.

116 Wagner 2022a, 22–23.

117 Karl Schütz in exh. cat. Vienna 2005, 86–87, no. 7.

118 Karl Schütz in exh. cat. Vienna 2005, 87, no. 8.

119 Cf. Wagner 2022a, 29.

120 See most recently exh. cat. Dresden 2022.

121 Schütz 2005, 101.

122 It seems unlikely that Bellotto came to Vienna on direct summons from the Imperial court or through recommendation by Maria Theresa's cousin, Queen Maria Josepha, who had died in November 1757. See Wagner 2022a, 33.

123 On Kaunitz see Mayer 2021.

124 Lorenz 2008, 128–33.

125 Cf. Meyer 1995, 45–63.

126 Nivelon 1737, E.

127 Schütz 2005, 101.

128 On Soliman see especially the essays in exh. cat. Vienna 2011/12.

129 Schütz 2005, 101.

130 Cf. Frank 2001, 27–32.

131 "XVI. Augusti. Anno M.D.C.C.LIX Prusso caeso ad Francofurtum ab exercitu Russo-Austriaco."

132 On the painting see Wolfgang Prohaska in exh. cat. Vienna 2005, 134–38, no. 2.

133 Cf. Maurer 2017, 88.

134 See Dobretsberger 2023.

135 Cf. Maurer 2017, 88. On carriages in Bellotto's paintings more generally see Kurzel-Runtscheiner 2005, 48–61.

136 Kozakiewicz was first to suggest such an identification. See Kozakiewicz 1972, 119.

137 Kerber 2017, 5–8.

138 On the painting see Wolfgang Prohaska in exh. cat. Vienna 2005, 138–42, no. 25.

139 Cf. Hajós 2000, 223–39.

140 Maurer 2017, 80, 90.

141 On sociological concepts of regulatory processes see especially Elias 1978/82.

142 Karl Schütz in exh. cat. Vienna 2005, 108–14, no. 17.

143 On the gardens see Berger 2020, 197–208 and Hajós 2008, 41–48.

144 On the interpretation of the panorama as a Catholic triumph see Maurer 2017, 89.

145 Fellinger 2018, 11–24.

146 Cf. Dolz 2022, 126–27 and Wiedemann 2014/15, 294–99.

147 Marinoni 1751.

148 I sincerely thank Gudrun Swoboda for bringing the drawing to my attention. On Lanci's instrument see Kemp 1990, 175–77.

149 Koja 2022, 10.

150 Cf. Edney and Sponberg Pedley 2019, vol. 4, 732–34, 919–20 and Rill 2001, 183–202.

151 Cf. Heinz and Mokre 1991/92, 93–122.

152 Fuhrmann 1738/39.

153 Cf. Steadman 2025, 64–65 and Bassett 2025, 15.

154 Marinoni 1745.

155 The vantage point is taken from the first floor of the former Jesuit convict erected between 1652 and 1654 (the location of today's Greek Catholic Church). See Karl Schütz in exh. cat. Vienna 2005, 130, no. 23.

156 Cf. Posch 2015, 417–28 and Steinmayr 2010, 169–85.

157 Karl Schütz in exh. cat. Vienna 2005, 127–30, no. 22.

158 Cf. Karner 2004, 397–412. On Messerschmidt's bust of Swieten see Pötzl-Malikova 2015, 249–51, no. 35 and exh. cat. New York and Paris 2010/11, 74–77, no. 3.

159 Schütz 2005a, 51–58.

160 On Hell's observations of the transit of Venus see Aspaas 2008, 10–20.

161 Cf. Posch 2015, 417–28 and Steinmayr 2010, 169–85.

162 Karl Schütz in exh. cat. Vienna 2005, 127–30, no. 22.

163 Cf. Crary 2001, 51–57.

164 Already Martina Frank understood the Viennese cycle as a celebration of Maria Theresa's reign. See Frank 2001, 27–32. See further Telesko 2018, 42.

165 Karl Schütz in exh. cat. Vienna 2005, 114–116, no. 18.

166 Cf. Nicolai 1784, 134–37. See further Knofler 1979, 29–30.

167 Maurer 2017, 71.

168 Cf. Kerber 2022, 137 and Karl Schütz in exh. cat. Vienna 2005, 114–16, no. 18.

169 On the monstrance see Czernin 2009, 280.

170 On the abbey's brotherhoods see Hübl 1918, 1–21.

171 Cf. Maurer 2017, 70–71 and Gugitz 1949/50, 94–104.

172 "Alle Tage wird alles frisch gekauft, und im vornehmsten Herrschaftshause findet man weder Ey noch Mehl, weder Butter noch Schmalz vorräthig." Cf. Nicolai 1784, 255 and Knofler 1979, 30–36.

173 "Ein in Wien residirender Bottschafter, der sich über solchen Uberfluß nicht genug verwundern konnte, machte lusthalber den Versuch, ob in den Sachen denn gar kein Mangel. Er befahl seinen Leuten, alles grüne auf dem Marckt auf einmal, und zugleich aufzukauffen. Es geschahe, aber der Marckt ward nicht so geschwind leer, als er mit allen aufs neu wiederum besezet ward, und man vermerckte nicht, daß etwas gemangelt." (An ambassador residing in Vienna, who could not be amazed enough at such abundance, decided, for amusement, to try whether there was really no shortage of anything. He ordered his servants to buy up all the green produce at the market at once. This was done, but the market was not emptied as quickly as it was newly filled again with everything, and one did not notice that anything was lacking.) Fuhrmann 1766, 235.

174 "In dem Gasthofe, worin ich abgestiegen, war im buchstäblichen Verstande jeden Tag Jahrmarkt. Die Kaufleute und Krämer scheinen nichts im Hause zu verkaufen, sondern schleppen ihre Waaren von Hause zu Hause, wie die Hausirer." Burney 1773, 152.

175 Cf. Golzar 2013, 32–39 and Wolfgang Kos in exh. cat. Vienna 2013, 47–53.

176 On Greek merchants in Vienna see Mildnam 2013, 158–65 and Do Paço 2011, 53–72.

177 See Anna Grochła and Karl Schütz in exh. cat. Vienna 2005, 235, no. 69.

178 Kiefer and Hattendorff 2022, 165–86.

179 "Ein sicherer Cavalier hat von der Stadt Wien folgende Verse verfertigt: / Wien / Ein Klumpen Häuser und Paläste, / Voll Ungeziefer, voller Gäste, / Ein Mischmasch aller Nationen, / Die in Ost, West, Süd-Norden wohnen: / Gestank und Koth in allen Gassen ..." Schütze 1751, 1214. See also Knofler 1979, 22.

180 See Maurer 2013, 13. Maurer drew on historical records held at the City and State Archive of Vienna (Stadtarchiv, Alte Registratur, Zusammengelegte Akten, 135/1759 and 216/175).

181 Cf. Bassett 2025, 81–82 and Stollberg-Rilinger 2017, 720–26.

182 Weddigen identified the same principle in Bellotto's Dresden views. See Weddigen 2008, 34–36. For similar interpretations of depictions of the poor in eighteenth-century British landscape paintings see Barrell 1980.

183 On the painting see Karl Schütz in exh. cat. Vienna 2005, 121–23, no. 20.

184 Maurer 2017, 75.

185 Gugitz 1949/50, 94–104.

186 On the Mehlgrube see Sabine Leitner in Lorenz 2008, 42–45.

187 "Die Redouten, welche die Carnevals-Zeit hindurch zu Wien gehalten werden, werden gemeiniglich in Hof- und Stadt-Redouten unterschieden. Die Hof-Redouten werden wöchentlich dreymal auf dem prächtigen kayserlichen Redouten-Saal gehalten, woselbst die kayserliche Herrschaft mit tanzet, die Stadt-Redouten aber werden auf der so genannten Mehl-Grube gehalten." (The masquerade balls held in Vienna throughout the Carnival season are generally divided into court balls and city balls. The court balls are held three times a week in the magnificent imperial Redouten Hall, where the imperial household also takes part in the dancing, while the city balls are held in the so-called Mehlgrube.) Willebrandt 1761, 302.

188 On the painting see Karl Schütz in exh. cat. Vienna 2005, 124–26, no. 21.

189 On the Palais Lobkowitz see Inge Nevole in Lorenz 2008, 46–49.

190 Cf. Pichlkastner 2015, 117–32 and Pichlkastner and Swatek 2017.

191 Cf. Hanzl-Wachter 2005.

192 On the painting see Wolfgang Prohaska in exh. cat. Vienna 2005, 145–48, no. 27.

193 On the painting see Wolfgang Prohaska in exh. cat. Vienna 2005, 142–45, no. 26.

194 On Bellotto's technique see Bendfeldt 2022, 180–95; Zech 2014/15, 302–13; Schwabe 2014/15, 334–41; and Bendfeldt 2011, 69–85. I also sincerely thank Anneliese Földes for discussing with me her observations whilst cleaning the KHM's pictures by Bellotto in preparation of the exhibition.

195 "Ich habe alles in der Art von Befestigungen ausgeführt, um sicher zu sein, falls einmal ein feindlicher Angriff erfolgen sollte." Cited after Brauneis 1981, 54.

196 Cf. Wolfgang Prohaska in exh. cat. Vienna 2005, 148–51, no. 28 and Martina Frank in exh. cat. Houston 2001, 206–07, no. 66.

197 On the Königstein views see exh. cat. London 2021.

198 On the picture see especially Karl Schütz in exh. cat. Vienna 2005, 151–52, no. 29 and Martina Frank in exh. cat. Houston 2001, 208–09, no. 67.

199 Weber 2005, 39–49.

200 Weber 2005, 43.

201 See Karl Schütz in exh. cat. Vienna 2005, 151–52, no. 29; Weber 2005, 47; and Martina Frank in exh. cat. Houston 2001, 208–09, no. 67.

202 For a transcription of the relevant passage see Schütz 2005, 106. See further Gruber 2006/07, 354–400.
203 Frank 2001, 30.
204 "Madame ma chere cousine. Je n'ais put voir partir Canaletti sans le charger de ces lignes et le lui recomander; il s'est conduit ici tres bien et nous at fournit plusieurs pieces des ces ouvrages tres belle. Je lui porte envie de vous voir peut-etre 8 mois plutot que moi. Je souhaite bien que la nouvelle année me procure ce bonheur et qu'elle soit plus heureuse que les autres, nous avonts actuellement pour peu des jours les princes Albert et Clement chez nous qui m'interessent infiniment et je le aime d'autant plus vous etant si tendrement attachee. Ils ont bien regretée de n'avoir eut la permition de vous voir; il l'esperent a leurs retour, et je suis tonjours de Votre Altesse tres affectionnée cousine Marie Therese." (Madam, my dear cousin, I could not let Canaletti [=Bellotto] leave without entrusting him with these few lines and recommending him to you; he behaved very well here and provided us with several pieces of his work, which are very beautiful. I envy him for getting to see you—perhaps eightmonths before I do. I sincerely hope that the new year will grant me this happiness, and that it may be a happier one than the others. We have at present, for a few days, Princes Albert and Clement with us. They interest me immensely, and I am all the more attached to them since you are so tenderly devoted to them. They greatly regretted not having had permission to see you; they hope for this on their return. I remain, as always, Your Highness's most affectionate cousin, Maria Theresa) Maria Theresia to Maria Antonia, Vienna, 4 January 1761, Sächsisches Staatsarchiv, Hauptstaatsarchiv Dresden, 12528 Estate of Maria Antonia, Electress of Saxony, No. 104, letter No. 35. French transcription cited after Lippert 1908, 97–98, no. 67.
205 On the Munich pictures see Andreas Schumacher in exh. cat. Munich 2014/15, 250–59, nos. 51–53.
206 Cf. Manikowska 2022, 65–77; Marinelli 2016/17, 39–49; Manikowska 2014; and Manikowska 2012, 32–36.
207 Wagner 2022a, 36–39.
208 Cf. Aurelia Zduńczyk in exh. cat. Warsaw 2022, 297–99, no. 65 and Julia Thoma in exh. cat. Munich 2014/15, 260–61, no. 54. See also Karl Schütz's entry on Bellotto's etching after this painting in exh. cat. Vienna 2005, 237, no. 70.
209 "Canaletto, Bernardo Belotti, Mahler, zieht 1650 r [= Taler] Besoldung und 100 r Hauszins. Scheint mit vielen Mahlereyen und Vorstellungen der Prospecte, die in der Gallerie überflüßig seind, hingegen füglich die Landschlößer zieren können, der Absicht seines Hierseyens ein völliges Genüge geleistet zu haben." (Canaletto, Bernardo Bellotto, painter, receives a salary of 1,650 r. [= thaler] and 100 r. in house rent. He appears, through many paintings and representations of views which are superfluous in the gallery but can suitably adorn the country palaces, to have fully fulfilled the purpose of his stay here.) Sächsisches Staatsarchiv, Dresden, 10026 Geheimes Kabinett, Loc. 894/5, fol. 51r. Cited after Wagner 2022a, 36.
210 Cf. Wagner 2022a, 36–39 and Wagener 2014/15, 130–34.
211 Cf. Kerber 2022, 140–42; Magdalena Królikiewicz in exh. cat. Warsaw 2022, 299–301, no. 66; Manikowska 2014, 161–222; Gottdang 2014/15, 96–103; and Kemp 1990, 147–48. On a related drawing see exh. cat. Darmstadt 2022/23, 180–81, no. 53.
212 Wagner 2022a, 39.
213 On Bellotto's Warsaw period see most recently Rottermund 2022, 145–59.

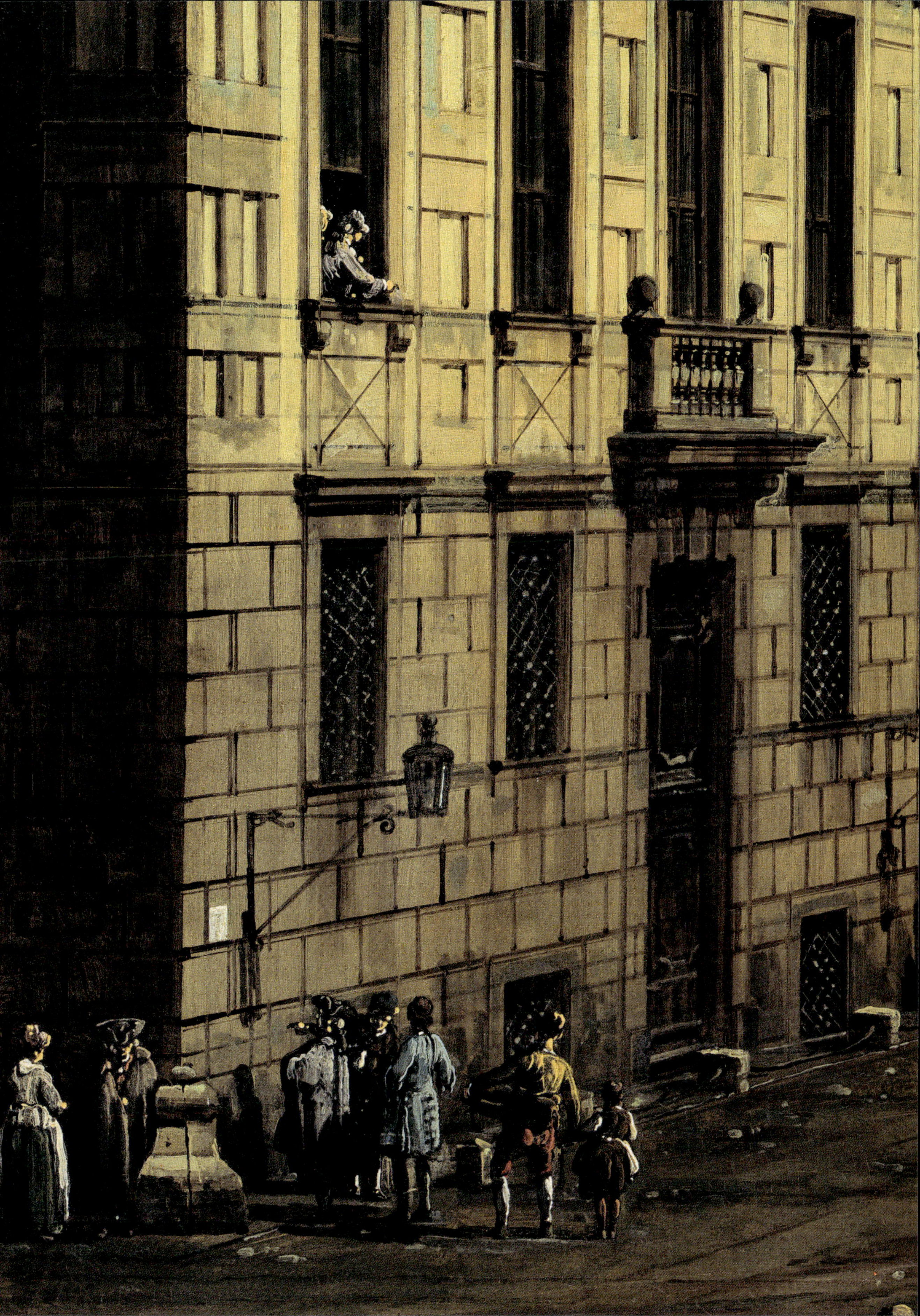

REFERENCES

Exh. cat. Bath 2021
Charles Beddington, *Canaletto: Painting Venice. The Woburn Series*, exh. cat. Bath (Holburne Museum) 2021

Exh. cat. Birmingham 1993
Michael Liversidge and Jane Farrington (eds.), *Canaletto & England*, exh. cat. Birmingham (Museum & Art Gallery) 1993

Exh. cat. Darmstadt 2022/23
Mechthild Haas (ed.), *Remember Venice! Bernardo Bellotto zeichnet*, exh. cat. Darmstadt (Hessisches Landesmuseum) 2022/23

Exh. cat. Dresden 2022
Stephan Koja and Iris Yvonne Wagner (eds.), *Bellotto: Zauber des Realen. Bernardo Bellotto am sächsischen Hof*, exh. cat. Dresden (Staatliche Kunstsammlungen) 2022

Exh. cat. Houston 2001
Edgar Peters Bowron (ed.), *Bernardo Bellotto and the Capitals of Europe*, exh. cat. Houston (The Museum of Fine Arts) 2001

Exh. cat. London 2021
Letizia Treves, Lucy Chiswell, and Stephen Lloyd (eds.), *Bellotto: the Königstein Views Reunited*, exh. cat. London (The National Gallery) 2021

Exh. cat. Milan 2016/17
Bożena Anna Kowalczyk (ed.), *Bellotto and Canaletto: Wonder and Light*, exh. cat. Milan (Gallerie d'Italia) 2016/17

Exh. cat. Munich 2014/15
Andreas Schumacher (ed.), *Canaletto: Bernardo Bellotto malt Europa*, exh. cat. Munich (Alte Pinakothek) 2014/15

Exh. cat. New Haven and London 2006/07
Charles Beddington (ed.), *Canaletto in England: A Venetian Artist Abroad 1746–1755*, exh. cat. New Haven (Yale Center for British Art) and London (Dulwich Picture Gallery) 2006/07

Exh. cat. New York and Paris 2010/11
Maria Pötzl-Malikova and Guilhem Scherf (eds.), *Franz Xaver Messerschmidt*, exh. cat. New York (Neue Galerie) and Paris (Louvre) 2010/11

Exh. cat. Venice 2001
Alessandro Bettagno and Bożena Anna Kowalczyk (eds.), *Canaletto: prima maniera*, exh. cat. Venice (Fondazione Giorgio Cini) 2001

Exh. cat. Vienna 2005
Wilfried Seipel and Karl Schütz (eds.), *Bernardo Bellotto genannt Canaletto: europäische Veduten*, exh. cat. Vienna (Kunsthistorisches Museum) 2005

Exh. cat. Vienna 2011/12
Philipp Blom and Wolfgang Kos (eds.), *Angelo Soliman: Ein Afrikaner in Wien*, exh. cat. Vienna (Wien Museum) 2011/12

Exh. cat. Vienna 2013
Wolfgang Kos (ed.), *Wiener Typen: Klischees und Wirklichkeit*, exh. cat. Vienna (Wien Museum) 2013

Exh. cat. Vienna 2018
Stella Rollig and Markus Fellinger (eds.), *Der Canalettoblick*, exh. cat. Vienna (Belvedere) 2018

Exh. cat. Warsaw 2022
Artur Badach (ed.), *Bernardo Bellotto on the 300th Anniversary of the Painter's Birth*, exh. cat. Warsaw (Zamek Królewski) 2022

Algarotti 1739
Francesco Algarotti, *Sir Isaac Newton's Philosophy Explain'd For the Use of the Ladies, in Six Dialogues on Light and Colours* (London, 1739)

Algarotti 1764
Francesco Algarotti, *An Essay on Painting Written in Italian* (London, 1764)

Allen 1987
Brian Allen, "Topography or Art: Canaletto and London in the Mid-Eighteenth Century," in Malcolm Warner (ed.), *The Image of London: Views by Travellers and Emigrés 1550–1920*, exh. cat. London (Barbican Art Gallery) 1987, 29–48

Anonymous 1734
Anonymous, *A New Critical Review of the Publick Buildings, Statues, and Ornaments, in and about London and Westminster* (London, 1734)

Anonymous 1744
Anonymous, *A Trip from St. James to the Royal Exchange* (London, 1744)

Aspaas 2008
Per Pippin Aspaas, "Maximilian Hell's Invitation to Norway," *Communications in Asteroseismology* 149 (2008): 10–20

Badach 2022
Artur Badach, "Die frühen Jahre: Bernardo Bellotto in Italien," in exh. cat. Dresden 2022, 88–105

Barrell 1980
John Barrell, *The Dark Side of the Landscape: The Rural Poor in English Painting 1730–1840* (Cambridge, 1980)

Bassett 2025
Richard Bassett, *Maria Theresa: Empress* (New Haven, 2025)

Beddington 2006/07
Charles Beddington, "Canaletto in England," in exh. cat. New Haven and London 2006/07, 8–29

Bendfeldt 2011
Sabine Bendfeldt, "Die Restaurierung des Canaletto-Blicks und Betrachtung zu Bellottos Malweise," in Andreas Hennig, Sebastian Oesinghaus, and Sabine Bendfeldt (eds.), *Bernardo Bellotto: Der Canaletto-Blick*, exh. cat. Dresden (Staatliche Kunstsammlungen) 2011, 69–85

Bendfeldt 2022
Sabine Bendfeldt, "Betrachtungen zur Maltechnik: die Dresdner Veduten Bernardo Bellottos," in exh. cat. Dresden 2022, 180–95

Benjamin 1936
Walter Benjamin, "L'œuvre d'art à l'époque de sa reproduction mécanisée," *Zeitschrift für Sozialforschung* 5, no. 1 (1936): 40–66

Berger 2020
Eva Berger, "Gartengestalter und Gärtner am kaiserlichen Hof und in Wiener Adelsgärten vom 16. bis zum 19. Jahrhundert in bildlichen Darstellungen und Schriftquellen," *Die Gartenkunst* 32, no. 2 (2020): 197–208

Bettagno 1969
Alessandro Bettagno, *Caricature di Anton Maria Zanetti* (Venice, 1969)

Bibiena 1711
Ferdinando Galli Bibiena, *L'architettura civile preparata sú la geometria, e ridotta alle prospettive. Considerazioni pratiche …* (Parma, 1711)

Bolla 1995
Peter De Bolla, "The Visibility of Visuality: Vauxhall Gardens and the Siting of the Viewer," in Stephen Melville and Bill Readings (eds.), *Vision and Textuality* (London, 1995), 282–95

Bradley 1805
Edward Bradley, *The Work of the Late Edward Dayes* (London, 1805)

Brauneis 1981
Walther Brauneis, *Die Schlösser im Marchfeld* (St. Pölten, 1981)

Burford 1988
Ephraim John Burford, *Royal St James's: Being a Story of Kings, Clubmen and Courtesans* (London, 1988)

Burlini 1758
Biagio Burlini, *Raccolta di macchine, ed istrumenti d'ottica …* (Venice, 1758)

Burney 1773
Karl Burney, *Carl Burney's der Musik Doctors Tagebuch seiner Musikalischen Reisen. Zweyter Band. Durch Flandern, die Niederlande und am Rhein bis Wien* (Hamburg, 1773)

Buttery 1987
David Buttery, "Canaletto at Warwick," *The Burlington Magazine* 129 (1987): 427–45

Campbell 2007
James W. P. Campbell, *Building St Paul's* (London, 2007)

Capdeville and Kerhervé 2019
Valérie Capdeville and Alain Kerhervé (eds.), *British Sociability in the Long Eighteenth Century: Challenging the Anglo-French Connection* (Woodbridge, 2019)

Cassidy-Geiger 2007/08
Maureen Cassidy-Geiger, "Princes and Porcelain on the Grand Tour of Italy," in Maureen Cassidy-Geiger (ed.), *Fragile Diplomacy: Meissen Porcelain for European Courts ca. 1710–1763*, exh. cat. New York (Bard Graduate Center) 2007/08, 208–55

Cassidy-Geiger 2018
Maureen Cassidy-Geiger, *Die Grande Kur 1738–1740: Prinz Friedrich Christian von Sachsen auf der Suche nach Heilung und Kultur in Italien / The Grand Cure 1738–1740: A Disabled Saxon Prince and his Tour of Italy* (Dresden, 2018)

Clayton 2006
Martin Clayton, *Canaletto in Venice* (London, 2006)

Coke and Borg 2011
David Coke and Alan Borg, *Vauxhall Gardens: A History* (New Haven, 2011)

Constable 1962
W. G. Constable, *Canaletto: Giovanni Antonio Canal 1697–1768*, 2 vols (Oxford, 1962)

Constable 1989
W. G. Constable, *Canaletto: Giovanni Antonio Canal 1697–1768*, revised by J. G. Links, reissued with supplement and additional plates, 3 vols (Oxford, 1989)

Conti 1756
Antonio Conti, *Prose e Poesie*, vol. 2 (Venice, 1756)

Corboz 1985
André Corboz, *Canaletto: una Venezia immaginaria*, 2 vols (Milan, 1985)

Crary 2001
Jonathan Crary, *Techniques of the Observer: On Vision and Modernity in the Nineteenth Century* (Cambridge [Mass.], 2001)

Czernin 2009
Martin Czernin (ed.), *Museum im Schottenstift: Kunstsammlungen der Benediktinerabtei Unserer Lieben Frau zu den Schotten in Wien* (Vienna, 2009)

Dallinger von Dalling 1780
Johann Dallinger von Dalling, *Description des tableaux, et des pièces de sculpture, que renferme la galerie de Son Altesse François Joseph Chef et Prince Regnant de la Maison de Liechtenstein etc. etc.* (Vienna, 1780)

Delneri 2007
Annalia Delneri, "Scenografia e sperimentazione prospettica: il nuovo spazio urbano di Bernardo Canal", in Giuseppe Maria Pilo, Laura De Rossi, and Isabella Reale (eds.), *Un'identità: custodi dell'arte e della memoria* (Gorizia, 2007), 315–21

Diderot 1753
Denis Diderot, *Encyclopédie ou dictionnaire des sciences, des arts et des métiers*, vol. 3 (Paris, 1753)

Diderot 1772
Denis Diderot, *Recueil de planches, sur les sciences, les arts libéraux, et les arts méchaniques: avec leur explication. Seconde livraison, en deux parties. Seconde Partie. 202 Planches. Troisième édition* (Livourne, 1772)

Dobretsberger 2023
Christine Dobretsberger, "Geschichte des Langstreckenlaufs in Wien: Als Wien laufen lernte," *Wien Museum Magazin* [online journal] (June 6, 2023) <https://magazin.wienmuseum.at/geschichte-des-langstreckenlaufs-in-wien> accessed 1 Oct. 2025

Dolz 2022
Wolfram Dolz, "Landesvermessung in Sachsen am Anfang des 18. Jahrhunderts," in exh. cat. Dresden 2022, 126–27

Do Paço 2011
David Do Paço, "Le marchand grec existe-t-il? Remarques sur les représentations collectives et les identités sociales viennoises dans le Kaufruf de Johann Christian Brand de 1775," in Christine Lebeau and Wolfgang Schmale (eds.), *Images en capitale: Vienne fin XVIIe – début XIXe siècles* (Bochum, 2011), 53–72

Duffy and Hedley 2004
Stephen Duffy and Joanne Hedley (eds.), *The Wallace Collection's Pictures: A Complete Catalogue* (London, 2004)

Edney and Sponberg Pedley 2019
Matthew H. Edney and Mary Sponberg Pedley (eds.), *The History of Cartography* (Chicago, 2019)

Elias 1978/82
Norbert Elias, *The Civilizing Process*, 2 vols (Oxford, 1978/82)

Ellis 2012
Markman Ellis, "River and Labour in Samuel Scott's Thames Views in the Mid-Eighteenth Century," *London Journal* 37, no. 3 (2012): 152–73

Fellinger 2018
Markus Fellinger, "Der Canalettoblick: Stadtbilder zwischen Kontinuität und Wandel," in exh. cat. Vienna 2018, 11–24

Frank 2001
Martina Frank, "Bellotto in Vienna and Munich," in exh. cat. Houston 2001, 27–32

Fuhrmann 1738/39
Mathias Fuhrmann, *Alt- und Neues Wien oder dieser Residenzstadt chronologische und historische Beschreibung*, 2 vols (Vienna, 1738/39)

Fuhrmann 1766
Mathias Fuhrmann, *Historische Beschreibung und kurz gefasste Nachricht von der Röm. Kaiserl. und Königlichen Residenz=Stadt Wien, Und Ihren Vorstädten*, vol. 1 (Vienna, 1766)

Golzar 2013
Elisabeth Golzar, "Bilder führen durch den Klang der Stadt: Die Entwicklung der europäischen Kaufrufgrafik," in exh. cat. Vienna 2013, 32–39

Gottdang 2014/15
Andrea Gottdang, "Die Verführung des Blicks: Architekturfantasien der 1760er-Jahre," in exh. cat. Munich 2014/15, 96–113

Gravesande 1711
Willem Jacob 's Gravesande, *Essai de perspective* (A la Haye, 1711)

Gruber 2005
Gerlinde Gruber, "Bernardo Bellotto in Italien (1738–1747)," in exh. cat. Vienna 2005, 61–69

Gruber 2006/07
Gerlinde Gruber, "Das Bilderverzeichnis der Pressburger Burg von 1781: Ein Beitrag zur Sammlungsgeschichte der Gemäldegalerie des Kunsthistorischen Museums," *Jahrbuch des Kunsthistorischen Museums* 8/9 (2006/07): 354–400

Gugitz 1949/50
Gustav Gugitz, "Die Sesselträger in Alt-Wien," *Jahrbuch des Vereins für Geschichte der Stadt Wien* 8 (1949/50): 94–104

Gwynn 1766
John Gwynn, *London and Westminster Improved* (London, 1766)

Hajós 2000
Beatrix Hajós, "Der Park von Schönbrunn: Das kaiserliche Lieblingsprojekt," in Renate Zedinger (ed.), *Lothringens Erbe: Franz Stephan von Lothringen (1708–1765) und sein Wirken in Wirtschaft, Wissenschaft und Kunst der Habsburgermonarchie*, exh. cat. Schallaburg 2000, 223–39

Hajós 2008
Beatrix Hajós, "Schönbrunn: The Garden Designer Jean Trehet around 1700 and the Modernization of the Gardens by the Colonie Lorraine around 1750," *Die Gartenkunst* 20 (2008): 41–48

Hallett 1993
Mark Hallett, "Framing the Modern City: Canaletto's Images of London," in exh. cat. Birmingham 1993, 46–54

Hallett 2000
Mark Hallett, *Hogarth* (London, 2000)

Hanzl-Wachter 2005
Lieselotte Hanzl-Wachter (ed.), *Schloss Hof: Prinz Eugens tusculum rurale und Sommerresidenz der kaiserlichen Familie. Geschichte und Ausstattung eines barocken Gesamtkunstwerks* (St. Pölten, 2005)

Haskell 1956
Francis Haskell, "Stefano Conti, Patron of Canaletto and Others," *The Burlington Magazine* 98, no. 642 (1956): 296–300

Heinz and Mokre 1991/92
Markus Heinz and Jan Mokre, "Über Joseph Daniel von Huber (1730/1731–1788) und seinen Vogelschauplan von Wien," *Jahrbuch des Vereins für Geschichte der Stadt Wien* 47/48 (1991/92), 93–122

Hübl 1918
Albert Hübl, "Die Bruderschaften an der Schottenkirche in Wien," *Berichte und Mitteilungen des Alterthums-Vereines zu Wien* 50 (1918): 1–21

Karner 2004
Herbert Karner, "Wien: Vom Jesuiterplatzl zum Universitätsplatz. Architektur und Programm," in Martin Scheutz, Wolfgang Schmale and Dana Štefanová (eds.), *Orte des Wissens* (Bochum, 2004), 397–412

Kemp 1990
Martin Kemp, *The Science of Art* (New Haven, 1990)

Kerber 2017
Peter Björn Kerber, *Eyewitness Views: Making History in Eighteenth-Century Europe* (Los Angeles, 2017)

Kerber 2022
Peter Björn Kerber, "Subjektive Lebens-Perspektive: Bernardo Bellottos menschliche Stadtporträts," in exh. cat. Dresden 2022, 128–43

Kiefer and Hattendorff 2022
Marcus Kiefer and Claudia Hattendorff, "Hugo von Hofmannsthal und das Wien des Canaletto: Zur Bildrezeption im Anatol-Prolog (1892)," in Peter Bell (ed.), *Maraviglia: Rezeptionsgeschichte(n) von der Antike bis in die Moderne* (Vienna, 2022), 165–86

Klein 2002
Lawrence Klein, "Politeness and the Interpretation of the British Eighteenth Century," *The Historical Journal* 45, no. 4 (2002): 869–98

Knofler 1979
Monika J. Knofler, *Das theresianische Wien: Der Alltag in den Bildern Canalettos* (Vienna, 1979)

Koja 2022
Stephan Koja, "Anspruch des Realen: Bernardo Bellotto und die Erneuerung der Vedute," in exh. cat. Dresden 2022, 9–11

Kowalczyk 1999
Bożena Anna Kowalczyk, "I primi sostenitori veneziani di Bernardo Bellotto," *Saggi e memorie di storia dell'arte* 23 (1999): 189–218

Kowalczyk 2001
Bożena Anna Kowalczyk, "Bernardo Bellotto: The Formation of an Original Style," in exh. cat. Houston 2001, 3–13

Kowalczyk 2012
Bożena Anna Kowalczyk, "Bellotto and Zanetti in Florence," *The Burlington Magazine* 154 (2012): 24–31

Kowalczyk 2016/17
Bożena Anna Kowalczyk, "Bellotto and Canaletto: The Success of Separation," in exh. cat. Milan 2016/17, 15–37

Kozakiewicz 1972
Stefan Kozakiewicz, *Bernardo Bellotto genannt Canaletto*, 2 vols (Recklinghausen, 1972)

Kurzel-Runtscheiner 2005
Monica Kurzel-Runtscheiner, "Von der barocken Karosse zum sportlichen Coupé: Die Entwicklung des europäischen Wagenbaus im Spiegel der Veduten Bellottos," *Vernissage* 142, no. 02 (2005): 48–61

Liebsch 2022
Thomas Liebsch, "Bellottos Arbeitsmethoden: Die Verwendung der Camera obscura," in exh. cat. Dresden 2022, 196–97

Links 1982
J. G. Links, *Canaletto* (Oxford, 1982)

Links 2010
J. G. Links, *The Soane Canalettos* (London, 2010)

Lippert 1908
Woldemar Lippert (ed.), *Kaiserin Maria Theresia und Kurfürstin Maria Antonia von Sachsen: Briefwechsel 1747–1772* (Leipzig, 1908)

Liversidge 1993
Michael Liversidge, "Canaletto and England," in exh. cat. Birmingham 1993, 10–29

Lloyd 2015
Christopher Lloyd, "Canaletto and the Depiction of Rome," in Bożena Anna Kowalczyk (ed.), *Venezia Settecento: Studi*

in memoria di Alessandro Bettagno (Milan, 2015), 85–93

LORENZ 2008
Hellmut Lorenz (ed.), *Das barocke Wien: Die Kupferstiche von Joseph Emanuel Fischer von Erlach und Johann Adam Delsenbach* (Petersberg, 2008)

MAGRINI 1998
Marina Magrini, "Giambattista Recanati collezionista di Canaletto e Tiepolo," *Rivista dell'Istituto Nazionale di Archeologia e Storia dell'Arte* 21 (1998): 273–81

MAGRINI 2001
Marina Magrini, "Canaletto e dintorni: I primi anni di Canaletto attraverso le lettere dei contemporanei," in exh. cat. Venice 2001, 221–45

MANIKOWSKA 2012
Ewa Manikowska, "The Rediscovery of Bernardo Bellotto's Inventory," *The Burlington Magazine* 154 (2012): 32–36

MANIKOWSKA 2014
Ewa Manikowska, *Bernardo Bellotto i jego drezdeński apartament* (Warsaw, 2014)

MANIKOWSKA 2022
Ewa Manikowska, "Bernardo Bellottos Dresdner Wohnung: Sozialer Anspruch und Status des Künstlers," in exh. cat. Dresden 2022, 64–77

MARIETTE 1853
Pierre-Jean Mariette, *Abecedario de J. P. Mariette et autres notes inédites de cet amateur sur les arts et les artistes*, edited by Charles Philippe de Chennevières-Pointel and Anatole de Montaiglon, vol. 1 (Paris, 1853)

MARINELLI 2016/17
Sergio Marinelli, "Black Lights of the Enlightenment's Painter," in exh. cat. Milan 2016/17, 39–49

MARINONI 1745
Giovanni Jacopo de Marinoni, *De astronomica specula domestica et organico apparatu astronomico libri duo* (Vienna, 1745)

MARINONI 1751
Giovanni Jacopo de Marinoni, *De re ichnographica: cujus hodierna praxis exponitur, et propriis exemplis pluribus illustratur* (Vienna, 1751)

MAURER 2013
Maximilian Maurer, *Bernardo Bellottos Ansichten der Freyung in Wien* (unpubl. manuscript, 2013)

MAURER 2017
Maximilian Maurer, "Mehr als schöne Ansichten? Ikonografische Beobachtungen zu Bernardo Bellottos Wiener Veduten (1759–60) aus der Sicht eines Historikers," *Mitteilungen des Instituts für Österreichische Geschichtsforschung* 125 (2017): 68–91

MAYER 2021
Gernot Mayer, *Kulturpolitik der Aufklärung: Wenzel Anton von Kaunitz-Rietberg (1711–1794) und die Künste* (Petersberg, 2021)

MEYER 1995
Arline Meyer, "Re-Dressing Classical Statuary: The Eighteenth-Century Hand-in-Waistcoat Portrait," *The Art Bulletin* 77, no. 1 (1995): 45–63

MILCHRAM 2013
Gerhard Milchram, "Auswärtige Händler in Wien: Tiroler Teppichhändler, Figurini, Zwiebelkroaten, jüdische Hausierer und griechische Kaufleute," in exh. cat. Vienna 2013, 158–65

MORITZ 1886
Karl Philipp Moritz, *Travels in England in 1782*, edited by Henry Morley (London, 1886)

NEPI SCIRÈ 1997
Giovanna Nepi Scirè, *Canaletto's Sketchbook*, 2 vols (Venice, 1997)

NEWTON 1704
Isaac Newton, *Opticks: or, a Treatise of the Reflexions, Refractions, Inflexions and Colours of Light* (London, 1704)

NICOLAI 1784
Friedrich Nicolai, *Beschreibung einer Reise durch Deutschland und die Schweiz im Jahre 1781*, vol. 3 (Berlin-Stettin, 1784)

NIVELON 1737
François Nivelon, *The Rudiments of Genteel Behavior* (London, 1737)

NOLLET 1764
Jean Antoine Nollet, *Leçons de physique expérimentale*, vol. 5 (Paris, 1764)

O'BYRNE 2008
Alison F. O'Byrne, "Composing Westminster Bridge: Public Improvement and National Identity in Eighteenth-Century London," in Maximillian E. Novak (ed.), *The Age of Projects* (Toronto, 2008), 243–70

PACKER AND BEDDINGTON 2025
Lelia Packer and Charles Beddington, *Canaletto and Guardi: Views of Venice at the Wallace Collection* (London, 2025)

PEMBERTON-PIGOTT 1989
Viola Pemberton-Pigott, "The Development of Canaletto's Painting Technique," in Katharine Baetjer and J. G. Links (eds.), *Canaletto*, exh. cat. New York (Metropolitan Museum of Art) 1989, 53–63

PEMBERTON-PIGOTT 2001
Viola Pemberton-Pigott, "Canaletto 'prima maniera': tradizione e innovazione nelle tecniche pittoriche degli esordi di Canaletto," in exh. cat. Venice 2001, 207–17

PICHLKASTNER 2015
Sarah Pichlkastner, "Insassen, Personal und Organisationsform des Wiener Bürgerspitals in der Frühen Neuzeit: Eine Projektskizze," *Mitteilungen des Instituts für Österreichische Geschichtsforschung* 123 (2015): 117–32

PICHLKASTNER AND SWATEK 2017
Sarah Pichlkastner and Manuel Swatek, *Fürsorge und Ökonomie: Das Wiener Bürgerspital um 1775* (Vienna, 2017)

PIRENNE 1970
Maurice Henri Pirenne, *Optics, Painting and Photography* (Cambridge, 1970)

POPE 1720
Alexander Pope, *Windsor-Forest* (London, 1720)

POSCH 2015
Thomas Posch, "Zur Geschichte der Astronomie an der Universität Wien," in Karl Anton Fröschl (ed.), *Reflexive Innenansichten aus der Universität: Disziplinengeschichten zwischen Wissenschaft, Gesellschaft und Politik* (Vienna, 2015), 417–28

PÖTZL-MALIKOVA 2015
Maria Pötzl-Malikova, *Franz Xaver Messerschmidt 1736–1783* (Weitra, 2015)

POZZO 1693
Andrea Pozzo, *Perspectiva pictorum et architectorum* (Rome, 1693)

REDFORD 1996
Bruce Redford, *Venice & the Grand Tour* (New Haven, 1996)

RILL 2001
Robert Rill, "Die Anfänge der Militärkartographie in den habsburgischen Erblanden: Die Josephinische Landesaufnahme von Böhmen und Mähren nach hofkriegsrätlichen Quellen," *Mitteilungen des Österreichischen Staatsarchivs* 49 (2001): 183–202

Rottermund 2021
Andrzej Rottermund, "An Artist's Prestige: Bernardo Bellotto between Dresden and Warsaw," *Artibus et Historiae* 83 (2021): 215–54

Rottermund 2022
Andrzej Rottermund, "Ansichten von Warschau und Rom: Zu Genese und Chronologie der Gemäldezyklen von Bernardo Bellotto," in exh. cat. Dresden 2022, 144–59

Russell 2006/07
Francis Russell, "Patterns of Patronage," in exh. cat. New Haven and London 2006/07, 38–47

Sabbattini 1638
Nicola Sabbattini, *Pratica di fabricar scene e machine ne' teatri* (Ravenna, 1638)

Saussure 1902
César-François de Saussure, *A Foreign View of England in the Reigns of George I and George II: The Letters of Monsieur Cesar de Saussure to his Family*, translated and edited by Madame Van Muyden (London, 1902)

Savérien 1753
Alexandre Julien Savérien, *Dictionnaire universel de mathématique et de physique*, vol. 1 (Paris, 1753)

Schumacher 2014/15
Andreas Schumacher, "Viel Kunst für viel Wahrheit: Wie der Vedutenmaler der Stadt ins Gesicht blickt," in exh. cat. Munich 2014/15, 16–45

Schütz 2005
Karl Schütz, "Bernardo Bellotto in Wien und München (1759–1761)," in exh. cat. Vienna 2005, 101–07

Schütz 2005a
Karl Schütz, "Bernardo Bellottos Wirklichkeit: die Korrektur der Realität zum Kunstwerk," in exh. cat. Vienna 2005, 51–58

Schütze 1751
Gottfried Schütze (ed.), *Johann Georg Keyßler's Neueste Reise durch Deutschland, Böhmen, Ungarn, die Schweiz, Italien und Lothringen*, vol. 2 (Hannover, 1751)

Schwabe 2014/15
Bettina Schwabe, "Fluchtpunkt und Fadennetz: Das Schloss Nymphenburg von der Parkseite – Die Bildkonstruktion," in exh. cat. Munich 2014/15, 334–41

Selva 1761
Lorenzo Selva, *Esposizione delle comuni, e nuove spezie di cannocchiali, telescopj, microscopj, ed altri istrumenti diottrici, catottrici, e catadiottrici perfezionati ed inventati da Domenico Selva* (Venice, 1761)

Serlio 1545
Sebastiano Serlio, *Il secondo libro d'Architettura* (Paris, 1545)

Solkin 2015
David H. Solkin, *Art in Britain 1660–1815* (New Haven, 2015)

Sperber and Stenger 2016
Roxane Sperber and Jens Stenger, "Canaletto's Colour: The Inspiration and Implication of Changing Grounds, Pigments and Paint Application in the Artist's English Period," *British Art Studies* [online journal], 2 (2016) <https://doi.org/10.17658/issn.2058-5462/issue-02/rsperber-jstenger> accessed 1 Oct. 2025

Steadman 2025
Philip Steadman, *Canaletto's Camera* (London, 2025)

Steinmayr 2010
Pater Johann Steinmayr, "Die Geschichte der Universitätssternwarte Wien," in Jürgen Hamel, Isolde Müller and Thomas Posch (eds.), *Die Geschichte der Universitätssternwarte Wien* (Frankfurt am Main, 2010), 169–85

Stollberg-Rilinger 2017
Barbara Stollberg-Rilinger, *Maria Theresia: Die Kaiserin in ihrer Zeit* (Munich, 2017)

Succi 2011/12
Dario Succi, "Bellotto in Italia, da Venezia a Verona," in Dario Succi (ed.), *Bernardo Bellotto: il Canaletto delle corti europee*, exh. cat. Conegliano (Palazzo Sarcinelli) 2011/12, 18–51

Telesko 2018
Werner Telesko, "Canalettos Wienansicht vom Oberen Belvedere: Eine Stadtvedute zwischen Konstruktion und Wirklichkeit," in exh. cat. Vienna 2018, 35–45

Vertue 1933–34
George Vertue, "Notebooks, vol. III," *The Walpole Society* 22 (1933–34)

Vivian 1971
Frances Vivian, *Il Console Smith mercante e collezionista* (Vicenza, 1971)

Wagener 2014/15
Theresa Wagener, "Bernardo Bellotto genannt Canaletto: Ein venezianischer Blick auf Mitteleuropa," in exh. cat. Munich 2014/15, 114–43

Wagner 2022
Iris Yvonne Wagner, "Eine Bretterhütte als Camera obscura? Bernardo Bellotto zeichnet die Festung Sonnenstein," *Dresdner Kunstblätter* 66 (2022): 58–62

Wagner 2022a
Iris Yvonne Wagner, "Dem Adel verpflichtet: Bernardo Bellotto in Dresden, Wien und München," in exh. cat. Dresden 2022, 20–41

Weber 2005
Gregor J. M. Weber, "Zwischen Kunst und Natur: Anmerkungen zur Staffage auf Gemälden Bernardo Bellottos," in exh. cat. Vienna 2005, 39–49

Weddigen 2008
Tristan Weddigen, "Ansichtssache: Bellottos Veduten und die städtebauliche Bilderpolitik," in Sigrid Brandt and Hans-Rudolf Meier (eds.), *Stadtbild und Denkmalpflege: Konstruktion und Rezeption von Bildern der Stadt* (Berlin, 2008), 28–41

Wiedemann 2014/15
Wolfgang Wiedemann, "Geodätische Analyse der Ansicht von München," in exh. cat. Munich 2014/15, 294–99

Willebrandt 1761
Johann Peter Willebrandt, *Historische Berichte und Praktische Anmerkungen auf Reisen in Deutschland, in die Niederlande, in Frankreich, England, Dännemarck, Böhmen und Ungarn* (Frankfurt, 1761)

Woolf 1928
Virginia Woolf, *Orlando. A Biography* (New York, 1928)

Wortley Montagu 1861
Mary Wortley Montagu, *The Letters and Works of Lady Mary Wortley Montagu*, edited by Lord Wharncliffe (London, 1861)

Wroth 1896
Warwick Wroth, *The London Pleasure Gardens of the Eighteenth Century* (London, 1896)

Zanetti 1771
Antonio Maria Zanetti, *Della pittura veneziana e delle opere pubbliche de' veneziani maestri libri V* (Venezia, 1771)

Zech 2014/15
Wolf Zech, "Maltechnik und Restaurierung der Stadtansicht," in exh. cat. Munich 2014/15, 302–13

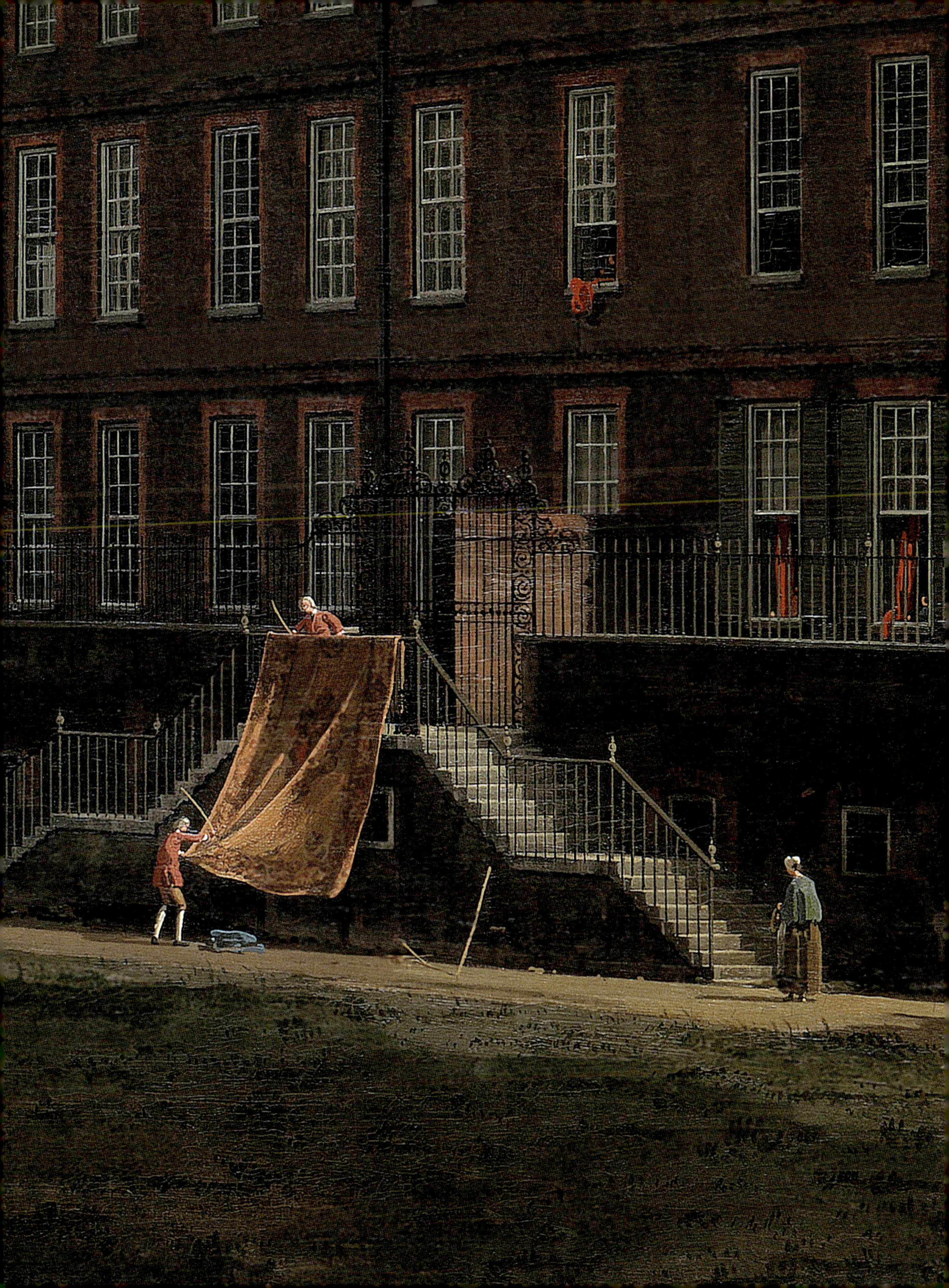

INDEX

Names

Works

Canaletto

Bellotto

IMAGE CREDITS

Unless stated otherwise
© KHM-Museumsverband,
photo: Andreas Uldrich

Cover: Canaletto, *London: The River Thames on Lord Mayor's Day* (detail), c.1748
© The Lobkowicz Collections, Lobkowicz Palace, Prague Castle, Czech Republic, photo: Jon P. Stokes

Full bleed images:
p. 2–3: fig. 1
p. 4: fig. 36
p. 6: fig. 26
p. 12: fig. 1
p. 46: fig. 19
p. 86: fig. 37
p. 152: fig. 66
p. 172: fig. 67
p. 179: fig. 25
p. 185: fig. 59
p. 190–91: fig. 37

Allen Phillips / Wadsworth Atheneum: p. 29, fig. 11
© Archivio fotografico G.A.VE – su concessione del Ministero della Cultura – Gallerie dell'Accademia di Venezia: p. 26, fig. 7; p. 39, fig. 14; p. 40
Austrian National Library, Vienna: p. 26, fig. 8; p. 106, fig. 40; p. 111, fig. 42
© Compton Verney, photo by Jamie Woodley: p. 70, fig. 26; p. 71, fig. 27; p. 72
© The Dean and Chapter of Westminster: p. 46; p. 55, fig. 19
© Collection of the Duke of Northumberland / Bridgeman Images: p. 63, fig. 24
© Fondazione Giorgio Cini: p. 31, fig. 12
© Gemäldegalerie Alte Meister, Staatliche Kunstsammlungen Dresden. Foto: Elke Estel / Hans-Peter Klut: p. 44, fig. 16; p. 79; p. 81, fig. 30
Gemäldegalerie der Akademie der bildenden Künste Wien: p. 106, fig. 39
Getty Research Institute, digitized by Internet Archive: p. 26, fig. 6
Image: ALBERTINA, Wien: p. 128, fig. 55
Kupferstichkabinett der Akademie der bildenden Kunste Wien: p. 139, fig. 60
Leica Microsystems GmbH: p. 166, cat. 33
Library of Congress: p. 106, fig. 41
© LIECHTENSTEIN. The Princely Collections, Vaduz–Vienna: p. 91, figs. 33, 34; p. 92, fig. 35
© The Lobkowicz Collections, Lobkowicz Palace, Prague Castle, Czech Republic, photo: Jon P. Stokes: p. 51, fig. 18; pp. 52–53; p. 59
© The Lobkowicz Collections, Lobkowicz Palace, Prague Castle, Czech Republic, photo: Oto Palán: p. 61, fig. 22
© P. Christoph Merth, Schottenstift: p. 168, cat. 39
Metropolitan Museum of Art, gift of David and Elizabeth Tunick 1991: p. 16, fig. 2
Metropolitan Museum of Art, gift of Sarah Lazarus 1891: p. 56, fig. 20
Metropolitan Museum of Art, Purchase, George Delacorte Fund Gift, in memory of George T. Delacorte Jr., and Gwynne Andrews, Victor Wilbour Memorial, and Marquand Funds, 2002, inv. 2002.22: p. 16, fig. 3

Musée des Beaux-Arts de Troyes © Carole Bell, Ville de Troyes: p. 152; p. 155, fig. 66
© Museo Nacional Thyssen-Bornemisza, Madrid: p. 23, fig. 5; p. 24; p. 75, fig. 28; p. 76
Photo: Giacomelli © Photo Archive – Fondazione Musei Civici di Venezia: p. 161, cat. 4
Photo: Hans Thorwid / Nationalmuseum: pp. 42–43; p. 44, fig. 15
Photo: National Gallery of Ireland: p. 82; p. 84, fig. 31
Photo: Wien Museum: p. 116, fig. 46; pp. 126–27, figs. 50–54; p. 131, fig. 56; p. 135, fig. 58
The Royal Castle in Warsaw – Museum; photo Andrzej Ring, Lech Sandzewicz: p. 156, fig. 67; p. 159
© Royal Collection Enterprises Limited 2026 | Royal Collection Trust: p. 27, fig. 9
Sächsisches Staatsarchiv, Hauptstaatsarchiv Dresden: p. 154, fig. 65
Szepművészeti Muzeum / Museum of Fine Arts, Budapest, 2026: p. 89, fig. 32
Tate – on permanent loan from The Andrew Lloyd Webber Foundation, London, UK: p. 65, fig. 25; pp. 66–67
Technisches Museum Wien: p. 166, cat. 30; p. 167, cat. 34
© The Trustees of the British Museum: p. 58, fig. 21; p. 61, fig. 23
By permission of the Trustees of the Goodwood Collection: p. 49, fig. 17
© Wallace Collection, London, UK / Bridgeman Images: p. 18, fig. 4
Wellcome Collection: p. 18, fig. 4; pp. 20–21; p. 34, fig. 13
Yale Center for British Art: p. 75, fig. 29

COLOPHON

This accompanying volume is published on the occasion of the exhibition *Canaletto & Bellotto*.

Kunsthistorisches Museum
www.khm.at
24 March to 6 September 2026

Director General
Jonathan Fine

EXHIBITION

Curator
Mateusz Mayer

Exhibition management
Elisabeth Kainberger

Exhibition design
ARTVIS

Partner

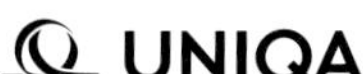

Sponsor

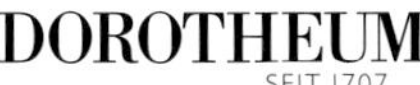

PUBLICATION

Publisher
KHM-Museumsverband, Vienna

Author
Mateusz Mayer

Editorial coordination
Rafael Kopper

Project management Hirmer Publishers
Jutta Allekotte

Design and layout
Michaela Noll

Copy-editing
Phoebe Collins

Image rights and coordination
Jeannette Mayer-Severyns

Image editing
Thomas Ritter

Production
Sophie Friederich

Paper
Magno Volume, 150 g/m²

Typeface
Rialto

Printing and binding
Printer Trento s.r.l., Trento

Printed in Italy

Bibliographic information published by the Deutsche Nationalbibliothek
The Deutsche Nationalbibliothek lists this publication in the Deutsche Nationalbibliografie; detailed bibliographic data is available on the Internet at http://dnb.d-nb.de.

ISBN 978-3-7774-4755-1 (English edition)
ISBN 978-3-7774-4754-4 (German edition)

Hirmer Publishers
(Hirmer Verlag GmbH)
Managing Director: Kerstin Ludolph
Bayerstraße 57–59
80335 Munich
Germany

www.hirmerpublishers.com
www.hirmerpublishers.co.uk

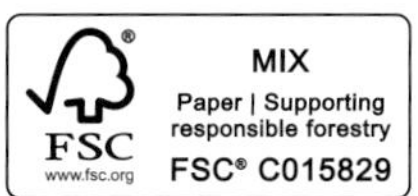

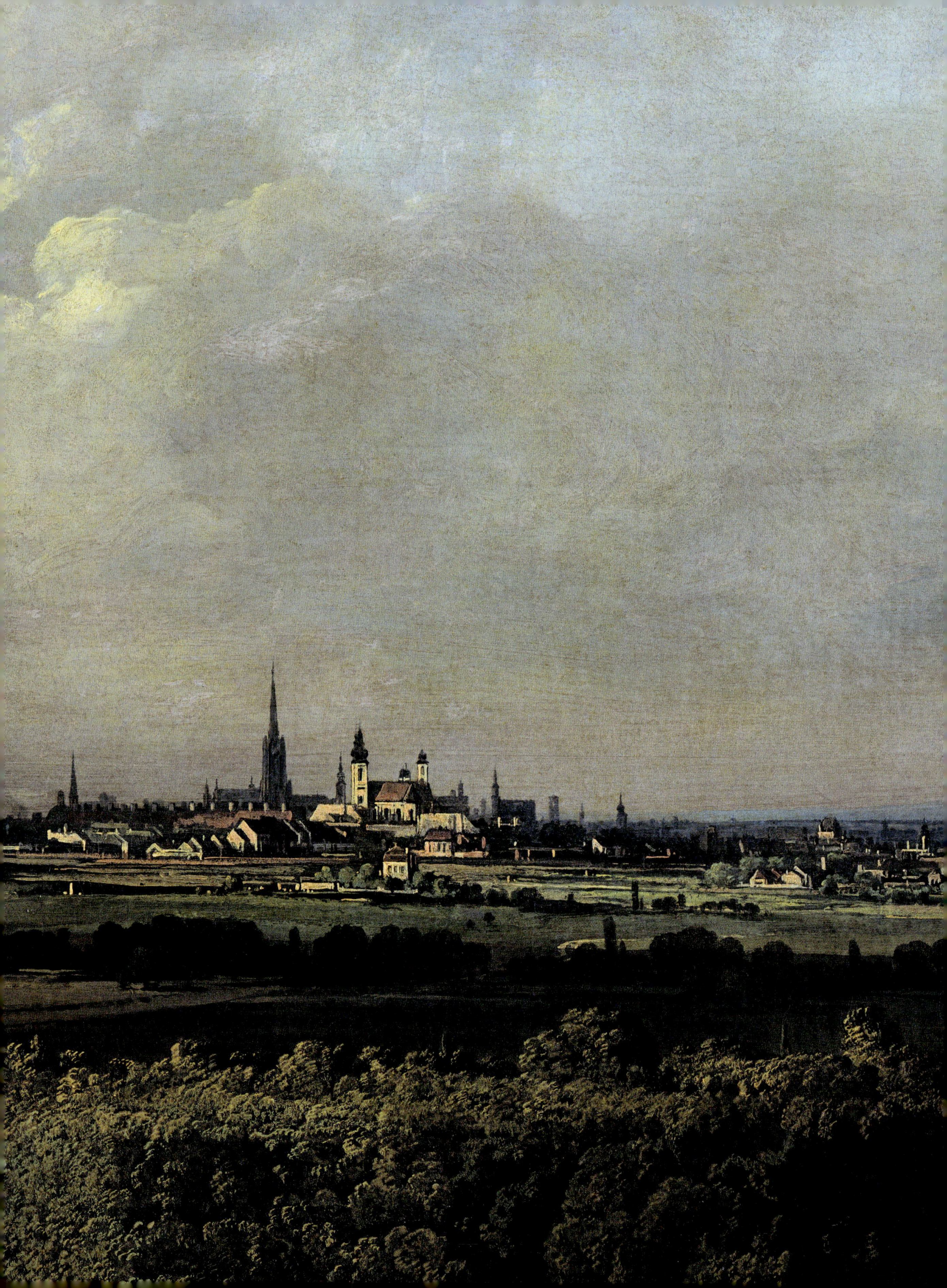

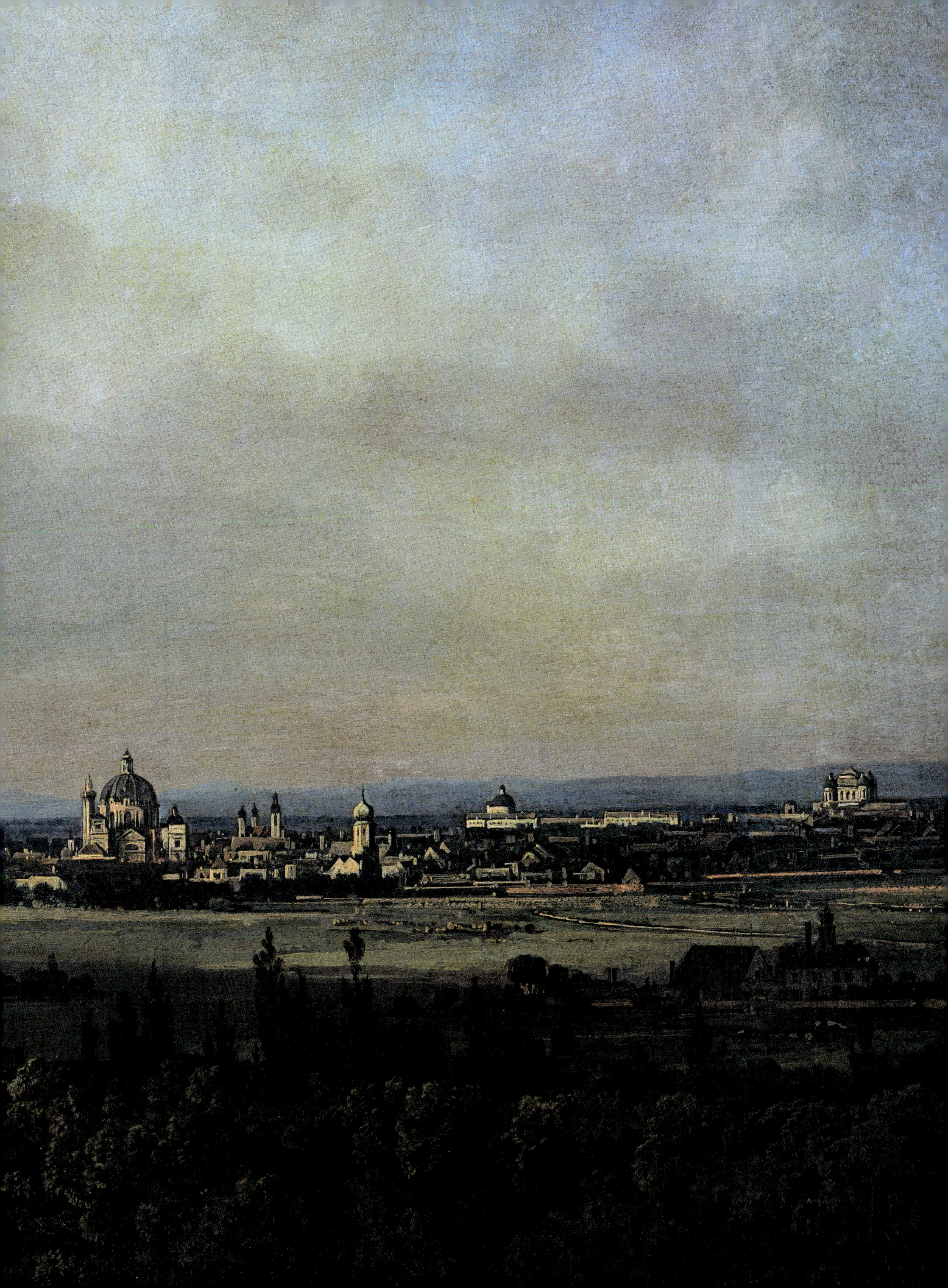